With Justice for Some

With Justice
for Some:
an Indictment of the Law
by Young Advocates

Edited by
Bruce Wasserstein
Mark J. Green

With an Introduction by
Ralph Nader

Beacon Press *Boston*

To Laura Lynelle

Contents

Introduction
by Ralph Nader

Every profession has its own myths, totems, and taboos. In the legal profession these serve to camouflage the dependency of the legal status quo on the established power systems. To begin with, most Americans cannot use the legal system for the vast majority of their grievances. These grievances individually represent causes of small dollar amount or important quests for rights which are not dollar-structured. Retainer astigmatism being what is it, lawyers in the aggregate are uninterested in most of these potential clients. Judicial and administrative politics, archaic-authoritarian procedures, and endemic delays comprise an additional layer of obstacles to the use of the law. Finally, civil rights, poverty rights, consumer rights, environmental rights, and procedural rights are expected to be defended by single or small-group parties who cannot afford the costs of the legal system. As a result, the paradox of a wealth of abuse (consumer fraud, for example) and a poverty of access by individual victims grows more acute as society grows increasingly complex.

Despite the reality of the legal system—designed largely for the powerful to contend among themselves or against the weak —the myth of equal justice moves on. Past legions of graduating law students assumed that widespread paper rights and the presence of public defenders, legal aid offices, and two thousand OEO lawyers satisfied the many in need of legal services. Lawyers and students rarely thought quantitatively in evaluating the quality of justice. Rights were confused with both the availability of remedies and the ability to endure the attrition necessary to secure such rights.

In a rawer dimension, most lawyers have not been distressed at all to have the law define violence in such a way as to exclude most of the large-scale violence from the embrace of the law. Environmental pollution, mass malnutrition, rotting tenements, defectively designed or constructed consumer products, and job injuries and diseases are major forms of violence. Yet the law has remained mostly silent as the destruction of people's property, health, and safety has continued to climb and as new risks to unborn generations accumulate.

In the making of a lawyer, law schools for decades neglected or refused to ask the hard questions, seek the hard data, and provide opportunities for the students themselves to understand and prepare to deal with the injustices challenging the pretensions and canons of the profession. Indeed, law schools did not even see the need to investigate the politico-economic power that deployed the legal system to its special advantage. There was little attention, for example, during the fifties, to the questions dealing with minorities and indigents which the Supreme Court confronted in the sixties. The law schools, allegedly the vanguard of the profession's concerns and conscience, were rigorously irrelevant to the deepening crises in the law which reflected the conflicts in the country's political, economic, and social relationships. Aristocratic pedagogy flitted before the students one uncritical image after another of the society's power alignments—big business, big bureaucracies, racial oppression, control of information and technology, and hypocritical electoral and legislative processes. If there were widespread taboos on openly discussing or challenging such systems, the law schools adapted easily in parallel muteness. Even so close a phenomenon as the role of large law firms in the legal system was considered either not pertinent or not appropriate for law students to study. The very spectrum of lawyer roles was narrowed by law schools in the design of their curriculums to meet the needs of Wall, State, and LaSalle Streets, and their lesser satellites.

Now comes a new wave of young lawyers. In this book, sixteen contributors bring to their subjects normative as well as analytic concentrations. They are describing situations and rendering judgments which are decades overdue. Written by law students and recent graduates, the quality of the chapters is a tribute to the self-education, experiences, and sensitivities which they have engaged in along with formal classwork. There were just as bright law students in the forties and fifties and early sixties. But lacking in general the normative framework for their intellectual talents, they came out well tuned to serve power but not to shape, distribute, curb, or displace power in accordance with their presumed professional allegiance to a just legal system. Such latter initiatives were not considered their responsibility as lawyers or attorneys. It is this attitude which is giving way to the broader, system-directed focus of the public interest lawyer.

Most of the topics treated in this volume are continuing front-page events. They have been treated in congressional hearings, court testimony, administrative hearings, and other investigations. What these young authors are saying is that this is the law's moment of truth, that it can no longer hide behind the public's ignorance of its failures or the complicity of the organized bar's tokenism when massive re-developments of legal manpower are necessary. And as an indication of a more profound awareness, most of these contributors are living their concerns in public interest legal careers that require a stamina of commitment quite beyond perception or observation. Unlike past reformist legal schools of thought, these young lawyers and increasingly more like them are "staying with it." They are determined to make the law a force in reducing the institutional injustices and in shaping an *initiatory* democratic system of active and skilled citizens.

Editors' Note

Justice in America is more an assumption than a fact. We have an adversary process in which the accused, the ignorant, and the inconsequential have at best token representation while the most skilled counsel is reserved for those who need it least. Yet, there are some rumblings of change in criminal law, legal aid, minority rights, and consumerism. These reforms are, however, only first, faltering efforts which have served to state the problems rather than to solve them. The criminal law has *Miranda*, but accused indigents wait in jail for months before trial because they cannot raise bail; legal aid is in a constant battle against politicians seeking to emasculate it; city dwellers watch TV ads on the ecological responsibility of oil companies while being smogged to an early death; peaceful dissidents believe their phones are tapped by a Justice Department which revels in its injustice.

The chapters of this book probe the failures of contemporary law, offer proposals for change, and describe some victims—blacks, women, students, servicemen, consumers, the poor. The scope is deliberately broad, going beyond description of political trials to less visible but equally pressing legal problems. Many people think of law as dispensed by white-haired judges in taut courtroom dramas with the defendant having a Raymond Burr or at least an E. G. Marshall as his counsel. Not only is this a distortion of the judicial process—except for the white hair—but it ignores the point that most legal decisions are made by legislatures, administrative agencies, and enforcement personnel. The blemished performance of the cop on the beat, the local welfare agency, the giant corporation, and the government regulator are the reality of our legal system.

An attempt is made to avoid the pedantry of legalese without sacrificing thorough analysis. Although perhaps disagreeing with the precise contours of each other's contribution, we will concur in a common bias: whatever the views of the President, Vice President, Attorney General, or recent Supreme Court nominees, we believe in the vitality of civil rights and civil liberties. When J. Edgar Hoover was reappointed Director of the FBI by Mr. Nixon, the nation's top police officer told a reporter that, "Justice is incidental to law and order." Not too respectfully, we dissent.

We would like to thank Daphne Ehrlich and Arnold Tovell for their encouragement and our authors for their good humor.

Bruce Wasserstein
Mark J. Green

Cambridge, Massachusetts
Washington, D.C.
November, 1970

With Justice for Some

The law, in its majestic equality,
forbids the rich as well as the poor
to sleep under bridges, to beg in the streets,
and to steal bread.

Anatole France

. . . in a modern democracy social problems
become translated into legal problems
—if the democracy coheres.

de Tocqueville

The Law of the Young

MARK J. GREEN*

*. . . neither the Fourteenth Amendment nor the Bill of
Rights is for adults alone.*

— *Justice Abe Fortas*[1]

Paternalism is deeply embedded in America's national character,
converting our most oppressive actions to a noblesse oblige
benevolence. Consequently, Slavery was an institution for raising
helpless Negroes; women have historically been protected against
their own frailties; and we are now destroying Vietnam—for its
welfare, not ours. This national hubris reflects a successful past:
we have attracted émigrés, won wars, avoided revolutions, and
prospered. Yet when the recipients of our good will—blacks,
women, Vietnamese—rebel at our offerings, ingratitude embitters
the donor.

Youth are today's paternalized and oppressed group. They are
considered undisciplined spirits, marginal citizens, in need of
training and social control. Schools, therefore, exercise *in loco
parentis* dominion over them, courts exercise *parens patriae* command over them, and the family leverage of economic support
binds them to the home. Yet, like predecessor groups protected

* Mark Green is a lawyer working in Washington with Ralph Nader. He
was the Editor-in-Chief of the *Harvard Civil Rights–Civil Liberties Law
Review* in 1969–1970, and his articles have appeared in *The Nation, Commonweal, The Village Voice, The New Republic,* and *The Progressive.* He is
currently working on books dealing with Washington law firms and with
antitrust enforcement, the latter with co-contributors Bruce Wasserstein
and Beverly Moore.

for their own benefit, the young do not passively accept their predetermined roles. Boxed in by these three insensitive institutions, they often fight to break out.

In this contest between the national character and the youth culture, the law is not a neutral bystander. It reflects the national policy and character of voting and/or influential adults. As a result, minors are controlled by rules imposed by others and designed to wind them through sanitized corridors to citizenship and maturity. And minors are legally called "infants," since the law only knows two classes of people: adults and infants. The latter category comprises nearly 40 percent of our entire population, with 18 million individuals included in the 16–21 age group alone. Considered below is how high school rules, laws against victimless vice, a juvenile court system, and legal barriers by age all conspire to keep Junior down.

I. SCHOOL-BOY: GOODBYE TO ARCHIE AND VERONICA

In the first place, God made idiots; this was for practice; then he made school boards.

— *Mark Twain*[2]

That's the Public school system all over. They may kick you out, but they never let you down.

— *Evelyn Waugh*[3]

A few weeks before his 1969 graduation, Walter Crump became involved in a minor argument with a stern teacher. An intense, intelligent, and black high school senior, Walter was then suspended summarily, despite a New York City Board of Education rule that a parent be notified prior to suspension; informed twelve days later that a hearing would be held (a Board rule permitted a maximum of five days between the suspension and hearing); denied representation in violation of a state law allowing counsel for suspensions of more than five days; and was found guilty of an unstated offense without his presence.

In January, 1969, 670 students, mostly black and Puerto

Rican, were summarily expelled from the Franklin Lane High School in New York. While the actual reason for the purge, as later shown by interested attorneys, was to put the crowded school back on a single session, the stated reason was that all the children expelled had both missed more than thirty days of school and had maintained unsatisfactory academic records during the Fall semester. They received no notice, nor were they given any opportunity to contest the action against them. Many of the students, unsurprisingly, had not been absent more than thirty days, had justifiable reasons for absences, and had satisfactory academic records.

Fortunately, the local ACLU was informed of these cases and filed successful suits to reinstate the students. Yet usually Walter Crump—and the thousands like him—would simply disappear into the shadows of the city, lacking both a diploma and respect for law. For most instances of official illegality are not unearthed by an attentive ACLU lawyer, organized into a lawsuit, and favorably resolved before a sympathetic judge. The telling point in both these cases is not that constitutional wrongs were righted, but that school autocrats felt free to ignore the law while inflicting arbitrary punishment.

"Student Unrest" should consequently not be greeted with dramatic surprise by high school authorities. Fifty-nine percent of all high schools and 56 percent of all junior high schools, according to the National Association of Secondary School Principals (NASSP), experienced student protest within their recent history, with over three-fourths of these protests involving conflicts over school rules.[4] Many of these protests thus go beyond "unrest" into the arena of political struggle—as students organize themselves out of their own serfdom. For example, 200 students formed the New York High School Union in an attempt to organize the 275,000 secondary school students and to "heighten their radical consciousnesses." Their nonwhite counterpart was the Committee of the Black and Puerto Rican Coalition, which presented fifteen nonnegotiable demands to the New York City School Board, such as: removing police from the schools, purging racist literature from their curricula, and establishing holidays to honor Malcolm X and Martin Luther King.

Besides these nonsanctioned efforts, in February of 1970 the elected representatives of all of New York City's high school students sought to restructure student-administration relations by proposing that Committees of Twenty, one-half students and one-half administrators, govern each school. They further demanded the abolition of tracking systems, which institutionalized inferior education for minority groups, the end of illegal use of the police in the schools, and the end of penalties for exercising their freedom of speech and press—whether antiwar views in school newspapers or counseling on the draft, on drugs, or on contraception. School officials, according to the *New York Times*, "view the proposal as part of a new campaign by high school and college militants to sow discord in the schools."

Yet those who sow discord are not outside agitators but school personnel themselves, and as students come to perceive this reality, the high schools reap the returns. What were formerly bastions of culture indoctrination become microcosms of society, with its loves, hates, prejudices, wars, and warts. And a system of law whose ethic left control of the student to the principal and teacher is being pushed to the constitutional wall. The nonrecognition or suppression of student activities, aside from escalating the reactions, raises difficult legal issues. These grievances are finally working their way into the judiciary, a branch of the government historically quiescent toward high school student rights.

Free Speech and Press

However valuable an education is to the student—as *Brown* v. *Board* famously stated—it is also clear that the local school administrator can control the condition of the education. Thus, as criminal law is what the cop on the beat says it is, school law, in the first instance, is what the local school board says it is. School boards are public authorities which operate under a legislative delegation of authority; they function as parent surrogates under *in loco parentis*, being given wide discretion to formulate policy and exact punishments—to a limit.

One of these limits is the First Amendment guarantee to free speech and free press. As long as high school newspapers reported the team scores and the election of class officers, this amendment had as much relevance as the following amendment on the "well regulated Militia." Yet with the Vietnam War, students' interests turned outward, and school newspapers began to reflect the reorientation. If they did not, competing underground newspapers often surfaced. It is now estimated that more than 500 of these publications exist, with 150 alone subscribing to the *High School Independent Press Service*. They are wildly funny, irreverent, biased, opinionated, and, occasionally, obscene, ranging in title from *The Finger* to *The South Dakota Seditionist Monthly* to *The Neo-Dwarf*.[5]

Some administrators cooperate with these vanguard efforts in education, efforts which prove that students may have learned more than they have been taught. Other officials adopt a more Agnewistic view. Schoolboard Chairman William Freienmuth of Montgomery County, Maryland, forbade the distribution of the *Washington Free Press* in his high schools, because "it advocates revolution and makes disparaging remarks about the CIA and the police. Part of our job is to teach students to live within the law. After all, everyone had a little trouble with conformity sometime." In Delaware, two high school students were arrested and charged with blasphemy under a 143-year-old law for writing an article entitled "The Purple Jesus, or the Grape of the Virgin," in their paper, *The Acid Flash*. There is also the case of John Freeberg, high school senior from Seattle, Washington. He was an honor student, student council representative, winner of the VFW "What Democracy Means to Me" Contest and editor of his school newspaper. For his anti-war editorials in the latter, he was suspended before graduation. Such situations are not mere aberrations. The NASSP has estimated that of those schools they surveyed, one-half had attempted to suppress nonsanctioned publications.

The most prominent high school rights decision to date is a free speech case with numerous free press implications—*Tinker* v. *Des Moines Board of Education*.[6] Three school children wore black armbands to school in 1965 as a silent protest against the Vietnam War. They were suspended for violating a school regulation forbidding the wearing of armbands—a rule created after the principal learned of the protest plan. (The school had not prevented students from wearing Nazi Iron Crosses.) The district and appellate courts upheld the action of the school, but the Supreme Court reversed, saying that a school could prohibit such protest only if it materially and substantially interfered with school operations; it was a standard which unsettled Justice Black, who complained that ". . . it is the beginning of a new revolutionary era of permissiveness in this country fostered by the judiciary."

The test of "material and substantial interference" would seem to encompass the above newspaper cases, unless it could be proven that the written word was in fact a trigger to disruptive action. Yet, when courts deal with student rights, they are often uncharacteristically indifferent to precedent, being unable to comprehend that students are citizens with rights rather than undisciplined spirits in need of paternal control.*

For example, a 1969 Court of Appeals decision—*Scoville* v. *Board of Education*[7]—upheld the expulsion of two seventeen-year-old Illinois students for "gross disobedience and conduct" due to certain articles in their publication *Grass High*. The piece described the senior dean as having a "sick mind" and it called compulsory attendance laws "idiotic and asinine." Yet the court considered no evidence on the actual likelihood of disruption, as *Tinker* commands. The sixteen-page newspaper, however, containing original poetry, essays, short stories, and graffiti, reflected a refreshing creativity and should not have been banned because of the discomfort it caused some readers. Then, in April, 1970, *mirabile dictu*, the appeals court reversed itself on rehearing, acknowledging that, in fact, the school had failed to hold the required evidentiary hearing and therefore could not suspend the students.[8] Of course, by this time the culprits were safely in college anyway, but the decision is still a significant one, telling school rulers that they—like welfare administrators who had

* Courts seem to be in a state of disarray over these student issues. For example, on the question of whether a student, for nonreligious reasons, can refuse to salute the flag, one judge in the Brooklyn District Court said "yes," while a later judge in the *same court* said "no."

thought that the Rule of Law did not apply to *their* domain—had to heed the Constitution and would be watched over by an increasingly alert judiciary.

Three other 1969 and 1970 high school press cases advance the First Amendment rights of students. A Michigan District Court said that the school principal overstepped permissible discretion in expelling students caught with an "obscene" publication, since the offending word in the periodical also appeared in the school's own library—in Salinger's *Catcher in the Rye* and in *Harper's*.[9] Another District Court held that a New Rochelle, New York, principal had no right to censor an antiwar advertisement in the school newspaper on the grounds that it did not relate to a school activity,[10] and a Connecticut District Court held that a student group did not have to submit a privately printed newspaper to the school administration for predistribution approval.[11]

Despite these cases, most high schools run themselves without fear of court interference or any kind of accountability. Many continue traditional suppression. Yet it is critical to permit high school students a vehicle to express their atypical, dissenting views. This school stage too frequently inoculates its captive audience with the rote and plasticity of patriotic catechism, training students how to adjust, not think—a point well argued by Paul Goodman, Edgar Friedenberg, and, most recently, Charles Silberman. Encouraging free speech and press—considered "preferred rights" in our constitutional galaxy—can stimulate the dulldom of many secondary schools, expose administrative ineptness and illegality, and release student hostilities. Censorship, on the other hand, can be educationally disastrous. By teaching the young our constitutional guarantees and then by denying these rights to them, students will learn something, but one wonders what they will learn. What *Tinker* and its progeny emphasize, reiterating the views of John Dewey, is that the process of education in a democracy must be democratic.[12]

Stylistic Censorship

"Style," defined differently in different times, has long been a sensitive issue in the schools. One early variant dealt with moral

style, as the Charleston School Board in 1851 expelled a Miss
Sherman for engaging in a "continued course of open and notorious familiarities, and illicit intercourse, and that for hire and
reward."[13] The court reasoned that since a school could eject a
student with lice, due to contamination problems, it could do
likewise with a licentious student who was, supposedly, the
equivalent of a moral pollutant. In the early 1920s an eighteen-
year-old girl was expelled from an Arkansas high school for
wearing excessive talcum powder on her cheeks, thereby violating a rule which stated: "The wearing of transparent hosiery,
low-necked dresses or any style of clothing tending toward im-
modesty in dress, or the use of face paint or cosmetics is prohibited."[14]

Today, it is long hair. Largely a post-Beatle–Vietnam phenomenon, it is also something of a traditional American heresy,
blurring gender lines by its transsexual implications, and over-
lapping a hip style with a Left political ideology. And the schools
assumed the burden of this stylistic acculturation, as the California Administrative Code points out: "[A]ll pupils who go to
school without proper attention having been given to personal
cleanliness, or neatness of dress, may be sent home, to be properly prepared for school. . . ."[15]

The early hair cases were one-sided contests, with schools controlling their students without the threat of court actions. In
1966, the principal of Oyster Bay High School confined five
long-haired students to a special room during school hours because they refused to get haircuts. Although fellow students
picketed on their behalf—carrying signs reading "Better flowing
locks than throwing rocks"—the quarantined offenders submitted themselves to a selected "hair stylist." In 1968, there was a
near pogrom in one Connecticut high school, as 53 boys were
suspended after class-by-class inspections. In a note to the parents of the students, the principal said: "Hair must be kept away
from the collar bone. Hair must be neat (not bushy) around the
ears and must not overlap the ears. Sideburns are not to extend
beyond the midpoint of the ears." Another species of stylistic
control was the disciplining of black students for wearing

dashikis in a Boston high school. White costumes, not black, were required.

One Ohio incident, in particular, articulates just why this issue is not wholly humorous. High school student Carl Towner, son of a hirsute Englishman, was ordered by the school principal to get a haircut. Backed by his parents, he refused, and was promptly suspended. Carl was then sent to juvenile court as a truant and jailed for twenty-four hours. The judge gave him an ultimatum: be in school by November 20 with a haircut or face a six-month jail term. On November 18 the family escaped back to their native England.

When these horrors finally got into the courts, the early decisions paid the usual deference to school rules "necessary for the maintenance of an orderly system." A 1967 Federal District Court in Louisiana upheld the suspension of a bushy-headed highschooler by a principal who asserted, "I am very concerned with preventive discipline." The opinion called long hair on males a "gross deviation" which could lead to "disfunction in the social adjustment of children."[16] A year later, another Federal District Court, this time in Texas, affirmed the suspensions of some boys who comprised a singing group called "The Sounds Unlimited."* "[S]ociety expects public education to concern itself with building young citizens as well as teaching the '3 R's,' " the court stated.[17] By 1970, one court held a student in violation of a *student*-passed hair code, as if authoritarianism by the majority is any more palatable to the individual than if by

---

* The group immediately cut a record, played on television, radio, and in court, called "Keep Your Hands Off Of It":

> Went to school, got kicked out,
> Said it was too long, now we're going to shout
> (Chorus)
> Keep your hands off of it,
> Keep your hands off of it,
> It doesn't belong to you.
> Bopped upon the steps,
> Principal I met,
> You're not getting in now
> What do you want to bet?

the minority. The court reasoned that if billboards and junk-
yards could be esthetically regulated, why not hairy students?"[18]

These protectionist decisions simply assumed their conclusion, that ill-grooming was disruptive to the school, a point
asserted but not proven. Three 1969 cases, however—one a Court
of Appeals ruling—have upheld long-haired students just because
the state can offer no valid justification for the attempt at
militaristic control over its pupils. In one, a Chicago judge accurately asserted, "We can't mold people who are going to run
the world in the 1980s into the shapes of the 1920s. . . ."[19]
And the well-respected Judge Charles Wyzanski permanently enjoined the principal of Marlboro High in a Boston court from suspending a student whose hair met with his disapproval. The
judge observed that there had been no showing of any disease
or disruption dangers, and he took judicial notice that Samson,
the Founding Fathers, and "the English singers called 'The
Beatles' " all had long hair. Judge Wyzanski emphasized that
these school children had a right "to look like themselves."[20]

Finally, *Breen* v. *Kahl*, in a United States Court of Appeals,
held that a public high school cannot enforce a rule that students must get a haircut of a certain length or face expulsion.[21]
On appeal, the Supreme Court refused to review that judicial
conclusion, letting it stand as law.[22] Although the Court wrote
no opinion for its refusal to review the decision, the grounds to
do so are straightforward and compelling:

(1) *First Amendment.* It was premature for Justice Fortas to
state in his *Tinker* opinion that the "symbolic speech" rubric
clearly did not encompass student hair and dress issues. And it
was naive for the Louisiana Court to state, "But just what does
the wearing of long hair symbolize? What is the student trying
to express? Nothing, really." In today's McLuhanesque world,
style *is* substance; a beat-hippie gestalt has clear antiestablish-
ment denotations, and the long-haired or short-skirted student
may indeed be communicating ideas. It would be illogical to
allow symbolic speech on specific issues, such as the Vietnam
War in *Tinker,* but not on a more general controversy over competing ideologies—old versus young—a conflict with traditional
political and social implications. Clearly, a student's long-haired

style says *something*, since schools get sufficiently exercised to ban it. In fact, this vehicle of expression may be one of the only ways a student can publicly communicate his point of view, for whatever it is worth, given his lack of access to the adult media.

(2) *Right to Privacy.* The case of *Griswold* v. *Connecticut*[23] gave form to Justice Brandeis' phrase "the right to be left alone." There the Supreme Court held the Connecticut anti-contraception statute unconstitutional because it violated the right of marital privacy, a right "lying within the zone of privacy created by several fundamental constitutional guarantees."

The "right" to personal style, while not presenting as dramatic a context as invasion of the marital bed, is an analogous situation. To order a student to change his appearance in order to conform to an officially accepted style epitomizes the state intrusion on a personal right. The ultimate insult that an official body can level at a student, it is an arbitrary act, unrelated to any provably valid state purpose.

Yet the hair issue is but one example of a larger student-rights theme: the extent to which the state can compel uniformity among its pupils. And such coercion conflicts with a new ethic among students—what one sociologist has called "privatism"—which insists that the state and school leave him alone in his exercise of personal, nonharmful rights. Justice William O. Douglas, iconoclast-on-the-mount, has capsulized the situation best:

> I suppose that a nation bent on turning out robots might insist that every male wear a crewcut and every female wear pigtails. But the ideas of life, liberty and the pursuit of happiness [include] of course freedom of expression and a wide zone of privacy.

Privacy

Personal privacy, as in the hair and style issue, has other manifestations. The search and seizure of students' lockers and belongings is one. In October, 1969, the day before the Administration's Operation Intercept at the Mexican border was ended,

Max Rafferty, ex-senatorial aspirant and superintendent of California schools, suggested that all student lockers be blitzkrieged and searched for marihuana. This position exemplifies the niggerdom of the student who is subject to the rule of such men.

Fortunately, this mass invasion failed to occur, yet individual and little-publicized cases of illegal searches are appearing around the country. In Mt. Vernon High School in New York, a vice-principal allowed police to inspect a student's locker for marihuana, pursuant to a search warrant, a warrant which later turned out to be defective for lack of "cause." The lower courts upheld the search based on the vice-principal's permission to see the lockers, ignoring the obvious fact that he opened the locker only because he felt the (invalid) search warrant compelled him to do so.[24] The United States Supreme Court remanded the case back to the lower court for further consideration in light of another court opinion, which held a similar search under a false warrant illegal. *Nevertheless,* the lower court ignored the hint and affirmed their ruling; the case, therefore, will most likely return to the Supreme Court for a final ruling.

In Kansas, police entered a high school, with school approval, and searched lockers for leads to a recent robbery. Their search uncovered incriminating evidence against one of the students, and their dragnet tactics were upheld by the Kansas Supreme Court, which said that school authorities had plenary power "to inspect the lockers under their control and to prevent their use in illicit ways or for illegal purposes."[25] Yet such searches undermine the entire warrant system—based on the Fourth Amendment—which requires that all searches must be either pursuant to a valid warrant, in a narrowly circumscribed manner incident to a lawful arrest, or in response to an emergency. A fourth category is now created: as a condition of attending school (to which the student has no choice, given compulsory attendance laws), the student must waive his constitutional rights against "unreasonable searches and seizures." Yet such waiver rules cavalierly assume that school is a "privilege," with conditions attached, rather than a basic "right" of citizenship, as the *Brown* case states.

Privacy is also invaded by the casual dissemination of personal data, compiled by school authorities, to any who ask for it. The president of a foundation which invited twenty education specialists to look into this problem, Dr. Orville Brimm, Jr., concluded: "It is very difficult for you, as a parent, to get information about your own child from school files. Yet those same school records frequently are opened to truant officers, the FBI people in the social welfare field, and to official bodies who are agents of the government."[26] Such files often contain old and unreliable data, obtained by hearsay, which can trail a student through his years of schooling, making fresh starts from past incidents difficult. These practices also violate one's sense of self, of privacy, since intimate details are being viewed by an undetermined number of unknown eyes. The only clear remedy for such abuse is the periodic destruction of outdated material and the requirement that permission be obtained when unauthorized personnel seek to view the records.

Due Process

In the situations of Walter Crump and the Franklin K. Lane High students, discussed above, as in all the examples of when school rules are broken, the disobedient student is subject to suspension or expulsion. Often, in a manner unfortunately consistent with the repressiveness of the rules, disciplinary proceedings lack the legal formalities necessary to protect the defendant from very severe penalties. These include: irreparable harm to his education, effect on likelihood of college attendance, effect on future livelihood, and the deprivation of the full development of his capacities. For example, in Illinois there is no statutory provision for a hearing prior to expulsion, for a list of the specific charges, for the evidence against the student, for an opportunity to rebut that evidence, or for the identification or cross-examination of incriminating witnesses. And even in districts where such rules do exist, as some do in New York City, officials often ignore legal rules in favor of administrative expediency—e.g., Walter Crump.

Suspensions and expulsions are not infrequent occurrences. In New York City alone last school year, there were 10,000 five-day suspensions, a tactic "designed to be instruments of discipline, not justice," according to one ACLU attorney studying the situation. A *Village Voice* writer came to similar conclusions: "Many . . . result from violation of dress codes and first amendment protests. . . . And increasingly, although principals deny it, suspensions are being used to intimidate political activists and chill high school organizing." The way to insure that such substantive abuse of school rules does not occur is to guarantee that procedural fairness will always attend any punishment proceedings.

Between Rafferty and Emerson

Which way the high schools? While one can prescribe, the actual alternatives are diffuse. In California, a committee empowered by Max Rafferty has drawn up a *Guidelines for Moral Instruction in the California Schools,* a text "to lead California out of the moral decay in which it is presently descending." The *Guidelines* were critical of sex education, the Supreme Court, and the United Nations, and were admiring of J. Edgar Hoover, the Bible, and William F. Buckley, Jr. (Which answers Ronald Reagan's question why "we're hailed out here as some kind of regressive Neanderthal administration"?)

Beyond this hybrid of the Decalogue and the Girl Scout Oath stands the "Wellesley Incident," a 1968 phenomenon that featured criminal complaints against local teachers and the producers of a LeRoi Jones play entitled *The Slave.* In a town meeting over the situation, the school principal involved shouted: "I can pledge you a repetition of such a performance as *The Slave* will not again be given as long as it is my privilege to be the principal." A former student replied by reading excerpts from the play, including a passage which read "Sit the fuck down," for which he was arrested, handcuffed, and dragged away.

Happily, such responses to the student rights issue are not inevitable. In New York, hair codes have been essentially eliminated by Superintendent of Schools Ewald Nyquist (after his son had been suspended for having long hair), and the Board of Education in the city passed, in October, 1969, and, in revised form, in June, 1970, a significant "High School Bill of Rights."

It liberalized publishing restrictions and punishment proceedings, among other improvements. More ambitiously, the openly non-oppressive school authorities could someday simply state: if the faculty participates in determinations over student codes, the students should have a voice in any faculty codes, or hirings, or course creations or disciplinary hearings; if teachers strike for due process rights for themselves, they should guarantee that it also exists for their students; society should legalize: smoking in schools, marriage with consent, all hair choice, all dress short of nudity, all published words, all spoken words except those which imminently ignite disruption; we should outlaw: locker checks, data disseminations, bathroom passes, and immutable curricula. Yet even the mentioning of some of these possibilities has started a movement among some teachers to push for legalization of corporal punishment. The resolution of the issue, therefore, is suspended in doubt.

Yet, the indictment seems clear. Teachers and administrators have failed to protect pupils' rights both as citizens and as clients of the education industry. Such legal insensitivity has gone hand in hand with a simonizing, not humanizing, learning process, one in which you "prepare" the student by racing to keep him innocent of corrupting influences, rather than one in which you "educate" him by encouraging exploration and responsibility. And this latter goal can only be attempted when students are freed from the countless, trivial coercions which impede their development. Even the law, in its pristine application, cannot achieve this result, since cases filed and resolved years later cannot hope to include most or many or even a few of the consistent violations. The only lasting remedy is for those who daily rule the students to do so with a democratic, not tyrannic, hand—for them to realize, as did Ralph Waldo Emerson, that "The secret of education lies in respecting the pupil."

II. VICTIMLESS CRIMES

It's wrong because sexual promiscuity is an assault on an institution that is central to the survival of the hardiest Western ideal: the family. . . . It isn't surprising that the

cohabitating girls of this world shouldn't multiply like rab-
bits, whose morals they imitate.
                                    —*William F. Buckley, Jr.*[27]

I see no reason to limit the legislatures to protecting chil-
dren alone from pornography. The 'juvenile' delinquents I
have known are mostly over 50 years of age.
                                    —*Justice William Douglas*[28]

Mark: We will have steak and salad every night for a week
when you come home. All you can eat . . . Love, mommy.
                                    —*Berkeley Barb Classified*

High school students are clearly captive to discriminatory and
repressive control. Their serfdom continues when they enter
society, a point extrapolated from adult prohibitions against
moral crimes: nonmarital sex, marihuana, and pornography.
What is not adequately emphasized about these common practices is that they differentially bear down hardest on the young,
for the "evils" listed, especially the first two, are the accoutre-
ments of the youth culture. Laws and taboos against fornication,
cohabitation, and sodomy usually apply to the unmarried, who
are of course disproportionately the young; marihuana, similarly,
is the *youth's* cocktail-cigarette substitute, and its ban restricts
him while his double-martini father trips home. And even
pornography, which must include nonpornography since no
ready definition exists for either, is often consumed by those for
whom other pleasures must be delayed until customary man-
hood. All three of these areas stand as symbols of hypocrisy and
repression to the young, since each involves immediate, personal
satisfaction, for each there is no proven harm, and each can put
you in jail. Also included as a "victimless crime" is the young
runaway, since if anyone is theoretically hurt, as with the above
prohibitions, it is the participant himself.

Sex

Any discussion of a sexual revolution among the young has a
déja vu air about it; the real sexual revolution occurred in the

1920s, and our attitudes and expectations have ever since been trying to catch up with our practices. (See, *e.g.*, Bertrand Russell's *Marriage and Morals* in 1930.) Yet, if the reality of sex is not any greater, its visibility is. The *New York Times* front-pages the story of a modern Hester Pryn—Linda LeClair—a Barnard girl who was found to be living with her Columbia boyfriend. *Esquire, Life, et al.* run articles on campus cohabitants, complete with pictures and comments: "We're not just eating and sleeping together, we're protesting the war together"; "We are not sleeping together, we are living together."

Such candor contrasts with our sex laws, for though our mores change, the law is locked into the Comstockery of the early 1900s; and few, if any, legislators are bold enough to attempt reform on such an emotional issue. These laws, in sum, outlaw all sex which is not face-to-face and within the marital bond. They were passed during a moral-religious revival five decades ago, and were based on no more scientology and argument than that "it was wrong"—period. Thus, forty-nine states classify anal or oral intercourse as sodomy, and therefore illegal as a "crime against nature"; yet 59 percent of all males indulge in such love-making.[29] Until recently, these acts were punishable in New York by twenty years in prison, while at the same time the penalty for second degree robbery was fifteen years, and statutory rape was ten years. Forty-nine states also forbid fornication and cohabitation, acts so commonplace that most of the law's violators are unaware of their crimes. In Connecticut, until July, 1970, the punishment was five years at hard labor for fornication, and two and a half years for just trying. And two states still provide for the death penalty for fornication with a girl under eighteen, consenting or not. Consequently, it should come as no surprise that Alfred Kinsey had estimated that if all our sex laws were woodenly enforced, 90 percent of our male population would be behind bars.

Of course such statutes are curious anachronisms, yet their very existence carries an ominous implication. While arrests and prosecution on sex charges are declining, the existence of such laws allows enforcement officials wide discretion as to whom to suddenly apply the law against, and the victims are disproportionately society's outcasts—the black, the "weird," and the young. One Connecticut policeman let slip this kind of prejudice: "When you see a black boy and a white girl together, well, you just know what's going on." The implied problem is not rhetorical. The writer knows a married couple who, while engaged and at college in Connecticut, were invaded by five policemen during a weekend at a motel. This Orwellian episode ended with a morals charge against each.

Furthermore, corollary effects of these laws also adversely affect the young. Strictures against abortion and the sale and display of birth control devices discriminate against nonadults, for it is they who lack the money and sophistication to obtain an easy abortion in Hawaii or Puerto Rico, or New York, and it is they who are most ignorant in the ways of contraception. One idiotic example of the latter point concerns the case of a mother who warned her thirteen-year-old daughter, after she had given birth illegitimately, that "If you do have sex relations be sure the boy 'uses something' so you won't have another baby." She was convicted of impairing the morals of a minor and received a suspended sentence of one year in prison and a $200 fine.

These laws pose a chilling, deterring effect on overt premarital sex, causing many couples to sneak between motels to avoid detection, although detection is a remote possibility. It is pure class legislation, penalizing the sexual freedom of the young because of the sexual paranoia of the old.* It is one thing for taboos against early sex to exist; it is quite another to have such shibboleths reinforced by the respect and commandment of the law, which in combination exert an intimidating presence on the manipulated young. The necessary answer to this regulation and repression of the sex habits of one segment of society by another is to abolish the laws against such consensual acts. The 1962

---

* A 1968 Gallup Poll found that adult Americans disapproved of premarital relations by more than 3 to 1. College students, however, approved of it by 2 to 1. Since the adults tested came from the generation Kinsey studied, and since he found that 50 percent of the males and 25 percent of the females had intercourse before marriage (another 25 percent of the women wanted to but could not find the right man and moment), some of the disapproving adults have clearly forgotten their own youth.

American Law Institute Model Penal Code goes far in this direction, excluding from criminal sanction "all sexual practices not
involving force"; whether such rules will also apply to the 16–21-
year-olds remains to be seen. In addition, the recent Supreme
Court decision in *Stanley* v. *Georgia*[30] takes a timid step in this
general direction by holding it was not criminal for a person to
watch obscene movies in the confines of his own home; it should
be no different when he engages in consensual sexual acts within
the privacy of his own bed.

Marihuana

The youth use of marihuana raises analogous problems. Adult
society, having convinced itself of the non-evils of alcohol forty
years ago, has found a successor hobgoblin. Although pronounced illegal, and usually a felony, an estimated twenty to
forty million Americans have tried it, and as the *New York
Times* headlined a story, "Many Students Now Regard Marihuana as Part of Growing Up."

Like sex, there is no apparent danger to the normal use of
marihuana. The joint-to-junkie myth is post hoc reasoning and a
scare tactic, and was discredited by, among many others, the
President's Crime Commission. There is no known physical
hazard or dependency to this hallucinogen, unlike alcohol, which
causes an estimated 20,000 deaths a year and unlike smoking
which causes 300,000 premature deaths a year according to
former Surgeon General Luther Terry. Yet, for the 10 percent
or less chronic marihuana smokers, psychological difficulties
can occur, creating a stylistic dependence on the weed and its
subculture; the extent of this problem, and whether it is in fact
caused by the illicitness of illegality, is wholly speculative.

Arrayed against any criticism of marihuana are two salient
facts: first, like liquor and sex, grass is a permanent part of
American society, and the only issue is whether we shall criminally punish the few who are caught out of the many who
smoke; the law should realize its limitations—unlike the fourteen years of Prohibition when there was *more* drinking per
capita than there is today. And second, the person smoking has

chosen this vehicle of enjoyment, and without any second party harm, society should not interfere.

Rather than legalization, however, the trend is clearly the contrary. There were 7,000 marihuana-associated arrests in 1964, 15,000 in 1966, and 80,000 in 1968.[31] Of those persons arrested for sale or possession of grass or hashish in New York City in 1969, 60 percent were under twenty-one, confirming the reality that, as Tom Buckley has written, "It's the young who get 'busted' for using marihuana."[32] Yet whatever the arrest rate, "pot smoking is so widespread," says Time magazine, "that there are roughly 25 times as many users as there are places to hold them in all the nation's prisons."[33] Such a situation inevitably engenders disrespect for this law, and, accordingly, for all law.

The clearest fact about the marihuana controversy is the severity of the laws, which became especially publicized when the young sons of four U.S. senators and three governors and gubernatorial candidates were arrested on pot charges. Most state laws provide for penalties up to ten years for the first offender; for 98 percent of all juveniles arrested for possession, it was their first arrest of any kind.[34] While few suffer the maximum penalties, even partial penalty is strict enough "to ruin the life of a first-time offender," according to Dr. Stanley Yolles, former director of the National Institute of Mental Health.[35] Yet some offenders are not so lucky. In February, 1969, a long-haired nineteen-year-old was arrested with six and a half pounds of grass; a conservative, Southern judge sentenced him to twenty-five years in jail. In the same month, another nineteen-year-old was arrested in Virginia with three pounds of marihuana for school friends. He, too, was sentenced to twenty-five years, which is the minimum penalty in Virginia for possessing more than twenty-five grains and which is the same as the minimum penalty for first-degree murder. The outgoing governor of the Commonwealth, however, in one of his last acts in office, pardoned the offender. And in September, 1969, a twenty-year-old Texan was convicted of selling two joints, the equivalent in "high" potential of three to four lunchtime martinis. He was sentenced under state law to fifty years in prison.

These cases arose under state law. Equally severe federal penalties were reduced, after pressure was exerted on the Nixon Administration by medical experts, but the lowered penalties were passed along with a "no-knock" provision which would allow police to burst into suspect rooms if they fear that incriminating evidence may be destroyed. Such a rule raises the more general and ominous implications of marihuana arrests. Tom Buckley has written:

> Some observers believe that police zeal in seeking out marihuana offenders is proportional to their dislike of the life style it exemplifies, which is often associated with antiwar and civil rights protests, loud rock music, sexual freedom and what is described as a disrespect for law and order, rather than to the seriousness of the act itself.[36]

Both sex and marihuana offenses are convenient excuses for culturecide. Movies like *Easy Rider, Alice's Restaurant,* and *Joe* dramatically detail the syndrome. More realistically, it occurs when New Jersey Turnpike police stop all cars with freaky looking riders, ask for registration, which is legal, and then search the car for drugs or weapons, which is illegal. If they find grass they give the victim an alternative: pay over a $200–$300 fine now or we will press charges which might entail a jail penalty of up to five years. Faced with this Hobson's choice, the former alternative is invariably chosen, however illegal the search was in the first place. Culturecide also occurs when a rock festival in Chicago erupts into violence, which leads courts in Connecticut and Maryland to enjoin similar concerts from their states.

It is unclear the extent to which such stylistic warfare exists independent of laws like those against grass. There are enduring indications that it largely involves classic class struggle, lower class cops against middle class students, authoritarian figures versus humanistic figures. Richard Poirer concludes in an *Atlantic* article, "War Against the Young," that the struggle is "essentially a cultural one."[37] To the extent, however, that marihuana use is a symptom of the clash, perhaps the only publicly palatable reform would be to convene a prestigious commission, as Rep. Koch has suggested, to study scientifically the dangers of marihuana. Yet one cannot be sanguine even at this mild alternative; after California hired five professors to study the state's drug laws, they fired the group when, after three years of exhaustive research, the professors concluded that marihuana should be legalized. In addition, Attorney General John Mitchell has indicated that even *if* such a commission came out in favor of marihuana, he would still oppose its use since, "There is no rhyme or reason to it,"[38] a comment more applicable to itself than pot.

Most simply, the guiding principle concerning marihuana use by the young was articulated by Professor Neil Chayet of Boston University Law School: "The youth of America are our most precious asset. Let us remember this as we regulate this most crucial area."

Pornography

Unlike the above two vices, which may have only operationally discriminated against the young, pornography bans are specifically aimed at this group in an attempt to keep as unrestricted as possible adult reading matter. The 1968 Supreme Court case of *Ginsberg* v. *New York*[39] upheld the concept of "variable obscenity," which forbids the sale of obscene materials to those under seventeen. Most people consider this solution the best compromise to a complex problem, assuming so much by that simple assertion that they are unable to articulate social, psychological, or even constitutional reasons for their conclusions—reasons which must be uncovered before we tell our youth what to read and not read.

First, what is the definition of pornography? Even the use of the word is deceptive, since it seems to assume one homogenous identifiable thing; yet obviously no two articles or books or pieces of "pornograph" are the same. One early formulation of pornography was: art which tends to corrupt the most vulnerable readers. "The incidence of this enactment is to reduce the adult population of Michigan to reading only what is fit for children," wrote Justice Felix Frankfurter in *Butler* v. *Michigan;*[40] "surely this is to burn the house to roast the pig." The Court eventually settled on a definition in *Roth* v. *United States:* "whether to the average person, applying contemporary community standards, the dominant theme of the material taken as a whole appeals to prurient interest."[41] The "variable obscenity test" essentially replaces the word "person" with "child."

These existing standards suffer from an inevitable vagueness.* What is "prurient interest" that justifies the banning of that which stimulates it? The *Roth* dissent noted that: "Nearly 30 years ago a questionnaire sent to college and normal school women graduates asked what things were most stimulating sexually. Of 409 replies, 9 said 'music,' 18 said 'pictures,' 29 said 'dancing,' 40 said 'drama,' 95 said 'books,' and 218 said 'men.'" What is "contemporary community standards"? Is it judged by a Gallop Poll, or a guess by the writer, publisher, or distributor with the penalty being prison if they guess wrong, as Ginsberg did? "A poem," said Robert Frost, "is at its best when it is a tantalizing vagueness." The law should not be allowed such poetic license.

This problem surfaces in *Ginsberg*, where the New York Statute involved forbids the sale of material which "appealed to . . . their curiosity as to sex or to the anatomical differences between the sexes." Judge Fuld of the New York Supreme Court has suggested that, if taken literally, this would prohibit virtually all sex courses, or those in feminine hygiene, and could even forbid married sixteen- and seventeen-year-olds from seeking sexual instruction.

The second problem is: who judges the work? "Censors are, of course, propelled by their own neuroses," asserts Justice Douglas in the *Ginsberg* case. And organizational momentum contributes to this personal propulsion to make it likely that censorship will overleap any set standards.

Censorship is a dirty business. In Philadelphia, on September 29, 1963, in the presence of the Chief of Police, the superintendent of schools, a hymn-singing choir, and a large assemblage of

---

* New Jersey attempted to avoid the vagueness problem by describing all of the acts and words which were to be deemed obscene. The New Jersey printing office said it was the only government publication in the state's history to be sold out of its first printing.

persons, some 5,000 pieces of alleged pornography were burned. In 1969, Governor Lester Maddox urged his state teachers to "do your duty. . . . See what has been added to the curriculum at your school and burn it." Max Rafferty banned Eldridge Cleaver's *Soul On Ice* from California reading lists as obscene. It is relevant to realize that these men are not merely reactionary bruhahas; they controlled the education and minds of the children of their respective states. Of course, Rafferty was defeated in the November 1970 election, but the problem persists. The point is that censorship is always abused because it is undefined power in the hands of troubled people, to whose jaundiced eyes everything looks yellow. One wonders what books and films will be suppressed in the name of the welfare of children, since in the name of the welfare of adults, works of Hemingway, Salinger, Moravia, Maugham, Dumas, Voltaire, de Maupassant, Tolstoy, Zola, and Freud have been burned at one time or another.

The artistic taste of such censors—little old ladies of both sexes—should not control the minds of our future adults, injecting strains of orthodoxy now to kill potential nonconformity. Perhaps immature children would be easily influenced by some banned work, but such confusion is well worth the risk of mass Babbitry infecting our young. If a work has artistic or literary merit for adults, it should be no less true for teenagers in educational flux.

One attempted compromise in this area is the Motion Picture Association film rating code, which rates films to communicate to possible viewers the degree of licentiousness involved. Children are restricted only if the film is judged R (restricted, persons under sixteen not admitted unless accompanied by a parent or adult guardian) or X (persons under sixteen not admitted). Slightly more than 25 percent of all films are lumped into these two categories. Basically, the code is an effort by the movie distributors to keep the local censors off their backs; yet state and local laws operate regardless of the code. Of this attempt and of child censorship in general, *New York Times* movie critic Vincent Canby concluded: "Ideally, of course, there should be no rating systems and no censorship. . . . I also question a system that seems . . . concerned with keeping us sexually pure and with pretending that fourteen- or fifteen-year-old kids have never seen certain parts of our bodies and never heard certain four-letter words."[42]

Finally, there is the question of the harm involved with pornography, if any. In a series of juvenile delinquency studies, researchers at Harvard Law School repeatedly traced antisocial behavioral traits to the individual's physical constitution and home environment, rather than movies and books. "If he has a need for such outlets," the researchers found, "he will somehow get to them; deprivation is no cure."[43] The young consumer of pornography is most likely to be a shy introvert, deriving pleasure from quiet and private erotic experiences; yet this auto-eroticism may be just what censorship is aimed at, as D. H. Lawrence charged in 1929.

The counterargument, if it can be called that, was put best by J. Edgar Hoover: "Pornography, in all its forms, is one of the major causes of sex crimes, sexual aberrations and perversion. . . . Are we forsaking the simple teachings of right over wrong and good over bad?"[44] Among other flaws, this argument assumes too much: other than for rape, a nonconsensual act, it should be irrelevant if pornography leads to "sex crimes" or "sexual aberrations" since there should not be any laws against consensual, sexual acts. Furthermore, there is no evidence that pornography does lead to such sexual activity. To the contrary, a Presidential Commission on Obscenity and Pornography concluded in late 1970 that there was no such dangerous link. It therefore recommended, after attempts at political suppression failed, that all laws restricting pornographic films and books for adults be abolished. Although it could make no finding that pornography was harmful to children, the report weakly suggested that the fears and pressures of parents are enough justification to continue these laws against young readers. Thus is political fact dissimilar to empirical fact.

Pornography and sex were first made crimes for religious reasons. The former was a crime at Common Law, because the state thought it necessary to enforce religion in order to insure public order; the latter was a crime in order to encourage sex

within marriage, since early Christians and Jews felt compelled
to reproduce themselves to protect their faith against infidels.
Yet, as each justification ended, the concept continued, a rule
without a purpose but with an innocent victim: the young.

Runaways

"Runaways" is a new term for an old condition: when the child
leaves the family home. The latest characterization reflects the
current wisdom, since it makes the young seem foolish and
wicked. Thus, they are not called "adventurers," "independents,"
or "run-to's," but rather are considered to be running *away*
from something, with all the escapist, maladjusted innuendoes
intended.

It was not always so considered. Benjamin Franklin and
Horatio Alger were both runaways, at times when "society, rather
than send them back, usually applauded their courage."[45] And a
1924 *Nation* article stated with apparent approval that "Boys
leave home because they are always more eager to explore what
beacons [sic] to them from the window than to sit by the fire.
When they cease to do so we will have become an insufferable
dull people."[46]

Today, however, society has a more critical view of the way-
ward child. One police authority, reflecting the "preventive detention" underpinning for the runaway laws, intoned: "Like the
oak that grew from the acorn, the runaway is often the seed of
the future felon."[47] And the mass media periodically parade the
horrors of hippie runaways, citing drugs, disease, cohabitation
and crime. Yet one of the only detailed studies on runaways
contradicts these casual assertions. Researchers at the National
Institute of Mental Health, studying this issue, noted that "the
most striking feature to emerge from these findings is that the
great majority did not get into trouble at all either before or
after running away."[48]

Nearly every state has a "runaways" statute, which forbids
youth, usually defined as under twenty-one, from leaving home
without parental consent and which provides for police interven-

tion, if necessary, to retrieve them. The FBI reported 82,000 runaway arrests in 1965, 101,821 in 1966, and 129,532 by 1967. Most are booked and detained; yet the actual number of runaways is far greater, obviously, than those arrested. A 1967 *Look* magazine article estimated the total per year at 500,000.[49]

It is difficult to assess the motives of this illegal army. One expert, however, the Rev. Larry Beggs, who runs a home for runaways in San Francisco, said:

> The majority of runaways have no prior record. . . . [M]ost runaways leave for what they perceive to be very legitimate reasons. . . . It is a serious issue with them. In this context, when they are tracked down, taken by force in a police arrest, booked, and assigned a probation officer, a level of resentment is created which makes the reconciliation process at home much more difficult, if not impossible.[50]

Legislatures and courts should be sensitive to the fact that often the parents are the people who need treatment most, not necessarily the child. One commentator agrees that "running away seems to be a healthy mode of response to an intolerable situation."[51] Even if the child voluntarily returns home, as most do without the law's compulsion, the event can have a therapeutic effect on him and his family.

Children often leave to escape oppressive conditions—the family which sends them to bed without dinner, spanks them as punishment, or denies them their selected life-styles. Physical abuse is not uncommon. And abuse can be financial as well as physical and psychological, as fathers, by controlling the purse-strings, attempt to control the offspring's behavioral responses. Often the only way to break such economic control is to abandon it.

The law, however, reflects no such insights, as runaway rules violate three of our more lofty notions of civil liberties:

(1) It is a serious infringement of personal freedom to be compelled to live with undesired company; accordingly, the Thirteenth Amendment prohibition against "involuntary servi-

tude" applies. Just as this amendment was first used to free the
blacks, and end the Fugitive Slave Laws, it can be employed today to end the parallel "Fugitive Child Laws."

(2) The growing "right to be left alone," in Mr. Justice Brandeis' phrase, should encompass the runaway situation. Cases
discussed earlier carved out new constitutional terrain: that the
state cannot restrain people from private, personal acts if the
activity involved is not harmful to another or society. Thus,
in *Griswold* it was no business of the law to interfere with the
privacy of the marital bed; in *Stanley* it was no business of the
law to tell a man what movies he could view in his own home.
It is equally no business of the law to tell a seventeen-year-old
with whom he must associate and live.

(3) Runaway laws can be construed to violate the constitutionally established "right to travel." This concept first emerged
from cases where communists were denied passports to travel
abroad and has most recently been expressed in a Supreme Court
case which held that residency requirements for welfare recipients interfered with their freedom to travel. One of the
former cases summarized the importance of this right: "Freedom
of travel is a constitutional liberty closely related to rights of free
speech and association. . . . [T]he risk of abusing liberty so as
to give rise to punishable conduct is part of the price we pay for
this free society."[52]

This analysis does not *favor* children fleeing their homes; it
does oppose the use of state machinery—the laws, courts, and
enforcement agencies—to track them down, give them a record,
and bring them back. There exist less drastic alternatives than
legal compulsion to remedy this social situation. If physical
health of the young is the concern, free medical clinics could be
set up, and in fact are being established with significant success
on the West Coast. Board and beds could be provided through
a system of government hostels, as were established for the
shifting jobless during the Depression. Private institutions now
fractionally provide this service—for example, the Huckleberry
House in San Francisco, Project Place in Boston, the Terra
Firma Commune in New York City, and the Runaway House
in Washington. If emotional health is at issue, guidance coun-

selors could be provided; and if education indifference is the problem, then truancy from school could be the corrective mechanism. The cost for these reforms is likely to be far less than the financial and psychic costs of processing hundreds of thousands of runaways now arrested and extradited home—often to the same situation which caused the original exit.

III. SOCIETY'S CHILD:
IN COURT AND WITHOUT RIGHTS

The powers of the Star Chambers were a trifle in comparison with those of the juvenile courts.
                                        —*Dean Roscoe Pound*[53]

A society that does not recognize the rights of its youth will find more adults in its jails and mental institutions.
                        —*Editors' Note, American Bar Association Journal*[54]

Aside from the illegal artifacts of a forbidden culture, discussed above, how does the law affect the lives of youth? Considering what the law permits them to do, and then how the juvenile court system treats them, the answer is that the law protects them too much, and then not enough.

A. *In Court*

Of all the injustices inflicted on the youth because of their age, perhaps none is as harsh—given its lofty expectations—as the juvenile court system. In most states it deals with offenses of those eighteen and under; in 1964, this system processed 591,000 juvenile respondents. Originally created at the turn of this century, protected from publicity, and lacking need for adult procedural safeguards, the juvenile court and judges could give youths before them special attention and dispense justice as they saw fit. Its architects did not understate their attempt and technique: "[We] devised the best plan for the conservation of human life and happiness ever conceived by civilized man"; and, "Seated at a desk, with the child at his side, where he can on

occasion put his arm around his shoulder and draw the lad to
him, the judge . . . will gain immensely in the effectiveness of
his work."[55]

Unhappily, the ugliness of reality conflicted with the construct:

(1) Juvenile courts argued that lack of due process was justified since reform schools were not as evil or opprobrious as
prisons, a bromide unconnected to truth. Graduates of reform
school are as stigmatized as those of prisons, especially since
many juvenile offenders are either sent directly to adult jail
or are transferred there from juvenile facilities. A 1968 study of
1,214 juvenile courts found that 31,000 children were incarcerated in adult jails, with an additional 20,000 in juvenile
detention homes; the study also noted that in most of these instances the children would have been out on bail *if* they had
been adults, since many were detained until they were formally
tried or were convicted of offenses, like being an "incorrigible,"
of which an adult cannot be guilty.[56]

(2) Judges became despotic, not benevolent. Playing god
with a free hand, they often resented any moves to permit lawyers to defend juvenile defendants. The National Council of
Juvenile Court Judges conducted a study of young offenders,
finding hostility generated most when a child was lectured to and
incarcerated or not, depending on the judge's mood, and also
finding that the judge who was formal in his disposition of the
case had the most positive effect on those before him.[57] The
apotheosis of the juvenile judge is captured by the following
sentence of one of its clan: "If he is good, he can go home; if
he isn't good, I will keep him in detention."[58]

(3) Overcrowding is endemic, having a disastrous effect on
deterrence and rehabilitation. In Philadelphia, judges traditionally try 70 cases a day; in Washington, D.C., there were 3,547
cases waiting to be tried as of mid-summer, 1970. Many youths,
after their arrests, wait weeks before they ever see a judge; many
are not formally tried until two or three years after their alleged
offenses, often spending months at a time waiting in "receiving
homes" for court hearings. Yet, as juvenile experts (and parents)
realize, the longer the time between wrongdoing and correction,

the less meaningful becomes any corrective action taken by the court.

(4) Rehabilitation is a charade. Although the theoretical support for the whole system, rehabilitation efforts in the District of Columbia, for example, occupied only about 5 percent of the court's time in 1969–1970. The lack of remedial and counseling facilities compels judges to sentence or release those acknowledged as disturbed children in need of treatment.

(5) Finally, despite all these pitfalls, juvenile courts continued to consider due process safeguards as unnecessary. Although the Fourth and Fifth Amendments' use of the word "person" makes no distinction between child and adult, the rights accorded adults were denied to their children.

The gap between concept and reality was evident to all. Justice Fortas warned that "the condition of being a boy does not justify a kangaroo court,"[59] and Justice Douglas, apt as always, commented: "Despotism is never justified because it intends to be benevolent. Big brother is not necessarily either rational or wise."[60] The following three case studies chart some recent developments, with two leading to the first Supreme Court pronouncements in this area, and with one falling far short of it.

Morris Kent, sixteen, confessed to police that he committed a robbery and rape. The statute governing the District of Columbia Juvenile Court permitted a defendant on such serious criminal charges to be "waived" into adult court after a "full investigation." A psychiatrist's affidavit recommended hospitalization, but the judge, pressured by an overcrowded docket, waived Kent over to the criminal authorities without any hearing or factual findings. In a later trial, Kent was sentenced to a total of from thirty to ninety years in jail for various counts. The Supreme Court found fault with this decision in 1967, not on constitutional grounds, although they were hinted at, but on statutory grounds, that in fact no "investigation" or fact findings had occurred.[61] Sending a juvenile from a situation where the maximum penalty was five years (ages sixteen to twenty-one) to one where it was death could not be accomplished on such frivolous grounds.

Fifteen-year-old Gerald Gault was found guilty of making an

obscene phone call, was not notified of the charges against him, was not told of his right against self-incrimination, was not represented by counsel, and, for an offense carrying a maximum sentence of two months for an adult, was declared a delinquent and subjected to institutionalization until twenty-one, *six years* later. The Supreme Court in 1967 issued a historic opinion, going beyond its *Kent* rationale and finding that a juvenile had a right to a timely notice of charges and that notice at the first hearing was not timely, a right to counsel or appointed counsel, if indigent, a right to be informed concerning self-incrimination and a right to cross-examine the witnesses testifying against him.[62]

Finally, there was the case of Betty Jean, a black, seventeen-year-old girl; while appearing before juvenile court, her attorney requested a psychiatric examination for her: she had had sexual relations at ten, was the mother of an illegitimate child, was raped at sixteen, and had nightmares that people were staring at her while the lights were out. A physician recommended "nothing short of a complete psychiatric study," which was denied by the judge, who had wide discretion in this area. He claimed:

> Such experiences are far from being uncommon among children in her socio-economic situation with the result that the traumatic effect may be expected to be far less than it would be in a case of a child raised by parents and relatives with different habits and customs.[63]

Yes the poor and the black *are* different from you and me, rephrasing Hemingway to Fitzgerald; they have less money and are of a different color. Thus, the system at its worst reveals its overt bigotry, against race and against class, a trait which can be amply exercised given the disproportionate number of poor people and blacks who find themselves in the victim's seat at juvenile proceedings. Institutional racism also permeates the structure. A white child in trouble is more likely to be released to the custody of his parents than the black child, who often lacks any; and when a white child needs treatment he can often afford it on his own, while the lack of public facilities penalizes the poor black the most.

Although the Supreme Court has at last begun to insist that juvenile proceedings be conducted with certain due process rights, much remains to be done. Issues such as hearsay, right to a transcript, right to appeal, burden of proof, right to a public proceeding, and right to a jury trial have still to be favorably resolved. If all are necessary to insure adult fairness, they are necessary to protect those who are even less able to protect themselves. Yet a more crucial remedy lies in the amount of public resources which must be granted juvenile proceedings. Backlogged courts and harassed judges can never really guarantee individual justice. More judges and adequate treatment centers must be sought to relieve this adjudicatory fiasco.

Yet where is the public pressure to insure legal justice? It doesn't exist. There are no persistent pressure groups here, unlike those who push farm, maritime, and oil subsidies, which cost the taxpayers billions of dollars each year. Lawyers, who as a group could do it given their professional obligations, do not, magnetized by the immediacy of retainer interests. And the unexpressed public reaction is: why worry since it doesn't affect me? It is not realized that of all white children under twenty-one, 50 percent will at some time be arrested for a violation more serious than a traffic offense; the comparable statistic for blacks is 80 percent. Consequently, the problem admittedly goes beyond inadequacies in children's court; the whole administration of justice in the United States—from local courts to the Supreme Court—is appropriated $128 million, according to Chief Justice Burger, approximately the cost of the new FBI building alone or of two C-5A's.

B. Without Rights

Why is it that until an individual witnesses his 7,670th morning, he is considered an infant, and that after the great event, he is an adult? The facile, and probably most accurate, reason is that men in 1600 England were knighted at twenty-one, a tradition and age that have been passed down through the centuries, immune to changing eras and countries. There is actually little theoretical or statistical underpinning for the twenty-one-year-old cut-off other than the general sense that a certain level of maturity and knowledge is required for admission to full citizenship, and that twenty-one seems as good a place as any to draw the line. This age of legal maturity catalyzes with the phenomenon of large numbers of adult students—"institutions of higher education [are] warehouses for the temporary storage of a population it knows not what else to do with"[64]—to produce a nation of adolescents, legally and mentally. There seems to be a tacit policy of encouraging prolonged, dependent youth, which is both motivated by concern for their inexperience and for their complete training—luxuries affordable by a post-affluent society.

The result of this tradition and policy is that for those aged sixteen to twenty-one, excepting a few situations such as laws permitting eighteen-year-olds to drive and receive social security prepayments, legal immaturity results. The young cannot:

• sign a binding contract or hold and dispose of property.
• work in many occupations.
• represent themselves in divorce or will proceedings.
• sit on a grand jury or jury.
• vote, run for elected office, or be appointed to state agencies.
• marry or travel without parental consent.
• purchase liquor and cigarettes or attend many movies.

Yet the young can:

• be drafted and taxed.
• be subject, legally, to corporal punishment by family.
• be controlled by school authorities and be subject to juvenile curfews.
• be sent to adult prison.

The state of legal infancy imposes legal liabilities without compensatory rights. It is a policy which lacks any factual basis, yet affects millions and persists, passively accepted by adults and children alike who do not comprehend any alternative.

One factor in the acceptance and seeming permanence of this tradition is the failure of the legal system to make this problem an issue or to articulate decisions which bear on this point. Thus, while law students drivel away hours debating apportionment between life tenants and remaindermen, they do not discuss the law as it applies to nearly one-half our population—all those under twenty-one. It took the Supreme Court 177 years of existence before it reviewed an issue relating to children, in the *Kent* and *Gault* decisions. And finally, when concern *was* voiced for the rights of battered children, as early as 1874, there were no public authorities or legal precedents extant to aid in the effort. Eventually, one particular litigant convinced the ASPCA to help and a suit was filed and won on the grounds that children were members of the animal kingdom. Even today, laws dealing with animals are more specific than those dealing with children.

This situation, however, may not remain static. Great Britain can become our model of reform, since on January 1, 1970, the age of legal capacity there was dropped from twenty-one to eighteen. As of that date, eighteen-year-olds could vote, hold and release property, make enforceable contracts and wills, marry without consent, obtain credit, and be sued on the default of debts (with rights come responsibilities). And in this country, Congress passed a law in the summer of 1970 permitting eighteen-year-olds to vote in all local, state, and national elections, a law based on the principle that the equal protection of the laws demanded that eighteen-year-olds as well as their elders have the vote. Since the Constitution specifically leaves voting requirements up to the states, many charged that the law as passed was unconstitutional. On December 22, 1970, the Supreme Court decided the issue in Solomonic fashion: eighteen-year-olds could vote in all federal elections, but it was up to each state, not Congress, to set their own age requirements for other contests.

No doubt the divided vote will lead to confusion on election day, but the point to emphasize is the reasoning behind the lowered federal age limit.

The equal protection analysis should be adequate to support the law; the more important issue is the argument behind and purpose of this legislation as enacted. When the Constitution was passed, the average twenty-one-year-old had about two-thirds of a year of formal schooling; now the average is approaching eleven years. In 1920, only 30 percent of the high-school-age population was in high school, 17 percent were graduated, and 8 percent went on to college. Today, 85 percent attend high school, 75 percent graduate, and approximately 45 percent go on to higher education. While in 1920 the average age for marriage was twenty-five for men and twenty-one for women, today nearly one-half of those eighteen to twenty-one are already married.[65] Compounding the increasing formal education and family maturity are the twin facts that the omnipresent media can disseminate informed views to millions of children who need only sit and listen, and political involvement of those under twenty-one has sharply accelerated as the peace and race issues have found constituencies. The inevitable conclusion was drawn by Erik Erikson, student of the young: "There are more and better informed young people in the world today; and they are in better communication with each other, or, at any rate, connected through more and more uniform news media."*

This conclusion, however, does not *merely* support the change in voting age—a step already undertaken by thirty-six other countries—but should signal a change in *all* the laws which now keep down the sixteen to twenty-one-year-olds. If a taste of voting will make them more involved and responsible, so will participation in all our laws. Of course, such social facts have

* A *New York Times* article of January 24, 1971, discussed new evidence which supports this point: "From surveys involving thousands of girls, four generations of Harvard boys, records of the choir of Johann Sebastian Bach, and numerous other studies, researchers on human growth have concluded that the rate at which boys and girls mature has been increasing steadily. Not only are sexual and physical maturity coming earlier, but some researchers have also found a parallel acceleration in mental development, a phenomenon, they point out, that could have wide social and legal implications if confirmed."

been recently overwhelmed by the kind of political fear carica-
tured in a movie entitled *Wild in the Streets*, where the voting
age was lowered to fourteen, a pop-singer in his early twenties
was elected President, and all citizens over thirty-five were led
away to LSD centers. More realistically, as Chicagos and Colum-
bias increasingly occur, the electorate tends to penalize all youth
for the apprehended errors of some.

Yet sound public policy should announce that about 200
years after our founding, a class of people were discovered who
were neither classical infants nor classical adults, who were subject to governmental authority without any influence over it, and
who should be considered as adult citizens for the benefit of the
polity and of themselves. For a central assumption of this chapter has been that with the added responsibilities and respect that
attend the granting of these legal rights—from freer schools to
more contractual rights—the young will themselves rebound with
added self-respect and character growth due to increased personal
freedom. There are numerous primitive societies where post-
puberty children are inducted into the tribe, with full benefits
and responsibilities. Perhaps we too can reach this level of advancement.

The Courts and the Campus

BRUCE WASSERSTEIN*

A nation that has lost the allegiance of part of its youth is a nation that has lost part of its future.
　　　　　　—Report of the President's Commission
　　　　　　　　on Campus Unrest

Students are increasingly perceiving the courts as their enemy; the handling of campus disorders by the judiciary has done little to dispel this impression.

Much of the law governing campus conduct is a dangerous anachronism that should have died in the 1930s. For a dissident at a private college, judges still cite a 1928 case which allowed Syracuse University to expel a coed, Beatrice Anthony, on the basis that her sorority sisters did not think her a "typical Syracuse girl."[1]

Through the late fifties, students at publicly supported colleges got much of the same treatment as Miss Anthony did from private Syracuse. As Harvard law professor Warren Seavey pointed out, the courts denied to students the "protection given a pickpocket."[2] Finally, in the landmark *Dixon*[3] case of 1961, a federal court of appeals agreed with Seavey and ruled as a matter of constitutional doctrine that some minimal standards of fair play were applicable to students expelled from public universities. In

* Bruce Wasserstein has served as Managing Editor of the *Harvard Civil Rights–Civil Liberties Law Review* and is currently collaborating in a study of antitrust enforcement. At college he was executive editor of *The Michigan Daily*, and articles by him have appeared in publications such as *The New Republic*.

Dixon black students were summarily expelled from public Alabama State College after attempting to integrate a lunch counter in the county courthouse. No list of charges was presented and there was no hearing.

But the new dawn of the post-*Dixon* era is pretty gray. First, private universities are not at all covered by its constitutional rule. Second, aside from constitutional law, the courts still refuse to apply modern legal theories of such fields as trusts and contracts in determining student rights. Third, the *Dixon* rule is inadequate today for those public institutions it does cover because it has failed to evolve since 1961. The result is that our courts are presently incapable of dealing fairly with the current wave of student unrest.

The shooting of students at Kent and Jackson State Colleges on the one hand, and the blowing up of the mathematics building at the University of Wisconsin on the other, have fueled the mutual antagonism between the student and much of the rest of society. In the last two years, there has been a tendency for the courts, especially through their injunctive proceedings, to become more an enforcement arm of the administration than a neutral judicial body. In a national climate of repression and reaction, the reformation of judicial doctrine on college students which seemed to be commencing with *Dixon* has been stalled.

I. THE PRIVATE UNIVERSITY

As the *Dixon* court pointed out, *Anthony* remains the law governing the actions of private colleges. The reason for this sharp dichotomy in judicial standards between private and public universities is that the Fourteenth Amendment guarantees invoked by the *Dixon* court, such as due process, are directed against what the courts call "state action" rather than the acts of private parties. According to the Fourteenth, "No *state* shall . . . deprive any person of life, liberty, or property, without due process of law. . . ." In recent years, the Supreme Court has been taking an increasingly broad view of what constitutes "state action," and in a number of decisions the concept has evolved to logically encompass private universities. Underlying this redefinition of "state action" is the realization that many private institutions either function like a governmental unit or are inextricably interconnected with the state. Aside from more obvious cases, such as private schools financed by the state to avoid desegregation, the courts have also applied the Fourteenth "state action" concept to more subtle situations: a private park which seemed like part of the public park; a restaurant in a state-owned parking building; a state-funded medical hospital; shopping centers; company towns.[4]

As early as 1963, the *Yale Law Journal* concluded that no distinction could be made between private and public universities, given Supreme Court rulings on the "state action" issue.

> A school is as much a school whether it be named "state" or not. State schools today do not differ as a class from private schools in terms of size, organization, purpose, quality or functional importance. . . . To the extent that a school—state or private—is functionally a government, our social values demand that standards be imposed on the discretion of administrators—state or private—to protect justice and liberty in the school community.[5]

The fact that in 1968–69 31.5 percent of total expenditures of private colleges were paid with public funds strongly reinforces this viewpoint. To take a particular example, in 1967 Columbia University, a "private" institution, received $60 million in public funds out of a total budget of $134 million. Now Columbia, and all other nonsectarian private universities in New York State, is eligible to get under the recently financed "Bundy Program" a direct subsidy from the state of $400 for each bachelor's and master's degree and $2,400 for each doctoral degree conferred yearly. Under this program, New York's "private" colleges will receive an estimated $24 million from the state coffers, aside from the indirect subsidies of direct state tuition grants to students. Yet, in a recent case, a court refused to concede that Columbia was subject to any constitutional limitations in its actions.[6]

In Pennsylvania, historically "private" colleges are becoming increasingly dependent on the state. Temple University and the University of Pittsburgh are now officially "state-related" schools, and the University of Pennsylvania is called a "state-aided" institution. In early 1970, the legislature failed to deliver sums promised to these schools and a major crisis arose. Temple, which expected $41.4 million, had to borrow $30 million and was paying $6,600 a day interest. The University of Pennsylvania, which expected the state to pay 23 percent of its budget, was forced to stop hiring faculty and washing windows.

Another example is "private" Howard University, which was created by act of Congress. When students heckled General Louis B. Hershey, former director of selective service, they were expelled without notice or hearing. In upholding the school's action, the court contended that Howard was a "private" institution not subject to the Fourteenth Amendment even though it was "true a large percentage of its expenses are paid for with annual appropriations from congress. As a condition of receiving such money, the Secretary of HEW is given authority to visit and inspect Howard University and to control and supervise the expenditure of those funds."[7]

Looking at some other private universities, there are many historical interconnections with the state. Harvard originated in 1636 by action of the Massachusetts Bay Legislature. Until 1865, members of the state government chose some of the Board of Overseers. Six members of the state senate sat on the Board of Trustees of Yale until 1872, and as late as 1910 the governor of New Jersey still sat on the Board of Trustees of Princeton, ex officio.[8]

Recently there has been an increased connection between state governments and the campus through the passage of statutes cutting off state aid to schools that don't keep demonstrators in line. During the 1969 and 1970 legislative sessions, bills regulating campus activities were passed in thirty-two states as a reaction to student activism.[9] At the federal level, similar statutes have been passed requiring certification by university administrators that they have halted funds to student protestors.[10]

The bizzare results courts can reach in trying to differentiate between private and public universities is illustrated by the

Alfred University case.[11] Demonstrators peacefully formed a line between ROTC cadets and the viewing stand at an award ceremony in violation of the school rule that groups who wish to protest must inform the dean forty-eight hours in advance. The court differentiated between students who were in the liberal arts program and those who were enrolled in the Ceramic College, which was directly funded by the state. Although ultimately the court held that no constitutional rights were violated, the artificiality of this distinction among students who mixed in the dorms and in all phases of campus life is absurd. The campus officers for all students were the same, and so were the regulations. Certainly, the idea that "private" and "public" schools are inherently different is put to the test in this case, for one single university is legally both.

There have been a few cases in which the courts have held that private schools are subject to the Fourteenth Amendment, but they generally have been reversed on appeal. For example, Judge J. Skelly Wright, a jurist with a well-deserved reputation for being ahead of his time, ruled that Tulane University was subject to constitutional limitations in its student admissions policy. After noting that historically Tulane was the state-supported University of Louisiana until Paul Tulane gave it a substantial endowment, Judge Wright went on to say:

> One may question whether any school or college can ever be so "private" as to escape the reach of the 14th amendment. . . . Clearly the administrators of a private college are performing a public function. They do the work of the state, often in the place of the state. Does it not follow that they stand in the state's shoes?[12]

But Judge Wright was reversed by a higher court which supported the inconsistencies of past doctrine.

Aside from ignoring modern constitutional law, the courts are determined not to apply the modern law of contracts and trusts to these cases. In many of the earlier private college decisions, the courts supported the administrators through various theories of contract and fiduciary law. However, since these cases were decided, the law in these areas has changed and now dictates the opposite conclusion. For example, the *Anthony* court relied on contract law to support the expulsion of the Syracuse coed. Contract law has since changed and now the decision is theoretically unsound. Courts now recognize the disparity of power between large institutions and the individual citizen and therefore construe quite narrowly conditions of contracts which unduly favor the institution. In fact, if you examine the conditions of enrollment in *Anthony*, the supposed contract is no contract at all because one side, the university, is not bound to perform any services. According to the university regulations, the administration could dismiss a student for whatever reason it pleased, whenever it pleased. Even in 1928, the time of the *Anthony* decision, the courts realized that upholding such clauses contradicted existing law. The judge said that Syracuse should have reasons for its actions, although he also held in a puzzling contradiction that the administration need not disclose them. Yet, according to the judge, if Miss Anthony could have rebutted either the evidence or the pertinence of the charges, both of which he said need not be disclosed, she would have a strong case. This comedy of contorted legalese only began with the *Anthony* decision. Since that time, as courts have in general moved to protect the individual against harsh contracts and "boiler plate" provisions, judges have simply moved to other bases for defending their decisions in private college cases. For example, the notion of *in loco parentis*, which essentially maintained that the university had the rights of control of a parent over its child, was fashionable for a time but has gradually become discredited. The interesting point is that if the courts had consistently applied any one theory such as the contractual relationship, the modern law in that field could act as a positive instrument protecting student rights.

Beyond misapplied legal doctrines, the courts, however, do have an important policy reason for seeking to differentiate between private and public institutions. Traditionally the courts have been reluctant to interfere with the educational process fearing such action would constrain the diversity of approaches to education taken by different schools. Although the *Dixon* case imposed certain standards on public universities, the courts implicitly feel private colleges should be free to experiment with varying forms of student-administrative relationships without court intervention. Typical expression of this sentiment was made by the court in the Howard University case:

> An entering wedge seemingly innocuous at first blush, may lead step by step to a serious external domination of the university and college and a consequent damper and hindrance to their intellectual development and growth.[13]

Of course, what the court failed to mention after citing the glories of Harvard and other private universities, is that public universities subject to the *Dixon* rule have managed to retain their quality without sinking beneath a wave of court orders.

Other jurists are specifically fearful that the imposition of *Dixon* type standards to colleges with religious affiliations would conflict with their sectarian goals.

To illustrate the problem, take the case of Howard Carr and Greta Schmidt, seniors at St. John's University, a Catholic institution in New York City. In 1962, Howard and Greta decided to get married in a civil ceremony at the municipal building in Brooklyn and brought along fellow student Jean Catto as a witness. Hearing of the marriage, the university expelled all three students based on the following clause in the college bulletin: "In conformity with the ideals of Christian education and conduct, the University reserves the right to dismiss a student at any time on whatever grounds the University judges advisable." Although the lower court held that the university regulation was too vague to include a city hall marriage, a higher court upheld the dismissals. One judge in an indignant dissent commented "There is no basis for the University's exercise of discretion . . . a University may not enforce against a student ecclesiastical law."[14]

If St. John's were subject to the Fourteenth Amendment, there would be great tension between constitutional standards and the sectarian goals of that institution. But this reason is no justification to reject the applicability of any constitutional standards at all. The problem for the courts is to achieve the proper trade off between diversity and constitutional standards; the current approach which achieves a solution to this difficult quandary by completely dismissing the applicability of standards is unacceptable.

One possible resolution to this problem is for courts to admit that the Fourteenth Amendment applies to private colleges, but the standards should not be as rigorous as those applied to public schools. A better solution would be for the courts to examine with each private college its educational goals and see whether the imposition of due process standards as strict as those used for public university cases would negate these objectives. Another alternative is to maintain the view that the Fourteenth is inapplicable to private colleges, and then move toward the establishment of standards through some common law vehicle such as contract law. The advantage here is that the common law may prove to be a more flexible means of tailoring judicial rulings to the particular institution than constitutional doctrine.

The problem with any approach less than a bright line rule stipulating that the Fourteenth is applicable to private colleges is that the courts have a bad case of myopia when it comes to protecting the student interest. But at least the door would be open for a change of attitude. Current doctrine cuts off all possibilities of evolution by holding, in effect, that modern constitutional law and common law are not applicable to the 2,100,000 private university students.

Ultimately, the best solution to the diversity problem is to presume that the same standards of fair procedure are applicable to all colleges, whether private or public, unless a school can show that the imposition of such rules negates its legitimate educational goals. Thus, a military academy or a theological seminary would be able to rebut the presumption of standards, but schools like public UCLA and private University of Southern California would be subject to the same rules. Such an approach recognizes that the private-public dichotomy now used by the courts is a result of antiquated legal reasoning, and that preferable classification schemes would be closely related to the actual functions of the schools.

A step in the right direction has been taken in a recent Massachusetts decision. Frederick C. Sturm III was a junior majoring in biology at private Boston University when he was accused of cheating on his comparative anatomy course in May, 1968. When Sturm was brought before the school academic conduct committee, there were no witnesses, no information was given as to evidence, and legal counsel was not allowed to be present. Because of a mailing mishap, Sturm was not informed of his dismissal until the following November, even though he was enrolled in both the summer and fall terms. Judge Francis Good found that Boston University had deprived Sturm of fair process on a mixture of contractual and constitutional grounds.

Focusing on the contractual ground, Judge Good applied modern law by holding that Boston University could not arbitrarily break their implied agreement to offer the student an education. Moving to alternative constitutional grounds, Judge Good wrote:

> I take it that the day has passed when the courts would approve of a college disciplining a student for failure to tip his hat to the tutor as they were passing each other on the college grounds. . . . Boston University has argued that it is a private institution and this requires a different result. . . . However Boston University is not a small, isolated theological school in Vermont, but rather is a major university of over 23,000 students engaged in one of the most important duties of society.[15]

Judge Good specified procedural rules, including the right to cross-examine witnesses, have a lawyer present, and be presented with the evidence. "For the Court to approve anything less," Judge Good held, ". . . would be to bow in the direction of pure pretense and make believe and to approve a clearly unfair procedure with reference to this student."

Although Boston University did not appeal the Good decision, its precedential value is unfortunately minimal. Judge Good sits on the Suffolk County Superior Court, and his opinions are unlikely to have great effect on the federal judges involved in most student expulsion cases.

A recent case where the doctrine is hazier but the impact probably greater arose when twenty-four blacks tried to fight their expulsion from Lutheran-affiliated Wagner College in New York City.[16] The court of appeals remanded the case back to the district court to determine whether a recent statute passed by the state legislature requiring the filing of rules for retaining campus order was sufficient action by the state to give students at private New York colleges constitutional protection. The majority reasoned that if the statute expressed a mandatory "get tough" policy, the students would be covered by the Fourteenth Amendment. The case brings up more questions than it answers, and it is quite easy to see how the legal mind could subvert its spirit. But it could be a seminal decision, and if the social climate of the country were different, the maverick views expressed by Judges Good and Wright would definitely be, within a few years, the governing law. Today, unfortunately, the assumption of progress may prove to be fallacious.

II. THE PUBLIC UNIVERSITY

Compared to the plight of the private college student who is legally at the mercy of the administration, the public university student is well protected by the courts. But the law here is still inadequate. The innovation of the *Dixon* standard of fundamental fairness was commendable in 1961, but now it is outdated by the changing campus scene and the revolution in constitutional law as interpreted by the Warren court.

A. *Fair Procedure*

The *Dixon* court felt it could not endorse the expulsion without formal charges or hearings of Alabama State College students just because they had protested segregation in the Montgomery County Courthouse lunch counter. But the court did not go very far beyond these extraordinary circumstances in guaranteeing procedural rights to students.

For example, the court says "This is not to imply that a full dress judicial hearing, with the right to cross-examine witnesses is necessary. Such a hearing, with the attending publicity and disturbance of college activities, might be detrimental to the college's educational atmosphere and impractical to carry out."[17] This overemphasis of a college's interest to avoid publicity and possible turmoil reflects the willingness of courts to generally go along with the administration when weighing the competing interests of school and student. This tendency of the courts has gone too far. Many will argue that procedural safeguards given to students need not be as strong as those of criminals or "adults," but this conception fundamentally misunderstands the importance of education in our society. The right to remain in college is one of the most important possessions of the student. Aside from the more intangible benefits of prestige, a greater appreciation and understanding of the world, and access to more intellectually meaningful work, the hard fact is that a college degree is a valuable piece of property. Looking at the statistics that differentiate the high school graduate's salary from that of the college man, expulsion is equal to the deprivation of $167,000 in lifetime income. Certainly, a student's place in a university warrants the same procedural protection as any other property right.

Furthermore, the trend in constitutional law is against recognizing different procedural privileges for different age groups. For example, in the juvenile offense area, the Supreme Court has ruled that the old concept of paternalistic informality which allegedly made youngsters more at ease in court is outmoded and unconstitutional.[18]

Finally, the implicit notion that all university students are not adults in the legal sense is factually fallacious. Although the average age is between twenty and twenty-one, 1,207,000 students are over twenty-five. Are the millions of students who are over twenty-one to be denied the full privileges of citizens merely because they go to school? In many ways judicial attitudes toward students is a vestige of the days when few went to graduate school or adult education programs. But times have changed, even if the courts have not.

Dixon might have evolved into a more positive doctrine, but unfortunately the courts have generally limited its holding. For example, the judges in the western federal district court of Missouri assembled in 1968 to issue their interpretation of *Dixon's* impact on student rights. According to them, the discipline of students is part of the teaching process, and thus relevant to the goals of an educational institution.

> The nihilist and the anarchist determined to destroy the existing political and social order, who direct their primary attacks on the educational institution, understand fully the missions of education in the U.S. . . . By judicial mandate to impose upon the academic community in student discipline the intricate, time consuming, sophisticated procedures, rules, and safeguards of criminal law, would frustrate the teaching process and render the institution control impotent.[19]

One of the district court judges in the same judicial circuit even further limited *Dixon* by holding, "The legal doctrine that a prohibitory statute is void if it is overly broad or unconstitutionally vague does not in the absence of exceptional circumstances apply to standards of student conduct."[20] Similar indifference to constitutional principles about vagueness in governing regulations was announced by a Colorado federal court in dealing with some University of Colorado students who harassed CIA recruiters on the campus. The university disciplined these protestors on the basis of a "hazing" regulation which was designed for the days of freshman beanies and raccoon coats.[21]

If the courts were to approach student rights from a modern constitutional viewpoint, there would also be concern for the problem of double jeopardy when a student is both being prosecuted by the university and civil authorities for an offense. A particularly interesting twist here is the problem of the usability of evidence gathered in university proceedings at criminal trials. If universities are allowed to use flexible procedural devices, the fact that a student refuses to answer charges would presumably be held against him; but if he does talk, the local prosecutor can use the testimony against the student. Clearly there is a Fifth Amendment self-incrimination problem. In the Columbia building take-over case, the problem did arise, but the court avoided it by pointing out that the district attorney had signed an affidavit stipulating he would not use student testimony for evidence. Such a solution to the dilemma is, however, unsatisfactory, since federal authorities could still use the material. The important point is not the specific problem of double jeopardy and self-incrimination, but rather that a whole host of due process problems erupts when a university expulsion proceeding is insensitive to procedures protecting student rights both on and off the campus. If, for example, a student may not have an attorney present at a university hearing, he may not even have access to a source of advice as to how his statements before the dean can be used against him. Similarly, new statutes such as California's provision denying financial aid to any student who a university board determines willfully disrupted the ordinary operation of the campus, even without arrest and conviction,[22] make the fairness of university procedures extremely important.

Aside from the question of students' procedural rights given present regulations, a more fundamental question can be asked about the rights of students to somehow participate in the promulgation of the rules that apply to them. The fact that a rule is in some handbook is not particularly meaningful if the administration can write a new handbook overnight. Using a contract analogy, one party cannot rewrite the conditions of the contract without the other party participating. Of course, the courts are not likely to look with favor upon the use of legal devices to give students a meaningful participatory voice in university decision making. Nevertheless, if we use the same contractual model that the courts used in such cases as *Anthony*, we could say that indeed there is a contractual obligation between the students and the university, with the student council acting as agents for the class of students and the administration acting for the university. Such a structure would solve the fundamental problems of who makes the rules and who can judge or select the judges in a student dismissal case. At present, the administration generally both brings the charges and also decides which body should review the expulsion. If the university discipline process is a learning experience, as the Missouri courts contend, then it should not be a lesson in arbitrary procedures where the prosecutor, legislator, and jury selector are all the administration.

In June, 1967, a committee consisting of representatives from the National Student Association, the American Association of University Professors, and the National Association of Student Personnel Administrators, among others, drafted a Joint Statement on Rights and Freedoms of Students setting up *minimal* standards for procedural fairness in disciplining students. Among the specific minimal standards suggested when serious charges were made against students were the rights to a formal hearing, to cross-examine witnesses, and to have an attorney present offering advice. If the accused so requested, students as well as faculty should be on the disciplinary committee, and improperly acquired evidence should not be admissible.

Since 1961, when *Dixon* was decided, the definition of what is fundamental fairness in procedural devices has changed as the Warren court increasingly demanded stricter safeguards. Certainly, for university students, the definition of what is fundamentally fair should have also evolved. The balance the courts seek to strike between due process and effective college administration with minimal disruption is misconceived. Arguably, when delimiting the substantive rights of students to demonstrate, there is an important factor of maintaining the campus tranquility necessary for an effective learning process. But there the problem is actual physical impediments. If the notion here that due process is too volatile a condition for the campus is accepted, we would also by logic ban the controversial thoughts of speakers, professors, or students. The courts have no business giving such heavy weight to the speculative ill effects of a process of fairness.

B. The Right to Protest

Dixon was a procedural rights case which did not define the permissible scope of student protest. Although the logic of *Dixon* should have set the stage for the broadening of students' substantive rights, the courts have not pushed the point. The most that can be said about the current state of the law is that clearly a public university administration cannot enforce a rule banning *all* demonstrations. But the issue of how narrowly the administration can limit the right to protest is unclear. Again, the courts weigh very heavily the right of a public college to preserve an atmosphere conducive to "intellectual pursuits"; in effect, administrators are given wide scope as to how to define the nature of a positive intellectual experience.

Yet statistically, the reality of student protest differs considerably from its public image. A study conducted during the first six months of 1969 shows at least 215,000 students actually participated directly in campus protests. Three-quarters of these protests did not result in any destruction or violence of any kind. As the Scranton commission on campus disorders pointed out, "Most student protestors are neither violent nor extremist." Colleges with students who had high SAT scores were far more likely to have protests than other schools. The New Left participated in only 28 percent of all protests, and the 6 percent of the college population that is black was involved in 51 percent of all demonstrations.[23] Thus, despite Fred Hechinger, campus unrest is not a monolithic conspiracy by rabid anarchists. It is a general phenomenon encompassing a large number of the brighter students who question the war, racism, and depersonalization of our society.

The Free Speech and subsequent Filthy Speech movements in Berkeley illustrate the attitudes of courts and administrators toward student political activity and the consequences of repression. The current era of building seizures and campus demonstrations should really be known in education circles as A.B. (After Berkeley). The free speech controversy on that famous campus was the model of things to come; and yet many people forget that the controversy was sparked by a simple issue which had no business arising in the first place: the right to solicit for political causes on a university campus. If the courts had taken a more progressive view of students' rights, ironically, the situation might never have occurred.

In a subsequent disturbance, Art Goldberg and other Berkeley students protested the arrest of a fellow student for carrying an allegedly obscene sign by conducting "Filthy Speech" rallies on campus. Goldberg was expelled for having violated the following campus rule:

> It is taken for granted that each student will adhere to acceptable standards of personal conduct; and that all students . . . will set and observe among themselves proper standards of conduct and good taste.

Specifically Goldberg was charged with "acting as moderator for the rally and in the course thereof addressing the persons assembled by repeatedly using the word 'fuck' in its various declensions," and collecting funds for the "fuck defense fund."* [24]

A California state court upheld the dismissal of the participating students on the basis that the rally was loud, bawdy, and the rules banning it were necessary to further the university's goals. Although the interests of students in shouting four-letter words in defiance of administrative regulations may not be the most important constitutional right, the interests of the administration also seem minimal. This was not a case of physical obstruction, or building takeovers, but rather involved speech. Given Supreme Court rulings on obscenity, it would appear that expression that contains bawdy language still may contain important expressions of political and social ideas. In a way, the filthy speech was symbolic itself of the obscenity of censorship.

Furthermore, the gross subjectivity of a rule requiring "proper" conduct in "good taste" makes regulations such as Berkeley's conducive to serious abuse. To some, the "good taste" of the administration in keeping political solicitation off campus in the original free speech controversy is itself more questionable than the yelling of various declensions of a four-letter word.

---

* Incidentally, Goldberg has had a rather colorful career since his expulsion. He entered Howard Law School where he was again expelled. Then he enrolled at Rutgers Law School studying under civil liberties lawyer Arthur Kinoy. Now he is fighting in court to be admitted to the California bar, which has turned down his application because of its view of his moral character.

The important point is not the foul language, but rather the large scope of discretion courts give even public universities to determine what conditions are necessary for retaining an academic atmosphere. The seductiveness and potential maliciousness of this broad discretion are illustrated by examining the problems of college newspaper editors.

Garey Dickey, editor of the Troy State College Newspaper in Alabama, was expelled for trying to publish an editorial critical of state legislators. When the faculty adviser suggested a substitute editorial on dog-raising in North Carolina, Dickey simply ran a blank space with the word "CENSORED" across it. Although a court reinstated Dickey, it pointed out that his editorial did "not materially interfere with requirements of appropriate discipline in the operation of the school."[25] *Dickey* is a landmark decision leaning in the direction of favoring freedom of the student press, but its implicit logic can have some negative consequences. For example, the *Harvard Law Review* extrapolated from the case and concluded:

> Public criticism of the administration or the faculty by a student newspaper can undermine the confidence of both the student body and the public in the university and thereby impair both the quality of instruction and the maintenance of order and discipline. . . . A university might reasonably conclude that in view of the damage that can be done by false reporting, as well as the inexperience or possible irresponsibility of student editors, a rule banning criticism not based on demonstrable fact is justifiable in order to encourage responsible editorial comment.[26]

Such a position is inconsistent with the basic tenets of a free press. The law and order argument can be equally applied to the national mass media. In fact, the argument resembles that of the current Agnewstics. The concept of "demonstrable fact" is merely a cover for censorship since, as any journalist knows, the "informed source" is infinitely more valuable than the official press release. Besides, who determines what is demonstrable? When a story has two conflicting sides, whose facts are demonstrable? When an editor feels that the administration has mishandled a situation, how does he demonstrate it? Again, the point is that the courts and many legal commentators overemphasize the right of a university administration to be free from expressions of dissent if they foment dissatisfaction on campus. The right to speak, print, read, and think as one wants should be encouraged, not stifled at a public university. If the courts applied their logic elsewhere, free speech would be a nullity in this country. Again, we are talking about speech and expression, not action, which is a more difficult situation. The irony is that by stifling expression of dissent, the courts are merely encouraging direct action. If an administration were forced to react to the rumblings of change, it would not have to wait for student rampage to bring about needed reforms.

A recent case illustrates the reactionary tendency of the courts. Students at East Tennessee State University were suspended for distributing literature lambasting the school administration and calling upon their fellow students to protest. In complaining about parietal hours, the pamphlets referred to chastity belts and the administrators were called "despots." The court decided that, "This vicious attack on the administration was calculated to damage the reputation of the university. . . . The reference to 'chastity belts' for girls is a crude vulgar remark offensive to women students."[27] The learned jurists then held that college authorities could "nip such action in the bud" by expelling the protestors. If this is the type of constitutional protection that *Dixon* provides, the fight to give coverage to private school students may not be worth the battle.

The line between rhetoric and action, however, becomes more unclear in cases such as the disciplining of Berkeley student body president Dan Siegel. Siegel, a law student, delivered a speech at a rally protesting the university's construction of a fence around a vacant lot, which later became known as People's Park. Siegel exhorted the crowd, "Don't let those pigs beat the shit out of you, don't let yourselves get arrested for felonies, go down there and take the park."[28] And the students did, with a resultant wave of mass injuries and arrests. Siegel was put on probation and not allowed to hold official student office as a result of his speech. The court upheld the university's action, and ironically probably hurt the cause of nonviolence more than helped. By equating speech with action, the court is treading on very treacherous ground. Siegel's speech would not have been sufficient to have had him indicted in a criminal action, because of the First Amendment. Why should it have been sufficient grounds for a university subject to the Constitution to have disciplined him? In fact, the tactic seems to backfire. The student leader who seems to be advocating nonviolent tactics is punished, probably radicalizing other students and undermining the support of groups opposed to violence. Suspending Siegel as student body president reinforces the view that administrations are just interested in puppets as student leaders of official organizations; thus students must turn to more informal groups to get involved in meaningful actions.

Even more complex than the Siegel problem of the student saying or writing what he believes, is that of his right to act upon his beliefs. The recent wave of sit-ins, take-overs, and dean carry-outs has swept the national conscience and headlines.

To understand the legal position of students in such actions, it is necessary to look at the rather confused state of the law dealing with demonstrations in general. The most important case limiting the general right to demonstrate is *Adderley* v. *Florida*.[29] In *Adderley* the Supreme Court upheld the conviction of demonstrators who gathered on the driveway and grounds of a jailhouse to protest an earlier arrest. The Court relied upon the security needs of the jailhouse coupled with the problem of traffic flow to make its decision. *Adderley* thus defined a class of situations where the governmental interest in smooth functioning exceeded the public's interest in conducting a demonstration.

The specific conclusions of *Adderley* can be attacked on the basis that there wasn't, in reality, any tangible security threat. However, assuming there was a security problem, it would indicate a situation where the state interest was extremely strong. Such a rationale, however, should not be applicable to the college campus because the public university is perhaps the one public facility that should be consecrated to the concept of the free flow of ideas. To the degree that the courts have recognized demonstrations as "symbolic speech," such actions should be protected at public colleges. The problem arises when a university asserts that the demonstrations are in fact interfering with the everyday free flow of ideas in the classroom.

For example, if demonstrators took over a classroom and prevented discussion through their disruption, a balance would have to be made between the right of expressing ideas in the traditional classroom manner and more demonstrative means of expression. Assuming, however, that protestors cannot burst into classrooms claiming a monopoly of First Amendment protection, it is very hard to see how the interests of university administrators are strong enough to be able to flatly ban all demonstrations within buildings. There are many hallways, lobbies, and waiting rooms where no other idea dialog is taking place. Similarly, charging students with trespass because they stay in an administration building after closing hours completely disregards the importance of their political protest. True, an administration may have to pay more for electricity, and the hair of the distinguished businessmen and lawyers on the board of trustees may turn a little whiter; but a university building cannot be treated as just another item of private property that a college president can call his own. Of course, physical violence is another question, but it should be recognized that the university situation is the opposite of the circumstances in *Adderley*. There, the interest of the state in order and smooth functioning was inordinately high. In the case of the university, the interest in protecting demonstrations as a manifestation of the flow of ideas should be the presumption. Per se rules banning demonstrations in buildings, which may be the only meaningful place for students to protest, ignore that presumption. Administrators tend to view campus buildings as private landlords with the students being tenants-at-will. But merely because the dean goes home at 5:00 should not mitigate against students' staying in the administration building for the evening, if it makes a political point. Private property concepts are not appropriate in determining the students' right to demonstrate on the campus. Even from a technical legal viewpoint, it is extremely difficult, as the prosecution in the Harvard takeover cases found, to define when a trespass is taking place, especially when administrators bob back and forth debating whether any occurred. Rather than routinely applying simplistic trespass doctrines, courts should be attempting to delicately balance constitutional interests. Assuming we are dealing with a Columbia University rather than a Jesuit Seminary, these arguments for expanded student rights at public colleges should also apply to those at private universities.

The courts, unfortunately, do not agree with this analysis. Even in dealing with public universities, they cite *Adderley* repeatedly, as though a college and a jail were one, with the administration in the role of the jailers. A court upholding the conviction of students demonstrating against the Defense Intelligence Agency at the University of Kentucky put it this way:

> The privilege of an enrolled student to use and occupy the property of a school is and should be subject to the will of its governing authorities. If he is told to stay out of a particular room, building, or familiar trysting place, he enters it as a trespasser.[30]

In other words, the court gives absolute control to the administration to control demonstrations. Worse yet is the court which upheld the conviction of students at Central Missouri College under the following school regulation:

> Mass gatherings: Participation in mass gatherings which might be considered as unruly or unlawful will subject a student to possible immediate dismissal from the college. Only a few students intimately get involved in mob misconduct but many so called "spectators" get drawn into the fracas and by their very presence contribute to the dimensions of the problems. . . . When a breach of regulations involves a mixed group all members are held equally responsible.[31]

Obviously such rules chill protests in general for if one person happens to become "unruly," all demonstrators and spectators could find themselves dismissed from school.

Aside from stretching legal doctrine to find students guilty, courts are increasingly imposing heavier penalties for campus disruptions. For example, in early 1970 a California judge sentenced three students to state prison for one to twenty-five years on charges stemming from a building takeover at San Fernando Valley State College. Specifically, the students were convicted on one count of conspiracy, three counts of kidnaping, and twenty-nine counts of false imprisonment.

As the prosecutor in the case, Deputy District Attorney Vincent Bugliosi, admitted, the unprecedented charge of mass felonies for a building takeover was designed to stem similar demonstrations across the state. According to Bugliosi:

> Students have been getting amnesty in misdemeanor prosecutions and a slap on the wrist. If some of these students get stiff sentences, . . . the case could have an effect on campus militants. They've gotten away with murder, but they might think twice before doing it again.[32]

The takeover occurred after black students were spurned in their attempt to remove an allegedly racist freshman football coach; the students then marched on the administration building and got the president to accede to a list of their demands, which he later repudiated. The president charged that his staff was threatened by physical violence, although no actual injuries occurred. The judge, who, incidentally, had been called a "fascist pig" by the defendants, rejected the usually accepted recommendations of the probation department in sentencing the students. The defense lawyer charged the case was a "judicial lynching." It's obvious that the judge's political antennas were quite well tuned; the week before the trial began, Governor Reagan signed into law several bills stiffening penalties for campus demonstrators.

To further illustrate how the courts bend over to support the administration, take the new craze of the college dean—the injunction. In the Dartmouth College building takeover, for example, a court injunction was used to put the onus of calling in the police on the courts rather than on the campus administration. In essence, the students are no longer merely violating a campus regulation; they are in contempt of court. The temporary restraining orders universities are increasingly seeking are issued without notice to the students, and the penalty for violation can be far beyond that of the actual criminal offense. As one advocate of the injunction as an effective means of quelling student dissent points out, even though the penalties for offenses such as trespass may be minimal, the mechanism of an injunctive order can result in quite a stiff jail sentence.[33] The perniciousness of the court injunction is that a student who violates it is guilty of breaking the law, even if it were later determined that his activity before the injunction was issued was legal. The latest prominent statement of this contorted doctrine came in a civil rights case where Martin Luther King conducted a demonstration in the face of a ban on such activity.[34] Although the Supreme Court later acknowledged that the ordinance was unconstitutional, King was sentenced to a jail term for violating a court order. According to the Court, you simply cannot legally violate a court injunction no matter how capricious. Applying this doctrine to student cases, the administration can continually get injunctions from courts and seldom have to worry about the constitutionality of their position.

These injunctions are reminiscent of the days when courts undercut union organizers by issuing injunctions and sending in U.S. marshals to enforce them. As Felix Frankfurter pointed out then, "The injunction is not ordinarily sought to prevent property from being injured nor to protect the owner in its use, but to endow property with active, militant power which would make it dominant over men."[35] Of course, such antics ended generally in the union field with the passage of the Norris-LaGuardia Act, but in the college field they are just beginning.

Moving even further than issuing injunctions once the demonstration is in progress, some courts have now started issuing blanket injunctions before possibly illegal acts, such as building takeovers, even occur. For example, a Massachusetts judge has recently issued an injunction stopping the student senate of Southeastern Massachusetts University from interfering with the holding of classes. Wesleyan University officials obtained a court injunction restraining an all black campus group from disrupting "athletic, social or academic events." The order came after disturbances following the suspension of a black student at the school. Such prior restraints have historically been deemed offensive to the First Amendment because of the chilling effect they have on dissent. But with students, constitutional precedent applicable to the general citizenry seems to be ignored.

III. THE FUTURE: GAVEL v. GOWN?

In the case of private universities, the courts have managed to duck modern precedents in the fields of constitutional law, contracts, and trusts to maintain a system perpetuating the autocracy of the university administration. Implicitly, beyond the judicial rhetoric there is a desire to encourage diversity; but this goal does not justify the negation of all other legal doctrines, especially in the cases of private universities whose objectives are very similar to those of public institutions. As Eleanor Norton of the ACLU points out, "We are light years away from progress in private schools." Essentially the courts have locked themselves into a pro-administration stance through applications of obsolescent law.

In the case of public universities, the *Dixon* decision forced courts to balance the interests of students and administration. But the courts manage to consistently favor the administration in applying their balancing test. As the courts move beyond a supportive role for the administration to the more affirmative stature of issuing injunctions, students will increasingly view the courts as a repressive instrumentality, just as the labor movement considered them before the thirties.

But there are rumblings of change. The mere fact that experts are predicting hundreds of cases in the field each year is indicative of the attention current legal doctrine will be getting in the near future. At present, students and their attorneys are generally fighting losing battles, but their theory is that with increased litigation the courts will become sensitive to the students' position. Already there has been a sprinkle of court cases that indicate a more formalistic view toward public university students' procedural rights.

The only indication of the Supreme Court's attitude toward the college demonstration problem came in its refusal to review the case of ten Bluefield State College students in West Virginia who were suspended because their demonstration interfered with the university president's view of a football game. In clarification of his reasons for not hearing the case, Justice Fortas commented that the Constitution's protection did not extend to students "engaged in an aggressive and violent demonstration."[36] On the other hand, there is the seminal *Tinker* case which deals with the rights of high school students but should be even stronger as an argument for college student rights. Three children of the Tinker family in Des Moines were sent home from public school for wearing black armbands protesting the war in Vietnam. The Court held the school's actions were unconstitutional, reasoning, "In our system, state operated schools may not be enclaves of totalitarianism . . . Undifferentiated fear or apprehension of disturbance is not enough to overcome the right to freedom of expression."[37]

The pattern of future cases is indicated by the celebrated Columbia takeover litigation featuring defendants such as Mark Rudd and defense counsel such as William Kunstler, Arthur Kinoy, and Floyd McKissick. In six causes of actions Columbia students who occupied the administration building asked the court to: (1) Enjoin disciplinary proceedings and declare void a statute of the university which asserted vague disciplinary powers; (2) Drop the criminal prosecutions against the students because of their chilling effect on free speech; (3) Declare that D.A. Frank Hogan's position as a member of the board of trustees and prosecutor denied the students of due process; (4) Enjoin the police from further brutality; (5) Enjoin the university president from bringing in again the police and violating the integrity of the academic community; (6) Order a restructuring of the university which currently was "essentially unchanged since 1754, and affords no participatory power in the faculty or student body in the determination of policies."[38] The students, needless to say, lost. But some of the issues raised including double jeopardy, the relation between Columbia and the state, and the liability of the administration for brutal acts of the police, will be recurrent themes in the next few years. Current legal doctrine, especially in the private school field, will begin to crumble under the assault of precedent, logic, and analogy, and the courts will have to build anew. Of course, some schools are not waiting for the day when their policies are declared unconstitutional and are moving toward self-generated reform.

Edward Schwartz, a former president of the National Student Association, once commented while attending a conference of law and the college student, "The debate over legal rights is a substitute for a consideration of the real issues which we should be considering." He went on to say that instead of discussing use of police, injunctions, and hearings, the conference should focus on such issues as student power, the anomie of campus life, the relevance of the curriculum to social needs, and the interrelationships between the university, business, and the military. Schwartz scoffed at the concern of the administrators at the conference for the autonomy of their schools when "universities are willingly embracing the Department of Defense, the Federal Narcotics Bureau, and the neighborhood police force." He went on to tell the administrators present, "However adept you become in handling tactics, the protests will not end until you become adept at accepting change."[39]

To some degree, Schwartz is right. The current crisis in the legal rights of college students is merely a manifestation of underlying tensions between an outdated university structure grafted on an unresponsive political system and an activist generation of students who have the courage to question the assumptions of the past. Forcing universities to change by redefining students' legal rights is no panacea. As with all civil rights, it's just a start.

But the national climate at this time does not favor further broadening of student rights. While 80 percent of graduating seniors in a recent survey believe confrontation tactics are necessary to bring social change,[40] another poll shows campus unrest is regarded as the country's leading problem by adults.[41] Fred Hechinger is worried about cutbacks in financial support to universities by wealthy donors; Edward Teller frets over the jeopardization of defense research; the Army brass fear a loss of cannon fodder; middle America quakes in fear and anger at the questioning of its values.

A grand jury indicts students for burning a bank when they were in jail at the time of the incident.[42] President Nixon receives the Scranton report and calls for more FBI agents on campus. Chancellor Heard's warnings that students should be given a sympathetic hearing from their government are given a cold shoulder. Ontario County Sheriff Ray Morrow defends the activities of his infamous undercover agent Tommy the Traveler by saying, "There is a lot of difference between showing how to build a bomb and building one."[43] Blood spills into the streets and the National Guard is resupplied with even more rapidly firing weapons. Obviously, we are in the throes of a national insanity and the question of expanding student rights may be very academic. The immediate need is protecting the rights that already exist from further incursions.

At some point, we must explicitly ask ourselves whether the attempt to punish a few for violent acts justifies suppression of dissent. Although the Campus Unrest Commission did not examine how the courts were strangling the peaceful avenues of protest, its report did have moments of insight. As was pointed out, "To respond to peaceful protest with repression and brutal tactics is dangerously unwise. It makes extremists of moderates, deepens the divisions in the nation, and increases the chances that future protest will be violent."[44] Hopefully, the judges were listening.

The Civilianization of Military Law

EDWARD F. SHERMAN*

I. THE CHALLENGE

There is nothing like a war, and especially an unpopular war, to raise fundamental questions concerning the treatment of servicemen. The usual problems which crop up in the disciplining and training of men are always increased when an army suddenly has to expand its manpower and enters combat. The Vietnam War has produced not only these expected strains but also its own distinctive challenges. As a result, the military system of discipline and justice has been tested as never before, and often its performance has not been impressive.

The first challenge came early in the war from dissenting servicemen. It was inevitable in a war which has caused such deep divisions in American society that some soldiers would attempt to express their dissent from war policies. The dissent movement began with actions of individuals: Lt. Henry Howe, in 1965, dressed in civilian clothes, carried a sign critical of the President's Vietnam policies in an off-post peace rally; Captain Howard Levy, in 1966, made statements critical of the war to other servicemen and finally refused to teach medicine to Green Beret troops; Captain Dale Noyd, in 1967, refused to teach fighter pilots after being denied conscientious objector status. The reaction of the military through the court-martial system

* Edward Sherman graduated from Harvard Law School in 1962 and is now assistant professor of law at Indiana University School of Law. He served as a Captain in the U.S. Army from 1965 to 1967, and has written extensively on military law in law journals and for the *New York Times*, *The New Republic*, and *The Nation*.

was immediate and uncompromising. Howe received two years; Levy three years; Noyd one year. These courts-martial gave the public the first glimpse of some of the distinctive characteristics of military justice, which would continue to appear in the Vietnam War dissenter cases—vague and sometimes authoritarian military crimes (like "conduct unbecoming an officer and a gentleman" and "contemptuous words" against public officials); juries handpicked from their officers by commanders; intense interest in conviction by commanders who exercised a variety of functions in the trial process; and sentences which seemed overly severe.

As the war continued, a few dissent activities, especially if performed off-post and tailored to avoid clashes with the military, did not result in court-martial, a result due in part to slightly liberalized guidelines on dissent issued by the Secretary of the Army in 1969.[1] Thus Andy Stapp, an ex-private, has continued to obtain members for his American Servicemen's Union, some dozen antiwar coffee-houses have been opened around military bases, and over fifty underground antiwar GI newspapers are now being published. However, dissent continues to be risky: Pvt. George Daniels and Cpl. William Harvey received ten and six years for making "disloyal statements" about the war to other black marines; Pvts. Ken Stolte and Dan Amick received four years each for distributing antiwar pamphlets on post; and Seaman Roger Priest was given a bad conduct discharge for statements made in an underground paper. Thus the military courts continue to apply an extremely narrow view of servicemen's First Amendment rights (which is now being challenged in the federal courts in *Howe, Levy, Daniels,* and *Stolte-Amick*).[2] This view, together with the disciplinarian aspects of military justice, has not produced a favorable record concerning the protection of individual rights in courts-martial during the Vietnam War period.

A second challenge faced in the Vietnam War period has been the enormous increase in the number of AWOL's and the problems created by the disposition and incarceration of military offenders. The public first learned about stockade problems in

1969, when twenty-seven young prisoners participated in a peaceful sit-down strike at the Presidio in an attempt to present grievances concerning stockade conditions. The commander had them court-martialed, despite the finding of a lawyer investigating officer that there was no evidence of mutiny (the military appeals courts have now reversed the mutiny convictions), and the first three tried were sentenced to fifteen, fourteen, and sixteen years. The Presidio courts-martial displayed the evils of command-domination of the proceedings, and revealed the inadequate conditions existing in many military confinement institutions. As a result, a special committee of six penologists, headed by Austin H. MacCormick, was appointed to study the problem, and on June 21, 1970, it reported that there were serious deficiencies in the Army's treatment of offenders and recommended a major overhaul of both the army prisons and military justice.[3]

A third challenge has been the increase in racial tension in the services. Serious racial conflicts and riots have taken place during the Vietnam War. Many of the complaints of black servicemen concern rigid disciplinary policies which forbid expressions of cultural diversity and claims that courts-martial made up of officers (blacks constitute only 3.2 percent of the Army officer corps; 1.7 percent of the Air Force; 1.2 percent of the Marine Corps; and 1 percent of the Navy) do not provide a fair trial for blacks. Some of the tension regarding disciplinary policies was eased in late 1969 when the Marine Corps, followed later by the other services, promised to give more attention to black problems and to permit some cultural diversity such as Afro-haircuts and "soul music" in military clubs.[4] However, blacks continue to complain of discrimination in assignments and promotions, and the effects of military justice continue to be felt most severely by black servicemen (blacks often receive higher court martial sentences and make up an unduly large percentage of military prisoners).

A fourth challenge, and perhaps the most serious in terms of public concern, has come from events of the Vietnam War itself. First, in early 1969, the Navy completed its Board of Inquiry hearings concerning the seizure of the *Pueblo* and announced that it would court-martial Commander Bucher and certain other crew members. In response to a storm of public criticism, much of it implying that the defendants could not get a fair trial in a court-martial and that the Navy was seeking a scapegoat, the Secretary of the Navy dismissed the cases. Then, later in 1969, "the Green Beret defendants" were charged with the murder of a Vietnamese double-agent, and again, after claims were made that the Commanding General had a personal interest in the prosecution and that the defendants could not receive a fair trial, the charges were dropped by the Secretary of the Army. These unprecedented interventions by the civilian secretaries indicate the level of public skepticism and the questionable ability of the system to provide the type of impartiality which can be counted on in a time of crisis.

Finally, the My Lai cases have raised fundamental questions concerning its capacity to provide a fair trial in this most critical of national crises. Because of the structure of the military justice system which permits commanders to exercise substantial control over court-martial trials, there was an aura of command manipulation in the My Lai trials. The Pentagon played a key role, deciding who should be prosecuted, selecting the posts where the trials took place with an eye to which commanders could be depended upon to perform as desired, appointing the military personnel who participated in the trials, and exercising careful advisory control over the proceedings. As a result, the public had the uneasy feeling that the My Lai verdicts were all according to plan. It is ironic that the military is suspected of being both too harsh and too lenient in the My Lai cases, but this is an inevitable result where a criminal law system is as susceptible to command pressure as is military justice.

Public concern over military justice in the Vietnam War period has now led to the introduction of three major reform bills—by Senators Tydings, Hatfield, and Bayh.[5] However, the road to reform has always been a difficult one, and, before assessing the chances for success of such reform legislation, we should consider the past reform movements and the present structure of the military justice system.

II. MILITARY JUSTICE THROUGH WORLD WAR I

Military justice in the United States has always functioned as a separate system of jurisprudence independent of the civilian judiciary. It has its own body of substantive laws and procedures which come from a different historical tradition than the civilian criminal law. The first American Articles of War, enacted by the Continental Congress in 1775,[6] copied the British Articles, a body of law which was more influenced by the seventeenth century rules adopted by Gustavus Adolphus for the discipline of his army than the English common law. Dissimilarity between American military and civilian criminal law has been encouraged by the isolation of the court-martial system. The federal courts have always disclaimed power to interfere with courts-martial, as explained by the Supreme Court in 1953 in *Burns* v. *Wilson:* "Military law, like state law, is a jurisprudence which exists separate and apart from the law which governs in our federal judicial establishment. This court has played no role in its development; we have exerted no supervisory power over the courts which enforce it. . . ."[7] As a result, the court-martial system still differs from civilian courts in terminology and structure, as well as procedural and substantive law.

The procedural framework of the court-martial evolved over the years as a practical means of formalizing punishment of soldiers and sailors by their commanders. Its principal characteristic was control by the commander. Since military units were sometimes isolated from other units and the civilian population, it was necessary that court-martial authority be decentralized, with the power in lower echelon commanders to convene a court-martial and staff it with their own officers so that a determination could be made quickly and the unit could get back to its main task of fighting. Thus the court-martial had to be a relatively simple proceeding, with few legal formalisms, sometimes conducted right in the field with a drum as a desk, hence the term "drum-head justice." There was little pretense at providing an impartial and adversary "judicial" hearing. No one blushed in admitting that the court-martial was not a real trial, that the commander used it to enforce his disciplinary policies and incul-

70 WITH JUSTICE FOR SOME

cate military values in his men, that it was administered by officers alone, that there was no right to review, and that the sentences were calculated to set an example and not to provide equal justice.

Throughout the nineteenth century and well into the twentieth, the court-martial system remained an autonomous legal system relatively unaffected by civilian notions of criminal law and judicial due process. A good example of the military philosophy is the statement of General William T. Sherman, Command-General of the Army from 1869 to 1883, before a congressional committee in 1879:

> [I]t will be a grave error if by negligence we permit the military law to become emasculated by allowing lawyers to inject into it the principles derived from their practice in the civil courts, which belong to a totally different system of jurisprudence. . . . An army is a collection of armed men obliged to obey one man. Every enactment, every change of rules which impairs the principle weakens the army, impairs its values, and defeats the very object of its existence. All the traditions of civil lawyers are antagonistic to this vital principle, and military men must meet them on the threshold of discussion, else armies will become demoralized by even grafting on our code their deductions from civil practice.[8]

General Sherman's view of military justice was consistent with his emphasis upon professionalism in the small volunteer post–Civil War army, and until World War I it was generally accepted. However, as a result of court-martial abuses and outrageously severe sentences in World War I, a movement for the civilianization of military law took shape which asked, for the first time, why members of the military had to be subjected to a system of justice which failed to provide them with the constitutional and due process rights to which they would be entitled in civilian courts.

The World War I movement was led by General Samuel T. Ansell, the acting Judge Advocate General of the Army. In sharp contrast to the prevailing view as described by General Sherman, General Ansell argued that the military system itself was foreign to our American system of justice and injured the effectiveness of the armed forces:

> I contend—and I have gratifying evidence of support not only from the public generally but from the profession— that the existing system of military justice is un-American, having come to us by inheritance and rather witless adoption out of a system which we regard as fundamentally intolerable; that it is archaic, belonging as it does to an age when armies were but bodies of armed retainers and bands of mercenaries; that it is a system arising out of and regulated by the mere power of Military Command rather than Law; and that it has resulted, as it must ever result, in such injustice as to crush the spirit of the individual subjected to it, shock the public conscience and alienate public esteem and affection from the Army that insists on maintaining it.[9]

General Ansell's proposals for reform of the military justice system were largely contained in the Chamberlain Bill, introduced in 1919.[10] The bill did not undertake to replace the military structure of the court-martial, but operated on the premise that a number of traditional military procedures had to be altered. However, by the time that the Chamberlain Bill got into the congressional stream much of the force of the movement had been spent, and the growing atmosphere of "normalcy" made reform legislation difficult to pass. Its advocates, who had themselves invoked the patriotism of Americans against court-martial abuses, found that, with the war over, patriotism had begun to cut the other way. Professor Wigmore told a 1919 Maryland Bar Association meeting:

> The prime object of military organization is Victory, not justice. In that death struggle which is ever impending, the Army, which defends the Nation, is ever strained by the terrific consciousness that the Nation's life and its own is at stake. No other objective than Victory can have first place

in its thoughts, nor cause any remission of that strain. If it
can do justice to its men, well and good. But justice is
always secondary, and Victory is always primary.[11]

After hearings on the Chamberlain Bill were held in November, 1919, it became obvious that the proponents of the bill
could not muster enough support to overcome the opposition of
the military and the War Department. The Subcommittee failed
to report the bill out of committee, adopting instead a limited
revision of the military code, called the Articles of War of 1920,
which was passed as part of an Army Reorganization Act. Virtually all of the Chamberlain Bill proposals for limiting the
control of the commander over a court-martial were rejected.
Courts-martial would still only be made up of officers chosen
by the commander. There would still be no judge, although the
commander could detail a legal officer to give the court members
legal advice, but he could be overruled by a majority vote of the
court on all matters other than admissibility of evidence. A defense counsel would be appointed in all special and general
courts-martial, but he was not required to be a lawyer. Commanders would continue to review court-martial convictions and
sentences but could not revise sentences upwards or return an
acquittal to the court for reconsideration. The proposal for a
civilian Court of Military Appeals was rejected.

Thus ended the first major movement for reform of military
justice. There would be no further reform until after World War
II, and, as a result, some sixteen million Americans who served
in World War II would be subject to the Articles of War
of 1920.

III. THE POST–WORLD WAR II REFORM MOVEMENT
AND THE PASSAGE OF THE UCMJ

"When Johnny came marching home again from World War II,"
wrote Robinson O. Everett, commissioner of the Court of Military Appeals, "he brought with him numerous complaints about
justice as then dispensed in the Army and the Navy. Many of
these were prompted by a conviction that the administration of

military justice had not always lived up to the goals of fairness and impartiality which were accepted as part of the American legal tradition."[12] More American servicemen than ever before had experienced military justice first hand, and it was clear that they did not like it. There had been over 1,700,000 courts-martial during the war, most of them resulting in convictions. There had been 100 capital executions, and 45,000 servicemen were still imprisoned when the war ended. Some 80 percent of the courts-martial were for acts which would not have been crimes in civilian life, with AWOL and desertion the most frequent charges.

Undue severity of sentences was still a principal complaint. A Clemency Board appointed by the Secretary of War in the summer of 1945 to review all general court-martial cases where the accused was still in confinement remitted or reduced the sentence in 85 percent of the 27,000 cases reviewed.[13] Substantial numbers of servicemen who had never been in trouble with the law served time in military jails and came home from the war with military records showing court-martial convictions or less than honorable discharges. Senators and congressmen were flooded with complaints. Rear Admiral Robert J. White described the ground swell of criticism against military justice: "The emotions suppressed during the long, tense period of global warfare were now released by peace, and erupted into a tornado-like explosion of violent feelings, abusive criticism of the military, and aggressive pressures on Congress for fundamental reforms in the court-martial system."[14]

On March 18, 1946, the Secretary of War appointed a Board on Officer-Enlisted Men's Relationships, headed by General James Doolittle, to investigate the criticisms of unfairness and arbitrariness in the Army. After considering thousands of letters and holding hearings, it concluded that "the largest differential which brought the most criticism in every instance, was in the field of military justice and courts-martial procedure which permitted inequities and injustices to enlisted personnel,"[15] and recommended a sweeping recasting of the military structure and court-martial procedures to deemphasize rank. The Secretary of War also appointed a special committee to study military justice, headed by Arthur Vanderbilt, a former president of the American Bar Association, which concluded that there were serious deficiencies in the military justice system. It reported that "the command frequently dominated the courts in the rendition of their judgment"; "defense counsel were often ineffective"; "sentences originally imposed were frequently excessively severe and sometimes fantastically so"; "there was some discrimination between officers and enlisted men, both as to the bringing of charges and as to convictions and sentences"; and "investigations, before referring cases to trial, were frequently inefficient or inadequate."[16]

The Army and the Navy both offered drafts of new articles containing military justice reforms but retaining most of the basic features of the court-martial system. Hearings were held on the Army proposals, resulting in a somewhat more reformatory draft which was introduced as the Elston Act in the 80th Congress in 1948. Although advocates of broad reform opposed the Elston Act because it had rejected the recommendations of the Vanderbilt committee and various bar groups that command control of courts-martial should be removed, it was unexpectedly offered as an amendment to the National Defense Act of 1948 and quickly passed by both Houses.[17]

Since the Elston Act applied only to the Army, Secretary of Defense Forrestal, in an attempt to provide uniform rules for all services, appointed a committee in July, 1948, to draft a uniform code of military justice. The struggle for more extensive reform now shifted to the drafting committee. Correspondence, particularly from lawyers who had served in the war, poured in with suggestions. The letters, often critical, covered most of the traditional court-martial procedures. For example, Governor James E. Folsom of Alabama called for a court of the same rank as the accused:

When an officer orders a soldier court-martialled, before court-martial he is automatically convicted. I have one recommendation to make, that enlisted men try enlisted men and that officers try officers. This is an old common law which has been handed down for hundreds of years, that every man is entitled to be tried by his peers.[18]

Governor Ernest W. Gibson of Vermont urged that the commander's power to appoint and rate court members and counsel be removed, referring to his experiences as a JAG officer in the war:

> . . . we were advised, not once but many times on the Courts that I sat on, that if we adjudged a person guilty we should afflict the maximum sentence and leave it to the Commanding General to make any reduction. . . . I was dismissed as a Law Officer and Member of a General Court Martial because our General Court acquitted a colored man on a morals charge when the Commanding General wanted him convicted—yet the evidence didn't warrant it. I was called down and told that if I didn't convict in a greater number of cases I would be marked down in my Efficiency Ratings; and I squared right off and said that wasn't my conception of justice and that they had better remove me, which was done forthwith.[19]

The letters covered a number of different aspects of the court-martial system, but almost all the stories of unfairness, arbitrariness, misuse of authority, and inadequate protection of rights could be boiled down to the basic criticism that commanders exercised too much control over court-martial procedures from prosecution through review.

The military was opposed to any plan which would limit the individual commander's control over the operation of courts-martial. Secretary of War Patterson expressed the traditional argument that the military could not operate efficiently if commanders could not control courts-martial:

> Many of the critics overlook the place of military justice in the army or the navy. An army is organized to win victory in war and the organization must be one that will bring

success in combat. That means singleness of command and the responsibility of the field commander for everything that goes on in the field. The army has other functions such as feeding, medical care, and justice, but they are subordinate.[20]

A number of prominent military men, including Generals Bradley and Eisenhower, also forcefully defended the traditional court-martial structure.

Although the public debate over court-martial reform centered on removal of command control, there was never much likelihood that the drafting committee would not uphold the military position. A survey of the papers and correspondence of the committee, now part of the Morgan Papers at Harvard Law School Library, indicates that none of the drafts considered by the committee contained a provision for removal of command control of courts-martial. The committee's draft of the UCMJ (Uniform Code of Military Justice) was completed early in February, 1949, and introduced in the Senate and House. The advocates of broad court-martial reform set up a cry of opposition. The chairman of two bar association committees which had urged reform observed that:

"This Code embodies further improvements in the system of military justice, but incredible as it may seem, maintains intact the old system criticized by Senators Norris and Chamberlain as far back as 1919, whereby the commanding general appoints from his command the members of the court, the trial judge advocate and defense counsel, refers the case to the court and thereafter reviews the court's findings and sentences."[21]

The reformer's problem in marshaling popular support for broader reform was in the timing. Almost four years had passed since World War II, and even the raw wounds of servicemen who felt they had received unjust treatment in courts-martial had begun to mend. The country was now caught up in a struggle with a new enemy, and the anger at the "brass" had already been converted into the respect for the military might and technology which would characterize the cold war era. Hearings were held on the UCMJ in March and April, 1949, and the committee's draft was passed by both houses without substantial change. The act was signed into law by President Truman on May 5, 1950.[22] It is the basic law which governs the administration of military justice today.

The UCMJ was a product of compromise. It extended substantial new due process rights to servicemen, some of them more favorable than were then provided in civilian courts, and its changes in court-martial procedures, especially the general court-martial, considerably replaced the old disciplinary flavor with a judicial one. However, it did not alter a number of distinctively military aspects of the system.

First, it retained the traditional hierarchy of courts-martial. A serviceman could still be tried in any of the three types of court-martial chosen by his commanders—a general court-martial (which could give any sentence, within the maximum punishments prescribed for the offense, up to and including death, and which provided substantial due process rights); a special court-martial (which could give a sentence of not more than six months' confinement at hard labor, six months' forfeiture of two-thirds pay, demotion, and a bad conduct discharge, but which did not provide a lawyer defense counsel and other due process rights provided in general courts); or a summary court-martial (which could not give a sentence exceeding one month's correctional custody, one month's forfeiture of two-thirds pay, demotion, and restrictions, but which was conducted by one officer acting as judge and jury and provided few due process rights).

Second, the UCMJ made no substantial changes in the wording of the military crimes from the 1920 Code, retaining traditional military offenses imposing particularly authoritarian limitations on servicemen, such as "contemptuous words against the President" (Article 88) and "provoking or reproachful words or gestures towards any other person" (Article 117). It also retained the two extremely vague "general articles," "conduct unbecoming an officer and a gentleman" (Article 133) and "all disorders and neglects to the prejudice of good order and dis-

cipline in the armed forces, all conduct of a nature to bring dis-
credit upon the armed forces, and crimes and offenses not
capital, of which persons subject to the Code may be guilty"
(Article 134).

Third, the UCMJ left the commander who convened the
court essentially in control of court-martial machinery and appointment of court personnel. He still made the decision whether
to prosecute; had the power to appoint, either by himself or
through his subordinates, the members of the court, both counsel, the law officer (who carried out some of the functions of a
judge), and the other court personnel from men under his command; and could review the sentence with the power to remit or
reduce it.

Fourth, the UCMJ failed to make the court-martial a trial by
a jury of one's peers. Courts-martial would still be composed of
officers chosen by the commander. It was provided that, upon
request, an enlisted man would be tried by a court made up of
one-third enlisted men, but the commander convening authority
could appoint whomever he felt was "best qualified" and so
could, as has happened, always appoint high-ranking, noncommissioned officers who are often more disciplinarian than officers.

Fifth, the UCMJ left many of the nonjudicial trappings of
the court-martial intact. Although there would be a "law officer"
for all general courts-martial (but not special or summary courts)
to instruct the court as to the legal issues and rule on questions
of law, the members of the court continued to determine challenges for cause (such as prejudice) against any court member,
and could reject the law officer's rulings on certain motions. The
senior officer, called "the president," continued to preside at the
trial and to carry out a number of administrative functions, as
did also the prosecutor, called "the trial counsel." The arrangement of the courtroom was still military, with the law officer
seated at a side table and the court at a long table in front. A
military lawyer was provided as defense counsel in a general
court-martial, but defense counsel in a special court-martial
would usually be a non-lawyer officer.

Finally, the UCMJ did create a Court of Military Appeals

made up of three civilians appointed for fifteen-year terms by the President, but the court would only hear those cases it chose to hear where the sentence involved a bad conduct discharge or over a year's confinement. The court was limited to reviewing questions of law and had no equitable powers. Thus most court-martial decisions would only be reviewed by the commander convening authority and a JAG officer. In cases where the sentence included death, dismissal, dishonorable or bad conduct discharge, or confinement of a year or more, there would be an appeal to a board of review (now called Courts of Military Review) made up primarily of military officers in the office of the Judge Advocate General of the service.

IV. THE POST–KOREAN WAR REFORM MOVEMENT AND THE PASSAGE OF THE MILITARY JUSTICE ACT OF 1968

The UCMJ took effect on May 31, 1951, while the Korean War was still going on. The dire warnings of the military manpower difficulties in providing lawyers in general courts-martial and breakdowns of discipline due to the new availability of review by a civilian court did not materialize. The transition into lawyer-conducted general courts was smooth, without noticeable adverse effect upon military discipline or effectiveness.

Perhaps the most revolutionary provision of the UCMJ turned out to be the creation of the Court of Military Appeals. The court quickly indicated that it intended to act like an independent appellate court and that, as the Supreme Court of the military, it was the highest authority as to interpretation and application of the UCMJ. It considered itself bound by the standards of due process provided in the UCMJ and originally took the position that courts-martial were not bound by constitutional limitations. In an early case, *United States* v. *Clay*,[23] it coined the term "military due process" to describe those due process rights, derived not from the Bill of Rights but from congressional enactments concerning the military, which were requisite to fundamental fairness in a court-martial. However, this attempt to avoid direct application of the Constitution to military trials was not satisfactory, particularly after the Supreme Court's 1953 decision in *Burns* v. *Wilson*[24] upholding the right of federal courts on habeas corpus to consider denials of constitutional rights which the military had manifestly refused to consider. In 1960 in *United States* v. *Jacoby*, the court stated that "the protections of the Bill of Rights, except those which are expressly or by necessary implication inapplicable, are available to members of our armed forces."[25] The list of those rights which have been found to be applicable to the military has grown steadily by Court of Military Appeals decisions over the last twenty years, so that most procedural due process rights which are constitutionally required in civilian courts have now been applied to courts-martial. The Court of Military Appeals has felt its way carefully, and, due to its small membership, the attitudes of individual personnel have particularly affected its willingness to expand due process rights and grant relief. It still provides only a limited remedy for servicemen, but, nevertheless, it has accomplished more reform in the field of procedural due process than all the prior congressional military codes put together.

By the late 1950s, when some time had passed for evaluation of the UCMJ, criticism of military justice began to increase again. In 1959, the American Legion proposed a bill which particularly addressed itself to the problem of command influence.[26] It indicated that the UCMJ compromise had not removed the pall of improper command influence which continued to hang over courts-martial and that the only way to do that was to reduce significantly the commander's control over court-martial operations. It proposed that lawyers be required in inferior courts as well as general courts, that the commander's control over them be removed, that law officers be granted the status of judge, that boards of review be taken from the control of the Judge Advocate General and put under the civilian Secretary of Defense, and that jurisdiction over civilian-type felonies in time of peace be removed from courts-martial. The military reacted unfavorably to these proposals, saying they proposed "sweeping changes to correct a relatively minor evil,"[27] and the bill languished in Congress.

The next piece of legislation was proposed by the Powell

Committee, appointed by the Secretary of the Army in 1959 to study problems of order and discipline in the Army.[28] Composed of one lieutenant general, six major generals, and two brigadier generals, it offered a number of changes, indicating a disciplinarian philosophy and a predisposition for "decentralization" of military justice to lower command levels. Its proposal for expanding a commander's Article 15 power (the authority to give non-judicial punishment) was passed in a 1962 change to the UCMJ, and a few of its other proposals, such as streamlining court-martial proceedings by permitting trial by a law officer alone if requested, were incorporated into the Military Justice Act of 1968.

A third proposal for legislation was contained in the report of the Special Committee on Military Justice of the Association of the Bar of the City of New York in 1961.[29] It agreed with many of the sentiments expressed by the American Legion Bill but suggested that the basic court-martial structure need not be altered. It proposed that the role of law officers be increased so that they more closely resembled civilian judges; special courts-martial not be empowered to adjudge a bad conduct discharge; trial be permitted, on request, by a single-officer lawyer in a special court-martial; and summary courts-martial be abolished.

These three proposals, the changes recommended by a formal Code Committee established by the UCMJ, and the many suggestions which had been made to congressmen and senators were worked over by congressional committees in the late 1950s and 1960s. Hearings were held by the Subcommittee on Constitutional Rights of the Senate Judiciary Committee, headed by Senator Sam J. Ervin (D-N.C.) in 1962 and 1965. However, there was no significant support in Congress for broad reforms which would alter the basic UCMJ court-martial structure. The bill which finally passed Congress, known as the Military Justice Act of 1968,[30] left out the provision for reform of administrative discharge procedures and made no basic structural changes in courts-martial or in the commander's control over court-martial machinery and appointments. However, the act, which took effect on August 1, 1969, did replace the law officer with a military judge who is given a number of new duties and powers making him more comparable to a civilian judge, including the power to try the case by himself if the accused requests. It also contributed to the independence of military judges by requiring that the Judge Advocate General of each service establish a field judiciary from which military judges will be assigned for court-martial cases. Thus military judges are appointed from a pool of lawyers under the command of the Judge Advocate General rather than from the commander's staff judge advocate office, and are not subject to rating, assignment, or other control by the commander convening authority. The act provided that the accused "shall be afforded the opportunity to be represented at the trial" of special courts-martial by a lawyer "unless counsel having such qualifications cannot be obtained on account of physical conditions or military exigencies,"[31] and that a bad conduct discharge may not be adjudged unless a complete record of the proceedings and testimony has been made, lawyer counsel was detailed to represent the accused, and a military judge was detailed to the trial.

The Military Justice Act changed the name of the boards of review to Courts of Military Review and termed the members judges. The Courts of Military Review are still constituted under the judge advocate generals of each service, but there is a chief justice who divides the judges up into panels of not less than three and appoints a senior judge to preside. However, the members still have no tenure and are under the command of the Judge Advocate General and dependent upon him for ratings and assignments. The act also made some improvement in the availability of post-trial review. It authorized the Judge Advocate General, in any court-martial case that has been finally reviewed, to vacate or modify the findings and sentence because of newly discovered evidence, fraud on the court, lack of jurisdiction over the accused or offense, or error prejudicial to the substantive rights of the accused. The last ground—error prejudicial to the substantive rights of the accused—is important, for this means that, for the first time, a person convicted in a special court-martial who did not receive a bad conduct discharge (this type of case accounts for almost two-thirds of the total military courts-martial) can obtain a review of prejudicial errors by someone other than the convening authority and his staff judge advocate office. Although this is not an entirely satisfactory type of review—no standards are provided as to how the Judge Advocate General will conduct it, the term "error prejudicial" is unclear, and it provides only another administrative review rather than an appeal to an independent court—at least a serviceman can now seek review of a special court-martial conviction apart from that of the commander who tried him and the commander's lawyer.

Perhaps the most significant new due process right provided by the Military Justice Act was a provision for release pending appeal. The military practice, which appears directly contrary to the words of the UCMJ, had been to require convicted servicemen to begin serving their sentences immediately after conviction. Thus it is not uncommon for servicemen to have served their entire sentence before their appeal has been decided by a board of review and the Court of Military Appeals. A reversal of conviction was slim consolation to one who had already served his sentence. The act gave the convening authority power to defer the serving of the sentence until the appeals have been completed. However, no standards were provided to insure uniformity of application and preclude discrimination, and the convening authority was given absolute discretion as to granting release pending appeal or not.

V. THE CURRENT VIETNAM WAR MOVEMENT FOR REFORM

The movement for reform of seventeen years' duration which finally resulted in the Military Justice Act of 1968 brought valuable changes and additions to military justice, but did not affect the basic structure of the court-martial system. When President Johnson signed the act, he stated: "We have always prided ourselves on giving our men and women in uniform excellent medical service, superb training, the best equipment. Now, with this, we're going to give them first-class legal service as well."[32] To those who knew that the act had made only a few reforms of a relatively uncontroversial nature and had not addressed itself to the most highly criticized areas such as command control, court-martial structure, and administrative discharges, this statement was passed off as no more than the usual political puffing attending the passage of a legislative enactment. However, the military has not been so quick to drop the hyperbole. Within months, articles had appeared in legal magazines referring to the "sweeping reforms" of the Military Justice Act of 1968 and concluding that the military justice system had now achieved virtual perfectibility.

There has always been a tendency within the military to exalt the virtues of the present military justice system and discount the need for reform. Of course, the fact that the military has often failed to recognize the need for reform within the military justice system does not prove that further reform is needed today. The burden must be on the critics to prove the need and the workability of further reforms. However, the failures of the military to recognize and admit flaws in their system of justice should serve as a warning against accepting official pronouncements without question. The military, like any ingrown, highly traditional bureaucracy, displays tremendous resistance to change. Since the military is in control of most of the information concerning the operation of military justice, and, like any large and powerful agency, possesses the resources and manpower to present that information in a manner favorable to its official position, it has been at a decided advantage in turning back attempts to alter its system.

Two questions come to mind in considering whether further civilianization of military justice is desirable: Does the military justice system now provide as fair and just a system of criminal law as it should, and, if not, what reforms can be made without endangering the effectiveness of the military forces? Very little analysis has been made as to what standards of justice should be required of a military criminal law system and as to what the actual effects on the military would be of adapting to civilian standards. One difficulty encountered in speculating on the policy considerations behind the differences between military and civilian justice is that there are often valid policy reasons for both the military and the civilian position. As in so many other legal problems, one is often forced to weigh competing policy considerations in attempting to determine whether the military procedure should be made to conform with the civilian. For example, the policy justification for maintaining command control of court-martial machinery and appointments relates to the tradition-honored military concept of singleness of command and the necessity for a commander to exercise plenary powers over all operations within his command. This policy is quite different from the policy behind the civilian court emphasis on dividing up various administrative and judicial functions in a criminal prosecution among different and independent individuals in order to limit the possibility of arbitrariness and abuse of power.

Although there are some differences between the procedural due process rights guaranteed in military and civilian trials, they are today very similar, and therefore this is not the principal area in which the court-martial system is vulnerable to attack. The UCMJ provided a number of due process guarantees which were not, at that time, available in most civilian courts. However, the Warren Court's revolution of criminal due process in the 1950s and 1960s brought civilian court standards generally into line with the UCMJ, and, in some areas, instituted more demanding due process requirements. Probably the most objective assessment of military and civilian court procedural due process rights, such as protection against unreasonable searches and seizures, self-incrimination, and double jeopardy, and the right to a speedy and public trial, a transcript of the trial, and to discover evidence and subpoena witnesses, would find them roughly equal, with, perhaps, a slight edge for the civilian procedures primarily because of the command control aspect which still affects certain military rights.

However, as regards the manner in which crimes are charged, the court-martial is convened, the personnel chosen, the verdict arrived at, and a review made, the military comes off far less favorably. The weaknesses of the court-martial system lie particularly in its structure, which the UCMJ failed to change. These weaknesses will be considered in relation to certain primary categories of criminal law procedure:

1. *Crimes and Punishments.* Most of the individual military

crimes are stated with sufficient specificity in the UCMJ to avoid charges of unconstitutional vagueness and overbreadth. However, even a staunch supporter of the military justice system, Frederick Bernays Wiener, has conceded that:

> it cannot be denied that there is language in the void-for-vagueness cases broad enough to condemn as unduly indefinite the prohibition in Article 133 against "conduct unbecoming an officer and a gentleman" and the prohibitions in Article 134 against "all disorders and neglects to the prejudice of good order and discipline in the armed forces" and against "all conduct of a nature to bring discredit upon the armed forces."[33]

The question is whether a modern military code must retain these open-ended crimes which still survive from the day when the military did not find it necessary to inform its members in advance and with specificity as to what it considered to be criminal. The military views these vague crimes not as setting a trap for the serviceman but as providing the commander with the tools he needs for insuring good order and discipline. From the military point of view, efficiency in combat is the paramount consideration, and the idea that such efficiency can only be obtained by strict compliance by servicemen with military standards of conduct guided by an unwritten code of "honor" lies deep in military tradition. There is still a strong feeling among officers that the only alternative to strict discipline and absolute obedience to an undefined code of military conduct is chaos. The military sees the general articles as giving the commander the power to insure that his men live up to the "higher" standards required of servicemen, and the fact that failure to do so results in criminal penalties is accepted as a necessary part of the disciplinary process.

The civilian point of view, which increasingly tends to regard the serviceman as a technician whose role is not greatly different from that of such paramilitary forces as the police and fire departments, places less importance on these military values. In a day when most servicemen will not see combat, when substantial numbers of servicemen live off-post and lead a nine to five military existence, and when, even in combat, such qualities as initiative, creativity, and intelligent reaction have replaced the old standard of blind obedience to orders, military emphasis on obedience to a rigid and unspecified code of conduct administered by commanders with criminal sanctions is subject to question. Military demands for broad tools, like the general articles to enforce the conformity it feels is necessary to maintain military efficiency, are in basic conflict with civilian agitation for broader individual rights in the military and concern over the unfairness of prosecutions under vague and overbroad crimes.

It has been argued that particular specifications found in the *Manual for Courts Martial* define the crimes with specificity so that the general article is not unduly vague. However, although the *Manual* does contain a number of precise specifications which can be used to charge a serviceman with a crime under Article 133 (running from copying an examination paper to failure to pay a debt) and Article 134 (fifty-eight specifications running from wrongfully kicking a public horse to making disloyal statements), these are only examples of conduct which might be criminal under the articles. An infinite variety of other conduct, limited only by the scope of a commander's creativity or spleen, can be made the subject of court-martial under these articles. Furthermore, some of the specifications are themselves written in such indefinite and overbroad language—such as making "disloyal statements . . . with design to promote disloyalty among the troops"—as not to provide adequate notice of what acts will be called criminal. Specifications in the *Manual*, which are actually only a form to guide a prosecutor in filling out a complaint rather than the statement of a crime, do not seem to be the most satisfactory method of stating crimes in a modern criminal code.

There seems to be no reason why the present specifications under Articles 133 and 134 could not be rewritten as individual crimes so that each provides a clear statement of the elements of the crime charged. If there is other specific conduct which the military desires to make criminal, separate crimes could be drafted for such conduct. The military problem is not really so very different from civilian law in this respect. Drafters of civilian criminal codes run up against the same kind of problems when legislators indicate that they want to make criminal all conduct which might be "disruptive" or "dangerous to the economy" or "potentially violent." The old solution was to draft a beautifully vague crime so that almost any conduct which the police or prosecutor wanted to call criminal would fall under it. These statutes have been declared unconstitutional so frequently in recent years that drafters have now realized that a crime must be stated with specificity and definiteness and have begun to draft criminal codes accordingly.

The real question today is whether the military should be held to the requirements of specificity imposed on civilian crimes or should be permitted to continue to court-martial individuals for conduct which a military court finds transgresses a crime defined by unwritten standards which reasonable servicemen are supposed to recognize. General Ansell was disturbed fifty years ago by the vagueness of Article 134. He did not propose that it be abolished but that it carry a maximum sentence of six months. His reasoning would appear to have been that although a commander needs to have general disciplinary powers to control a wide variety of unspecific conduct of servicemen, no man should be given a lengthy sentence for violating an unduly vague crime. Many of the specifications under the general article now provide for maximum sentences of several years, the highest being twenty years, and Articles 133 and 134 have been particularly applied during the Vietnam War period to obtain substantial sentences against servicemen who have dissented in some manner against the war. It appears unlikely today that there would be an adverse effect upon military efficiency if these vague crimes were abolished or restricted to Article 15 proceedings. It is true that the commander would no longer be able to hold over his men's heads the threat of a major court-martial for unspecified conduct. But he would still have substantial "disciplinary" powers, which are the primary means of enforcing order in the military, and the removal of the power to court-martial under vague standards, which tends to encourage an arbitrariness of command, may itself have a favorable effect upon morale.

Other deficiencies in the manner of statement of crimes and punishments in the UCMJ include the retention of certain particularly authoritarian crimes which are stated in such vague terms as to violate First Amendment rights. These include the crime of "contemptuous words" against the President, Vice-President, Congress, secretaries of departments, governors, and state legislatures (Article 88), and "provoking or reproachful words or gestures" toward any other person subject to the Code (Article 117). These crimes are more honored in the breach than the observance. Since they are so rarely invoked (the prosecution of Lt. Henry Howe in 1965 for carrying a sign reading "END JOHNSON'S FASCIST AGGRESSION IN VIETNAM" and "LET'S HAVE MORE THAN A CHOICE BETWEEN PETTY IGNORANT FASCISTS IN 1968" in a peaceful off-post rally while off-duty and in civilian clothes was the first prosecution under Article 88 since the UCMJ took effect in 1951[34]), they appear to play no significant role in maintaining military discipline and efficiency. Furthermore it is unthinkable that the military would undertake broad enforcement of these articles, and so they seem to serve no other purpose than providing a means of selective and discriminatory prosecution for a commander.

Finally, as to punishments, the military code still follows the practice, contrary to that used in the federal courts and most state courts, of having the jury assess sentences. Thus, the non-lawyer officers who sit on the court-martial adjudge the sentences in each case without the benefit of the substantial experience with similar offenses which a judge possesses and without the aid of the probation officer's report usually required prior to sentencing in federal courts. As a result, military sentences vary a great deal depending upon the feelings of each individual court and there are often wide disparities in the sentences given to individuals convicted of the same offense under essentially the same circumstances.

2. *Pre-Trial Proceedings.* The UCMJ provided that before charges could be referred to a general court-martial, the commander had to appoint an investigating officer to make "a thorough and impartial investigation." The accused may present evidence and cross-examine witnesses, and so this pre-trial in-

vestigation provides greater rights to the accused than does the usual grand jury investigation in civilian courts. However, the commander is not bound by the investigating officer's report, and he can (as he did in the Presidio cases) refer the charges to a court-martial over the contrary recommendation of the investigating officer.

The absence of a right to a determinative pre-trial investigation in the military indicates a basic difference in judicial philosophy between the two systems. Civilian law places emphasis upon the role of an independent grand jury, selected at random from the community at large, which can prevent the prosecutor from going ahead with a criminal case if it refuses to indict in the belief that a separation of functions will prevent any one individual from exercising too much control over the criminal process and thus preclude arbitrariness and prejudice. Under military law, commanders have always exercised an absolute right to decide whether to court-martial their men, and the pre-trial investigation is still viewed only as an aid to the commander in insuring that he has all the facts before he makes his decision.

Once again a central consideration in weighing the competing military and civilian policies is whether, in fact, the military practice is needed to maintain discipline and efficiency. It is questionable whether the commander's absolute power to court-martial really adds much to the efficiency of the modern military. The fact that a commander could only prefer court-martial charges against one of his men, but that the final decision of whether there is sufficient evidence to court-martial would be made by a separate and independent individual, would not seem significantly to reduce the commander's effectiveness. There appear to be cogent reasons for extending to servicemen the right to a pre-trial investigation by someone independent of the commander convening authority which, if insufficient evidence is found to prosecute, is determinative of the case.

3. *Role of the Commander.* The most important difference between military and civilian justice after the passage of the UCMJ is in the role of the commander in a court-martial. Under the civilian criminal law process, different functions are per-

formed by independent individuals: the district attorney decides whether to prosecute; the Grand Jury determines whether to indict; the defense counsel has no connection with any of the other participants; the jury is picked at random from the community; the judge and other court officials have no relation to the district attorney; and the appeals courts are independent tribunals. In a court-martial, the commander plays a role, in varying degrees, in all of these functions. He decides whether to prosecute; he has the power to handpick the jury from his command and the trial counsel and defense counsel from his legal officers; he has certain supervisory powers over the administration of the trial; and he has the power to review the findings and sentence.

The Military Justice Act of 1968, by creating military judges independent of the commander convening authority, removed one of the functions from the commander's control. Also, in fact, commanders do not usually handpick court members or counsel, leaving this up to one of their staff officers, such as the staff judge advocate, and do not become involved personally in the administration of most courts-martial. However, the ultimate power still lies with the commander, and, in cases in which he is particularly interested, the commander not infrequently takes a hand in the selection of court and counsel and in various administrative matters. He has the power to enter into a pre-trial agreement with the accused to cut down the sentence in return for a guilty plea. This is an immensely important part of military justice prosecution; there are guilty pleas in 65 percent of all Army general courts-martial, and almost three-quarters of these are negotiated pleas. The convening authority rules on defense motions to subpoena witnesses and obtain other evidence before trial, unless this is changed under new practice rules. He can excuse court members both before, and, in certain limited situations, after the trial has begun. The Court of Military Appeals has even held that the convening authority can reverse a military judge's order dismissing charges, on such grounds as denial of a speedy trial, and order the court to try the man anyway.[35]

The UCMJ added provisions intended to prevent the commander from influencing the trial improperly. A commander is disqualified from appointing a special or general court-martial if he has a "personal interest" in the case, a limitation which has been strictly applied where the commander had some monetary interest or personal contact with the case but not when his contacts were in an official capacity. The convening authority is also disqualified from being "the accuser," that is, the person who brings the charges against the serviceman, but this technicality can easily be avoided by having a junior officer file charges against someone the commander wants court-martialed. Finally, Article 37 makes it improper for a convening authority, (1) to censure, reprimand, or admonish any court member, law officer, or counsel with respect to the findings or sentence, and (2) to attempt to coerce or, by any unlawful means, influence the action of a court-martial or any member. However, the commander is still permitted to write efficiency reports and ratings on court members and other court personnel and to exercise normal command authority over them, including such aspects as job assignments. He may also hold "informational" lectures for his officers to instruct them in general about court-martial duties. As a result, commanders have continued to have an important effect on the courts-martial held under their command, and command influence, sometimes overt but more often subtle, continues to be the principal problem in courts-martial today.

The military's justification for the commander's role in the administration of the court-martial and the commander-oriented structure of the legal corps relies upon a very different philosophy of the administration of justice than is found in civilian courts. The military tradition is exactly contrary to the civilian law's insistence that there should be separation of functions and independence of administrators. A commander is charged with insuring discipline and order within his unit. He can be held personally responsible by his superiors—and great importance is placed upon this personal liability of commanders in the military —for any failure or shortcomings of his unit. He is considered to have been given broad powers for disciplining and "shaping up" his men, and his failure to use these powers would be considered dereliction of duty. Command is a personal concept, and the military has always contended that division of command functions would be disastrous to discipline and order in the service. Removal of command control over certain phases of the court-martial is viewed as undercutting the commander's position, and "singleness of command" is seen as essential to efficient military administration. This is not to say that the military position assumes that the staff judge advocate or the defense counsel will compromise the interests of the accused under pressure from the commander. Members of the military are used to playing different roles, and the military takes pains to emphasize that although the staff judge advocate and the defense counsel are directly responsible to the commander, nevertheless they are also charged with insuring that the rights of the accused are protected.

The problem with this analysis is that, in fact, commanders and those accused often have different views of what rights the accused has and what is a fair and impartial proceeding. Commanders, no matter how conscientious, can become personally involved in disciplinary matters and court-martial cases, and this involvement can color their view of how the case should be handled. Likewise, the staff judge advocate and his legal officers often experience the inevitable conflict which arises when they are expected to maintain loyalties to two individuals whose interests are not, in fact, identical. The military, which tends to minimize possible conflicts between the interests of the command and servicemen and puts great faith in the ability of officers to perform conscientiously in a variety of assignments, sees no conflict of interest here; civilians who emphasize independence of administrators do.

"In the nature of things," the Court of Military Appeals has observed, "command control is scarcely ever apparent on the face of the record."[36] For this reason, critics claim, there is much more improper command influence than ever reaches the military appeals courts. They cite the 1967 cases at Ft. Leonard Wood as one of the rare occasions on which overbearing actions by commanders were detected and publicized. There the Court of Military Appeals reversed almost a hundred convictions on grounds of improper command influence by General Lipscomb—involving such actions as lecturing his officers concerning his desire for

severe sentences, personally talking to court members after trial
to indicate his pleasure or displeasure with sentences, systematic
exclusion of low ranking, non-career officers from court-martial
duty, and rearranging the courtroom to put the law officer at a
less favorable height. The military, however, argues that an
investigating officer found that the general had acted impru-
dently, but not illegally, and that this was just an example of
over-caution on the part of the court.

Until recently there was little objective evidence either way to
support or disprove claims of widespread command influence.
However, the Presidio courts-martial resulted in statements by
legal officers that substantial command pressures adverse to the
defendants were brought to bear on them.[37] Then, a former
career Army JAG officer, Luther C. West, completed a dissertation for the Doctor of Juridical Science degree at George Washington University entitled "The Command Domination of the
Military Judicial Process." This dissertation, recently published,
contains a detailed and documented description of improper
command influence in a number of cases of which Mr. West, as
an Army JAG officer, had personal knowledge. The accounts
make up a startling picture of command intrigue, staff judge
advocate compliance, and lower level acceding to command
wishes. The cases range from intense reprisals against a young
JAG defense counsel who raised the defense of command influence to documented proof of false or misleading testimony by
three field grade officers in an Article 32 investigation to cover
up the role a commanding general had played in incidents leading up to court-martial charges.[38] Mr. West's experience, of
course, is limited to a small percentage of the total courts-
martial, and many of his cases displaying extreme command influence involved circumstances which particularly aroused the
ire of the commander. There is probably truth to the claim by
the military that the average court-martial (a high percentage of
which are for AWOL) is not directly affected by improper overt
command influence. However, when a commander views a court-
martial case as a particular threat to the command—and cases
involving political dissent, alleged homosexual acts, barracks

thefts or any kind of disobedience often fall in this category—the court-martial system seems to provide an unduly attractive opportunity for a commander to influence the trial.

A reduction of commanders' powers over military justice is consistent with the civilianization trend which has been taking place in the nature of the military since World War II. There is a certain anachronistic ring to arguments that a commander needs to control courts-martial to obtain instant and unthinking response from his men and that any lessening of his powers would weaken his ability to maintain discipline. Servicemen today have more technical jobs, better education, and more individual rights than ever before. A whole new class of enlisted men, called Specialists, who perform technical jobs and are not placed in a troop environment, came into being after the Korean War. Many servicemen work in jobs not much different from a civil servant's or a corporation employee's, and substantial numbers live off-post. Only about 10 percent of today's servicemen have MOS's (job descriptions showing their occupational specialty) which involve combat skills, while 54 percent hold technical specialties (electronics, mechanics, crafts, etc.) and the rest hold service specialties (food, administration, clerical, etc.). Most servicemen are not given specialized combat training. In short, today's military is a big business with a substantial portion of its members noncareer civilian-soldiers who serve their country in a service job or at a desk.

This change in the nature of the military inevitably calls for a reevaluation of traditional military attitudes toward discipline and the role of the commander. Two of the traditional commandments of military discipline—absolute and unquestioning obedience to commands of superiors and absolute conformity to official attitudes—have already been seriously undercut. After Nuremberg, men in the ranks could not escape individual responsibility for acts they were ordered to do, and the Court of Military Appeals has created a number of areas in which a serviceman is not bound to follow the orders of a superior (such as an order which has only some private, rather than military, purpose or which seriously infringes upon a serviceman's individual rights). The following language of a board of review in *United States* v. *Kinder* (1953) indicates the change in attitude toward the relationship of a serviceman to his commander:

> The obedience of a soldier is not the obedience of an automaton. A soldier is a reasoning agent. He does not respond, and is not expected to respond, like a piece of machinery. It is a fallacy of wide-spread consumption that a soldier is required to do everything his superior officer orders him to do.[39]

The My Lai cases have made the Nuremberg principles of continuing vital importance in today's military.,

A similar alteration of attitude has taken place concerning the obligation of servicemen to conform to official attitudes and demands. No young man who enters the service today has escaped the influence of the individualistic and democratic values of our society, and it is more and more difficult for the military to command the absolute conformity to official views it once could. The current movement for expanded servicemen's rights, particularly as regards exercise of First Amendment rights involving reading and expressing dissenting views, has already led to rewriting of regulations to permit certain activities, and the substantial number of court cases still pending may further extend servicemen's individual rights.

There is also something unrealistic about the notion that a commander must himself possess all effective powers regarding the personnel under him or his authority and effectiveness will be undermined. This, of course, is the premise behind the contention that a commander must control all functions of a court-martial and that if these functions are divided among independent agencies or individuals, his ability to insure performance of the unit's mission will somehow be diminished. Today, with instant communications and easy mobility, there is no reason to believe that a commander's effectiveness would be destroyed if he had to rely upon other agencies to perform court-martial functions. Commanders may once have held their men in check by the fear they engendered due to their disciplinary powers and crude displays of retributory powers, but discipline in the modern military is a more complex matter. The fact that command authority is not absolute, or that it must be shared with other officials, seems to have little to do with the effectiveness of a commander. The young servicemen of today are often more sensitive to abuse of authority, brutality, and injustice than to the pettiness of bureaucracy. The fact that their commander, in order to court-martial them, must submit the charges to an independent court administered by impartial officials seems more likely to win their acceptance than the spectre of an all-powerful commander whose control makes a farce out of courts-martial. It is, of course, difficult to judge the reactions of millions of servicemen to removal of command control of courts-martial, and the foregoing analysis can hardly be considered a scientific prediction. However, it should indicate that there are a number of complicated dimensions to this question and that the obsession of the military with individual command powers as the only key to military effectiveness fails to take into account both changed conditions and a variety of other relevant factors. There is no concrete evidence on which to argue that removal of command control of court-martial appointments and machinery today would adversely affect military discipline.

4. *Membership and Selection of the Court.* The provision in the UCMJ for an enlisted man to be tried by a court containing one-third enlisted men has turned out to be a hollow right. Commanders have invariably chosen noncommissioned officers, and, as a result, enlisted personnel are rarely requested (they were requested in only 2.6 percent of the Army courts-martial in 1968). Since the UCMJ failed to provide for a random selection of court members, permitting the commander convening authority to continue to choose the members from his officers without limitations on his discretion, there is still a disciplinarian quality to trial by court-martial.

If court members were selected at random from the entire military community at the particular installation, as juries are chosen in civilian courts, it is likely that a heavy majority of the members would be young men in the lower ranks. The military views this as undesirable, arguing that class antagonisms might prevent lower ranking servicemen from rendering an honest verdict and cause undue sympathy with the accused. The military has also raised the somewhat contradictory objection that low-ranking enlisted men might be overwhelmed by the presence of officers on the court and therefore not exert their own independence. Finally, the military has argued, low-ranking enlisted men are not qualified to serve on courts-martial because of their lack of experience in the military and their lack of understanding and appreciation of the purposes and objectives of military discipline.

These arguments actually go to the heart of the jury system itself. Permitting an accused to be tried by a jury of his peers chosen at random always involves the possibility that jurors will be sympathetic to the accused, swayed by other members of the jury, or not appreciate the purposes and objectives of the prosecution and the criminal laws. These qualities, however, are only objectionable if they prevent a juror from judging a case with an open mind, and they have a valuable function in insuring trial by a jury whose members reflect the different experiences, attitudes, and biases found in the community. The all-officer court-martial is especially lacking in these qualities.

There seems to be little basis for arguing that lower ranking servicemen are not qualified to sit as members of courts-martial. Today, when a high percentage of enlisted men have a high school education and a substantial minority are college educated, they appear to possess as acceptable qualifications to determine the kind of fact questions which we seek from a jury as the average civilian juror. There may be, however, some risk that court-martial members from lower ranks will be more class-motivated and less objective than the average civilian juror. The young recruit, who has been forced to accept a highly disciplinarian way of life, may harbor deeper antagonisms against a military prosecution than does the average civilian juror toward the district attorney's case. The continued effects of antiwar and servicemen's union organizing in the military and of the movement for expanded GI rights have, no doubt, increased anti-establishment antagonisms among some servicemen. Of course, similar problems exist in civilian law, and it has not been suggested, for example, that the right to trial by a jury of peers should be suspended because, for example, a high percentage of the jury in a prosecution for acts connected with a labor dispute might be sympathetic to the aims of the workers.

A number of military justice reformers have maintained that trial by peers is not adaptable to the military because of the potential bias inevitably created by the military caste system. This view has been expressed by Charles Morgan, southern director of the ACLU and counsel for Captain Levy in his court-martial case, and by ex-JAG officer Luther West, and has been endorsed in a resolution by the National Conference on GI Rights which met in Washington, D.C., in November, 1969. They argue that military men can never shake off the disciplinarian attitudes which are basic to military life and that, since the military cannot provide the proper atmosphere for a fair and impartial criminal trial, all military crimes should be tried in civilian courts. The example of the West German army, which has no court-martial system, leaving servicemen to be tried in civilian courts, and of Great Britain, where civilian lawyers carry out judge advocate functions, lends weight to the feasibility of this position. The Supreme Court's recent decision in *O'Callahan* v. *Parker*[40] to remove court-martial jurisdiction over crimes committed by servicemen which are not "service-connected" was premised in large part upon the absence of a right to trial by jury of one's peers in a court-martial, and thus it seems clear that, at the very least, a broadening of the class from which courts-martial are chosen and removal of the commander's power to hand-pick the court members is essential to the reform of military justice.

5. *Defense Counsel.* The most serious weakness in the present law as regards appointment of military lawyers to represent defendants in general and special courts-martial is that the lawyers come from the office of the commander's staff judge advocate. The staff judge advocate, due to his close association with the commander as a subordinate and chief legal advisor, is not an impartial official. The staff judge advocate's office usually resembles a small law firm; there is usually a good deal of discussion of cases between opposing counsel and other lawyers in the office, and all actions are inevitably influenced by the staff judge advo-

cate. Law firms have recognized that they cannot avoid conflict of interest problems by claiming that different lawyers in the firm are handling each side of the case, and, despite the good faith of most JAG lawyers, the closeness in which they work and the overriding command interest of the staff judge advocate are not conducive to an adversary defense.

A second problem with military defense counsel is that, in some cases, the usually higher ranking members of the court prevent them from taking as adversary a position as they should. The only way to avoid such problems is to remove as many of the trappings of rank as possible from a court-martial trial, and to forbid any adverse action against a defense counsel on account of his zeal in the courtroom. Reformers like Charles Morgan and Luther West argue that military lawyers are not well-suited to providing an adversary defense and that, until the legal processes and personnel of the court-martial are civilianized, the court-martial will always display a disciplinary cast. The fact that JAG lawyers are part of a tight military establishment and, even when not under the commander, still reflect establishment attitudes, is one of the most disquieting aspects of attempting to make the military justice system into a genuine adversary system.

Finally, one substantial defect in the adequacy of military defense counsel results from the refusal of the Judge Advocate General to permit them to bring collateral suits for extraordinary relief (such as habeas corpus, injunction, mandamus, and declaratory judgment) in federal district courts. There are times when the only way a serviceman's rights can be protected is by seeking federal court relief, and if he is unfortunate enough only to be represented by a JAG lawyer, that avenue will be foreclosed to him. Lawyers, military or civilian, should be provided for servicemen's collateral actions in federal courts.

6. *Nature of the Trial.* Unfortunately, vestiges of the old court-martial administrative hearing still remain and serve as constant reminders that this is a military, and not merely a judicial, hearing. Military judges may still appear in military uniform rather than judicial robes. Military courtrooms still have a distinctively military design. Seating of court members by rank, saluting, and the ubiquitous use of "sir" when examining witnesses are prom-

inent in military trials. Transcripts are not required to be provided in all special courts-martial, and the prosecutor and commander still play a prominent role in the procedure for subpoenaing and discovery of witnesses. It may be difficult for military men, used to the military trappings, to do without them, but the usual court-martial defendant, a young two-year enlistee or draftee, would greatly benefit from a changed and less militaristic judicial atmosphere.

7. *Post-Trial Proceedings.* The appellate structure of the military justice system needs a thorough overhauling. The administrative reviews by the commander convening authority and legal officers all too often become a routine without any real scrutiny of the record. The power of the commander to review sentences, even though he can only remit or reduce them, encourages the undesirable practice of courts giving the maximum sentence so that the commander will have the option to cut it down or not, and this power should be removed. The Courts of Military Review are not independent, and the judges lack tenure, their availability on appeal is too limited, and they lack full equitable powers to provide a genuine forum for relief for servicemen in a variety of administrative matters. The Court of Military Appeals is too limited in membership for its caseload, its writs and equitable powers are too narrow, and its availability is restricted to too few cases. Finally, review by civilian courts is unduly restricted to a narrow area of review on habeas corpus, and direct appeal to the Supreme Court is forbidden.

VI. CONCLUSION

The movement for civilianization of military justice has achieved only limited success in the fifty years since General Ansell proposed an overhaul of the court-martial system. The legislative reforms were painfully won and the results all too often the products of compromise. However, a substantial movement for reform of military justice has developed in the late–Vietnam War period, and it now appears that Congress will not be able to avoid consideration of reform legislation. As was mentioned before, three major reform bills—introduced by Senators Tydings, Hatfield, and Bayh—are now pending which would make fundamental changes in the structure of the military justice system. First, all three bills would remove control over court-martial machinery and appointment of personnel from the commander who brings court-martial charges against a serviceman. All three propose some form of separate court-martial command independent from the commander, which would carry out many of the functions now performed by the commander, such as appointment of counsel and court members and review of sentence. The present commander-appointed, officer-dominated, court-martial jury would also be altered. Senator Hatfield's bill would require random selection of court members with one-half of the court officers and one-half enlisted men of the same rank as the accused, while Senator Bayh's bill would require random selection from a pool made up of all the officers and enlisted men at the particular installation or area who have served more than one year on active duty.

The Hatfield and Bayh bills would also make substantial changes in court-martial proceedings. The powers of military judges would be expanded so that they more closely resemble federal court judges, and they would exercise the power to sentence. Availability of civilian court review would also be expanded, in Senator Hatfield's bill by permitting federal courts to hear claims of denial of constitutional rights of servicemen by the military once military remedies had been exhausted, and in Senator Bayh's bill by permitting for appeal to the Supreme Court on certiorari from decisions of the Court of Military Appeals. The powers of the Courts of Military Review and the Court of Military Appeals would also be expanded, and judges of the Courts of Military Review would be appointed by the President to three-year terms, while the membership of the Court of Military Appeals would be expanded from three to nine. Senator Hatfield's bill would require court-martial rooms to be designed and arranged as nearly identical to federal courtrooms as possible, would abolish seating by rank, and would require military judges to wear judicial robes. It would also abolish the Article 88 "contemptuous words" crime, limit the "general articles," Articles 133 and 134, to nonjudicial punishment proceedings, and remove court-martial jurisdiction over a number of civilian-type crimes.

These reforms, of course, deal primarily with the structure of military justice and are not directly concerned with many other problems—such as undue authoritarianism in military discipline, inadequate procedures and facilities for handling AWOL's and other problem cases, and absence of protection for many basic individual rights of servicemen—which have surfaced in the Vietnam War period. However, the military justice system, as the ultimate sanction, plays a vital role in discipline, and reform will inevitably have beneficial effects upon other aspects of military life. The problem is that, despite the continued pressure for reform, history has shown that fundamental changes in the military approach to justice are hard to achieve. By the time current proposals emerge from the military-oriented Armed Services committees, they will very likely be blunted. Some critics feel that the only solution to the problem of military justice is to abolish the court-martial system and use civilian procedures. However, it is not probable that such a fundamental reexamination of the whole system will be attempted unless public dismay forces the issue. The opportunity for major change has come and past many times; we must not let history repeat her lessons or the servicemen of the future will not be able to enjoy the rights and freedoms to which all Americans should be entitled.

Liberating Women—Legally Speaking

JEAN MURPHY and SUSAN DELLER ROSS*

We live in a male-dominated society. The policy-making levels of government, business, religion, higher education, science, and the professions are virtually devoid of women. One cannot fail to see a parallel to the patterns of race and ethnic discrimination evident in America's past and present—patterns of exclusion and tokenism, to which women have too often responded by simply surrendering.

The woman's issue is not new. But, while past controversies focused primarily on ending particular discriminatory practices, today much broader questions are posed. The enthusiastic response to Betty Friedan's thesis—that staying home baking bread and celebrating motherhood is a false and frustrating ethic—has grown to an increasingly large and vocal Women's Liberation Movement.[1] Many women now challenge the entire structure of society.

Sexually defined roles are pervasive in American society. Men are the providers and protectors, the decision-makers and "heads-of-the-family," strong, aggressive, and wise. Women are the homemakers and child-rearers, innocent of the world's hard realities, intuitively competent only at a very personal level. It jars the whole American psyche to imagine a woman President,

* The writers were both Hays Civil Liberties Fellows at New York University Law School, from which they were graduated in June, 1970. Jean Murphy is presently working in a neighborhood office for Community Action Legal Services in New York City. Susan Deller Ross is an attorney with the Equal Employment Opportunity Commission and is co-teacher of a course on "Women and the Law" at George Washington Law School.

head of General Motors, Pope—or even a factory foreman. Nor can we seriously conceive of a Congress truly representative of the American people, that is, half female; a hospital, half of whose doctors are women and half the nurses, men; or an office with half women "bosses" and half men secretaries.

Of course, a woman can become a doctor, a senator, or a business executive. Exceptional women have always escaped society's restrictions. The point is the exceptional quality of the achievement and the requisite struggles against normal life patterns. Women *as a class* are not really free to become doctors, senators, or business executives. They are not expected or encouraged to achieve in this fashion, and indeed are actively hindered from doing so. Nor are men as a class expected or encouraged to devote their time and energy to managing a home or raising children.

To be sure, current attempts to dignify the woman's role abound. Home management and child rearing have become a "profession." Yet few men view with pleasure the suggestion of role reversal and most are angered by the mere thought. It appears that attempts to improve the housewife's image are but an example of society's protesting too much. The good and trusted servant is always most highly praised at that moment in history when his own awareness of exploitation signals the end of a "good thing" for the master.

Of course, women's low status does not mean that the work done by women has no inherent value. It does mean that however impressively denominated, women's work is not highly rated by a male-dominated society, when measured in terms of monetary compensation or status—the criteria which this society has always used to designate the value of a member's contribution. Thus, child care, housekeeping, and physical personal service, when done for pay, are among the lowest paid and lowest status jobs. Traditional women's jobs outside the home—such as secretaries, nurses, and elementary school teachers—bear the same onus.* In factories, women's jobs are the lowest paid, and in

* Women constitute more than 90 percent of the total employed in the following fields: housekeepers (private household), nurses (professional), receptionists, babysitters, chambermaids and maids, secretaries, dressmakers

organized political activity—be it old line political club or Movement office—the men can be found in the smoke-filled rooms
while the women lick envelopes.

The low monetary value assigned to women's jobs is not a
minor problem. Almost two-fifths of the nation's working force
is female, but the average woman earns only 58 percent of the
average man's salary.** Indeed, sex is as important as race in
determining wages. The white male employed full time had a
median income in 1966 of $7,164; the black male, $4,528; the
white woman, $4,152; and the black woman, $2,949.[4] This situation exists despite the fact that white women on the average had
more education than white men, and black women had more
education than black men.[5]

The economic oppression of women has always been bolstered
by the legal system. In fact, under traditional Anglo-American
common law, women were virtual nonentities. As Blackstone
said, "By marriage, the husband and wife are one person in law;
that is, the very being or legal existence of the woman is suspended during the marriage. . . ."[6] This meant that they could
not vote, get an education, serve on juries or hold public office.
The husband alone determined the woman's name, her domicile,
had sole right to custody of their children, and had complete
control and virtual ownership of all her property. A married
woman was considered incompetent to sue in her own name or
to make contracts. Indeed, she almost became a possession of her
husband, since he could control her behavior with physical force
and had a legally enforceable right to her services (including
sex).[7]

Of course, "We've come a long way, baby." Changes in the
law governing the rights of women reflect evolving social atti-

and seamstresses, private household workers, telephone operators, stenog-
raphers, practical nurses, typists, sewers and stitchers, nurses (student),
laundresses, attendants (physicians' and dentists' offices), dieticians and
nutritionists, demonstrators, milliners.[2]

** In recent years the gap between men's and women's median salaries
has actually widened. In 1956 a woman's median salary was 63 percent of
a man's. By 1966 this figure dropped to 58 percent.[3]

tudes toward women's role. A constitutional amendment gave women the vote and every state has adopted some form of the Married Woman's Property Act, which eliminates the harshest effects of coverture. And today women do go to college and wear short skirts. But have we really come so far?

The vitality of the Women's Liberation Movement attests that we've not come far enough. Legal restrictions on women remain and the entire organization of society perpetuates our oppression. Real equality requires radical changes in this social organization. Improving the legal status of women cannot itself bring about these changes, but it can facilitate them. Thus, exploration of both legal restrictions and legal tools is necessary.

The laws affecting women's employment reveal the handicaps laws can impose on women as well as the law's ability to bring about change. The employment area is particularly important because improving women's status there may well prove a key factor in changing her overall social status and self-awareness. It would mean ending her economic dependency on men and would free her to develop her intellect, talents, and creativity more fully.

I. EMPLOYMENT

A. *State Labor Laws for Women*

The shocking conditions under which America's working class labored in the early 1900s spurred legislative reform efforts, but the Supreme Court found the first maximum hours law unconstitutional.[8] Taking a hint from the Court, the reformers settled for less and focused their attention on women and children. The result remains with us today: a great variety and number of state labor laws which apply only to women.

Whether these laws ever really helped women can be doubted. Exempting men from their coverage guaranteed the continued existence of a pool of cheap and readily exploitable workers. Given a choice, an employer would prefer to hire men, since their working conditions were not hedged with legislative restrictions. Thus, one-sex laws did not end the exploitation of workers but did jeopardize women's jobs.

The crucial question is whether these laws help women today, laws which generally fall into two broad areas: (1) those *conferring supposed benefits* on women, such as a minimum wage, a day of rest, a meal or rest period, or maternity benefits, and (2) those *prohibiting women from working,* either by precluding them from certain jobs, such as mining or bartending, or by imposing restrictions on women, such as weight and hour limits, and the bans on nightwork and work before and after child-birth.

The rubric of "protective legislation" has been applied to all these laws, but the favorable implications of that label should be viewed with skepticism. One researcher found that:

> [business] observers of the early legislative period . . . allege that the motivation for "protecting" child and female labor was more the protection and advancement of the male's status at work than a humanitarian attitude for women and children in our society. The National Safety Council subscribes to this view by describing unreasonable statutory limitations and tacit unfair employment practices as "a deliberate attempt to exclude the possibility that a large group of workers [women] may enter into competition with those already in the trade [men]."[9]

Speaking in support of the sex amendment to Title VII of the 1964 Civil Rights Act, Congresswoman Griffiths subscribed to the same view:

> Some people have suggested to me that labor opposes "no discrimination on account of sex" because they feel that through the years protective legislation has been built up to safeguard the health of women. Some protective legis-lation was to safeguard the health of women, but it should have safeguarded the health of men, also. Most of the so-called protective legislation has really been to protect men's rights in better paying jobs.[10]

Whatever the motivation for the legislation, a closer examination of the laws will show that they do in fact hurt women. The most obvious harm is that both of the above categories of state legislation have been used as an excuse not to hire women or not to promote them to better-paying jobs. In addition, when all the state laws are examined together, more subtle patterns emerge. "Protection" has been very uneven. For instance, while women are graciously allowed chairs for use during rest periods in forty-five states,[11] no state gives job security for maternity leaves of absence and only two states provide monetary maternity benefits. Surely the latter are the more important to women. Yet male legislatures have overwhelmingly chosen meaningless chivalry over substantive protection in the one area where, because of a verifiable biological difference, all women as a class may at some time need protection that all men as a class will never need. Nor do maternity benefits represent an unattainable, utopian goal. Over seventy countries provide them.

Another pattern is that men do receive substantial protection in the important areas of the minimum wage and day of rest benefits. In fact, federal nationwide law guarantees both men and women a minimum wage, and at a higher rate than all but one state. Twenty-nine state minimum wage laws, out of a total of thirty-nine, apply to both men and women.[12] There has been no parallel trend to give men chairs, rest periods, or to limit their hours of work. One can only suspect that male legislatures knew very well which laws represented true protection, and acted accordingly in choosing which benefits to extend to men.

The final two types of benefit laws, which provide lunch breaks and ten-minute rest periods for women,[13] seem innocuous enough, but they can be harmful. In one case before the Equal Employment Opportunity Commission, the thirty-minute lunch break, required only for women, proved to be expensive. The men worked in three regular eight-hour shifts, but received no formal lunch breaks, eating "on the fly" instead. In contrast, women were given a formal lunch break, but the employer consequently cut their third shift to 6¾ hours. Under a weekly rotating schedule of shifts, every third week women were paid for only 33¾ hours of work. Over a work year of fifty weeks, the "protection" of a lunch break cost them 2⅗ weeks of take-home pay. Another example of the harm caused by this kind of benefit is found in an Oregon federal court case.[14] An employer claimed that he had denied a woman employee's application for the job of Press Operator B (and had given it to men with less seniority) in part because the union contract required two ten-minute rest periods for women. It is evident that such "benefit" laws hurt women by denying them job opportunities and hurt men by denying them the "benefit."

The same cannot be said about the second broad category of laws, those which prohibit women from working. To confer their "protection" on men would not help men but would only serve to eliminate many jobs—e.g., bartending, mining, jobs requiring the lifting of twenty-five pounds or overtime work (with their premium rates). These laws hurt only women: those women who are perfectly capable of performing the prohibited jobs and are, in fact, anxious to do so for the higher pay, the improvement in status, the increased job satisfaction and the preferred hours.

The most outrageous laws in this category are those which close jobs completely to women. A total of twenty-six states exclude women from various jobs: working in mining (seventeen states), bartending (ten), retail liquor stores (one), as a bellhop (one), and in dangerous or injurious occupations or with harmful substances (three). Ohio goes to the most absurd limits, forbidding women to work in fourteen specific categories.[15] One can only wonder at the stereotyped vision of women held by the legislatures in these states.

There are also the weight and hour laws. Ten states forbid women to lift more than a set amount, ranging from fifteen to fifty pounds. People should compare these limits with the weight of the weekly grocery bags and five-year-old children the average woman lifts all the time. Forty-one states forbid women (men are covered in three) to work more than a maximum number of hours, ranging from forty to sixty hours per week.

Fortunately, the courts have begun to question these laws because they are not based on proof that all or substantially all women cannot safely lift more than set weight limits or work more than set hours. One might have thought that such a simple fact was obvious. Yet the public clings to the notion that all women are weak, delicate creatures who prefer getting home to their babies rather than earning extra money at overtime rates. In fact, women head 4.6 million families (10 percent of U.S. families; 25 percent in the poverty area), one million working women have unemployed husbands (disabled or retired), and six million working women are single.[16] Legislatures assume that single men and male heads of household want and need extra money, but that single women and female heads of household do not. Why not allow women to make their own choice, based on their economic needs, just as men do?

Another type of law prohibits women from working at night; eighteen states have such laws. The rationale is again based on an obvious stereotype: it is not proper for defenseless ladies to be wandering about at night. Men must come to realize that many women prefer to work at night—for better pay or because husbands can take care of children at night or because a night-time job can be combined with daytime studies. The hypocrisy of these laws is exposed in the bitter remarks of Congresswoman St. George: "Women are protected—they cannot run an elevator late at night and that is when the pay is higher. . . . But what about the offices, gentlemen, that are cleaned every morning about 2 or 3 o'clock in the city. . . ."[17]

A final prohibition is found in seven state laws which force women to quit work when pregnant, or to stay away from work after childbirth. Women should have the right to make this decision. Housewives do not stop working just because they are pregnant. If a woman decides that she cannot safely perform a job, perhaps employers should be required to let her transfer to another one. We should not assume that these laws grew out of concern for women's safety; they might simply reflect male embarrassment at having pregnant women around.

In conclusion, analysis of state laws which apply only to women does not support the thesis that they protect women in any meaningful way. In fact, these laws do not protect women in the one area legitimately applicable only to women—maternity benefits and job security during maternity leaves of absence. They are ineffective in dealing with women's exploitation through receipt of lower pay and worse jobs than men. They are used to discriminate against women in job, promotion, and high-pay opportunities. And in those few areas where they might be said to have real value, they exploit men by denying them that protection.

Even more important, these laws reflect a basic perception of women and men as inherently different in the amount and kind of work they can do. This difference is in turn used to justify "protective" treatment but, as should be clear from the statistics, the crucial fact in the job market today is the exploitation of women, not their protection. This exploitation arises from the same perception of a difference between men and women. As long as we argue for a need for separate protective legislation for women only, we are reinforcing the idea of a crucial difference and thus helping to insure that the exploitation based on this idea will continue. Women are not a monolithic class with identical physical strengths, intellectual capacities, or job motivations, any more than are men. It is time to recognize that by opposing discriminatory, one-sex only, legislation.

B. *The Equal Pay Act*

The 1960s gave rise to new legislation concerned with employment discrimination against women. The Equal Pay Act[18] was designed to meet the widespread and blatantly discriminatory practice of paying women less than men for the same work. A government policy had already supported the principle of equal pay to women during both World Wars and the Korean War, when the female industrial work force became particularly valuable to the country.[19] After each war, as the country returned to peacetime conditions, sex discrimination in wages also returned. Despite sustained efforts to obtain national legislation against this practice, it was not until 1963 that the Equal Pay Act was finally passed.

This law requires employers to pay equal salaries to a man and a woman when their jobs require equal skill, effort, and responsibility and are done under similar working conditions. It also forbids labor unions "to cause or attempt to cause" an employer to violate this requirement. Four exceptions are set forth in the statute. Different salaries paid to men and women do not violate the act if they are based on a merit system, a seniority system, a system measuring earnings by quality or quantity of production or on "any other factor other than sex."

The equal pay provision is enforced by the Labor Department's Division of Wages and Hours as part of the Fair Labor Standards Act. Labor Department inspectors routinely check for equal pay violations as well as investigate specific complaints. Women who have suffered pay discrimination can recover the difference between their wages and those paid to men for up to a two-year period. By April, 1970, seventeen million dollars had been recovered for over 50,000 employees.[20]

When necessary, the Labor Department (or the employee herself if the department fails to act) can sue to recover the wages due because of equal pay violations. In most of the cases litigated the conflict has concerned whether the work involved is equal. *Schultz* v. *Wheaton Glass Company*[21] represents a typical fact pattern. In the company's plant, both men and women inspected bottles and operated the machines that packed them, but the men were paid more than the women. Other workers, called "snap-up boys," carried packages to and from the machines and did simple repair work. This assistance was available to both men and women but men sometimes performed these "snap-up" jobs themselves. The district court judge listed all the additional tasks sometimes performed by some men and, finding them to constitute a substantial part of the men's work, allowed the pay differential.

The court of appeals, however, reversed this decision, finding that the wage system was discriminatory because it was not rational to pay men significantly more than women because they sometimes did work usually performed by "snap-up boys" who were paid at about the same rate as the women. An employer would be justified in paying one group more only if all members of that group could and did perform the additional work and all members of the group paid less had the opportunity of doing the more highly paid work. Wheaton, however, was paying *all* men more because *some* men did the extra tasks that no women were allowed to do. The appellate court also considered the historical context of the pay differential which was originally based on sex and instituted because of union fears at the competition offered by the first women hired.

The criteria set forth in the *Wheaton* opinion make it difficult for employers to avoid the equal pay mandate by classifying jobs so that men and women appear to perform different work. Nevertheless, considerable leeway still remains to each court when deciding whether particular jobs constitute "equal work."

Employers have also tried to defend their discriminatory pay scales by claiming the differential is based on a "factor other than sex"—the fourth exception listed in the statute. In a series of cases involving bank tellers and clerks,[22] employers claimed that higher pay for men was justified because they were part of an executive training program. In fact, there was no formal program to which women could apply, an exclusion based on the expectation in the minds of the bank management that men were potentially promotable and women were not. Despite these facts, two lower courts accepted the employers' claim, and only on appeal did the women prevail.

Although the Labor Department has urged that the "factor other than sex" exception be interpreted narrowly, the courts retain great freedom to allow pay differences on this ground. One court looked to the "subtleties of personalities and attitudes," finding a male travel consultant's higher salary was not due to his sex but to his added "ambition and enthusiasm."[23] It seems unrealistic (and perhaps unfair to the female employee who, in another case, might be the more valued employee) to discount subjective factors entirely. But the assertion that pay differences are due to personality and attitudes can easily mask sex discrimination. This is especially true in a society whose members, including employers and judges, normally and "subjectively" assume men to be more valuable employees than women.*

* Psychological studies have shown that such assumptions can be totally false. When two groups of college students received the same essay to read

There is no questioning the importance of the Equal Pay Act. The prior pattern of viewing sex itself as sufficient reason for lower wages has been all but eliminated. Where men and women are holding identical jobs, enforcement of the equal pay principle is relatively easy. But a great deal of wage discrimination remains under job classification systems that ensure men higher pay. Half the jobs in the United States are not even covered by the equal pay provision and the funds available for its enforcement are inadequate.

If equal pay is truly to become a reality, the act must be amended to cover workers now unprotected,* and additional funds must be made available for its enforcement. Political pressure is needed as well. An increased consciousness and militancy among women workers could itself stimulate effective enforcement of the Equal Pay Act. Publicizing violations would encourage "voluntary" compliance and spur the Labor Department to more frequent and effective investigation. If more women would defy the social pressure against doing men's work,** the artificial distinctions between jobs relied upon by employers to avoid equal pay would break down.

A militant labor union position at the local level would also encourage government action and employer compliance. The union's role in negotiating contracts gives them an additional and unique power to ensure equal pay. In the past, union contracts have formalized the policy of paying women less and have also set up the sexually based system of job definitions that invariably lock women into the lowest paying positions. What a difference it would make if the same power were used to redefine jobs in

---

and evaluate, it was rated much higher by the group told it was written by "John T. McKay" than by the group told it was written by "Joan T. McKay."[24]

* Four bills that would do so at least in part have been introduced in this session of the 91st Congress: HR 15971, HR 16098, HR 18427, and S 3612.

** This pressure can be very strong and imposed by women themselves. One reporter has seen the reluctance of telephone operators to seek the more highly paid but traditionally male jobs even after the right to do so had been won in court.[25]

order to facilitate women's entry into higher paying jobs, and to eliminate the artificial differences on which unequal wages are based. Admittedly, the male-dominated unions are unlikely to make such a complete about-face on their own impetus. But women union members, if organized, should be able to exercise considerable political leverage on issues affecting them directly.

C. Title VII of the Civil Rights Act of 1964

A year after passage of the Equal Pay Act, a second law relating to women's employment passed Congress. Title VII of the 1964 Civil Rights Act[26] has an unusual history. Originally it dealt only with racial, ethnic, or religious discrimination in employment. Southern strategists proposed that sex-based discrimination also be prohibited, as they had suggested for every other section of the Civil Rights Act. The proposed amendment was designed to help defeat the entire bill, and when Representative Howard Smith introduced it on the floor, he made it clear that he considered sex discrimination a joke. He read a letter asking for "a bill to correct the present 'imbalance' which exists between males and females in the United States," and which shuts off "the 'right' of every female to have a husband of her own."[27]

The women in Congress, however, took the proposed amendment very seriously, and ultimately, the sex provision did become part of Title VII. Once passed, a new problem arose—ensuring that the sex provision would be enforced. Working women knew the problem was serious, and one-third of the complaints handled by the Equal Employment Opportunity Commission (EEOC)—the body charged with overseeing Title VII—came from women. But the mass media and even EEOC still thought it was all a splendid joke, asking whether a man could be a Playboy bunny—hence, the label, "bunny bill."[28] In essential agreement with Howard Smith's approach, even the *New York Times*[29] and *The New Republic*[30] could not refrain from issuing bigoted editorials, which shows the extent to which sex discrimination pervades all levels of American thought and cuts across the traditional political and philosophical boundaries.

What exactly does Title VII do, that it should evoke such ridicule? Broadly speaking, it prohibits discrimination in employment on the basis of sex; employers cannot fire employees, refuse to hire them, pay different rates, or give different "terms, conditions, or privileges" of employment because of the worker's sex. Employment agencies are also covered, and cannot discriminate on the basis of sex in their referrals. Likewise, labor unions cannot exclude members of one sex, discriminate against them, refuse to refer them for a job, or try to force employers to discriminate on the basis of sex. Finally, employers and unions are forbidden to keep one sex out of training or apprenticeship programs.

Yet there are some important exceptions to the prohibition on sex discrimination. First, employers and labor unions with fewer than twenty-five members are not covered, nor are employment agencies dealing with such employers. Second, the national, state, and local governments and their agencies are exempted, as well as United States public corporations. Other exempt categories of employers include Indian tribes, private clubs, religious groups, and educational institutions; this last proviso means that none of the nation's teachers is covered. Communist employees are not protected. Finally, and most importantly, where sex, religion, or national origin is a "bona fide occupational qualification," discrimination is permitted; significantly, this last exception does not extend to racial discrimination.

The "bona fide occupational qualification" exception (otherwise known as a "bfoq," with the letters read separately) was of crucial importance. If the courts had interpreted it broadly, Title VII could have become a dead letter for women, for under such an interpretation, many admitted cases of sex discrimination would be permitted as necessary to a business.

One of the major areas in which employers sought to utilize the bfoq exception was the restrictive state labor laws applying to women. Thus, if a state prohibited women from working more than forty hours a week, and a woman applied for a higher paying job requiring forty-two hours of work per week, the employer could refuse her the job. His argument would be that the

male sex is a qualification (a bfoq) for that job, because the job
requires forty-two hours of work and state law prohibits women
from working that long.

The EEOC's initial lack of commitment to fighting sex discrimination was reflected by a vacillating position on the conflict
between Title VII and the state laws. Starting in 1965, it
adopted successive, conflicting policies evidencing, at different
times, a desire to avoid the controversy, an idea that some of the
laws might genuinely be protective, and a possibility that Congress had intended to leave state laws in effect.[31]

Fortunately, the EEOC finally seems to have realized that
these laws really do harm women workers. In August, 1969, it
issued new regulations. Henceforth, the EEOC would not allow
state laws limiting women's employment (specific job prohibitions, and hour, weight, and nightwork laws) to be used by
employers as a legitimate excuse to discriminate against women.
The language showed that EEOC understood the injustice of
treating women as a class with stereotyped characteristics.

> . . . such State laws and regulations, although originally
> promulgated for the purpose of protecting females, have
> ceased to be relevant to our technology or to the expanding
> role of the female worker in our economy. The Commission
> has found that such laws and regulations do not take into
> account the capacities, preferences, and abilities of individ-
> ual females and tend to discriminate rather than protect.[32]

The federal courts expressed the same initial reluctance to
deal with the problem of the state laws. Women who raised the
issue in 1967 and 1968 saw their cases dismissed on various evasive grounds.[33] Since that time, the courts have begun to deal
with the issue and a trend toward invalidating restrictive state
laws seems to be developing. The three leading cases, all within
the last two years, are *Rosenfeld* v. *Southern Pacific Co.*, *Weeks*
v. *Southern Bell Telephone & Telegraph Co.*, and *Bowe* v.
Colgate-Palmolive Co.[34]

Leah Rosenfeld, an employee of twenty-two years, bid for the
position of agent-telegrapher with Southern Pacific. Although

she was the most senior employee bidding for the job, it was awarded to a male with less seniority, on the grounds that to award the job to plaintiff would violate the California hours and weight laws for women, and company policy. The court held that the California hours and weight legislation discriminates against women on the basis of sex, that it does not constitute a bfoq, and that the federal legislation controls.

In the *Weeks* case, an employee of nineteen years lost her bid for the job of switchman when it was granted to a man with less seniority. As switchman, she could have earned almost $3,000 a year more. The lower court supported Southern Bell's position that the Georgia weight law, a thirty-pound limit for women, forbade awarding the job to a woman, and came within the bfoq exception to Title VII. Georgia then repealed the specific weight limit, substituting a general limit ". . . to avoid strains or undue fatigue." The company still refused to consider Mrs. Weeks for the switchman position, and relied on its own privately imposed thirty-pound weight limit on women's jobs. On appeal from the lower court, Mrs. Weeks finally established her right to be considered for the job, with the appellate court setting forth a new standard which significantly narrowed the scope of the bfoq exception:

> the employer has the burden of proving that he has reasonable cause to believe, that is a *factual* basis for believing, that *all or substantially all women* would be unable to perform safely and efficiently the duties of the job involved. [emphasis added]

The company failed to meet this test, since it had submitted no evidence on the issue, but rather had relied on unproven, stereotyped assumptions about the lifting abilities of women.

The real significance of this decision is the test it established for the bfoq exception—a test which could play a decisive role in invalidating restrictive state laws. It is difficult to imagine how states, employers, or labor unions are going to prove, for example, that all or substantially all women cannot lift more than thirty pounds, work more than forty hours a week, or serve drinks safely and efficiently. Even the standard model of the suburban housewife and mother is required to do all of these tasks on a daily basis.

Another company-imposed weight restriction was invalidated in the *Bowe* case. Here, it was apparent that restrictive state laws can have an even greater impact than their strictly legal force. Even though there was no state weight law, Colgate-Palmolive deliberately set out to copy existing laws in other states. Revealingly, the company did not do so until after passage of Title VII, under which the existing sex-segregated job system in the plant would be illegal. By setting up a weight limit, the company had managed to retain an essentially sex-segregated job system. Women were limited to jobs which did not require lifting thirty-five pound weights and which, "coincidentally," all paid less than any over–thirty-five pound job. Women also were disadvantaged in layoffs, since men could compete for under–thirty-five pound jobs before being laid off, but women could not compete for the men's over–thirty-five pound jobs before layoff. Fortunately, the weight limitation was not allowed as a valid bfoq. Here, as in *Weeks*, the court realized that a broad construction of the bfoq would in effect nullify Title VII itself.

These three cases, and others following them,[35] indicate a trend toward invalidating restrictive state laws applying to women only and company policies that parallel state laws. But the act still presents serious problems. The definition of "discrimination based on sex" is one of them. Some courts have adopted such loose definitions that Title VII could lose all effect. One case presented a challenge to Delta Air Lines' policy of firing their stewardesses when they got married.[36] No male employees of Delta were subjected to such a policy. The court commented that "sex . . . just sort of found its way into the . . . Civil Rights Bill," and held that the Delta discrimination was based on marriage, not sex, and therefore was permissible.* It is im-

* One court recently went even further and found that only women were capable of being stewardesses! The judge was impressed by Eric Berne's testimony that male passengers would be threatened by a virile male steward, and respond negatively to a less masculine steward, but would feel "more masculine and thus more at ease" with female stewardesses. The air-

portant to realize that the airlines' policy is economically very advantageous, since it ensures high turnover rates, difficult unionization, limited seniority, and, consequently, low salaries. And it is interesting to reflect on the sexual undertones of the entire stewardess role and the special implications of the "single girl" policy. Perhaps the real basis for the court's decision was an assumption that the status of marriage connotes something very different for a woman than for a man. In effect, employers and society in general can impose special disabilities upon married women which the courts will enforce.

The same assumption was made about the status of parenthood in a very recent case,[38] where an employer refused to hire mothers, though he would hire fathers, of pre–school age children. The court upheld the employer's policy because it was not based on sex alone but on sex plus another factor—having pre–school age children. The reasoning that discrimination is not discrimination under Title VII as long as only a sub-class of women is discriminated against seems patently absurd, yet the courts are obviously having trouble with it. A dissenting judge accurately remarked that "If 'sex plus' stands, the Act is dead."[39]

Recently, the Supreme Court reversed this decision, but its opinion is nevertheless disappointing. This was its first sex discrimination case in the last ten years, and the Court showed a less than lukewarm concern for women's rights in its written opinion. The attitude displayed during oral argument was worse, and reached its absurd height in a final exchange between Chief Justice Warren Burger and the company's lawyer. Upon learning that the job in question was assembling small electric components and that although the company refused to hire mothers of preschool-age children, 75–80 percent of its assembly workers were women, Justice Burger observed sympathetically,

> Q. . . . I would take judicial notice of, from many years of contact with industry, that women are manually much

---

lines' job, it appears, is no longer to fly passengers to a destination, but to coddle weak male egos.[37]

more adept than men and they do this kind of work better
than men do it, and that's why you hire women.

A. Mr. Chief Justice—

Q. For just the same reason that most men hire women as
secretaries, because they are better at it than men.

A. I am so pleased—I couldn't say that because it appears
to fall into this stereotype preconception concept that—

(Laughter)

Q. It's a preconception that—

A. We don't think it appeals to reason.

Q. The Department of Justice, I am sure, doesn't have
any male secretaries. This is an indication of it.

Presumably, the United States Supreme Court would not take judicial notice today of a special black capacity for manual labor, as
evidenced by the all-black janitorial force of some major employer,
but the same attitude toward women is evidently respectable.
Thus, although *Phillips* v. *Martin Marietta Corp.* does break
the tradition of notoriously bad decisions in the sex area, it also
warns women that they still cannot expect the Supreme Court
to champion their cause.[40]

II. SKETCHES IN SEX OPPRESSION

Aside from employment, women are severely discriminated
against everywhere, and law reflects and reinforces that tendency.
Some other areas of this discrimination will be sketched in order
to suggest where further legal research and action are necessary.

Acceptance of women's oppression runs so deep in our country
that it is largely unstudied. Thus, we do not know how many
girls are denied an education by men-only educational policies;
we do not know how many women are serving longer sentences
than men or are in jail for crimes for which men are not prosecuted; we do not know how many women are forced by the law
to have and care for children. We do not know these things because, very bluntly, the men who have been running the legal
system have not noticed a problem. So the study of how law has
oppressed women has only just begun.

A. *Education*

Discrimination is particularly offensive in the field of education, since this area supplies the key to both personal development and job opportunities. Sixteen years after *Brown* v. *Board of Education*,[41] it is still permissible to deny women public educational opportunities. The Supreme Court had a chance to rule on the issue in 1959 and 1960[42] when some women tried to get into Texas A. & M. This school was the only college in the state where they could have studied floriculture and many other subjects, but the Court did not think the exclusion of women from a state college was even worth a hearing. Until last year, one of the best public schools in New York City, Stuyvesant High School, kept out girls. Other schools were available, it was argued, and Stuyvesant's special reputation and long history as an all male top science school should be preserved. A few girls have finally been admitted after Alice de Rivera brought a suit challenging the exclusion of girls. Before the case reached a final decision, the Board of Education stipulated that Alice could enter Stuyvesant, thereby avoiding a legal test of the no-girl policy.[43]

Related to the outright exclusion of women is the use of quota systems. The low number of women lawyers, doctors, dentists, engineers, and scientists is usually attributed to lack of ambition on women's part, but it is strange that women in other countries have been born with so much more ambition than American women. Institutionalized quota systems, whether officially admitted or not, are very effective in excluding women from the professions. These practices could have been corrected by outlawing sex discrimination in public education as part of the 1964 Civil Rights Act. An amendment to do that was actually offered by Congressman Dowdy (again, as part of the Southern strategy), but there was no support for the proposition that women as well as blacks were entitled to an equal education.

Education offers other examples of discriminatory practices that should be brought under legal attack. Colleges routinely impose curfews on women, although they usually would not dream of imposing them on men, and the courts have upheld the practice.[44] High schools force girls to take home economics and boys to take shop, provide thousands of dollars for boys' athletics but none for girls', counsel boys to achieve and girls to take typing. Some college scholarships are barred to women or are limited through quota systems. Job discrimination enters into the educational world, too. Qualified women are repeatedly passed over for the top jobs—high school principal, full professor, head of the department, president of the college.

There are a few signs of change. A lower federal court temporarily ordered the University of Virginia to admit women,[45] and another court said a college could not impose the burden of paying for the college dormitory system unequally on women by forcing women, but not men, to live in college dorms.[46] But overall, the legal system still operates on the assumption that men have a right to education and all that goes with it, and that women do not.

B. Child Care

One of the reasons both employers and schools have felt free to discriminate against women derives from the notion that women will be tending babies anyway. Law plays a part here, too, since it often effectively compels women to fulfill this role.

The central fact is that there are extraordinarily few day care centers in the United States, although there are 10.5 million working mothers, one-third of all mothers.[47] When the economy needed women workers during World War II, it was able to supply places for 1.6 million children in child care centers; by 1967, there were only 200 thousand places.[48] The psychologists and sociologists, by giving day care a bad name, are probably the worst culprits of keeping women home. For example, the Director of the Children's Bureau Division of Social Services has said: "The basic problems that create the necessity for day care for most children who need it are the root problems of all child welfare: poverty, low income, broken homes, desertion, separation, divorce, minority status, physical and emotional problems."[49] Day care is seen as being meant only for "problem children" and women are made to feel guilty for leaving children in these centers. Margaret Mead has found ". . . a new and subtle form of anti-feminism in which men—under the guise of exalting the importance of maternity—are tying women more tightly to their children than has been thought necessary since the invention of bottle feeding and baby carriages."[50]

The laws have also enforced this trend by imposing stringent licensing restrictions, which make day care centers too expensive for the average couple. New York City's Health Code provides one example. Until recently, day care for children under two was actually illegal, and the commentators to the code had the gall to apologize for letting in two-year-olds:

> Although it is recognized that as an ultimate goal it is not desirable to permit children under three years of age in a day care service, and many services now have a policy of not admitting such children, the presently practicable limitation of prohibiting only the care of children under two has been adopted.[51]

Another section of the code literally forces women to care for children, by providing that only women can care for children under two in a "family care" setting.

In addition, the tax laws exacerbate the problem. No deductions for day care costs are allowed unless the family is very poor;[52] therefore, the financial burden of child care is increased and the incentive for women to work is decreased. Even from the standpoint of increased tax revenues, this policy seems to be a mistake. When women stay home, their work product is untaxable, being entirely outside the economy. When they work, the government gets taxes not only from their salaries, but also from the salaries paid for child care and from the increased profits of businesses taking over work traditionally done at home for nothing (laundry, sewing, cleaning).

C. Control of the Body

Related to the problem of child care is the problem of control over one's body. Although people usually do not think of birth

control and abortion laws in this light, to deny women the right
to birth control information and abortion effectively forces them
to submit their bodies to a use they have not voluntarily chosen.
And if a woman's involuntary choice is reduced to going full
term and submitting a baby to adoption, her body has been used
as an incubator to produce a child for someone else to rear. The
rationale that abortion amounts to killing life ignores the fact
that the definition of conception as the beginning of life is a
religious one. A vital American tradition is the principle that
society does not have the right to impose religious ideas (also
formulated by men) on those who do not believe in them.

A further consequence of the abortion laws is that some five
to ten thousand women in effect receive the death penalty each
year for undergoing abortions. This total represents the estimated number of deaths that occur when over one million
women resort to illegal abortions.[53] The lesser penalty of imprisonment is also possible in those states where undergoing an
abortion is a felony.

Recently courts in several states have found abortion laws to
be unconstitutional. The laws themselves have been substantially
liberalized in others. Yet New York's experience indicates that
even repeal of abortion laws does not eliminate the problem.
New York City has restricted abortions to hospitals and hospital-
connected clinics. It was questionable for some time whether
Blue Cross insurance would cover single women's abortions.
Hospital decisions to limit the number of abortions performed
each week have led to long waiting lists and, for many women,
transformed what in early pregnancy would be an easy, safe
operation into a far more serious one. Male control of other
institutions can thus subvert the victories women win in the
legislature.

D. Criminal Law and Juvenile Delinquency

Criminal laws keep women in their place by threatening imprisonment and fines to those women who refuse to adhere to
the sexual double standard. Prostitution is the obvious example.
In some states, it is a crime, under a specific statute, for a man

to have intercourse with a prostitute, and in every state, under traditional legal doctrines, men should be liable for aiding and abetting the commission of this crime. It takes two, as the saying goes; yet men are never prosecuted. If we realize that men, not women, pass laws, serve as district attorneys, and sit as judges, this fact is not hard to understand. One judge, with amazing candor, explained that men are not prosecuted because many judges, faced with an accused man, feel that, "There, but for the grace of God, go I."[54] Male judges obviously cannot empathize with prostitutes in the same way.

Statutory rape presents a less obvious example of forcing girls to be "pure" or suffer the consequences. It is less obvious because it is the men who are sent to jail for cohabiting with girls under a certain age (as high as twenty-one in some states); the sexual act is called rape, even though consensual, because women below this age are considered too immature to give their consent to such an important act—though they are mature and intelligent enough to get married and raise babies without parental consent at age eighteen, three years before the boys. Even though men bear the brunt of this particular enforcement of the double standard, the law also has the intended effect of making it more difficult for a girl below the "age of consent" to choose her own sexual life.*

One horrifying example of the traditional treatment of women by the criminal law was exposed in two recent cases.[55] State sentencing laws were declared unconstitutional because they effectively required judges to give longer sentences to women than to men for having committed the identical crime. New York and Maine still have similar statutes on the books.[56] The rationale for these laws is apparently that prison does women more good than men, so women should be protected by allowing them more time to be rehabilitated.

In the field of juvenile delinquency, there are similar laws. For example, the enlightened state of New York confines girls up

* The most absurd result of refusing to see women as human beings with sexual needs is shown in the Washington State Law which only requires men to prove that they have no venereal disease before marriage, because all women who get married are virgins—of course.

to eighteen years old for the offense of being a "person in need of supervision" (a PINS), while only boys under sixteen can be confined for this offense.[57] It should be realized that the outlawed acts do not constitute a punishable crime if done by an adult, and can encompass such misdeeds as being pregnant. Thus, this offense amounts to the very special one of being a girl, aged sixteen to eighteen.

E. The Problem of Sex-Based "Privileges"

A serious discussion of the law's discriminatory treatment of women cannot leave out those areas where the law does in fact discriminate in favor of women. Too often, the final and triumphant answer to anyone challenging the second-class status of American women is, "But what about alimony—or the draft?" It is difficult to be sure whether the tone implies that the system is unfair to men as well, so women have no cause to complain, or whether it implies women are so well taken care of by a "privileged" position that they should be happy in their "place."

The discussion of state labor laws makes clear that we should be wary of a distinction in legal treatment even where it confers a benefit. For that same benefit is too easily and too often used to justify treating women as "different" in other areas, depriving them of far more valuable benefits. Exempting women from an obligation imposed on men implies a second-class status in general.

Exemption from jury service is one example. Today women do serve on juries, but the obligation is not yet universal and usually is weakened by automatic exemptions for women based on sex alone or on having young children.[58] Such exemptions adversely affect the rights of all citizens. Every citizen has a right to trial by a jury of his peers, which implies a jury made up of a cross-section of the population. If a significant economic, racial, or sexual group is not even considered in a jury's selection, this right is denied.

The denial particularly harms women defendants. The most extreme example is a 1961 case in which a Florida woman was convicted of killing her husband, after suspecting him of infidelity, by an all-male jury. There were no women on the jury because in Florida, women, unlike men, were considered for jury duty only if they first registered with a court. Although it has long been recognized that a black defendant's rights are violated if he is tried by a jury from which blacks as a class have been excluded, the Supreme Court upheld the woman's conviction.[59]

The special exemptions for women with small children not only limit the number of women on juries, but also illustrate the special connotations the law confers on the woman's status of marriage and parenthood. Neither status is exclusively a female one and there is no rational basis for granting exceptions because a woman has young children, when fathers are not allowed the same option. The point is obviously the work (child care)* that the status involves, not the status itself. But there is no reason to treat the necessity for a woman to remain at her job any differently than a man's necessity to remain at his. Special hardship could be considered for women, as it is now for men.

Alimony raises a more difficult question. Historically, married women were deprived of virtually all their property, including their own earnings, but the law counterbalanced this inequity by requiring the husband to support his wife. When he did not fulfill his duty, she could enforce the obligation in several ways: a suit for support during the marriage, for alimony if the marriage were dissolved, and to claim inheritance rights after his death. Alimony can also be looked at in terms of the historical emphasis on the contractual nature of marriage. Support and services were exchanged. Since divorce was originally allowed only on the theory that one partner was at fault, a wife's right to alimony was a form of remedy for breach of contract—she was paid in damages what she could have expected from performance of the contract.

The present attitude toward marriage and divorce in this country has greatly changed, a change reflected by our laws. Divorces are more often than not consensual. Throughout marriage, women retain their property and an ability to earn money. Yet, although the absolute legal dependency on the husband no

---

* Of course, many of the women granted automatic exemptions do not even spend their working hours in child care, but earn salaries instead.

longer prevails, the actual dependency remains, maintained by a society that still sees women's primary role as homemaker, by parents who train their daughters to be attractive to men rather than able to support themselves, by husbands who see a threat to their own egos in their wives' working, and by schools that send girls to family education courses. The actual dependency is also partly attributable to the discrimination within the labor market, which makes it difficult for even a very determined woman to remain the economic equal of her husband.

Alimony today can be viewed as a private tax on individual male members of the society to compensate individual female members of society for some of the discrimination women have suffered in the course of their lives. Alimony also imposes costs on women, although they are less visible. It undermines a woman's self-respect and independence and encourages her to forego a serious commitment to a career, which ultimately hurts the husband, who must pay alimony, and society, which often loses her most productive talents.

The ideal, of course, is a society where alimony is unnecessary —where women have not been forced into dependency. But to abolish alimony now would have a disastrous effect on those women who have lived their lives in dependency. Unfair as it seems to a young man forced to pay alimony to his childless, college-educated ex-wife, it is no less unfair to deny alimony to a woman who has for twenty years stayed home to keep house at the insistence of her husband. He steadily advanced in position and salary, while her employment options declined.

Imposing an equal obligation of support on a woman could have a significant effect on the choices young women make. Compelled to regard employment as a necessity, she will be far more likely to make a careful career choice so that when she works it will be at a job as consciously chosen as a man's. And if alimony were awarded on the basis of a wife's or a husband's actual dependency, husbands would be more likely to encourage, rather than discourage, their wives to work.

Along these same lines, exemption from the draft must be viewed like other privileges granted women because of their sex. The privilege harms women because it reinforces a negative view of them and permits discrimination in other areas. Women who volunteer for military duty do so under far less beneficial terms than their male counterparts. Married women in the armed services do not receive equal survivorship benefits for their spouses nor do they receive equal housing and other benefits while serving overseas. Nor do young women receive the job training which makes the armed forces a source of upward mobility for poor men.

Whether the draft should exist at all is a question currently under serious reconsideration. But so long as it does, the burden of fighting—and the burden of resisting if one's politics or conscience requires—should fall equally.

IN CONCLUSION

Achieving equality for women is, of course, far more than a legal problem. Oppression is basically a social, not a legal, fact. To end it, women must reject the roles imposed on them by society and assert themselves as equals. Yet, as evidenced by the black struggle for equality in the last two decades, law can be effective in eliminating some kinds of discriminatory behavior immediately and legal efforts can serve as a catalyst for political organization and individual change.

To date, in some areas the law has acted directly to keep women in a second-class status, forcing them to conform to stereotyped expectations. Women are too weak to lift weights and work long hours, too emotional to send to prestigious science schools, too unimportant to decide whether to bear children, too maternal to want more than raising a family, too pure to need sex but so easily corrupted as to require special supervision. The laws enforcing these stereotypes must be eliminated.

But the law can also be instrumental in ending sex discrimination. Total enforcement of the two recent statutes covering employment discrimination could significantly change the position of women in the labor market. If these laws were amended to expand their coverage and strengthen their enforcement procedures, the change would be even greater. Passage of the many bills now pending in Congress would make similar changes possible in other fields. State laws, too, are needed where the application of federal legislation is limited. And although it would seem that the Fourteenth Amendment should guarantee equal protection of the laws to women as well as other citizens, the Supreme Court has never struck down any distinction based on sex, no matter how blatant. Thus, women need an Equal Rights Amendment. However, last year's events—when the Amendment was first passed by the House, but then rejected by the Senate—show that the Amendment is far from a certainty. Congress, after all, is still virtually all-male, and the men appear just as reluctant today to give up sex discrimination as they did during the bitter fifty-year struggle for the vote.

Women must therefore organize politically to achieve legal change. They have already started to do so. The National Organization for Women (NOW) is one of many groups that have undertaken sustained lobbying efforts for legislative changes. Women's Liberation, too, has helped create a more favorable climate for change. Many individual lawyers and some groups (the American Civil Liberties Union for one) have sued on behalf of women attacking discrimination. A woman's organization modeled after the NAACP Legal Defense Fund could be even more effective in seeking change through the courts. Viewed in this way, legal action can play a major role in the movement to liberate women and end the male dominance of society.

White Debt and Black Control:
of Missionaries and Panthers

RONALD BROWN

A missionary was going through the grasslands in Africa when he suddenly came upon a panther. Frightened, the missionary began to run and the panther promptly gave chase. Looking back and seeing the panther gaining on him, the missionary attempted evasive action, but to no avail. At last, unable to continue, the missionary stopped and started to pray that his life might be spared by a miracle. After a few minutes he opened his eyes and was amazed to see the panther on two legs, forepaws clasped in a prayerful manner. "Thank you, Lord, thank you for saving me from becoming a meal for this savage beast," the missionary exclaimed. Turning his head and opening one eye, the panther responded, "Shut up, man, I'm saying grace!"

In America, as in Africa, things are not always what they seem. The issues of reparations and preferential treatment for blacks in various phases of American life are examples. At first glance, the two issues might seem separate, reparations being a payment for criminal conduct or inhuman treatment by a society—as in Germany's reparations to Jews after World War II— and preferential treatment being a conscious and affirmative, non-monetary award of privileges. However, the two issues both relate to the same historical raison d'etre for compensatory action: Slavery. And if there are not enough funds to cover pay-

---

* Ronald Brown is a 1971 graduate of Harvard Law. He was an associate with the Boston Legal Assistance Project in Roxbury, Massachusetts, and has served as an officer of the *Harvard Civil Rights–Civil Liberties Law Review*.

ment of the debt envisioned by reparationists, then the debt has to be paid in a non-monetary form, for example, preferential treatment in jobs, admissions in colleges, and representation in decision-making processes. Thus, the two remedies logically and ultimately converge.

The late Reverend Dr. Martin Luther King, Jr., in the 1963 March on Washington, spoke of a check for justice that had come back from America marked "insufficient funds." This metaphor raises a major problem with the issue of reparations: are there enough funds to cover payment of the debt? Alternately, what forms will preferential treatment take in practice in an effort to "retire" this same debt? In fact, what kind of a debt at all is owed to blacks which is so outstanding as to be the subject of ersatz Sunday sermons in New York by James Forman, and is so clearly defined as to receive a vote of approval for payment from delegates at the Bankers Conference on Urban Problems in Chicago? The answer again lies in the legacy of slavery.

THE LEGACY OF SLAVERY

In cultural, economic, and political terms black people have historically been the objects of prejudicial treatment and exclusion in America. The benefits of citizenship and the rights of human beings were long marked as reserved for whites only. The history of past practices and programs which legalized white racism—preferential treatment for whites and special burdens for blacks—is one measure of the extent to which structural preferential treatment for blacks is owed and justified.

In myriad ways, white slavers prevented the development of black culture. Though there was no such place as Negroland in 1619, white slave owners redefined the first persons from Africa, i.e., Africans, as Negroes. Rationalizing that deculturalization was necessary, among other reasons, for religious conversion; white slave owners forbade blacks to use African languages, dances, or drums—the African mass communication medium. Since much of West African tradition was transmitted orally, blacks were effectively prevented from insuring a continued sense of heritage from one generation to the next. White slavers also redefined black tribal units or national identities with two different categories of identification: house niggers and field niggers.

Regardless of whether slaves were "house" or "field," they were the property of their owner for life. As slaves, blacks had no standing in courts, could not enter into a contract, assemble in public without a white person being present, or travel without written permission. The fact of blackness was one of the reasons slavery was so successful; how could blacks melt into a white pot even if they escaped from its southern to its northern half? As early as 1705, a New York law was passed under which any slave caught at a distance greater than forty miles north of Albany, New York, as verified by the oath of two witnesses, could be executed on the presumption that he was a runaway bound for Canada.[1] But for the blackness of one's skin, these burdens were inapplicable.

In the eighteenth century, blacks, whether free or slave, were subject to additional discriminatory treatment not accorded whites. In Maryland, Pennsylvania, and North Carolina, free blacks who loitered or "misused" time or were fit to work but failed to do so, regardless of reasons, could be indentured for unlimited periods by magistrates.[2] It was against the law to teach a slave to read or write and a crime for a black either to use insulting language to a white or to strike a white in self-defense.[3] These penalties exemplify the extent to which blacks as a class or group were the object of institutionalized white racism.

In the nineteenth century blacks were subject to even greater discriminatory burdens. In 1822, South Carolina enacted a law which required the imprisonment of all Negro seamen during the stay of their vessel in port. In the North, free blacks were often required to pay school taxes, some as high as $500, even though their children were not allowed to attend the public schools supported by the tax.[4] Mississippi went so far as to forbid free blacks from selling alcohol and from operating grocery stores or places of entertainment.[5] Several states even required free blacks, as does South Africa, to register with courts and local officials, limiting the registrant to seeking employment in the town where he was registered and requiring possession of the registration papers at all times as proof of free status.[6]

Blacks were faced with more invidious discrimination in the Civil War and Reconstruction periods. Though initially rejected from volunteering in the Revolutionary and Civil Wars, they came to be considered by some union officers as "contraband of War, property owned by the enemy which the union army should at least sequester, if not use themselves."[7] The idea that blacks were property thus continued, strengthened both by the *Dred Scott*[8] case and by the Black Codes which denied blacks the rights to vote, serve on a jury, own property, or practice certain professions. Laws were passed, such as the eighteenth-century laws in Maryland, Pennsylvania, and North Carolina, under which unemployed blacks were to be arrested as vagrants. The invidious discriminations of the Black Codes in the South also had analogies in New York, Rhode Island, Delaware, and Massachusetts laws—applicable to blacks only—which denied the right to vote through property tax qualifications or requirements relating to the ability to read the United States Constitution.[9]

After the Civil War, black hopes for better treatment were deflated by President Andrew Johnson's plan for the reorganization of six southern states. Under Johnson's plan, only southerners who had been voters in 1860 and who took an oath of allegiance could participate in the reorganization. What was feared by blacks soon materialized as the reorganized governments rewrote their state constitutions to make the ability to read, understand, and interpret articles of the federal Constitution a condition precedent to exercising the franchise. Since the rewritten state constitutions allowed those who failed the test to vote anyway if their ancestors were able to vote in 1860, blacks were unable to qualify because at that time most were slaves and property, and thus not able to vote.

The controversial Freedman's Bureau—which was supposed to *help* the freed black man—again imposed unjust burdens on a class defined by color. Some of the bureau's more discriminatory regulations ordered "the arrest of Negro vagrants, forbade freemen to travel without passes, provided for registration of former slaves, prohibited their leaving the plantation of their erstwhile owners and compelled them to enter into annual labor contracts." In Georgia, agents of the bureau were instructed to make contracts for blacks who refused "reasonable" offers, such contracts to be as binding as though made by the freedmen themselves. But perhaps the most startling example of unjust discriminatory treatment on the basis of color is Circular No. 2 of the bureau's commissioner Samuel Thomas, addressed to "the colored people of Mississippi," and threatening them with arrest as vagrants if they did not sign labor contracts for the year 1866.[10]

Segregation or exclusion by race became a way of life throughout the country after the Civil War and Reconstruction periods. In 1896, the Supreme Court in *Plessy* v. *Ferguson*[11] approved the "separate but equal" doctrine, and with segregation and Jim Crow laws, blacks as a class were subjected to specific negative treatment not accorded whites. Segregation practices in accommodations, transportation, hospitals, cemeteries, schools, and churches were extended in 1913 to federal lunchrooms, offices, and shops in Washington, D.C. The practice of segregation was to hold sway virtually unchecked until 1954 when *Brown* v. *Board of Education*[12] declared its demise in education with all deliberate speed.

Even when the country was engaged in war, blacks, as seen in the Revolutionary and Civil Wars, were treated as chattels. Through World War I, the navy rejected black sailors except as menials. The marines were less "liberal" and rejected blacks altogether. The army took a middle position by placing blacks in separate non-white units. These practices largely continued through World War II, with the exception that the quantity of separate units created by the army was in proportion to the percentage of blacks in the entire population. The blood of black donors was segregated from the blood of white donors with the government's approval, even though the idea of a blood bank was largely that of a black physician, Dr. Charles Drew. The discriminatory and segregated treatment of blacks continued in the military until 1949, when desegregation became the pronounced, if not the practiced, policy.

This brief historical sketch documents numerous instances of white racism institutionalized to give blacks harsh and unjust treatment. In contract, tort, voting, freedom of movement, choice of occupation, courts, the armed services, and even the United States Constitution, blacks were treated as a class with less status, dignity, and humanity than whites, with few if any vested rights, and with no worthwhile culture or traditions. Since these policies made blacks victims en toto, they are thus justified in demanding preferential treatment restricted to them as a class defined by color, applied en toto. This demand fairly uses the extent of injury and deprivation to measure the scope of compensation.

Slavery's legacy of institutionalized white racism is partly reflected in statistics indicating that in June, 1969, for example, "40.6% of non-white Americans live in poverty as opposed to only 11.9% of white Americans; the black unemployment rate is over 7% although the white rate is only 3%, and average black family income is only 58% of white family income."[13] Further indications of this legacy are that blacks in the United States own only 7 of 17,500 authorized automobile dealerships; only 8 of 16,000 radio stations; only 20 of 13,762 commercially owned banks and non-deposit trust companies. Though constituting 12 percent of the total population and 11 percent of the civilian work force, blacks constitute only 2.8 percent of the business managers, officials, and proprietors of America. The persistence of this racism is further revealed by the fact that less than 1 percent of the nation's business receipts are obtained by black businessmen, 25 percent of whom operate either beauty or barber shops, and that less than 1.5 percent of all construction and wholesale trades and 1 percent of all manufacturing firms are controlled by black owners.[14]

This history indicates the tenacity of policies awarding preferential treatment to whites as well as disadvantages to blacks. If in fact it has only been in recent years that the idea of equality has come to diminish this tenacity of dual treatment, then it will prove difficult to convince whites that blacks must be given preferential treatment, *in the short run*, because of past unequal treatment, *in order to achieve long-run equality*. Whether or not this educative goal is realized will largely determine the future relations between white debtors and black creditors.

THE IMPACT TODAY

Accompanying the immediate goal of preferential treatment of blacks must be the realization on the part of whites that slavery and its legacy prevented blacks from developing and expressing blackness in cultural, economic, and political terms, and also prevented the transmission of black traditions. It is now imperative that individual blacks define themselves in these areas, thereby expressing the collective Black Self, which slavery and its legacy have so consistently devalued and denied. Whites have to realize that blacks must "do *their* thing" and whether this "thing" is expressed with Afro-Sheen or Black Power, it must and will express blackness affirmatively.

To a limited degree the cost of compensating these disadvantages forced on black people is capable of reduction to calculable figures. But even ignoring the political and cultural costs, calculation in the economic area itself can become difficult. For example, Group A, five blacks, serves ten times longer at apprenticeships with RWB firm than does Group B, five whites with similar background and aptitude. Weekly wages for apprenticeships are $100. Rates for journeymen, the next stage at RWB, are $200 per week. If it is shown that racial discrimination was the reason for the longer period served by black apprentices, then calculation of back wages due, in order to raise the blacks to the same pay level they would have occupied had it not been for discrimination, is not difficult. Suppose, however, that the practice continues for five, ten, one hundred, or three hundred years. The economic effects of the discrimination for individuals, families, and groups become infinitely more difficult to determine.

The RWB company example raises a corollary issue. Suppose that C is a white worker at RWB and not an executive or a foreman; he as an individual may be "innocent" of any connection with the past discriminatory practices which were imposed on Group A. To the extent that there are a limited number of promotions—foreman or manager positions and associated benefits—C, the argument goes, would be discriminated against if RWB adopted a policy of preferential treatment for blacks in rewarding these promotions and positions. The argument continues that in principle:

> preferential hiring is unjust because it classifies persons by race rather than as individuals in order to distribute favors and disadvantages. It is just as unfair an employment practice to discriminate against a qualified white worker because of his race as it is to discriminate against a Negro because of his race.[15]

Further, if blacks are preferred today, some other group—Puerto Ricans, Indians, or women—will be preferred tomorrow, and an endless number of innocent people will be victimized.

The "white victim" argument is a canard. First, it is an argument grounded in terms of the impact of a program on *one* white person and ignores that past practices have operated against blacks in a *class manner*; thus, *all* whites as a class have benefited from racism in that they are *not* discriminated against, and any reversal of this situation merely redresses the historic imbalance rather than takes anything unfairly away. Second, blacks *are* different from any other oppressed or quasi-oppressed group; no other people were "brought" here, stolen from family, homeland, and culture; none needed a constitutional amendment to free them from slavery. Yet if other groups can show similar degrees of racist subjugation—as surely the Indians can—then they too at that point should be preferred over whites to be repaid for this historic debt. Third, the "white victim" lacks the usual stigma of victimization: subjugation, inferiority, and exclusion. He is still white and in the majority, not in any fear of institutional slavery. Judge J. Skelley Wright therefore concluded in the 1968 *Cornell Law Review*: "[C]ompensatory legislation favoring Negroes would be constitutional because in American society it would be rational and would not stigmatize whites."

If anything is clear from the black experience, it is that there are no innocent white people, just some who are less guilty than others. Though whites may write books about their experiences as "temporary blacks,"[16] white individuals collectively forming white society have not acted to undergo such an ideological transformation on a permanent basis. Had this change occurred, then no one would have supported the institutionalizing of benefits and burdens on the basis of color because there would have been no difficulty in treating people as people. The "white victim" argument thus rests on an equal treatment and fairness test rejected by whites throughout the history of suppression of black people. Though strict adherence to and enforcement of a policy of equal treatment for all might have avoided the development of preferential or discriminatory treatment on the basis of color in America, imposition of such a policy simply perpetuates the exploitation of black labor and ignores over 350* years of preferential treatment for whites. This would be both inadequate and anachronistic.

Though preferential treatment will not in itself restructure existing institutions, it may be a transitional tool for bringing about reform in the institutional practices which have placed unjust and unequal burdens on blacks. Recognition of these practices may impose affirmative obligations to take special action where blacks are involved, as in the case of *Norwalk CORE* v. *Norwalk Redevelopment Agency*.[17]

In *Norwalk*, it was found that black people displaced by urban renewal faced problems in finding relocated housing which were not faced by whites of the same renewal area. The court held that "the Renewal Authority must recognize and seek to counteract special problems faced by black families . . . otherwise the Renewal Authority incorporates into its own conduct [the] discriminatory patterns of the housing market."[18] If a reasonable solution to the problem in this case is a higher relocation allowance for blacks because of racially inflated rents, then clearly the significant fact is that the discrimination blacks will face necessitates additional compensations, not that displaced whites do not receive an equal relocation allowance.

---

* Though enslaved blacks did not reach Jamestown until 1619, the slave trade had commenced in the Western Hemisphere within twenty years after Columbus's arrival and had enchained a half million blacks by 1600.

Suppose those displaced were all black. The significant fact would still be the discrimination they will face, not that they receive a greater or higher allowance than, for example, whites in Hartford. Suppose further that the situation is not urban renewal in housing, but rather admission to a college or university, application for a loan from a bank, or for employment by a company. Supporting test scores measuring white middle class values as admissions criteria, making decisions whether or not to loan on white standards of collateral and risk, and using profiles of projected employment success based on an all-white working force, all exemplify the same structural racism which produced the housing situation. Preferential treatment is just as drastically needed for reform in these areas as in housing. The form of the "preference," however, must of course be adopted to counteract the degree of discrimination which has historically developed. Just as an additional relocation allowance would be accepted as a fair and reasonable way of counteracting discrimination in our housing example, so is an additional allowance necessary in counteracting discrimination faced by blacks in other areas.

Contrary to statements made by Vice-President Agnew in February, 1970, preferential admissions of blacks into medical and law schools for example, would not result in inferior professional service to the public. Only 2 percent of the medical profession and 1 percent of the legal profession is black. To argue against the use of preferential treatment to correct this discriminatory ratio perpetuates racial inequality. Further, if a student is admitted on standards more relevant to his life experience, is graduated by his school, and certified by the state, there is no need to fear incompetence.

A significant question remains: what response have American public institutions and private organizations made to the demand for lost wages, as in the RWB example, or for remedying the debt owed by means of special treatment for blacks?

The construction field has received an increasing amount of attention on the question of compensatory treatment and merits examination as one indicator of America's response to the de-

mands of black people for economic justice. The center of much
of the publicity on compensatory treatment and the subject of
much congressional concern is the so-called Philadelphia Plan,
instituted in Philadelphia by Secretary of Labor Shultz and soon
to be implemented in New York, Seattle, Los Angeles, San Francisco, St. Louis, Detroit, Pittsburgh, Chicago, and Boston. Simply
stated, it makes the goal of a specified number of man-hours
supplied by workers from minority groups a condition to the
awarding of a government construction contract of $500,000 or
more. The parties are not unconditionally obligated to fulfill the
goal but simply required to make a good faith attempt to do so.
Granting that there has been discrimination in the past which
has resulted in a limited number of opportunities for black
people to be represented in the construction field, it is relevant
to measure the plan and its approach against the size of the
underlying problem and its causes.

The precise procedure under which the plan is to work is
fairly simple and includes four steps. Step one is the development
of a profile of minority involvement in construction trades for
each city under consideration; step two is a prediction of the
growth of construction crafts for the next four years; step three
is the percentage of the growth in step two being earmarked as
a goal for the hiring of minority workers; step four is the expectation that contractors and the city involved will show "good
faith" in attempting to meet step three. Further, despite the
opposition of U.S. Controller General Elmer B. Staats, Senator
Sam J. Ervin, and others on the Senate Judiciary Subcommittee
on Separation of Powers, who argue that the plan violates the
Civil Rights Act of 1964 by setting minority hiring quotas, U.S.
Attorney General John Mitchell, whom no one has accused of
being a reverse racist, has ruled that hiring goals are not hard
quotas and that the plan is therefore legal. The plan is now law.

Since more than a year has passed since the Philadelphia
Plan was put into effect by Executive Order, blacks remain skep-
tical as to when enforcement can be expected. In Chicago, for
example, the Department of Labor supplied $1 million for ad-
ministering the program and training four thousand minority

workers within one year. After more than six months, no training
has taken place. Thomas Nayder, Secretary-Treasurer of the Chicago and Cook County Building and Construction Trades
Council, has acknowledged that some unions accepted the plan
only to "stop the demonstrating" for the summer. Others, such
as Wagner D. Jackson, compliance officer in the Department
of Housing and Urban Development, have found it difficult
to implement the plan because of its man-hour loophole. This
allows a contractor to defer hiring minority workers until the
remaining project man-hour requirements match the total minority work hours stipulated by the plan. Efforts to induce compliance may drag on long after the project has been completed.
As Michael L. Desmond of the Pittsburgh Black Construction
Coalition sees it: "We've been meeting; we've been raising hell;
we've been calling each other a bunch of dirty names, but we
haven't accomplished a damn thing yet."

On September 22, 1969, a statement on the hiring of minorities was issued by the Executive Council of the Building and
Construction Trades Department (BCTD), AFL–CIO, and
unanimously approved by a hundred delegates attending the department's fifty-fifth annual convention. The position paper
stated that whether or not legally required to do so, the department and its affiliates "have undertaken affirmative action to
increase Negro employment in the building and construction
trades."[19] The department and the delegates went on record as
"unalterably opposed to the quota system."[20] Controller General
Staats had, according to the department, drawn attention to a
distinction, which merits quotation:

> There is a material difference between the situation in those
> cases where enforcement of the rights of minority individ-
> uals to vote or to have unsegregated educational or housing
> facilities does not deprive any member of a majority of its
> [sic] *rights* and the situation in the employment field where
> the hiring of a minority worker as one of a group whose
> number is limited by the employers' needs in preference to
> one of the majority group *precludes the employment of the
> latter.*[21] (emphasis supplied)

Finally, C. J. Haggerty, president of the department, stressed the accomplishments of the BCTD "Outreach" program which, since 1967, had recruited, counseled, and tested 27,000 minority youths and indentured 3,826 into apprenticeship programs.

The ideas expressed in the BCTD statement embody a concern for change and a commitment to competence of workers. But the concern for change echoes the popular song by the Impressions: "If you have a choice of colors, which one will you choose, my brothers?" And the rhetorical commitment to competence of workers, as it operationally turns out, seems aptly to translate: "If you're white then your work's got to be all right."

An examination of the BCTD position bears out these assertions. The controller general's statement sets up rights against a preclusion of employment. The BCTD seems to hold for a kind of "white right" of employment which must not be denied or violated by the hiring of a number of black or minority workers. When an employer is faced with the question of hiring a minority member his decision should be not to hire the worker if doing so would "preclude" employment of a "member of the majority." These propositions are sustainable only if one suffers from amnesia regarding the history of preferential treatment for whites and discriminatory burdens for blacks. The only reason whites as a group are more qualified than blacks for the limited number of positions is the favoritism they obtained in the past —a favoritism which must be undone and reversed.

The status of blacks in the construction field reveals the extent of the racism the BCTD tried to ignore. Only 7.2 percent of the 2.9 million building trades jobs and 2 percent of the 800,000 highest paying construction jobs are held by blacks.[22] Of the annual $100 billion worth of national construction handled by 500,000 construction contractors only one-half of 1 percent is handled by the less than 8,000 black construction contractors. Of 130,000 current apprenticeships, blacks are filling only 5,000 and "less than 4% of the black apprentices are in skilled-craft training programs."[23] While blacks are required to spend three to five years in apprenticeship at half pay, "most white workers are not trained in apprenticeship programs; more than 80% train on the job."[24] Though plans for more than $1½ trillion in construction work over the next ten years would seem to indicate that "build, baby, build" is the phrase of the next decade, a perpetuation of the institutionalized racism seen in the statistics above could well replace that phrase by the less appealing but more appropriate "burn, baby, burn." In fact, the Equal Employment Opportunity Commission reported in February, 1971, that not only had the number of blacks in the building and construction trades actually declined by .6 percent between 1968 and 1969, but blacks had made little progress out of the lower paying jobs—carpenter, bricklayer, asbestos worker—into the better paying job categories of electrical worker, elevator constructor, and iron and sheet metal workers.

Black frustration, however, might even be kindled by a program such as the Philadelphia Plan, which sets out to achieve a minority employment goal, for example, of 20 percent. Thus, it is established that only 20 percent of minority applicants will be employed even if there are 25, 30, or 40 percent available for employment. If the goal becomes a ceiling instead of a floor, it will insure that a much higher percentage of whites will be guaranteed employment than minority workers. This would clearly exemplify institutional racism and exacerbate black grievances.

One method of getting into unions and thereby into the "action" is through an apprenticeship program, as for example the BCTD Outreach program. Such a program combines on-the-job training with relevant education courses at a vocational high school. Yet as of 1968, only 3 percent of registered apprentices were blacks.[25] If there were an equal proportion of black people in the construction work force to their share of the population, "there would be 37,000 more black carpenters; 45,000 more laborers; 97,000 more mechanics; 82,000 more metal craftsmen, and 112,000 more construction foremen."[26] Perhaps we should multiply these figures by 350 years, at some minimum wage level, for example, $2.00 per hour, times a 40-hour week and a 50-week work year. Roughly, this computation comes to about $1½ million in lost wages. If we multiply this by the total of 373,000 workers above, we get a figure of about $500

billion. Though mathematicians and economists may question
the method of computation, it is unlikely that the meaning of
our conclusions, based on data even as meager as this, will be
as easily dismissed.

First, it seems clear that any program which tried to compensate or rectify the effect of past practices by a quasi-quota or
goal system will be inadequate because the number of victims
of past discriminatory practices will always exceed the number
compensated by the quasi-quota or goal program.

Second, measuring what was lost, by whom, at what rate of
compensation, and for how long a period is dependent on the
subjective criteria of the evaluator and what end is being sought
by him. Black creditors would surely include interest in their
calculations. White debtors would surely seek to avoid payment
of the debt by denying personal responsibility, or diminish the
debt by citing their financial support of such organizations as the
NAACP or such programs as JOBS, sponsored by the National
Alliance of businessmen. Alternatively, the white debtor might
offer to make a *de minimus* payment based on the "white victim" argument. The dilemma of valuation is further complicated
by such distinctions as made by James Forman, of the Economic
Development Conference, and by Roy Innis, National Director
of CORE, between economic reparations and political recoupment.*

Third, the type of solution offered by the Philadelphia Plan
seems to depend on a number of factors which are not stable
enough for black people to depend on for the kind of consistent,
vigilant, and aggressive action that comes when there is identity
of interest. The composition of Congress, the pressures on
Pennsylvania Avenue, the director or head of a commission or
agency, the president of a university or dean of admissions are
all subject to such change or variance in mood and motive that
it would be unrealistic for black people to commit themselves
to dependency on any of these actors; there must be some degree

* Forman would use reparations only to reform existing institutions, while
Innis would not preclude restructuring or creating new institutions with
the money to serve black people.

of control exercised by black people themselves. Reparations, a form of green power to the people, is one means by which control can be acquired.

Since James Forman presented his Black Manifesto and demands for $3 billion in reparations at Riverside Church, May 4, 1969, the drive for reparations has fared better than the quest for preferential treatment. A number of American clerical bodies have committed themselves to raising funds for black programs. Riverside Church has made a $350,000 grant for poverty work over three years. The Unitarian Universalist Church has voted $1 million to the Black Affairs Council for community organization work. Targets of $9 million, $50 million, and $70 million also have been voted respectively by the Episcopal Church, Roman Catholic Bishops, and the General Assembly of the United Presbyterian Church. The quality of these responses will be determined by the extent to which the goals are realized and the funds distributed without restrictions.

THE SEARCH FOR SELF-DETERMINATION

Black people are seeking control over or at least participation in the decision-making processes which affect their lives. For example, Senate Bill 3876, the Community Self-Determination Bill, provides for federally chartered community development corporations acquiring, managing, and creating all business in a poverty area, with the corporation being owned by ghetto residents who hold shares at $5.00 par value. The bill also envisions attracting national corporations to ghetto areas, where they would establish plants managed and operated by blacks, later selling the plants to the community development corporations. This goal can be seen as the by-product of black dissatisfaction with exploitation by whites, and as a commitment to changing the conditions of contemporary ghetto life.

The intermediate goal of such programs, according to Phase II of CORE's plan, is not only controlling "every single institution that takes tax monies and is supposed to distribute goods and services equitably" to blacks, but also to accord blacks proportional representation "in directing and forming the policy of

any other institution functioning inside their communities."[27]
Although Roy Innis and Harold Cruse both seek a black philosophy of economics and politics which describes blacks and
their life style, Innis also seeks an award to blacks of a per capita
share of all political power; yet, as a pragmatic black nationalist
he believes this is impossible under the present U.S. Constitution. Preferential treatment for blacks, proportional representation on institutional decision-making bodies, and community
control over bodies providing goods and services for tax monies
are each intermediate goals in assisting blacks to develop institutions which protect, express, and relate to their dynamic life
styles.

Black people can and will no longer wait for white people to
pass judgment on whether or not the creation of such institutions
will be acceptable. An example from Harold Cruse seems well
taken:

> Take the notion . . . that holds slavery as a human institu-
> tion to be a good thing. [If] the slaves waited for the slave-
> masters to change their views on slavery before fighting for
> freedom, they would never be free. For even after the slaves
> won their freedom there would still be ex-slavemasters . . .
> who thought slavery was a good thing.[28]

Black people simply cannot take time to negotiate for their dignity,
march for their freedom, or to verbalize over the injustice so
clearly perpetrated against Fred Hampton and other black
brothers and sisters. The development of black institutions cannot wait on the "ex-slavemaster," his descendants, contemporary
whites, their society, or their institutions; the birth of black
institutions must come out of a sound black ideology. This is
an imperative prerequisite if on one level—perhaps the most important—they are to demonstrate how much more effectively
than white institutions they protect, express, and relate to the
black *zeitgeist*, or on another more fundamental level, they are
to resolve black history's constant theme of "conflict between
integrationist and nationalist forces in politics, economics, and
culture."[29]

Reparations are a possible means by which the goal of such institutions may be realized. Seeking funds for change, James Forman demands $3 billion in reparations from white churches and Innis demands $6 billion from American banks in recoupment as economic development funds for black banks. These two sums are surely conservative since they total just 2 percent of the money due blacks from institutionalized racism in the construction field alone. While Innis sees the recoupment going to black banks for economic development as opposed to black capitalism, a good portion of Forman's reparations would be used to set up a publishing house, acquire a radio station, and start a newspaper chain—The Inner City Voice—in Detroit, Cleveland, and Chicago, as well as for "supporting community organizations, a black university, and help for Welfare Rights Organizations."[30]

As suggested earlier, preferential treatment in the form of admissions to colleges or black employment goals may become a form of reparations when or if monetary compensation is insufficient to extinguish the debt claimed by reparationists. It is relevant to consider how reparations per se might be put to use in reforming or ameliorating existing conditions for blacks in America or in assisting blacks to acquire and exercise control over practices which influence their lives, especially in black ghettos.

The black ghetto today has been described as a "social, political, and above all an economic colony,"[31] and an area whose poverty "changes all of the rules of classic economics."[32] It produces such creatures as the "povertician," who deals in or profits from the politics of poverty, and it witnesses one garnishment suit for every $2,600 in consumer sales as opposed to one in every $232,000 for the economy as a whole. It is an area in which one pays a so-called tax on being black in that credit costs more. The Washington, D.C., Urban League has even proposed issuing ghetto credit cards, so that ghetto residents who hold cards would pay a 1 percent credit charge per month on consumer purchases, as an alternative to the present practice of paying credit interest charges three to four times higher in the ghetto than in the normal credit economy.

Specifically, blacks in Boston's Roxbury district, Washington, D.C., and Harlem, who own small carry-out shops, beauty or barbershops, exemplify the contemporary black entrepreneurial ownership of property and assets which is receiving less than 1 percent of the nation's business receipts. These shops can be seen as minimum vehicles for establishing growing enterprises of value to black communities and as means for personal advancement of black individuals. One reason for this conclusion is that of two thousand small businesses in Harlem, for example, 85 percent are owned by white merchants who live outside of Harlem.[33] If it is considered beneficial that indigenous enterprises should increase, expand, diversify, incorporate, and employ more black people, and that the number of white entrepreneurs in Harlem should be reduced as a way of avoiding racial tension and riots, then it would seem that there should be some transitional institution or agency, for example, the Small Business Administration (SBA), addressing itself to these business-social problems. For all intents and purposes, SBA has not.

SBA, like many of the existing structures, such as the Federal Housing Authority (FHA), has yet to adapt to the changing needs of the people it should be designed to serve. The SBA regulations, for example, have forbidden loans to "small grocery, beauty parlors, and carry-out food shops."[34] They have also stated that a loan made by a bank is not ordinarily eligible for an SBA guarantee of payment "if the purpose of the loan is to effect a change in the ownership of the business."[35] Under such conditions it was not surprising that more violent means were employed to change ownership of businesses in Harlem, and that no "pieces" of the action materialized in the ghettos.

Like the SBA, the FHA has not been effectively responsive to the needs of black people. The National Urban League has estimated that 30 percent of black homes are purchased through "loan speculators whose interest rates start at 10%,"[36] these speculators being dealt with because black family income profiles do not meet the so-called standards of lending institutions. It has been noted that the FHA throughout most of its history "has been dedicated to building in suburban areas, virtually ignoring the inner city" and further that "because of the high element of credit risk, the FHA has been reluctant to insure mortgages for low income families." High risk FHA ghetto programs have also often failed "because of the agency's dependence on Congressional approval and appropriations."[37]

One program designed to reduce the black "capital gap" is the fledgling Minority Enterprise Small Business Investment Company (MESBIC), which seeks to aid black businesses through private investment. MESBIC sponsors interested in assisting black entrepreneurs pledge to make investments in small businesses which are at least 50 percent owned and managed by minorities. Corporations interested in becoming sponsors include General Motors, The Prudential Insurance Company, International Telephone and Telegraph, as well as General Foods. A MESBIC must start with at least $150,000 in assets—a stipulation of its SBA license—which is loaned to small minority businesses. As the money is loaned, the MESBIC can borrow twice that amount from the SBA on a long-term basis. A MESBIC starting with minimum assets ends up with a $450,000 investment in minority enterprise. Where a borrower has one MESBIC dollar, he theoretically can borrow up to $15 from a commercial bank. The program thus merely seeks to increase the leverage available to black businesses.

Though they can function to reduce the impact of institutional and individual racism, SBA, FHA, and perhaps MESBIC cannot completely remove that impact because they are by-products of such racism. No matter how conscientiously these agencies strive to be responsive to the needs of black people, the results produced by their endeavors will never completely remove that lingering doubt whether agencies controlled by blacks would not have done a better job.

If, as black people gain greater control over the institutions which control and influence black lives, their lingering doubt becomes permanent belief, then such agencies as SBA and FHA will be increasingly considered incapable of expressing or relating to black economic culture. Blacks will thus recognize the same ideological inconsistency in perpetuating the domination or influence of SBA and FHA which led other Third World groups to reject neocolonialism in the form of colonial administrators;

this conflict also led the Congress of Racial Equality to reject white leadership in its organization. Ideological consistency will further demand awareness that blacks are not members of a minority, as that term is traditionally used, because their experiences with white America and institutional racism parallel those of two billion non-whites around the world. Like these groups, blacks are a minority only in terms of power, not in terms of color or numbers. Blacks, like Third World nations, will become real members of the majority when they have the power to define and create institutions which relate to their own cultural styles. The reform of agencies such as SBA and FHA can be but a transitional step in entirely restructuring the status of black politics, culture, and economics to exercise and achieve Black Power.

As Harold Cruse has noted in his book, *The Crisis of the Negro Intellectual:*

> . . . black ghettos today, especially Harlem, subsist on two kinds of economics: laissez faire–free enterprise capitalism, and welfare state–anti-poverty economics. Are either of these schools of economic method compatible with racial equality? They are not.[38]

Since these two schools of thought are not compatible with racial equality, Cruse reasoned further that:

> . . . logic demands that a movement for social change must be motivated by some other school of economic thought or else it is fooling itself and wasting the public's time. This is especially true in view of the fact that both free enterprise capitalism and welfare state economics are *administered and controlled from the top down.*[39] (emphasis supplied)

Cruse's thought raises the question of how these economic schools have operationally expressed facts and figures relevant to black people.

The expression of past economic schools can be seen in South Bronx, Harlem, and Bedford-Stuyvesant in New York; in Newark,

New Jersey; and in Washington, D.C., where one is startled by the ratio of blacks to the number of businesses blacks own which employ ten or more black people. In the New York areas, the ratio expresses itself as 200,000 blacks owning 10 percent of such businesses. These statistics and Cruse's observations underscore the unacceptability of current patterns of social programing both in terms of the ephemeral "piece" of the action President Nixon invoked during the 1968 election campaign, and in terms of the viability of existing bodies, such as the SBA, to respond to the needs of black people.

It is clear that reparations could be used to provide a number of specific services to black people. These are a total program, not independent or alternative suggestions, and constitute evolutionary reforms rather than revolutionary changes because they do not alter the structures of the involved institutions. Any money received by reparationists should be expended on a broad range of problems present in black communities, and not on a single, limited problem. Not to do so is to waste resources and exacerbate interrelated social cancers.

First, reparations could in part be used to finance, support, and create new black businesses as well as the type of community control envisioned in the Community Development Corporation Bill. Second, reparations could in part be used to finance concerted legal efforts to end the tax on being black by driving credit shark merchants out of business through prosecutions under the Truth in Lending Act or by creating community controlled cooperatives dealing in the same goods as the dishonest merchant. Funds could in part be used to fulfill the functions where SBA has failed, e.g., in guaranteeing loans where the purpose of the loan is to effect a change in the ownership of the business. Fourth, reparations could be used in part to support community cultural development, such as supporting groups like the Alvin Ailey Dance Troupe, the Olatunji Center in New York, or Elma Lewis's National Center of Afro-American Artists in Roxbury. Fifth, reparations could well be used as part of a fund for electing blacks to decision-making bodies, and for establishing a black "think-tank" considering solutions to problems submitted from all spectra of black experience. Such a "tank" could also serve as an information distribution center making sure that all spectra of the black community were aware of the platforms and programs of SCLC, NAACP, CORE, US, Black Panthers, Urban League, Black Muslims, and OAAU, both as they historically developed and as they are contemporarily articulated. Such a "tank" would be significant also when either by natural death, or political assassination, various leaders were no longer able to articulate the philosophies upon which black institutions will rest and develop. Lastly, based on projections that blacks will be the majority population in fourteen major cities when the 1970 census is completed,[40] reparations could wisely be used to support such organizations as the National Afro-American Builders Inc., a consortium of black contractors through which resources of small businessmen are pooled, enabling the builders to bid on and perform major contracts. Reparations could thus be used to support blacks employing and training other blacks in meeting construction needs in largely black cities and in correcting inadequacies in FHA programs.

THE LEGAL PROBLEMS

Conceding the insufficiency of using cash alone to pay the debt created by slavery's legacy of white racism, two questions remain regarding preferential treatment. Since accomplishing an allocation of slots for blacks in universities, labor, or business may necessitate using classifications by race, is the use of such classifications legal? If it is, what tests are there by which the use of such classifications might be evaluated?

Though the courts have not passed on the question of racial preferences per se as yet, a number of fundamental guidelines have been established. It is patent, for example, that the equal protection clause of the Fourteenth Amendment does not mean that *all* instances of different treatment by race is or would be unconstitutional. In *McLaughlin* v. *Florida*,[41] a case involving a Florida statute forbidding interracial premarital cohabitation, the court held that racial classifications bear a far heavier burden of justification and should be upheld only if necessary to the accomplishment of a permissible state policy; the court therefore struck down the law. In *Brooks* v. *Beto*[42] the court also said that racial classifications must be "necessary" and not merely rational.

Perhaps the most succinct statement of possible standards for judicial review of classifications by race are the three established by Victor Navasky in the *Howard Law Journal*. Navasky sets forth these three standards as:

1. Public racial classifications like other state classifications are unconstitutional only if they are unreasonable. But prejudice inspired classifications are *per se* unconstitutional, even if reasonable.
2. Public racial classifications as a rule are presumed to be unconstitutional even if they are reasonable. But benevolent racial classifications are unconstitutional only if they are unreasonable.
3. Public racial classifications are presumed to be unconstitutional; only overriding necessity—a war for instance—can justify such classifications as reasonable.[43]

Classifications are used for many reasons in society and it seems clear that the use of classifications by race should not be any more arbitrary than the use of non-racial classifications. All are familiar with the extra $625 exemption allowed to blind persons on federal income tax returns and with benefits available to veterans which are not available to non-servicemen; and few would argue that these classifications and the treatment attached to them are "wrong" because of the large number of persons excluded—sighted people, non-veterans—from receiving these benefits. If it is admitted that some classifications serve a useful purpose, then why not racial classifications attaching beneficial treatment on the basis of race, when it is shown that the persons so classified, received "disadvantages" like the blind, "wounds" like the veterans, or some other special burden.

A classification by race is one of those suspect classifications which, as indicated, in constitutional law bears a heavier burden of justification. The examples above, blindness and service in the

Armed Forces, have dealt with non-racial classification. But an example of a positive use of racial classifications is Title VII of the 1964 Civil Rights Act directing the Census Bureau to compile registration and voting statistics based on race, color, and national origin wherever recommended by the Civil Rights Commission. Section 703 (j) of Title VII does, however, provide that courts may not use Title VII to overcome racial imbalance in employment through compelled preferential treatment. It should be noted, however, that preferential treatment is not prohibited under other laws and regulations or where the goal is other than correcting racial imbalance.[44] The following argument by the *Harvard Law Review* cogently summarizes the justification for benign racial classifications.

> Where a state voluntarily chooses to adopt a program of benign racial quotas or measures that explicitly subject individuals to different treatment solely on the basis of race, courts have to choose a standard to test constitutionality. Traditional standards of review would require the state demonstrate an overriding justification for the use of racial distinctions and show that the purpose of the action could not be accomplished by a non-racially focused alternative.[45]

Although the historical legacy of slavery, institutionalized burdens for blacks, and the legitimacy of black demands seem to provide such an overriding justification, a residue of doubt remains. The question remains whether special treatment of blacks, such as under the Philadelphia Plan or the granting of economic concessions analogous to those declared under the Indian Claims Commission Statute, would mean an infringement on the rights of white people. Part of the answer was given above in discussing the "white victim" argument in the context of preferential employment hiring. Also relevant to this point is Professor Graham Hughes's example on the issue of infringed admission "rights." What if white student A is denied admission to Civil University, so that a place can be found for black student B, whose qualifications for admission to Civil University have been found to be lower as measured on standard white middle-class criteria?

> The white student will almost certainly feel aggrieved and might reasonably raise a complaint of injustice. We must acknowledge that the large institutional changes which will be necessary in order to achieve a rectification of major social injustices can only be accomplished at the cost of some individual injustice. The cost must of course be minimized and nobody should be asked to bear too heavy a burden of sacrifice.[46]

It is readily seen that if the situation for student A is either Civil University or no college education at all as opposed to Rights University, a less desirable second choice college, then the latter choice is more equitable when balancing degrees of hardship and may be one which in the short run "we may have to demand if there is to be any acceleration of the social advance of under-privileged groups."[47] By analogy, the balance weighs heavily for compensating blacks for 350 years of preferential treatment for whites rather than against such compensation. Whites will merely be deprived of their traditional benefit, i.e., not being burdened by discriminatory treatment faced by blacks. It is this unjust benefit that whites must no longer be allowed.

A public confession of past injustice followed by recognition of the need for compensation is not without precedent in America. In 1946, a federal statute created an Indian Claims Commission,[48] which was to have jurisdiction for the hearing and resolution of claims "arising from the seizure of property and breaches by the United States of its treaties with the Indian nations and tribes."[49] As Professor Hughes has indicated, "it was held that the government of the United States was liable to pay compensation for, among other places, the whole of Kansas."[50]

If the United States can be held liable for at least one state where it victimized distinct tribes and nations, then perhaps the claims of so-called radical blacks either for reparations or six southern states because of United States racism toward black people may be deserving of reevaluation. Further, as Hughes inquired, "if a public confession can be made in statutory form of the just claims of American Indians for compensation (a phenomenon uncomfortably close in time and nature to postwar Germany's reparations to Jews), why should we not initiate similar schemes for reparations to black Americans?"[51]

We have seen that the legacy of treatment by color, originating with institutionalized racism in slavery, has largely burdened blacks because of their color. Culture, economics, poverty, credit, and unemployment assumed distinct meanings when given a black prefix. Existing institutions such as the SBA and FHA have failed to adequately respond to the size of the problems encountered by black people. Independent institutions such as the BCTD have largely ignored the needs and demands of black people for "all" or "pieces" of the action. Black demands for non-dependency outcomes have been seen in labor, economics, culture, politics, and business. The call for reparations or preferential treatment, though presenting difficult constitutional and practical questions as to who or what group is to be paid and at what cost to whom, raises issues, like the call for forty acres and a mule and "freedom now," which challenge the commitment of whites to true equality. It remains to be seen whether or not whites will respond to the claims of black people for justice as the missionary responded to the panther's pose.

The Politics of Poverty Law

FRED J. HIESTAND*

I. INTRODUCTION: POVERTY
AS A PRIVATE PROBLEM

Juan Alviso[1] shifted anxiously in the high-backed wooden chair, his hands kneading the brim of his weathered straw hat. This was not the first time he had come to the law office (a recently refurbished meat market). Last spring he came to this same small, green stucco building hoping, but only faintly expecting, that an *abogado* (attorney) could convince his landlord to let the Alviso family—Juan, his wife Alicia, and their six children—stay in the two-bedroom, wooden frame house until they could find another place to live. Juan was two weeks behind in paying the landlord his $95-a-month rent. He was unable to pay. The three-week-old mailing from the welfare department contained not the expected monthly check of $349—the Alviso family's sole source of income—but a terse notice that their checks were being terminated at once because "full-time work was available." But work was not available then, at least not farm work, which was Juan Alviso's special, and only marketable, skill. It was the end of the dead season, *el tiempo muerto*, and unemployment in the rich agricultural county of Madera, California, hovered near 12 percent for the general work force, and over 45 percent for farm workers.

* Fred Hiestand graduated in 1968 from Berkeley's Law School and is now working in San Francisco for California Rural Legal Assistance (CRLA). This article is based on his opinions formed while working for CRLA in Madera, California.

Juan was certain the welfare department had made a mistake; he was less certain, however, that the mistake would be corrected and his family would receive their money. Still, he did not blame his landlord for serving them with eviction papers. After all, his landlord was simply acting as a good businessman with a product many were able and willing to buy if Juan could not (Madera has less than a 1 percent vacancy rate in housing rentals). Nonetheless, Juan was worried that his family might be arrested or forcibly thrown out of their house. The eviction notice that the sheriff handed Juan's wife said they had to pay their rent or get out within three days. He had only two days left when he went to *asistencia legal rural*. He didn't really believe a lawyer could help him—the law seemed always to be used against the Alvisos —but he didn't know where else to turn.

To his surprise, the young *anglo* lawyer he had visited that spring morning three months ago proved something of a gold mine for the Alvisos. Juan never fully understood all the intricacies of the lawsuit he soon filed against his landlord—who does except lawyers and judges?—but he was pleased with the result: the landlord agreed to let the Alvisos stay in the house rent free for six weeks. Juan, in turn, promised to leave at that time and to drop his lawsuit against the landlord for failing to repair the house as he had so often promised the Alvisos. In addition, his lawyer had filed some papers with the welfare department ("request for a fair hearing" is what Juan remembered his lawyer calling them) to get his family their money for at least the month they were so suddenly cut off.

All these events seemed far in the past to Juan, yesterday. It had been over a month since his family had moved out of their rent-free house and dropped their lawsuit against the landlord. And the welfare money, which they finally got a month late, was spent at once and the Alvisos were again taken off welfare. For this was late August, the height of the raisin and grape harvest, when work generally was available. Indeed, just yesterday Juan had been stacking trays of grapes in one grower's field, confident that though there was no more work in this field he could join his friends tomorrow on a new job at a large Madera olive-packing company.

That was yesterday. Today he found himself sitting across from a young *chicano* lawyer. Juan explained in rapid Spanish the new problem that had once again brought him to this same small office. Juan had mixed feelings about this new lawyer. He had been disappointed when the secretary in the front of the office told him his lawyer had left Madera, confirming in his own mind the rumor that young poverty lawyers did not stay in Madera for more than a year or two. Yet he was pleased to have a *chicano* lawyer now, one who could speak and understand Spanish.

"I need work, farm labor. Yesterday I was told that the Oberti Olive Company needed a lot of pickers. So this morning I go to Oberti, but they tell me they don't need any workers. Twenty others were turned away with me this morning. A friend working at Oberti tells me they're not hiring now because they have given jobs to over a hundred *alambristas* (wetbacks). I hear other growers have hired *alambristas* too."

Juan Alviso paused now, leaned back in the chair and hit his leg once with his clenched fist to punctuate the frustration and anger he was about to express. "If Cesar Chavez was in Madera County we'd picket Oberti, shut them down. Without the Union though, everyone's too afraid. I have all the *mala suerte* (bad luck). I know you probably can't get me a job with any grower, but maybe you can give me and others a chance by making sure the *alambristas* don't get all the jobs."

II. POVERTY AS A PUBLIC ISSUE

Juan Alviso had an ambivalent, and perhaps contradictory, view of what caused his unemployment on that hot August morning. At first he sensed it was due to personal and group powerlessness: "If Cesar was in Madera . . . we'd shut them (Oberti) down." A moment later, he blamed his plight on unavoidable misfortune: *"Estoy de mala suerte."* His ambivalence was shared by many other clients of California Rural Legal Assistance (CRLA), a federally funded law firm representing the rural poor of California since 1966. But for the more than forty CRLA attorneys, the poverty of their clients was experienced as less due to personal misfortune than institutional design.

To understand this important distinction between private problems and social issues, it is useful to begin with an observation of C. Wright Mills:

> When, in a city of 100,000, only *one* man is unemployed, that is his personal trouble, and for its relief we properly look to the character of this man, his skills, and his immediate opportunities. But when in a nation of 50 million employees, 15 million are unemployed, that is an issue, and we may not hope to find its solution within the range of opportunities open to any one individual. The very structure of opportunities has collapsed.[2]

For California's more than 400,000 *campesinos*—46 percent of whom are, like Juan Alviso, Mexican-American[3]—"collapsed opportunities" have long been, and still are, institutionalized. Their employers are not the yeomen of yesteryear, friendly family farmers, but big businessmen, often absentee landlords who operate their factories in the field by phone from air conditioned corporate offices in San Francisco and Los Angeles. In 1969, "agribusiness" (growers proudly banter about the phrase to epitomize the fusion between agriculture and big business) in California produced a gross income of close to $4 billion.[4] The precise financial contribution of farm laborers to this gargantuan figure is difficult to ascertain, but it undoubtedly looms large. Clearly the bulk of more than 727 million man hours invested in California agriculture annually are from *campesinos*.[5] Yet the earnings of farm laborers pale in comparison to the profits of corporate growers. Not until 1968 was the hourly wage for farm work increased to $1.65, and then it took a lawsuit with CRLA representation to get this wage level enforced.[6] The seasonal nature of farm work precludes employment for more than four months of the year, so the average annual earnings of farmworker families like the Alvisos is about $4,000. Farmworkers are excluded from unemployment insurance.[7] If, however, a farmworker is willing and qualifies, his family might get public assistance during the dead season. Given the glacial pace of the welfare bureaucracy in processing claims and its jungle of eligibility restrictions, it should not be too surprising that only 7 percent of Mexican-American farmworkers in California received any public assistance in 1965.[8]

Low wages, of course, are central to California's *latifundio* system.

> High wages, in many California crops, have a tendency to reduce the supply of labor, since the work is so thoroughly undesirable that workers will pick for a short time and then quit. It is important, therefore, that wages be kept at the lowest possible level, not merely to minimize labor costs but to keep workers on the job.[9]

Agribusiness has successfully kept farmworker wages at rock bottom through a variety of devices, not the least of which is the maintenance of a surplus labor pool. Almost every schoolboy knows that when the supply of a commodity exceeds its demand, the price for that commodity falls accordingly. So it is with the commodity of farm labor. Quite logically, then, one of the first lawsuits of national prominence filed by CRLA was to reduce the chronic oversupply of agricultural labor by shutting off the importation of *braceros*.

Braceros, or Mexican nationals imported by the United States under an agreement between the two countries, were first used on a large scale by agribusiness as World War II approached and domestic labor became more scarce. They soon became a mainstay of agribusiness. In 1963, in response to pressure by organized labor and others, Congress enacted and President Kennedy signed a bill legally killing the program. The *bracero* program, however, was only dead in theory; in practice the legislation provided a convenient loophole for growers—the United States Secretary of Labor could certify *braceros* for importation if convinced there was a shortage of domestic labor. Convincing the Department of Labor that a farm worker shortage existed proved quite easy for growers. They simply filed applications

The Politics of Poverty Law

The Politics of Poverty Law   165
with the department alleging a shortage and inflating their real demands for farm work so the scarce labor supply would appear real. Though obligated to verify the need for *braceros* before certifying them for importation, the Department of Labor always managed to be preoccupied with matters other than verification. In 1967, CRLA lawyers reminded Secretary Willard Wirtz of his duty by asking a federal district court to enjoin him from certifying for importation more than 8,000 *braceros* to work in California fields.[10] A prompt settlement was reached between the Department of Labor and CRLA's attorneys after the court issued a temporary restraining order. The settlement, called a "new low in groveling submission to blackmail" by one pro-grower California congressman, established procedures for disclosure of pending applications for foreign labor and for hearings before any future certifications. As a result, in 1968, for the first time in a quarter of a century, the Secretary of Labor announced that no *braceros* would be imported into the United States.

Shutting off the supply of *braceros* in 1968 only temporarily diminished California's surplus farm labor pool. Indeed, agribusiness had another source of extra farm labor on hand to replace the *bracero*—the commuter alien. Commonly called "green carders" because of the green registration cards they are required by law to carry, the commuter alien is a citizen of another country (Mexico, in the case of California farmworkers) who resides in that country but works in the United States. Mexican nationals have not, since 1965, been legally permitted to commute to the United States for farm work unless, as with *braceros*, the Secretary of Labor first certifies that appropriate wage levels and working conditions have failed to attract sufficient domestic workers to meet employer demands. At least that was what many thought when the Immigration and Nationality Act was amended in 1965. But the Immigration Service and the Attorney General of the United States soon found a statutory loophole that would permit commuters to bypass the certification procedures contained in the 1965 amendments. Commuter aliens were simply shoved into another legal category, that of immigrants, "lawfully admitted for permanent residence, who (are) returning from a temporary visit abroad." Such clever classification permits the Attorney General to admit commuter aliens—numbering 50 thousand persons in 1970—under documentation requirements much more informal and lax than those intended for commuters.

In 1968 farmworker clients suffering depressed wages and unemployment because of the commuters' presence sought legal help from CRLA. The result was *Gooch* v. *Clark*, an unfortunate two-to-one opinion from the federal court of appeals allowing commuters to displace domestic farm workers even though the Secretary of Labor refused to certify that a domestic labor shortage exists.[11] The battle over commuter alien traffic still rages, however; the United Farm Worker's Organizing Committee (UFWOC), plagued by strike-breaking alien commuters, is pressing litigation similar to CRLA's in a Washington, D.C., federal court.[12] If UFWOC wins, the conflict between the federal courts will increase chances that the United States Supreme Court will take jurisdiction of *Gooch* and finally resolve the commuter conflict.

The third source of surplus farm labor, the *alambrista* or wetback, is what brought Juan Alviso to CRLA's Madera office seeking legal help. The traffic in wetbacks, so-called because many originally gained illegal entry to this country by swimming across the Rio Grande, increased tremendously after the importation of *braceros* was stopped. The United States Border Patrol, for example, apprehended 37,343 deportable aliens—most of whom were Mexican farmworkers—in California in 1967; 48,827 in 1968; and 69,933 in 1969.[13] It is estimated by federal labor sources that for every apprehended *alambrista*, two go undetected. Thus, in 1969, over 180,000 illegal entrants were displacing California laborers, chiefly in agriculture. The hiring of these illegal entrants cost northern California farmworkers approximately $2.7 million in lost wages in 1969 and costs the public increased annual welfare expenditures of not less than $1.4 million for the support of domestic farmworkers and their families.

To halt this practice, CRLA has represented clients like Juan Alviso in numerous suits throughout California against growers hiring *alambristas* but refusing to employ qualified domestic farmworkers. Unlike the *bracero* and green card commuter litigation, the defendants in the wetback cases were all private growers, not government agencies. A novel adaptation of traditional theories (the statutory offense of an unlawful business practice and court enunciated principles of equity) provided the legal basis for the wetback suits. But in 1970 a California court of appeals denied domestic farmworkers injunctive relief against the defendant growers because:

> The federal government could, if it would, reduce the flow of illegal entrants to a trickle or virtually dry it up . . . Plaintiffs seek the aid of equity because the national government has breached the commitment implied by national immigration policy. It is more orderly, more effectual, less burdensome to the affected interests, that the national government redeem its commitment.[14]

The court admitted that "(w)eighed alone on any scale of human values, the farmworker's need is vastly more acute than the predicament of injunction saddled employers," but felt compelled to refer the aggrieved farmworkers to Congress. Yet it is precisely because Congress has been so indifferent to the plight of farmworkers that the judiciary was asked to intervene in the first place. Farmworkers, while not eschewing congressional remedies, are likely to continue to look to the courts for relief against growers who hire wetbacks; but the relief sought now that the injunction weapon has been judicially confiscated will be in the form of money damages, the language agribusiness understands best.

One common theme inherent in the *bracero*, commuter alien, and *alambrista* litigation is the breakdown of law and order. True, the lawbreakers in these three cases don't carry switchblades and lurk near dimly lit street corners; they sit at the highest levels of government (the Secretary of Labor and Attorney General) and business, dress nicely and speak favorably of social justice and free enterprise. Yet their willingness to flaunt the law when it suits them, and in so doing wreak misery on tens of thousands of California *campesinos*, is probably only exceeded by their local counterparts in government and business. Indeed, if rural areas like Madera, California, are viewed as the satellites or colonies of metropolitan financial centers like Los Angeles, San Francisco, and Washington, D.C., then Alexis de Tocqueville provides a further clue to understanding why and how government and business use and abuse the law in their relations to agricultural laborers: "The physiognomy of a government may best be judged in its colonies, for there its features are magnified and rendered more conspicuous."[15] Madera, California, where factories in the field are managed by corporate and financial offices in distant urban centers, is a logical place to test the veracity of de Tocqueville's observation.

III. OPPRESSION AT THE GRASS ROOTS LEVEL

Madera County, it should be noted at the outset, makes no pretense of its bias in favor of large growers and against the poor. It is, on the one hand, the thirty-seventh wealthiest agricultural county in the nation; and, on the other hand, it has the highest concentration of poor families (29.8%), and one of the highest infant mortality rates in the state of California (10.0 per 1,000). Motorists who pass through Madera—it lies at the exact geographical center of California, about mid-way between San Francisco and Los Angeles on Route 99—are often struck by the numerous pickup trucks with rifles mounted on rear view window racks. Usually these pickup trucks have two stickers prominently juxtaposed on their rear bumpers. One reads, "Eat California grapes, the forbidden fruit"; the other says, "Kick out CRLA—waste of taxpayers' money." The visitor to the Madera County Government Center, which houses the only superior court in the county, is greeted in the foyer by a prominent display of canned olives from the fields of the very grower and packer that Juan Alviso is suing for hiring wetbacks. If one engages a local resident of Madera in conversation, he is likely to encounter the same attitudes expressed by the 185 Madera County growers surveyed in 1968 who receive over $3 million in federal farm subsidies.[16] More than half of these growers (57%) were opposed to federal welfare for the poor. Nine out of ten (94%) were opposed to providing a minimum of $4,000 to a family of five in order to avoid depressing wages in a period of high unemployment. Less than one in ten (8%), of course, admittedly recognized the parallels between the federal assistance they were receiving not to plant crops and the federal assistance they were opposed to poor persons receiving. It is from this milieu that CRLA cases arise.

In September of 1967, at the height of the raisin grape harvest, numerous growers appeared before the Madera School Board to ask that the schools be shut down for four days so that pupils would be available to help pick the grapes. Without hesitation, the school board granted the growers' request by a vote of 4–2. Many of the fields in which the public school pupils would be picking grapes were in violation of state health and sanitation laws. Some fields lacked toilets, making it necessary for farm-workers to defecate and urinate on and near the grapes. Many fields failed to provide hand-washing and drinking facilities for the farm laborers, as required by law. These and other violations of California laws by growers both threatened the health and dignity of farm laborers and revealed an utter disregard for the sensibilities of the nation's grape consumers. The Madera public schools, in closing for four days so that pupils could pick grapes, had a duty to insure that any pupil issued a school work permit would be working in safe and sanitary fields. Not surprisingly, the schools made no inquiry of field conditions before issuing work permits. Consequently, CRLA brought suit against the Madera Unified School Board to enjoin closing the schools in callous disregard for the health and welfare of Madera's children.[17]

At the same time the Madera Welfare Department did all in its power to cooperate with the growers and schools in providing an available and cheap labor supply for the grape harvest. All families receiving assistance with children over the age of ten were ordered to put their children to work in the grape fields or have their assistance terminated. CRLA responded by suing the Welfare Department on the grounds that (1) children under 16 may not be forced to work to obtain public assistance, (2) no welfare recipient could be required to work in fields that were in violation of state health and sanitation laws, and (3) the Welfare Department's action constituted involuntary servitude, a violation of the Thirteenth Amendment to the U.S. Constitution.[18]

The Madera Welfare Department, with the necessary approval of the Board of Supervisors, obtained a private attorney to represent them in this case. During the course of the lawsuit, this private attorney took the deposition of an elderly welfare mother and her young daughter. It is normal, of course, for attorneys in major lawsuits to engage in extensive discovery proceedings before trial and CRLA had no reason to suspect that the deposition of these two clients would be used for anything except the defendant's preparation for trial. Shortly thereafter, however, a criminal fraud charge was filed against this same woman. When CRLA attorneys examined the deposition that the private attorney had taken, it became apparent for the first time that his questions had primarily been directed at setting the woman up for a welfare fraud charge. This was later confirmed when the deputy district attorney, during the criminal prosecution of the welfare mother, relied heavily upon the civil deposition that had been taken by the Welfare Department's private counsel. Since the Madera Welfare Department was normally quite lax in seeking out and prosecuting cases of fraud, the message gotten across by this particular prosecution was clear to Madera's poor. As one CRLA client aptly observed, "If you question the Welfare Department, they will mess you up for good." The woman was convicted in the local Justice Court for Madera County, but the case is presently on appeal.

In the summer of 1969, two years after Madera's schools and Welfare Department had acted to aid growers, the Welfare Department moved again to provide additional farm labor during the harvest season. This time, the Welfare Department informed all families with unemployed fathers who were receiving assistance that work was available in Madera and that they were therefore being terminated from aid. The law did require that if a father in such a family refused a bona fide offer of employment without good cause, his aid could be terminated. However, the Madera Welfare Department was unconcerned whether any father had actually been offered a job by the Department of Employment or anyone else. Instead, they were basing their determination that work was available upon informal communications from an official of the State Department of Employment that farm labor jobs were available. In reality, many of the purported jobs were nonexistent. As already noted, growers depend upon a surplus of farm labor to depress wages and discourage unionization. Therefore, it is not uncommon for exaggerated calls for workers to be made to the State Department of Employment by agribusinessmen. When jobs are actually filled by farmworkers, growers rarely notify the Department of Employment, so job openings remain on the records.

Several clients, all Mexican-Americans, came to the Madera office of CRLA bearing their notices of termination of welfare on the alleged grounds that "full-time work was available." CRLA attorneys prepared affidavits for three of the affected families, including that of Juan Alviso, stating that none of the families had specifically been offered any work and denying that full time work was available. These affidavits were filed along with administrative appeals demanding immediate restoration of aid for the families pending a fair hearing. An Alameda County Superior Court had formerly issued a written mandate requiring the State Department of Social Welfare to restore aid to terminated applicants pending a hearing, if an applicant filed an affidavit factually denying the department's reason for termination.[19] Upon receipt of the administrative appeal and affidavits, both the Madera Welfare Department and the California State Department of Social Welfare refused to grant aid to the clients. Finally, the directing attorney of Madera CRLA was forced to file an action in the Alameda Superior Court where the original writ to the State Department of Social Welfare had been issued. Argument was heard before the court, 165 miles from Madera, and an order was issued to the State Department of Welfare that all three families be immediately restored to aid.

The Madera Welfare Department complied with the court order in part; it restored two families to aid, one of which was the Alvisos. The third family, however, that of Mr. Jose Fuentes, received a letter instructing them to come to the Welfare Department with records and books on their income for the past year so that the department could determine the proper amount of aid to be restored. Mr. Fuentes was unable to appear on the scheduled date, so his wife went to the Welfare Department with what records she could find. Upon arriving at the Madera Welfare Department, Mrs. Fuentes was surprised to be met by a prominent private attorney. Since she did not have all the income records, and was unaccompanied by her husband, the attorney asked her to come back the following week with her husband and the records.

About the same time, CRLA attorneys were informed from a reliable source that the Department of Welfare was planning to bring another one of its infrequent welfare fraud charges. When Mrs. Fuentes then informed CRLA attorneys that she was met by a lawyer for the Welfare Department at her scheduled appointment, the suspicion was that her family might be the intended victims. The suspicion was all but confirmed when investigation revealed that the attorney retained by the Welfare Department to interview the Fuentes was the same attorney who had taken the 1967 deposition of a CRLA welfare mother client for the purpose of building a criminal fraud case against her.

At the next scheduled meeting at the Welfare Department with Mr. and Mrs. Fuentes, all three attorneys from the Madera CRLA office accompanied these clients. They were again met by the private attorney representing the Madera Welfare Department. The attorney was asked the exact purpose of the meeting and he informed everyone that it was solely to obtain needed information to determine the exact amount of aid to be restored. The CRLA attorneys then informed him that they had reason to believe that the real purpose of the meeting was to gather evidence to be used against their client for criminal prosecution. The Welfare Department's counsel was asked whether this was true. He admitted that there was some question as to whether the Fuentes had been reporting all of their income. He then reminded the CRLA attorneys and the Fuentes that anything said during the interview could be used against them. When this attorney was asked by CRLA if he originally had any intention of informing them of this additional purpose for the interview, he refused to answer and advised all four of the Welfare Department officials in the interview room to also refuse to answer the question.

CRLA attorneys then informed the Welfare Department through their counsel that the client had nothing to conceal, and was willing to furnish them with the information they had requested. However, given the suspicion of the criminal fraud motivation on the part of the Welfare Department, the attorneys also informed the Welfare Department that they would advise the clients not to answer any questions that might be incriminating. The Welfare Department attorney agreed to this procedure and began asking questions of the welfare recipients. After the questioning had gone on for a few minutes, the directing attorney of CRLA, who had become quite distrustful of government agencies in his previous five years of New York criminal practice, got up and walked across the room as if to look out the window. The room in which this interview took place was divided by a ceiling to floor sliding partition which was drawn across the large room so as to create a smaller interview room for the clients. A small space of about one foot existed between the end of the partition and the window to which the CRLA attorney had walked. While the questions were proceeding, the attorney at the window looked behind the partition and found the county's welfare fraud investigator hiding and listening in on the conference. This fraud investigator was challenged to come out from behind the partition and identify himself. The CRLA attorneys demanded of the private attorney retained by the Welfare Department that he disassociate himself from the deplorable conduct of the fraud investigator and the Welfare Department in this interview. Instead the attorney meekly murmured that he had asked the fraud investigator to hide behind the screen as a possible bodyguard should any trouble develop.

As a result of this entire episode, plus the knowledge CRLA attorneys had of this particular attorney and of the Welfare Department's action in the previous case brought against that department, the Fuentes filed an action against the Welfare Department in Federal District Court.[20] That suit, which is still pending, contends that the Madera County Welfare Department intended to use the selective enforcement of the criminal law to deter welfare recipients like the Fuentes from asserting their rights. It also contends that the Welfare Department violated the Fifth and Fourteenth Amendments of the U.S. Constitution by seeking to elicit information for a criminal fraud prosecution against the Fuentes on the false pretense that they were merely getting the information to restore the Fuentes' assistance. Since the federal action was filed, an administrative fair hearing was held for one of the other two families whose aid had been restored pending a hearing by order of the court. A decision by the State Department of Social Welfare in that hearing found that termination of the client's aid by the county under the so-called "available work policy" was illegal.

The crowning irony of this entire story was delivered by the Madera County Bar Association. In October, 1969, one month after the Fuentes brought suit against the Madera Welfare Department, the Bar Association elected a new president. The man chosen to lead the local bar was the attorney who had represented the Welfare Department in the 1967 suit brought by CRLA and in the 1969 incident with the Fuentes.

IV. THE GOVERNMENT AGAINST ITSELF

To reduce the oversupply of California farm labor and improve employment opportunities for clients like Juan Alviso and Jose Fuentes, CRLA has had to sue government agencies. Some view litigation against government agencies by a federally funded program like CRLA as, to use California Senator George Murphy's words, a "ludicrous spectacle" where the taxpayer loses "coming and going."[21] Yet the spectacle is no different in principle from Justice Department lawyers filing suit against the Federal Communications Commission's approval of the ITT-ABC merger. And the taxpaying public, at least in the case of CRLA, receives far more in savings and benefits than the $1½ million spent on the legal services program. In the *bracero* case alone, for instance, it is estimated that an additional $3 million in annual income was created by opening jobs to domestic workers that would have been taken by *braceros*, at least until the commuter aliens and *alambristas* took the jobs. And in *Morris* v. *Williams*[22] indigent and ill Californians received an additional $210 million in Medi-Cal benefits that would have been slashed by Governor Ronald Reagan's budget cuts but for CRLA's successful suit.

What is surprising—and alarming to the Nixon Administration—is not that CRLA has occasionally sued governmental agencies, but that it has had to do so quite often. This, of course, is more consistent with the conservative creed that government unchecked erodes power, than with the liberal notion that government must provide for the welfare state. At a minimum, it conflicts with the common law notion that "the sovereign can do no wrong," a quaint notion in a country saddled with Vietnam, urban erosion, and environmental pollution. Yet CRLA's experience would seem to confirm the need for an official ombudsman, a watchdog agency to police governmental abuses on all levels—federal, state, and local. The real question in the immediate future is whether the ombudsman of legal services will be strengthened or smothered. There are disturbing signs that legal services—at least as practiced by CRLA—will not long continue.

The signs come mostly from Congress and, ironically, the Office of Economic Opportunity. Some of the stifling measures, such as the abortive Murphy and Quie-Green Congressional amendments of 1969[23] that would have placed legal service programs under the thumb of state governors, were visible enough to arouse public opinion and defeat the legislation. Others, such as OEO's proposal for re-regionalization,[24] a euphemism for giving control of legal services to regional directors of OEO, while less likely to result in front page news headlines, are every bit as destructive to the future of an independent and strong legal services program. The origin of certain measures designed to cripple or kill legal services belies their purported purpose. Thus, when George Murphy moved to give an item line veto to state governors over legal services, it was less likely intended, as claimed, to decentralize legal services than, as he acknowledged about the consequence of his measure on the floor of the Senate, to permit governors to stop litigation against growers hiring illegal entrants. When the Justice Department resorts to collecting dossiers on legal service attorneys—a clandestine activity, so there is no rationale provided by the department as yet[25]—it is logical to infer that they are resentful of defending, and losing, numerous cases in which the federal government is sued by legal service attorneys. (CRLA has won over 80 percent of the cases it has brought against governmental agencies.) Similarly, OEO, an office created by a Democratic administration and inherited by Richard Nixon, is most certainly less interested in giving "power to the people" or "keeping with the original intent of Congress in enacting the War on Poverty"—two rationalizations for re-regionalization—than in accomplishing administratively what Republicans and conservative Democrats failed to achieve with the Murphy and Quie-Green amendments.

The proposal most likely to succeed in destroying legal services is "Judicare." When Governor Ronald Reagan vetoed CRLA for the first time in 1970, he told Frank Carlucci, then acting director of OEO and the man with authority to override Reagan's veto, that Judicare "holds enormous promise for truly serving the rural poor." Perhaps, but Judicare, like its medical analogue Medicare, is pregnant with dangers.

The details of Judicare plans vary, but the essential concept is that a poor person be given a judicare card (like a Medicare card) which he can take to private attorneys participating in the program and receive certain legal services. The private attorney then bills the government for the service he renders each eligible client. Cries of socialized law? To the contrary, local bar associations around the country are agreeing with Ronald Reagan that Judicare is the poor's salvation from injustice.

Of course, local bar associations expect to set fees for Judicare reimbursement, a practice that doctors under Medicare and Medicaid initially found quite lucrative and taxpayers inordinately expensive. If the government sets maximum Judicare fees, as has been necessary under Medicaid to control inflationary costs and overservicing, then serious price-fixing problems and violations of the Sherman Antitrust Act are raised. Moreover, unless government fees at least approximate minimum fee schedules for private attorneys—which presently far exceed what legal service attorneys are paid per hour of client service—private lawyers will not even take Judicare clients. What is worse, where local or state bar associations determine the nature of cases entitled to reimbursement, as many Judicare plans provide, the poor will likely be left with ineffective representation. In California, for example, the Washington Township Judicare Program in South Alameda County has, since its inception in 1966, never filed a class action, appealed a case, been involved in a jury trial, or filed an action in federal court. Indeed, over 60 percent of the Washington Township Program funds have been spent on domestic relations matters. Both the Washington Township and Wisconsin Judicare (where over 60 percent of the total cases handled are divorces) programs demonstrate that the poor cannot be well represented by local lawyers who depend upon a clientele—landlords, collection agencies, local government, and merchants—whose interests conflict with or are adverse to the poor. Even where Judicare is proposed to be run by state bar associations, less susceptible to local pressures than county bars, the poor will receive diluted representation. The Board of Governors of the California State Bar, for instance, primarily comprised of lawyers from prestigious corporate firms, has never included on its Board a single Negro, Mexican American, Oriental, woman, or lawyer under the age of 35. Finally, it is a significant irony that OEO, committed by law to "maximum feasible participation of the poor" in its programs, is besieged, not by the poor, but by lawyers and politicians like Reagan to scuttle legal services programs which the poor have praised for Judicare programs from which the poor have been excluded in both formulation and operation.

There is, however, little point in arguing with a George Murphy, John Mitchell, or even Donald Rumsfeld about the merits of their proposals for legal services. They know what they want and no amount of moral or factual suasion—unless it is coupled with political power equal to that of agribusiness—will deter them. However, opponents of legal services employ a rhetoric to neutralize or win over others not knowledgeable about legal services. Often the rhetoric, as already noted, is along the lines that government should not be paying both sides of a lawsuit, an argument that undoubtedly strikes a responsive chord in southern governors faced with Justice Department–initiated school desegregation suits. This rhetoric serves to obfuscate reality, to shield the political and economic forces at play in the struggle to shape the character of legal services. Since it also confuses or neutralizes some potential supporters of legal services, however, it is worth examining.

V. THE LAW REFORM BOGEYMAN

Two favorite charges made by opponents of legal services—particularly of CRLA—center about law reform. For legal service attorneys law reform means using the law—either through litigation, legislation, or administrative rule-making—to attack root causes of poverty, to enhance the power of the poor. Law reform litigation frequently takes the form of class actions, suits brought by a few named persons for themselves and others similarly situated. The *bracero*, commuter alien, and *alambrista* litigations are all examples of law reform; they were all class actions brought to reduce the chronic oversupply of farm labor. Some are disturbed by these cases and charge that law reform should be left to the legislatures, not the courts. The problem with judicial buck passing, as the *alambrista* case so well illustrates, is that injured poor persons are not left with any viable remedy—a perhaps not unintended result. Legislatures, on both the national and state level, generally represent those with political clout. This political fact, by definition, nearly precludes the passage of legislation furthering the interests of the poor and powerless.

If there was ever any doubt about the skewed representation of legislative bodies, one need only compare the recent actions of Congress respecting two welfare measures. In 1967 Congress acted to place a future freeze on grants to mothers with needy children (AFDC), thereby arbitrarily denying public assistance to hundreds of thousands of needy children. Yet in 1969, the very year the AFDC "freeze" was to take effect, Congress rejected an amendment that would have placed a $20 thousand maximum on federal subsidies to individual farmers. Rural interests were reflected in these two divergent pieces of legislation, but they were the interests of the wealthy, not the poor.

Juan Alviso's suit to enjoin a Madera agribusiness concern

from employing wetbacks amply illustrates the frequent futility of domestic farmworkers resorting to the legislature for relief. Federal law has long made it a crime to harbor or conceal illegal entrants, but also exempts "mere employment" of wetbacks from the net of criminality. Powerful agricultural interests were responsible for removing the act of employing wetbacks from the ambit of criminal sanctions. In so doing, agribusiness made it extremely difficult, if not impossible, to obtain criminal convictions against those who knowingly hire cheap foreign labor that has entered the country illegally. Thus, the prominent social status of growers, the onerous burden of criminal charges and problems of proving the acts of harboring or concealing all combine to make federal laws an impotent deterrent against the widespread practice of employing wetbacks as farm laborers.

CRLA, in representing clients like Juan Alviso, has merely tried to implement what the judiciary, at least the Supreme Court, has been saying since the late 1930s: that the courts, not the legislatures, are the branch of government least responsive to immediate pressures, the branch with the greatest flexibility and opportunity, and thereby the greatest responsibility, to safeguard and vindicate the rights of the poor.[26]

This is not to say that CRLA has written off either Congress or the California legislature as political institutions capable of representing the interests of the rural poor. To the contrary, in 1968 CRLA established a full-time legislative office in Sacramento, the California capital. This office reviews bills of particular interest to the rural poor. When hearings are held in the Assembly or Senate on matters of importance to CRLA's clients, the Sacramento office contacts and coordinates the necessary expertise and political pressure to support or oppose the legislation. In 1968, for instance, CRLA was instrumental in defeating, through testimony at legislative hearings, a bill introduced by apartment owners that would have reduced the notice requirements for evicting tenants. The office also provides a liaison with legislators, informing them of problems facing the rural poor that require remedial legislation. In several instances the Sacramento office of CRLA has drafted legislation to benefit the client community that has been introduced by friendly legislators. The Sacramento office thus complements the litigation brought by CRLA's attorneys; both programs are seen as essential to any viable attack on the causes of poverty.

The second allegation made by critics of CRLA is that law reform is antithetical to individual service work, that, as one Congressman charged, "it leaves the little guy with the greatest need for a lawyer out in the cold while legal service attorneys are out crusading for abstract social reform." This charge misconstrues the nature of law reform. To begin with, named plaintiffs in all successful class actions filed by CRLA receive the same services and tangible benefits they would receive if the cases were filed in simply their individual names. The interests of the individual and the class of persons he represents are not antithetical but synonymous—both seek social justice. True, a clever defendant can, by offering lucrative settlements restricted to named plaintiffs in a class action, render their individual interests technically adverse to those of the class they purport to represent. Indeed, this tactic has frequently been employed to nonclass actions with the result that a suit is rendered moot, and since there is no longer a present legal dispute between the parties, the court is robbed of jurisdiction to decide the case. A lucrative settlement is less likely to be offered in class actions, however, since the defendant realizes that, unless the entire class is party to and benefits from the settlement, the case is not rendered moot. Hence defendants in class actions are realistically left with a clear choice: fight all the way and hope for a judicial victory or make an offer of settlement so appealing that all named plaintiffs—and unnamed plaintiffs supporting the suit—press their attorneys to drop the litigation. Those who have decided to fight all the way have lost to CRLA attorneys in 90 percent of the class actions that have been filed and decided in the period from December, 1966, to January, 1970.

The charge of overemphasizing law reform also does not come to grips with the disparity between legal service attorneys and eligible clients. As of 1970, approximately forty lawyers and twenty-five community workers were scattered throughout eleven CRLA offices ranging north from Marysville to El Centro in the south. These offices served sixteen California counties with a total eligible client population in excess of 550 thousand persons. When all the other legal service programs serving these same potential clients are included, this means that only 73 full-time attorneys provide representation to over 550 thousand people with legal problems of a civil nature. Since nationally there is approximately one lawyer for every 640 persons,[27] the rural poor in these sixteen California counties are short 786 attorneys, if they are to have representation on the 1 to 640 ratio.

Moreover, the legal problems of the poor are both more numerous and complex than those of the middle class. The poor tenant about to be evicted from a dilapidated shack is often plagued by additional legal problems—repossession of his car or furniture, wage garnishment, and harassment from creditors. The poor, due to mis-education and ignorance, rarely keep records, understand the transactions into which they have entered, or make effective witnesses. Statutory and case law, traditionally shaped by interests and needs of the wealthy and powerful, is usually unserviceable to the poor. Only exhaustive and imaginative research can reverse this historical bias and make the law work for the poor rather than against them. Consequently, a lawyer desirous of providing a poor person with top quality legal representation must, according to estimates of former private practitioners turned poverty lawyers, spend roughly five times the amount of time he would have to spend in giving equally competent counsel to a middle income client.[28]

Given insufficient resources to provide competent counsel for all eligible clients, CRLA decided early in its existence that it would limit attorney caseload to not more than 500 cases per attorney per year. This is consistent with a study conducted in New York several years ago showing that 98 percent of the private attorneys surveyed handled less than 500 cases per year. Yet imposing a maximum caseload of 500 is neither easy nor consistent with practices in most other legal service programs.[29] It is difficult because many poverty law offices are besieged by demands from the client community to provide services for all eligible clients who come in the door.

Despite pressures for undertaking a large volume of traditional service work, CRLA has managed to limit its attorney caseload to insure that each client receives appropriate attention. In 1968–69, for example, CRLA attorneys handled an average of 429 cases each, permitting lawyers to research adequately the facts and law of each case. One reason for this situation is that CRLA is not subject to funding control by local community action agencies, but instead must look to the national director of OEO who is relatively insulated from local political pressure.[30] To be sure, California's governor presently can veto CRLA's annual funding, but since the national director of OEO can override his veto, it has only been exercised once. The 1970 veto of CRLA resulted from a coincidence of political events. Ronald Reagan was elected in November, 1970, to his second, and what he announced would be his last, term as governor of California. The election demonstrated well Republican Reagan's vote-getting ability, as practically every other important contested office—from the U.S. Senate seat to State Superintendent of Public Instruction—was won by California Democrats. An announced foe of CRLA since its attorneys stopped his $240 million Medi-Cal cut in 1967, Reagan took comfort that a Republican President presided over OEO for the first time since it was established under President Kennedy. In fact, this same President had just brought OEO national director Donald Rumsfeld into the White House as an advisor, suggesting approval of the firing by Rumsfeld in November, 1970, of the pro-CRLA national director of Legal Services, Terry Lenzner. Moreover, President Nixon, obviously needing California to win in '72, was waning in popularity according to statewide polls. Reagan calculated that the President would either welcome the veto of CRLA or, at the very least, not risk a dispute with Reagan over the anti-poverty program that could cost him Reagan's support and California in election '72. Hence, Reagan handed agribusiness a post-Christmas present by vetoing CRLA on December 26, 1970. But the White House, surprised by the strong nationwide reaction favoring CRLA, decided to compromise in an effort to appease Reagan and woo liberal support; the veto was sustained, but CRLA was given a new grant for one-half year pending a "blue ribbon commission" hearing on charges of CRLA misconduct made by Reagan's poverty chief,

Lewis K. Uhler, an ex-John Bircher. If CRLA receives a fair commission hearing it can easily refute the charges, which range from the libelous ("CRLA attorneys tried to arrange a meeting between Angela Davis and the Soledad Brothers") to the ridiculous ("CRLA attorneys appear in court barefooted"). Reagan will then have to decide if he wants to put political pressure on the White House again to terminate CRLA despite the absence of alleged misconduct, or rely instead on Congressional and OEO reform of Legal Services à la Judicare. In any event, the traditional independence CRLA enjoyed because of direct national funding has been seriously threatened.

Removing the purse strings from local pressures guaranteed greater independence for CRLA, at least until the veto, than other poverty programs, but has never permitted the program to simply ignore pressures for undertaking service cases. Indeed, CRLA has of necessity sought to involve members of the client community in establishing equitable guidelines for restricting attorney caseload. Primarily this is accomplished through consultation with local advisory committees for each of the ten regional offices, bodies comprised of representatives from groups, areas, and organizations of the poor within the particular communities served. Moreover, CRLA's thirty-one man Board of Directors, representing a variety of interests, disciplines, and organizations that share a common concern for the welfare of the rural poor, review, revise, and approve methods for restricting caseloads. Finally, CRLA attempts to inform the client community of the rationale behind limiting caseload through publicity surrounding its activities.

Ultimately, of course, the ability to limit attorney caseload depends on the criteria adopted for that purpose. Many programs have, for example, kept the number of clients represented by an attorney to a manageable level by simply refusing to take additional clients once an attorney is handling fifty at any one time. This method is irrational, and results in bad relations between the poverty law office and the community it supposedly serves. More affirmatively, CRLA attorneys establish priorities for accepting and rejecting cases with the overall goal being to attack the causes, not merely the symptoms, of poverty. Thus

emphasis is given to cases that will enhance employment opportunities for the rural poor, augment the political power of the
poor, and reallocate government benefits more equitably between
poor and wealthy. On the other hand, cases that affect only the
individual client, particularly if the other party to the dispute is
also poor, are almost never taken. Specifically this means that
domestic matters and bankruptcies are rarely accepted. Neither,
for instance, are landlord tenant cases where the potential client
is a poor landlord desirous of evicting an impoverished tenant.

Yet it would be erroneous to conclude that, through application of an affirmative case selection criteria, CRLA is completely
successful in minimizing service cases and focusing on law
reform. Though CRLA has earned itself a reputation within legal
services as an exemplary law reform organization, the vast majority of legal problems it actually handles are still traditional,
individual client situations. In 1969, for example, of the entire
15,486 legal problems handled by the organization's attorneys,
only 63 were class actions and 1,603 were problems involving
groups rather than individual clients. This leaves 13,820 legal
problems, or 85 percent of the total, that were individual client
situations involving mostly orthodox poverty law problems. Thus
far the crude ratio of 85 percent service cases to 15 percent law
reform has satisfied both community desires and program objectives.

VI. INNOCENT CRIMINALS AS NON-DEFENDANTS

Not all criticism of legal services is from the outside. Poverty
lawyers are frequently heard to complain about attempted political interference from Congress and the Office of Economic Opportunity. The fight against the Murphy and Quie-Green
amendments was barely six months old when OEO's re-regionalization proposal surfaced. Quipped one CRLA lawyer, "We
spend so much time now fighting to defend our integrity against
political interference that we don't have any time to represent
our clients. It's getting so even if we win, we lose." Besides constantly fending off politicians and administrators seeking to
meddle in the attorney-client relationship, poverty lawyers are

constantly struggling to work within a web of internal administrative restrictions. Only the very poor qualify as clients, and OEO has a niggardly fee schedule that screens out the working class poor. Yet the very poor do not qualify if they have a legal problem that is fee generating, that has potential for winning the client money damages. These restrictions are irritating, but certainly not fatal to a viable legal service program. The ban on representation of criminal defendants is, however, another matter.

The ban on criminal cases for legal service lawyers was not originally a part of the program. Two almost contradictory kinds of experiences with OEO attorneys representing criminal defendants were responsible for promulgation of the prohibition on criminal cases in 1968. The first set of experiences occurred in 1966–67 in counties like Madera, where OEO law offices were present but where there was no public defender. Legal service attorneys in these areas found themselves heavily burdened with appointed criminal cases, usually everyday drunk driving defenses. The reasons for this peculiar and unequal allocation of cases to OEO lawyers were twofold: first, the counties expected to save money by appointing federally funded attorneys rather than reimbursing private lawyers out of county coffers; and, second, there was undoubtedly a feeling, at least in the case of CRLA in Madera, that if OEO lawyers were terribly busy defending drunk driving charges they would have neither the time nor resources to bring discomforting law reform suits. Hence, many poverty lawyers in counties without public defenders were in favor of OEO or Congress placing some restrictions on their handling of criminal cases.

The second contributing event took place in the summer of 1967 when Detroit erupted in flames. OEO lawyers rushed to represent many alleged "rioters" who were arrested en masse by an uptight police force. The lawyers did a good job; so good that many, if not most, accused rioters were acquitted. Detroit's establishment was displeased by the result and put enough pressure on OEO that, combined with requests from poverty lawyers deluged with appointed criminal cases, a blanket prohibition on representation of criminal defendants was enacted.

The present regulation against poverty lawyers handling criminal cases is crippling for legal services. It only permits OEO attorneys to advise clients before the indictment or arraignment stage of criminal proceedings unless a judge will attest that the defendant cannot otherwise obtain competent counsel. This rule practically precludes poverty lawyers from representing clients facing criminal charges. Since the criminal law is frequently employed to harass and intimidate efforts at group organization—witness the widespread prosecutions of the Black Panther Party—it is imperative that organizations of poor people have ready access to an attorney of their own, a lawyer who can act as the organization's house counsel. Legal services are theoretically committed to perform this function. The program is based upon the need for poor persons to come together and convert their individual powerlessness into group power. Yet if poverty lawyers help a group organize only to withdraw when the leaders are slapped with criminal charges, their effectiveness with the group clients would approach zero. Imagine the kind of reception a legal service program would get in a poor community if it advised a tenant union in the initiation of a rent strike but then refused to represent the same tenant union against criminal contempt charges for violating an injunction prohibiting the strike. The poverty lawyers would likely be viewed as classic "copouts"; they would alienate themselves from the very clients they aim to serve.

The complete repeal of the OEO restrictions on criminal representation is not the solution. That could place legal service attorneys in counties without public defenders in the position of being saddled with appointed criminal cases that would not appreciably further the interests of the poor. Instead, affirmative guidelines setting forth the kinds of situations where legal service attorneys can undertake criminal representation are needed. These guidelines would permit representation of criminally charged indigents when (1) the case was of widespread concern and interest to the poor community, and when (2) the prosecutions were approximately related to parallel civil actions in which a legal service program was already representing many of the same clients. The current prohibition is clearly overbroad; it sweeps within its ambit many cases in which CRLA and other

OEO attorneys should be actively involved. Unless this regulation is changed, the potential of legal services to truly further the cause of justice among the poor will never be realized.

VII. CONCLUSION:
SOCIAL REVOLUTIONARIES OR DON QUIXOTES?

Opponents of CRLA have an apocalyptic view of the organization's activities. "Self-styled social revolutionaries"[31] is the epithet hurled by one congressman at the program's attorneys, a view due largely to the headline publicity given CRLA's law reform victories. Reading that CRLA successfully sued the United States Department of Agriculture requiring sixteen California counties to institute federal food programs, gives the feeling that the organization obtained a judicial decision of major impact on the lives of poor people.[32] Or when one learns that CRLA, in reliance on the "one man, one vote" principle, struck down a California law requiring a two-thirds majority vote before school bonds are approved, he probably thinks an important shift in educational funding is portented.[33]

These perceptions, of course, are partially correct on both counts. But there is another equally correct view of CRLA—one often shared by a majority of the program's attorneys who are frustrated over the glacial pace at which poverty is being eradicated. Certainly statistics from the War on Poverty confirm that poverty is winning. In 1968, according to the McGovern Committee Report on Hunger, "government statisticians estimated there were between 22 and 27 million Americans living in poverty." By the beginning of 1969, however, the President's Council of Economic Advisors mysteriously dropped the highest figure in the estimates and optimistically declared that "only 22 million Americans lived below the poverty line." Then the Bureau of the Census astounded the nation a half year later (August 18, 1969) by reporting that 25.4 million persons were in poverty and alleging that the number of poor decreased by 2 million in 1968. Quite obviously the Census Bureau was able to allege a 2 million decrease of persons in poverty by resurrecting the earlier 27 million figure that had been dropped by the President's Economic

Advisory Council. All along, according to the McGovern Report, the real number of poor persons was between 25 and 26 million, and this number did not change appreciably from 1968 to 1969.

To be sure, the numbers game is a highly unsatisfactory way to measure progress in alleviating poverty, particularly when politics taints the figures. That is why optimistic statistical reports from the War on Poverty are as convincing to poverty lawyers as the body count statistics proving successful military gains are to the soldiers in Vietnam. A true victory needn't be proven by numbers or proclamations; it is self-evident because it necessarily implies a qualitative change. Law reform, like land reform, means more than a paper shift in rights and privileges; it means that the quality of people's lives has measurably improved. Judged by this criterion, many law reform cases are "much ado about nothing." To illustrate, abolition of California's notorious "divorce or deprivation" rule, a significant law reform case by most standards, was perhaps a hollow victory.[34] This rule, which required a mother to file for divorce against an absent father or wait ninety days after his desertion before her child could get public assistance, was successfully challenged by CRLA as violative of the equal protection of the laws and the Social Security Act. To replace the invalid ninety-day rule, however, the State Department of Social Welfare adopted regulatory standards for determining if a mother and her children are truly needy due to desertion of the father. There is a great deal of room for social worker arbitrariness in applying this new criteria to individual clients. Applicants who are denied aid must appeal and prove that there was genuine deprivation by reason of desertion. Each case is, therefore, *sui generis*. Law reform has largely knocked down an arbitrary law and in so doing has created a mountain of future service cases for poverty lawyers. Clearly the only way to minimize or eliminate unjust decisions denying qualified mothers public assistance is to reform the people who run the welfare departments, something the law has proven itself impotent to do. In this sense, witness the similar effect of the 1954 school desegregation opinion on Southern values—law reform is a slow road to social reform.

Fortunately, CRLA attorneys have witnessed remarkable

changes in the attitudes and abilities of both some clients and a minority of officials whom clients are dependent upon. Many have learned with CRLA that, in the words of one prominent attorney, "the law can be a friend to the poor and that the powerful, too, can be made accountable." Yet few believe that the War on Poverty will be won by these attitudinal changes any more than the system of racial school segregation has been substantially reformed by law. In fact, there is strong evidence that its failure is inherently predictable. The President's National Advisory Commission on Rural Poverty suggested as much when its 1968 report confessed that "(T)he sustained tight full employment . . . required for the War on Poverty to succeed may be impossible to achieve with the financial system of American capitalism."[35] If this is true, it will take far more than the War on Poverty—and a thousand CRLA's—to change the plight of the poor.

The Crime of the Courts

JOHN CRATSLEY*

The "adversary process" has been the cornerstone of the American system of law. In theory, the search for truth necessary to decide a case, to determine guilt or innocence, is best achieved through the efforts of two verbal warriors—with the impartial judge or jury rendering the ultimate decision. This process is thought to be particularly appropriate in the area of criminal law in which the state must put its case across "beyond a reasonable doubt," against a skilled defense attorney committed to his client's cause. The American public, rich and poor alike, know the criminal process best by this trademark of advocacy. In essence, each citizen participating in the legal system, whether defendant, complainant, or witness, looks to the adversary process to protect his rights and achieve a fair and just result.

Is this confidence well-placed? Tragically, it is not. And the nature of the problem is further hidden because the answer cannot be found in the figures on the volume of court cases or the total numbers of acquittals and convictions, or even in any of the highly touted, well-researched criminal justice studies.[1] Rather, the problem is one of a "crisis of attitude" generated by the methods and manners of lower court operation and marked by the disappearance of the adversary process. The evidence of this crisis is heard in the embittered attitudes of neighborhood workers, social activists, and street people, who are the lower

* John Cratsley graduated from the University of Chicago Law School in 1966, and is currently an attorney at Community Legal Assistance Office (CLAO) in Cambridge, Massachusetts, and teaching Clinical Practice at Harvard Law School.

court's most frequent participants and critics, and occasionally from one or another outraged middle-American who suffered through his "day in court." Contemporary commentators, ranging from the political to the establishment, have chronicled the horrors involved.[2] Why this has happened, and what has replaced the adversary process in the operation of the lower criminal courts, may be seen in the handling of criminal cases in the district courts of Massachusetts.

The district court is the portal to the criminal process in the Commonwealth of Massachusetts. Counting plaintiffs and defendants, as well as court staff (including clerks, probation officers, etc.), police, civilian witnesses, and related parties (bail bondsmen, court psychiatrists, public defenders, etc.), roughly two million people (about $\frac{2}{5}$ of the population of Massachusetts) have some contact with the district court system in a year. Close to one million legal actions, civil and criminal, bring all these persons through the district courts. The district court is the great gathering place of both the oldest and the worst in criminal society—the prostitute, the petty thief, the teenage hoodlum, and the gangster, as well as today's "newcomers" to crime—the drug users, the "hippies," and America's new groups of political defendants. The "American Dream" for all of them, is, of course, that as a result of the adversary process justice will be fairly and evenly dispensed—quite hopefully to their benefit. The "American Tragedy" is that the lower court system is crumbling under its own weight—a disaster of its own making.

Each town or group of towns in the Commonwealth of Massachusetts has a district court. All criminal matters, from drunkenness and traffic offenses to robbery and murder prosecutions, start in these lower courts.* Everyone charged with a crime, unless he is one of those special few who are proceeded against by

---

* Defendants charged with minor crimes (misdemeanors) are tried and sentenced in the district courts, while those charged with serious crimes (felonies) are given "probable cause" hearings. If the district court judge finds "probable cause" to believe that the defendant committed the crime charged, his case is "bound over" (sent on) to the county grand jury. If the grand jury returns an "indictment," the defendant is held for trial in the superior court (a countywide court).

secret grand jury indictment, makes at least one, and usually three or four appearances, in a district court. District courts dispose of 95 percent of the approximately 700 thousand criminal cases commenced in Massachusetts each year. Consequently, all citizens involved with the criminal process, including defendants, complainants, witnesses, and public officials, receive their first impressions of the administration of criminal justice—and often their last and most telling—in a local district courtroom. Obviously, then, a large quantity of justice is handed out in these courts. But the quality does not keep pace. One particular district court recently created a particularly vivid impression of "blind justice" by its parodied role in the "Alice's Restaurant" saga.

Unfortunately, data outlining precise patterns in these courts has until recently been quite limited. But in October, 1970, a landmark report on the Massachusetts district courts appeared.[3] Among the important conclusions of the study is that ". . . when the district court makes a determination affecting defendants—summons, bail, adjudication, or sentence—the poor defendant fares less favorably than the non-poor defendant."[4] Particular statistics show (1) that poor defendants receive summons (rather than being arrested) at half the rate of non-poor defendants, (2) that poor defendants are released on personal recognizance less often than non-poor defendants (47 percent of poor defendants as opposed to 53 percent of non-poor), (3) that poor defendants who plead "not guilty" and go to trial are actually found "not guilty" less frequently than non-poor defendants (27 percent of poor defendants as opposed to 55 percent of non-poor), and (4) that poor defendants are jailed following conviction more frequently than non-poor defendants (25 percent of poor defendants as compared with 13 percent of non-poor). The daily impact of the system, however, goes far beyond mere numbers. The heart of the district court system is quite obviously the people who pass through it—whether as defendants, complainants, or witnesses. The emotions or psyche of the district court system is the sense of "justice" or fairness left after participation in it. One obvious example of an "emotional breakdown" in this system is the confused reaction of the defendant who insists he has not committed a crime and who relates a plausible story in his defense, but who is told to plead guilty to a lesser offense because, as the result of "plea-bargaining," he is assured of remaining out of jail.

All of these preliminaries are to make but one point; if people —their lives, their futures, and their attitudes toward law—are the heartblood of the criminal process, then the local municipal court must fulfill the needs and expectations of those people, needs and expectations which focus not on conviction or acquittal, or getting off on a technicality, but on fair and speedy treatment and representation by a trustworthy advocate.

The crisis in our municipal courts stems from a variety of pressures on all the official participants in the system—judges, prosecutors, defense counsel—which robs them of their ability to respond to human needs and expectations. For example, the sheer volume and apparent similarity of certain types of cases in the district courts render it impossible for the probation officers to prepare either detailed information about, or individualized rehabilitation "plans" for, each defendant. For example, the only available alternatives for handling the 75 thousand drunk cases yearly are a penal sentence, commitment to one understaffed, overcrowded alcoholism treatment center, or complete release without supervision. And when probation is used, the individual probation officers have such large caseloads that they can do little more than talk to their probationers occasionally on the phone. All too frequently, the probation officer's invitation to "come in and talk" turns out to mean "come in and wait an hour for me to finish in court." Even the most patient and concerned judge or probation officer is subject to the financial whims of legislature and local communities which fail to establish and fund rehabilitation programs with adequate staff and facilities.

A local district court judge is subject to the particular pressures of public image, on one hand, and the crowded docket of the higher trial court on the other.* Most district court judges prac-

---

* Cases go from the district courts to the Superior Court either (1) as a result of a probable cause hearing and indictment in a felony case, or (2) on appeal for a new trial in a misdemeanor case.

ticed law for many years in the town or city where the court is located, and were "elevated" to the bench when their party came to power in the State House. The unseen, and usually unacknowledged, pressure on them to reflect and preserve traditional community values can be easily understood in terms of their background and governmental ties. While they are willing to give lenient treatment to a young mother on welfare charged with shoplifting, they show no such judicial sympathy for a young college dropout similarly charged who is loosely identified with radical politics by the local police. Consequently, the "attempted murder" charge which after the probable cause hearing turns out to be merely a case of simple assault and battery is still sent to the grand jury. So, too, is the "car theft" felony against a black eighteen-year-old who has no adult record, despite a pre-hearing agreement between defense counsel and the police to reduce the charges to a misdemeanor. Both occur because the judge says he does not want a "whitewash" in his court. But the "breaking and entering in the nighttime" case, in which the defendant was caught inside the store with money from the broken cash register, is disposed of in the district court with a light jail sentence to avoid crowding the higher court with an appeal. This was achieved only after defense counsel was asked by the judge how high a sentence he would accept and not appeal.

The quality of district court justice is also adversely affected by the variety of matters the judges must handle. In Massachusetts, a district court judge can hear, all in the same morning, cases which would be heard by four different judges sitting in separate sessions in other states (i.e., criminal cases, traffic cases, family matters, and juvenile cases). It is virtually impossible for a district court judge who at 9:30 A.M. handles a number of adult cases (including those of eighteen- to twenty-year-olds) to shift his entire judicial outlook and philosophy to properly conduct juvenile court at 10:30 A.M. Considering the caseload and the significance of the juvenile court experience for the individual young person, it is a sad comment that Massachusetts has only three special juvenile courts, and that yearly more than 14 thousand juvenile cases are handled in other courts.

Local police departments and their non-lawyer prosecuting officers are under similar pressures. Frequent defense requests for continuances, appearances of defendants without counsel, and uncooperative civilian witnesses hamper their ability to prepare and present cases promptly, or even to discuss alternative dispositions of cases with defense counsel before trial. These limitations on local police prosecutors can only result in the complainants and witnesses losing pay and feeling bitterness toward the courts and police, particularly when some personal property of the complainant is involved and he cannot recover it until the case is completed. When the defense attorney is ready for trial with a well-prepared case, unnecessary police delays (witnesses or officers who fail to show up, incompleted drug or fingerprint tests, etc.) result in the accused having higher attorney's fees, losing pay, and becoming disillusioned about whether he will ever have his day in court.

Often this unhappy chain of events leads to the defendant making some "deal" with the prosecution just to get the case over. The other side of the coin finds the police, months after the original arrest, making "deals" in strong cases simply to get a conviction on record before further delays destroy their case altogether. This most frequently occurs when a clever defendant or defense counsel delays the case so long that the government witnesses grow tired of and frustrated with attending court and finally refuse to come for any future proceedings.

A clever defendant can win himself four or more continuances by using the following formula: first time, he says he has no lawyer and that he will hire one; second time, he says the lawyer cannot appear that day; third time, he says he can no longer afford an attorney and wants a public defender; and fourth time, he seeks to discharge the public defender and hire a new attorney. This is not to mention the delays that his attorney (assuming he ever gets one) can achieve.

Defense counsel, and particularly the public defenders, work under equally severe pressures. A conscientious defense counsel who wishes to discuss his client's situation with the police before trial will often have trouble reaching the police prosecutor, and once he contacts him may well learn that he has not had time to discuss the case with the arresting officer. All too often defense attorneys will actually visit the police station, or repeatedly call the police prosecutor, only to be told, if they ever locate him, that "no police report is ready yet, see me before trial." Consequently, most discovery and "plea-bargaining" with the police must be done, chaotically and unprofessionally, the morning of trial in the court lobby—a veritable market place of "deals" and dispositions. In addition to the difficulties of contacting the proper policeman to discuss the case prior to trial, there exists the basic inability to prepare a proper defense and plea regarding sentencing in the brief period between arraignment and trial in the district courts. This is particularly true for the public defender who is receiving new cases daily while preparing older ones for trial. Most district court judges are unwilling to continue a case once the defendant has an attorney because of the "heavy" caseload and desire to finish before noon.

Defense counsel may also be concerned that he cannot get all his client's witnesses present in court on the day of the trial, and that if they do show up, the matter will only be continued because the police are unprepared. The impact of delay and court inefficiency on citizen "bystanders" who have reluctantly agreed to come to court as witnesses for either side is as harmful to the image of justice as these experiences are for the direct participants.

Competent defense counsel is also constantly concerned that the probation officer will not know enough about his client, or have the resources available to help his client, should he be found guilty. As a result, the defense attorney must take valuable time away from the preparation of the case to do the "social work" necessary to prepare an otherwise non-existent, pre-sentencing report suggesting treatment programs, job opportunities, halfway houses, and other alternatives to jail. Frequently, a well-prepared defense counsel is able to win probation for his client because he has sold the judge on a rehabilitation plan or agency placement that was unknown to the probation office.

Unquestionably the public defender's difficulties are among the most severe found in the district courts. Underpaid, understaffed, and overworked, the public defender is both the victim of the overloaded municipal court and, in turn, another cause of the breakdown. As Edgar Rimbold, the chief counsel for the public defender agency in Massachusetts has pointed out, the sixty-two attorneys on his staff are about half of the staff he requires.[5] Frequently, the single public defender who is covering one district court will be in demand in two or possibly three different courtrooms of that court at the same time. In one district court, the chief judge would simply order the defender to stay in his court until all his cases were finished, thereby making two other judges and many citizens wait hours till their cases could be heard. Furthermore, the defender is rarely able to interview his clients personally until the morning the case is called for trial. Occasionally, a hardworking defender will make office appointments with his clients in upcoming cases, and only be able to see them after court, usually between 3 and 5 P.M. This, of course, leaves no time for investigation. The result is frequent requests for continuances for one very good reason—"I am unprepared, your Honor." When the defender can no longer get a continuance and must go forward, he is subject to the pressures of over-generalization, i.e., he treats each case like the one before it and succumbs to similar techniques in each. This method results in a failure to file written motions, a lack of prepared cross-examination, and an overemphasis on wheeling and dealing with the police and probation officers. Similarly, the public defender has little time or resources to prepare a presentation on his client's behalf at time of sentencing. Therefore, with few exceptions, the defender is forced into a regular routine at time of sentencing—reciting the defendant's age, family situation, and work record, and asking for leniency—thereby failing to exercise any creativity on the defendant's behalf in searching for or proposing useful alternatives to incarceration.

With the pressures on the participants, it is little wonder that the courtroom hearing—the so-called adjudicatory process —is a crazy quilt of trial and error, patchwork and shortcuts. For example, because of the high caseload in the district courts, the pressure on the court and the police to dispose of as many cases as possible as quickly as possible, and the pressure on defense counsel to keep their clients out of jail, the concept of "admitting to a finding" has developed. Traditionally, a defendant in a criminal case either enters a plea of "guilty" to the charges, (and then is sentenced and cannot appeal his admission of guilt), or stands on his plea of "not guilty" and goes to trial. Occasionally, a defendant will enter a plea of *nolo contendere* ("I do not wish to contest the case") which may be accepted by the court in its discretion.

In the district courts of Massachusetts, however, a defendant is permitted to "admit to a finding" which is neither a plea of "guilty" nor a trial. Rather, it is an indication by the defendant that he will let the government prove him guilty and not contest the case, yet retain his right to appeal if he does not like the sentence he receives. In many district courts, "admitting to a finding" is a direct invitation to the judge to give any sentence he wishes short of a jail term; the implicit understanding being that the defendant has saved the court the time necessary for a trial in return for the court not jailing him.

While the practice of "admitting to a finding" may not seem disturbing, much less illegal, the manner in which such pleas are entered or "bargained" robs the individual defendant of any sense that his attorney engaged in an adversary process or that he himself participated in the decision-making affecting his life. Since the defendant's attorney enters this plea in a whispered conversation with the judge at the bench (often coupled with some humble statement to the court about how much time he is saving everyone since there will not have to be a trial), the defendant is not involved. Frequently, this plea is entered, the probation officer's report given, the defense attorney's plea for leniency made, and the sentence rendered, all at the bench (some distance away from the defendant and out of his hearing) before the defendant realizes that his case has been concluded. All he eventually hears is an announcement by the clerk that he has been found guilty and given a certain sentence. With a public defender or busy private attorney, the hapless defendant is lucky at this point to have his attorney stop and explain what has happened to him before he leaves court or, if things have gone particularly badly, is jailed.

Even more confusing to the defendants in the district court system is the process by which his attorney decides to "admit to a finding" on his behalf. Having told his attorney his version of the events in question, the defendant watches his counsel disappear among a group he vaguely knows to be police officers, district attorneys, probation staff, and opposing witnesses. He may or may not be consulted sometime later by his counsel. If he is, the conversation may run along the following confusing lines:

> I know you said you were innocent, but the police will recommend a suspended sentence so we're going to admit to a finding;

or

> if you admit to a finding, the police will drop one charge, so you'd better take that deal;

or

> if you admit to a finding, the probation officer says he will go to bat for you.

Most defendants sense one of two things—either the deal must be good because it was "worked out" with the police, or the deal keeps him on the street regardless of the hypocrisy involved. Consequently, they accept their attorney's advice to "admit." Some discover that they have accepted it only after the clerk reads their sentence. For those who do not, and who insist on going to trial, a number of unfortunate consequences can follow.

The worst possible result of going to trial, and one which smacks of unconstitutional conduct, is the possibility that the defendant will be punished more severely simply for exercising his right to go to trial. This punishment is exercised in a subtly sophisticated form by the judge who sentences more harshly after trial and conviction because the defendant has burdened the court's limited time and because the judge believes that the conviction indicates that the defendant was lying all the time. Lying, in the judge's thinking, is a factor which he may take into account in sentencing. Such "lying," however, is merely the defendant's attempt to present his version of the facts and prove his innocence. Upon a determination of guilt, his punishment should be based on his crime and his background, not on his use of the adversary process—even if he lost out in that effort.

A second result of going to trial in the district court is the problem of appeal. As mentioned previously, any defendant in Massachusetts can appeal from a finding of "guilty" in the district court to a trial *de novo* (a wholly new trial unrelated to the results of the first one) in the superior court. Because of the burdens to all parties from a retrial of the entire case in an already overcrowded superior court, district court judges are under heavy pressure not to generate too many appeals. While judges cannot always control the defendant's decision regarding appeal, they exercise a prime deterrent in their power to sentence and place conditions on appeals. Consequently, a regular scenario in district court is as follows: the judge finds the defendant guilty, sentences him to a term in the House of Correction, and then suspends the sentence if the defendant "waives his right of appeal." The jail sentence is not suspended, however, if the defendant does appeal, and quite possibly a new, higher bail is then imposed on the defendant "to secure his presence in the superior court." This bail can be reduced by motion in the superior court, but it may take one or two days to bring the case before the higher court. The defendant's predicament is obvious. If he has a job, or some other reason not to want to make numerous future appearances in court, the defendant will unhappily accept the suspended sentence and probationary term. The consequence is that the suspended sentence which was not appealed can be later "executed" (the defendant forced to serve it) following any future law violation, no matter how minor, with no possibility of appeal at that time.

This problem of alternative sentences works its greatest hardship on the defendant who insists on his innocence at trial, but is found guilty. This is particularly true for the defendant who has no prior convictions. Since he wishes to clear his good name, and does not want the blemish of a conviction on his record, he will insist on taking an appeal. But the personal costs of doing so, in both time and money, are great. A far fairer system would be one which required the sentencing judge to render one sentence, which the defendant could accept or reject, rather than an alternative one.

The "coerced waiver of appeal" just described exemplifies the worst in the lower criminal courts. Here the accused gives up his statutory right to appeal and his constitutional right to a jury trial for the tenuously assured "freedom" of a suspended sentence, simply because the court system will require too high a personal price in future time and money from him if he is ever to obtain his day in court. The hypocrisy of the system is nowhere more self-evident. Legal scholars for years have condemned procedures whereby one right is conditioned on giving up another (here both the right to appeal and to jury trial are quickly swapped for certain freedom), yet district court judges engage daily in such a practice—all in the unspoken name of expediency.

An equally serious defect with respect to appeals is the lack of a transcript of the proceedings in the district court. Since the district court is technically not a "court of record" (i.e., all proceedings in it are subject to review on appeal by a *de novo* trial as a matter of right), no court reporter is present. Only the rich are able to have transcripts because only they can afford to hire a court reporter and pay for his transcript. In addition to the value of a transcript in the higher court for discovery, impeachment, and refreshing recollection, veteran attorneys agree that the presence of a court reporter in the district court curtails arbitrary conduct by the trial judge. Although his statements and rulings are not reviewable as a matter of law, his conduct now is.[6] There is no better way to draw attention to a district court judge's outrageous asides (e.g., the comment to a welfare mother arrested as a passenger in a stolen car, "So, out drinking the Commonwealth's money.") or illegal orders (e.g., $5,000 bail appeal bond for a female first offender pending trial *de novo*), than by way of an official transcript.

Another weakness in the district court criminal justice system is the creation and use of "criminal records." Each defendant coming through the court accumulates some sort of record in the court probation office—it tells when he was arrested, and for what, and the finding and sentence, if any, in his case. These records are cumulative and begin with one's juvenile court experiences. By themselves, as bare factual data, they serve the relatively innocent function of informing the court at the time of setting bail or sentencing of the prior involvement of the defendant with the law. Their discretionary use by probation officers, however, is of real concern. First, a defendant's juvenile record, which under the original theory of the juvenile courts was not to be used detrimentally against him at all, is usually presented to the district court in all its detail. One of the worst uses to which probation officers put the juvenile record is to try to establish a pattern of conduct to characterize an adult defendant. Frequently, an adult will have had a troubled youth and a resulting serious juvenile record, but will have matured and gotten into little trouble during his early adult years. Once he is in court with his first serious adult charge, however, his juvenile record is trotted out to show that he has a "pattern of crime." The theoretical "non-record" from a young man's experience in a so-called "rehabilitative" court proves to be his own worst enemy. Second, some probation officers take wide latitude to explain each charge on the record, regardless of the outcome —"there's a not guilty noted here, your Honor, but that was on a technicality." Others use the data to draw unwarranted conclusions—"all these arrests show that he's been quite a problem to the court" (with no mention of whether any of the arrests resulted in conviction). And third, in the rare case in which an enlightened judge will remove a guilty finding after a probationary term (so as to eliminate the defendant's "having a record"), the probation office still keeps the record so it reads "guilty, finding removed on such and such a date." This is hardly in keeping with the purpose of the procedure, which is to eliminate the conviction altogether once probation is successfully completed.

Having examined the pressures on the lower criminal courts, and seen the resulting chaos, one must ask if anything short of total overhaul will provide relief. One radical approach would be some form of neighborhood-oriented, "peoples' courts." Such plans do not, however, really answer the question of who shall be the judges and how they shall be selected. Nor does the proposed informality of these "courts" assure either regular procedures (akin to due process), uniformity of decisions (somewhat like the use of precedent), or effective representation of individual interests (the adversary process). It therefore seems fair to assume that the problems which presently riddle the district courts would likely remain.

A more traditional approach—"traditional" only because frequently repeated, but never carried out—is court reform. The list of "reform" measures presently affecting the Massachusetts district courts is lengthy and impressive. To date, none of these changes has significantly improved either the operation of the courts or the quality of "justice." Certain sweeping, and unfortunately expensive, reforms could, however, go a long way to achieve these desirable ends. These would include:

(1) providing court reporters for all district court proceedings with indigents entitled by statute to a free transcript;

(2) increasing the staff of the public defenders office and substantially improving their salaries, training, and investigative resources;

(3) requiring the imposition of a single sentence upon conviction, thereby eliminating the alternative sentencing process in which the lighter sentence is conditioned upon waiving one's right of appeal;

(4) appointing prosecuting attorneys for each court who could make judgments, independent of the arresting officers and their superiors, about appropriate charges and dispositions in each case, and who would be regularly available prior to trial to discuss cases with defense attorneys;

(5) establishing separate, specialized juvenile courts in all large cities, and traveling juvenile court judges who would hold the juvenile sessions in all other district courts;

(6) eliminating from use in the adult criminal court any evidence of the defendant's juvenile record;

(7) destroying all arrest records (or at least barring their use in court), where the case was dismissed at the Commonwealth's request;

(8) authorizing more probation officers for the district courts in larger towns and cities so that more attention can be paid to preparing pre-sentencing reports and to post-conviction supervision;

(9) establishing judicial conferences during which judges, probation officers, clerks, and other court personnel would regularly discuss policies, rules, and administrative problems; and

(10) eliminating the "special justices" who are attorneys specially appointed by the governor from private practice to sit periodically when needed, but who are often unfamiliar with the daily court procedures and needs, and who may well have conflicts of interests based on their private practice.

Various court reform groups have recommended some of these changes in their reports and proposals. But when one considers that one key reform frequently advocated is that judges should follow the rules of evidence rather than the ad hoc invention of their own arbitrary rules, the depth of the problem becomes clearer.[7]

A different type of solution, not inconsistent with the changes previously recommended, but one which speaks more directly to the problem of citizen alienation and disillusionment, is the return to a visible "adversary process" in the district courts. Veteran attorneys may vigorously argue the intellectual and practical imperfections of the adversary "search for truth," and they may also suggest that it is particularly inappropriate for local district courts; yet citizens who participate in these courts view that process as protecting their interests and assuring them of fair treatment and a just result.

The return to the adversary process should begin with those persons most disillusioned with lower court justice—the participants, and particularly the clients. The greater the time spent in consultation and explanation between the defendant and his counsel, between the complainant and the prosecutor, the greater will be the benefits in terms of citizens' understanding and confidence. Secondly, those professionals involved in many capacities as "officers of the court," including probation officers and courtroom staff, should patiently and willingly explain the mechanics of the district court system to all involved. One particular lower court judge in Washington, D.C., begins each day in court with a detailed explanation to everyone present about the nature of his judicial work and what is expected of them as citizen-participants. It is complicated enough for a citizen to understand that he has "admitted to a finding," but it is shocking that he often learns that fact, as well as the terms of his suspended sentence, from his probation officer or a court clerk, rather than his attorney. And third, no official participant, be he judge, prosecutor, or defense counsel, should compromise the values of advocacy and the ethics of the legal profession to efficiency, expediency, or opportunity. It will be a rare, but noble day when the public defender in a crowded district courtroom announces that he refuses to take another case because he cannot adequately serve his present clients. Even rarer will be the probation officer who refuses to supervise another probationer because his present load already precludes proper supervision by rendering impossible effective tools like weekly counseling sessions and home visits.

It remains true, however, that the crux of the adversary process for the client comes not in a detailed explanation of court operations, but in the manner in which his case is handled. A true advocate will carry his client's cause forward vigorously in trial, whether it be detailed and probing cross-examination or a sharp and clear presentation of his client's own case on direct examination. And where the attorney and client conclude together that a plea of guilty or admission to a finding is best, a dedicated advocate will press his client's case equally vigorously in the process of "plea-bargaining." Once they have decided to plead guilty or "admit," all too few defense counsel press hard for a marginal improvement in the sentence their client receives —i.e., straight probation instead of a suspended sentence, or "continued without a finding" instead of having the charges "placed on file." Similarly, complainants and citizen witnesses expect the police and the prosecutor to press their complaint actively. Half-hearted advocacy by defense counsel only harms individual clients, but careless prosecution can both free criminals and create public mistrust of law enforcement officials.

In essence, the advocacy required is a spirit of concern for the individual by his counsel. Whether he be an assistant district attorney or a public defender, the lawyer has an affirmative obligation to advance his client's interests. Although affected by numerous contingencies, these interests demand a fair, competent, and thorough job. This advocacy is lost in today's crowded courts somewhere between "plea bargaining" and "continuances." Regaining it is essential to a restoration of citizen confidence in the "justice" of our lower municipal courts. But until the legislators, the electorate, and the bar are ready to support extensive and very expensive reforms, the adversary process of justice in our lower courts will continue to be merely preached.

Taming GM ... and Ford,
Union Carbide, U.S. Steel,
Dow Chemical ...

DAVID P. RILEY*

Legitimacy, responsibility, and accountability are essential to any power system if it is to endure.

—A. A. Berle

—The Honeywell Corporation in Minneapolis makes cameras; it also has $250 million worth of government contracts to make anti-personnel weapons like cluster bombs that rain down thousands of pellets and "flechettes" or fishhooks that will stick you up against a tree or a comrade. American correspondents and officers in Vietnam have seen people shredded and impaled on trees by such weapons. (The Hague Conventions on the laws of war, which the United States signed and is bound by, state in Article 23 that "It is especially forbidden to employ arms, projectiles or materials calculated to cause unnecessary suffering.")[1]

—In April, 1970, a Honeywell shareholder went to court to get Honeywell's stockholder lists and records on war weapon production as part of a campaign to stop the company from making such weapons. A state judge threw the suit out of court saying it was just an attempt by the shareholder to advance his own

---

* David Riley, a graduate of George Washington University Law School, was formerly associated with the Institute for Policy Studies in Washington. His articles have appeared in *Potomac Magazine* of the *Washington Post*, *The Washingtonian Magazine*, *The Village Voice*, *Commonweal*, *The New Republic*, the *George Washington Law Review*, and other publications.

"political-social views." The shareholder's lawyer called the decision "an abomination" that would be "perfect propaganda" for radicals.[2]

—Three weeks later, during Honeywell's stormy, fourteen-minute annual meeting, with several thousand antiwar demonstrators marching outside, Honeywell Chairman James H. Binger was asked if the meeting was being conducted under Robert's Rules of Order. "We are operating by rules of the chairman," Mr. Binger replied, "and I'm the chairman."

—When a group of protesting proxy-holders prepared to leave the annual meeting, Mr. Binger pointed to two exits, "One on my right and one on my left." To a burst of cheers and jeers, someone shouted, "We'll take the one on the left!"[3]

It was the usual pattern: corporate practices with devastating social consequences, the law protecting such practices from serious public scrutiny, corporate arrogance in the face of a challenge to its authority, and finally angry citizen demands for change. That's been a recurring pattern in periods of the American past, and it's the emerging pattern again today. The strength of the environmental movement and the radical movement generally, the prominence and power of Ralph Nader and Saul Alinsky's campaign against corporations—these are some of the indications that today we may stand on the verge of another resurgence of the antibusiness popular instinct that held sway over the country during the Jacksonian Era, the Populist and Progressive movements, and the New Deal.*

In this country, where the 200 largest corporations (out of a total of 350,000) control over 60 percent of the manufacturing assets,[4] one must critically probe the large corporations, their

---

* There are other indications as well, including some striking parallels to the earlier periods. In 1908, Wisconsin Senator La Follette gave a senate speech documenting the interlocking directorates through which economic power was so highly concentrated; during the New Deal, the Temporary National Economic Committee investigated corporate consolidation and business power. In 1969, Wisconsin Senator Gaylord Nelson extended his Monopoly Subcommittee's investigation into an examination of the "Role of Giant Corporations" and in 1970, Montana Senator Lee Metcalf gave a senate speech calling for a full-scale investigation of economic concentration in America.

power, their responsibilities, their irresponsibilities, and their legitimacy. A. A. Berle, the distinguished, generally friendly critic of corporations in America, said that large corporations—"these instrumentalities of tremendous power"—presently "have the slenderest claim of legitimacy. . . . They must find some claim of legitimacy, which also means finding a field of responsibility and a field of accountability. Legitimacy, responsibility, and accountability are essential to any power system if it is to endure."[5] Berle thus raises the question of this chapter: *How can corporations be made accountable to the public interest* and to the society of which they are a part?

Many economists, from the conservative Milton Friedman to the left-oriented Douglas Dowd, argue that corporations should not be responsible for anything other than the narrowest definition of their purpose: making money. "Their business is to make the thing and try to sell it," says Dowd; "and I am not too sure that I would be happy having General Motors . . . making decisions about how our cities should function, and so on."[6]

The argument's importance, however, has been blown out of proportion. It is not a substantive argument (except in the staunch conservative's fantasy-land)* but rather a tactical one. Corporate action has tremendous effect on society**—no one

---

* Conservative economist Milton Friedman bases his argument against "corporate social responsibility" on the assumption that shareholders control corporations (and directors are their employees); that assumption has long been disproved, as discussed below.

** Andrew Hacker in *The Corporation Take-Overs* describes "the fulcrum of corporate power" as the "investment decision" made "by small handfuls of corporate managers" but with vast consequences as to "how much is to be spent; what products are to be made; where they are to be manufactured; and who is to participate in the processes of production. A single corporation can draw up an investment program calling for the expenditure of several hundreds of millions of dollars on new plants and products. A decision such as this may well determine the quality of life for a substantial segment of society: Men and materials will move across continents; old communities will decay and new ones will prosper; tastes and habits will alter; new skills will be demanded, and the education of a nation will adjust itself accordingly; even government will fall in line, providing public services that corporate developments make necessary."

ever denies that—and corporations are responsible for the action they take. They take action, and therefore they are responsible for taking it. And their actions are social. The question is whether we on the outside are to make the decisions about how they exercise that responsibility, thus forcing them to be accountable to us, or whether corporations themselves will make those decisions, thus imposing their "corporate social responsibility" on themselves. Actually self-accountability is, strictly speaking, a contradiction in terms; it means no accountability, because it is not enforceable or even reviewable by another party. Thus it's not surprising to find corporations increasingly accepting, on their own, their "social responsibility," at least in their rhetoric and sometimes in their action too. This chapter covers the abuses of corporate power, the lack of outside corporate accountability, and possible approaches to achieving it.

THE ABUSE OF CORPORATE POWER: WHAT IT DOES TO YOU AND ME

"America is a business civilization," says corporate critic David Bazelon. "Our chief assets are our great business institutions." The figures show it. General Motors, the wealthiest economic organization in human history, grossed $24 billion in 1969, which is more than the revenues of any country except the United States and the USSR; GM, Standard Oil of New Jersey, and Ford *each* has gross revenues much greater than those of any state in the Union.[7] Finally, Bazelon reports the amazing figure that "Out of the 55 organizations with a billion or more annual revenue (1958), only nine are official governmental units."[8] So when we talk about making corporations accountable, we are talking about the organizations that dominate our lives and our society.

We all know that corporations do good things: they make things for us to eat and wear and get around in. If they did only good things, there would be no need to talk about corporate accountability. But we know they do bad things too. Some of these things are spelled out in the following discussion.[9]

Deception

The Federal Trade Commission, long criticized for its caution and timidity in protecting consumers from unfair business practices, released a report in 1968 on trading, inspection, and marketing practices in the lumber industry. The FTC report stated that:

> The masquerading of low-grade lumber for high-grade lumber has bilked consumers of millions of dollars, has lowered the margin of structural safety in innumerable dwellings, and, in the affected market areas, has impaired competitive mores among surviving wholesalers, retailers, and contractors.

For those who don't believe governmental bodies, sometimes industry speaks for itself. The magazine *Food Technology* ran this advertisement:

> With Western Dairy Products' new *tasteless* (their emphasis) sodium caseinate called Savortone, you can now successfully use sodium caseinate as an emulsifier and binder for sausages, salad dressings, oil emulsions and egg substitutes. . . . *You can use it wherever you like, and never wonder for a minute what the consumers will think. They will never know.* (emphasis added)

Consumer Reports studied fresh pork sausages and found that one-eighth of federally inspected sausage and over one-fifth of non-federally inspected sausage contained "insect fragments, insect larvae, rodent hairs, and other kinds of filth." It also found that typically 30 percent of federally inspected sausage and 40 percent of infrequently Illinois-inspected sausage failed to pass tests for absence of filth or acceptable low bacteria. Meanwhile the meat industry vigorously opposed the U.S. Department of Agriculture's recent rule limiting fat content in sausages and other processed meat to 30 percent. No doubt they argued such a rule would seriously endanger the health of the meat industry.

In 1962, Congress gave the Food and Drug Administration

authority to test drugs not only for their safety but also for their effectiveness; if found ineffective, drugs could be ordered off the market. The result, when the FDA finally had the drugs tested in 1966: 300 drugs were found ineffective to do what they are prescribed or advertised to do. One of the many drugs ordered removed from the market, the commonly used Panalba (a combination of two antibiotics), had been bought by the public at a rate of $18 million a year, $12 million of which was the "net theft from the public" that is, the difference between the sales of Panalba and what it would have cost consumers to buy the one antibiotic in Panalba which *was* effective.[10]

Then there is the affair of the Pill. The FDA's original proposal for a written warning to the user to accompany birth control pills was 600 words long. It warned that women with blood clots, cancer, liver disease, and unexplained vaginal bleeding should not take the pill, and cautioned those with histories of heart or kidney diseases, high blood pressure, diabetes, epilepsy, migraine headaches, and other symptoms to use it with care. After the public controversy died down and the private pressure was applied, the final version of the complaint was less than 100 words long. It mentioned only blood clots as "the most important known complication," and suggested seeing the doctor if the user had symptoms like blurred vision, severe headache, unexplained cough, etc. "We decided it wasn't our role to play doctor," commented FDA Commissioner Charles Edwards. HEW Secretary Robert Finch said he thought the shorter statement was more likely to be read.[11]

Finally, there's the vast and fertile field of deceptive advertising. The FTC, for example, wants to stop mouthwash manufacturers from advertising their products as prolonged breath sweeteners. The FTC says such claims for mouthwash are a lot of hogwash. In 1968, consumers relied on such hogwash to the tune of $175 million worth of mouthwash.[12]

Danger and Death

In April, 1968, when cities across the country were in flames after the assassination of Dr. Martin Luther King, Jr., there were also flames in Richmond, Indiana. A leaky pipeline, which the company knew for some time was defective, blew up. Forty-one people were killed, and over one hundred others seriously burned. For a few days before the explosion, the gas leakage was so bad shopkeepers had to keep their doors open for ventilation. No federal or state law applied to the disaster, and the Indiana Public Service Commission didn't even think it could formally investigate it.

In 1965 and 1966, Edward Gregory, a Fisher Body Plant inspector for GM in St. Louis, repeatedly pointed out inadequate welding that caused lethal exhaust leakage into the passenger compartment of Chevrolets. He was ridiculed, abused, and then taken off the inspection line. Meanwhile people died from exhaust exposure. Three years later GM recalled two-and-a-half million Chevrolets for re-welding. The diligent Gregory was belatedly rewarded with $10,000 in savings bonds.

President Johnson's National Commission on Product Safety reported in June, 1970, that a wide array of dangerous household products "constitute an unreasonable hazard to the health and safety of the consuming public." The report called for mandatory federal safety standards and a permanent Product Safety Commission to enforce them and investigate further dangers. The Commission stated, a little redundantly, that industry self-regulation was "legally unenforceable and patently inadequate."[13]

Theft and Waste

All the above examples of consumers not getting what they thought they were paying for are instances of theft of consumers and wasted consumer spending. There are many other examples. One of the most obvious is that of automobile bumpers which cannot protect a car in collisions over two miles per hour. The result: an estimated $1 billion annual loss to motorists in repair costs for new fenders and front ends that the ornamental bumpers could not protect. A functional bumper that could take a ten-mile-an-hour collision would save consumers that amount in repair costs, according to a study done by Edward Daniels, an insurance executive and member of the Michigan Automobile

Club. When consumers buy new fenders and front ends, they often buy them from the parts divisions of the automobile makers. It is very hard to imagine that the car companies aren't aware of the benefit to them of a billion dollar annual repair business in fenders and related accessories. They would have to be pretty poor businessmen not to be aware of it, and no one accuses them of being bad *business*-men.

The list of theft and waste goes on and on. Senator Philip Hart, the low-key, level-headed consumer advocate from Michigan, compiled a list on wasted consumer spending recently, based on the extensive investigations of his Senate Antitrust and Monopoly Subcommittee over several years.[14] Among other examples, the Subcommittee found that consumers spend $8 to $10 billion a year on auto repairs not needed, not done, or improperly done; an estimated $45 billion a year on higher prices caused by monopolistic practices; and $5 to $8 billion a year on higher prices caused by the oil import quotas. On car insurance, consumers collecting for physical injury in 1968 paid $1 billion for coverage duplicating what they already had, such as through hospital insurance. Because of the inefficiency of our present auto insurance system, consumers pay $2.25 for every $1 of insurance benefits. And in credit insurance consumers overpay $216 million a year that goes back to lenders through commissions, rebates, and kickbacks.

Those are a few of the examples Senator Hart offers, and he often indicates the cautious nature of these estimates. Totaling them up, the Senator estimates that "easily 30 percent of all consumer spending is wasted," and it might well be as high as 40 percent. That means we consumers spend $174 to $231 billion a year buying nothing at all of value.

Another area of massive theft and waste through the exercise of corporate power is the defense industry, which thrives on $45 billion a year in military procurement contracts. Cost overruns in defense contracts boggle the mind, with the most celebrated, but not the worst, recent example being the C-5A built by Lockheed. This is the giant transport plane which PR flacks assure us will hold "58 Cadillacs or 100 Volkswagens or 150,000 lemon pies." This behemoth of American technology was originally pegged at a "target cost" of $1.7 billion to build 115 planes; it is now calculated to cost us taxpayers $4.6 billion for 81 of them. The cost overrun is usually figured at $2 billion (of which "less than $200 million can be attributed to inflation"); that's what Air Force procurement analysis expert A. E. Fitzgerald told a congressional committee a little before he was fired in a Pentagon "efficiency step." Actually the difference between $1.7 and $4.6 is $3 billion, not $2 billion, even ignoring the 115 to 81 plane reduction. But we must account for the fact that, according to SEC investigators, Lockheed knowingly lowered its original price below what it knew it could deliver in order to undercut the other bids.[15]

Lockheed's C-5A is just one example of how we finance the padding of the military-industrial complex. One study found that out of thirteen major Air Force and Navy aircraft and missile programs initiated since 1955 and costing $40 billion, less than 40 percent resulted in acceptable electronic performance. Two programs were canceled after $2 billion was paid on them; two others phased out after three years of poor results and a cost of $10 billion; and five others costing $13 billion are operating at "poor performance" levels, or 75 percent of original specifications.[16]

THE LACK OF LEGAL ACCOUNTABILITY FOR CORPORATE POWER

Originally corporations were "agencies of the state"—a private means of carrying out a public end without direct governmental administration. This private government quality of corporations was most obvious with the trading and colonizing companies built on the Dutch East India Company model. The Massachusetts Bay Company, a royally chartered corporation, was the government in northeastern America for many years. Private corporations also performed public functions for the American government during the development of the continent, particularly the railroad companies which the government favored with tax advantages and large land grants; they were given outright a quarter of the states of Minnesota and Washington. Today the most obvious example of a private corporation performing public governmental functions is the congressionally created Communications Satellite Corporation (COMSAT). The defense industry is another example; major private defense companies do 80, 90, and even 100 percent of their business with the Pentagon.[17]

But the law doesn't reflect the public function of corporations; there is no legal theory on which to hold corporations accountable to the public they serve. To understand this rather basic oversight in constitutional and public law, we need to review briefly the position of corporations in the development of American constitutional law.

The Constitution itself is a product of the more conservative, business-oriented leaders of the American Revolution. The men who met in Philadelphia in 1789 included none of the more radical Revolutionary leaders, men like Thomas Paine, Thomas Jefferson, Patrick Henry, or Sam Adams. And many of those leaders had strong objections to the Constitution that was written in their absence. For one thing, the very strong national government, constructed mainly to encourage interstate commerce and thus the growth of business, bothered these civil libertarians. For another, the Constitution prohibited the states from "impairing the obligation of contracts," a clause designed to counteract the "ignoble array of legislative schemes for the defeat of creditors" through which popularly elected state governments tried to help out hard-pressed debtors during the post-Revolution depression. The authors of the Constitution were frankly worried about the political power of such "men without property and principle," as Delaware's John Dickinson called them.[18]

Under Chief Justice John Marshall, the Supreme Court further strengthened the national government, favored the businessman's freedom of contract, and encouraged interstate commerce by striking down attempts of states to regulate business practices. With a few notable exceptions, this trend of decisions continued well into the twentieth century. When business got so big that the national government tried to regulate it, the Court struck down or seriously limited that too. Finally, in 1937, with the nation still struggling to pull itself out of the Depression and with Franklin Roosevelt elected by a landslide mandate for governmental action, the Court began to uphold legislation regulating business practices.[19] If it had not, the resulting chaos might well have led to socialism or fascism.

But we are still stuck today with the curious legal ruling (made in 1886 when it did not seem so curious) that a corporation is to be treated as a "person" under the Fifth and Fourteenth Amendments, which say that government shall not deprive any "person" of "life, liberty, or property, without due process of law." This sounds reasonable enough at first. But what it means today is that General Motors, with almost a fifth of the revenues of the federal government and with 750,000 employees, stands on the same footing before the law as you and I. Consequently, there is no legal way to provide constitutional due process (e.g., right to a hearing, notice of charges, impartial judge, etc.) for people within the corporate structure. The Constitution talks only about guaranteeing due process between government and "persons"; corporations are considered "persons," and the Constitution, not being a biological document, says nothing about due process *within* persons. Obviously the giant corporations are a lot more than individual persons; although they are not exactly states, they do exercise public, political power and do govern masses of people by making decisions that significantly affect people's lives. Law professor Arthur S. Miller would seem to be stating the obvious when he says that "Governing power, wherever located, should be subject to the fundamental constitutional limitation of due process of law."[20] But it isn't, not in America.

Virtually every economist and political scientist recognizes the public nature of large corporations, but constitutional and corporate law does not. The restraints on corporations that have developed come not from legal theory, but from organizing people, and generating political power to win reform through legislation. The most obvious example is labor. The National Labor Relations Act, and subsequent legislation, has provided union members with a certain amount of due process rights within the corporate structure that the Court's interpretation of the Constitution has denied them. Professional employees who are not union members are not so fortunate; David Bazelon put it this way:

> There is more law today running in favor of individual rights in the armed services than there is in any of our major corporate communities. I see no reason why the industrial army should not be at least as democratic as the other one. In fact, there is no good reason in the world why The People should not participate generally in the processes of our private governments.[21]

The reality is that the courts have not recognized the people's right to participate, and the people generally have not organized themselves politically to force recognition of it. There is now much legislation affecting business practices, as discussed below, but none of it establishes or even recognizes the right of corporate constituencies—particularly consumers and the general public—to participate in running our corporations.

Since we still persist in thinking of corporations as private institutions—which the giants clearly are not—there is a lot of private law (as opposed to public, constitutional, government-related law) that affects corporations. Traditionally, private law has worked mostly against the public and in favor of business, such as the tort doctrines of assumption of risk, master-servant rule, and contributory negligence. Though a proxy fight by shareholders to force changes in corporate management is theoretically possible, practically it is impossible, except for a few businessmen holding large blocks of stock. Cumbersome, expensive shareholder suits against corporate management are also acknowledged to be weak weapons.[22] Finally, class action suits by thousands or millions of dissatisfied customers have been severely restricted by court interpretation, a point other chapters discuss at length.

Some argue that private power should not necessarily be subject to legal control by government. Former Chief Justice Earl Warren has said that "Not only does Law in civilized society presuppose ethical commitment; it presupposes the existence of a broad area of human conduct controlled only by ethical norms and not subject to Law at all."[23] Reinhold Niebuhr has added another rationale: "You must allow quasi-sovereignties, whether they are corporations, church, or educational institutions. The more quasi-sovereignties you have, the better protection you have against totalitarianism."

Bazelon replies that "The gain against totalitarianism is certainly lost if the quasi-sovereignty is more authoritarian in nature than the alternative plenary national power." Nevertheless, some distinguished commentators have succumbed to the patently undemocratic (and downright un-American) notion that although authoritarian, such power has a "conscience" of its own, listening to the general "consensus" about how it should operate.[24] If we are to have a democratic society, concentrated economic power has to come under democratic control—perhaps not completely at every turn and with every decision; but in some general, and sometimes very specific, way, there must be some means of assuring that corporate power is accountable to, and therefore really serves, the public it is supposed to serve.

APPROACHES TO CORPORATE ACCOUNTABILITY

Because of the reservoir of popular antibusiness feeling that occasionally erupts with political force in America, the country has a long record of various attempts to curb corporate power. The result has been at least a vast change in business rhetoric. The original let-the-public-be-damned industrial tycoons have given way to today's "corporate statesmen," humbly offering pious public statements. GM Chairman James Roche concluded the company's stormy 1970 annual meeting saying: "We leave this meeting more determined than ever to fulfill our responsibilities. . . ."[25]

There have been some substantive changes, too, over the last century. Corporate tycoons do not operate with the same willful autonomy they once enjoyed. But the following review of the approaches taken to curb corporate power shows that truly accountable corporate power remains an elusive goal.[26] Three general approaches have been tried: antitrust action, general federal regulation through legislation and administrative agencies, and shareholder democracy. Despite the past failures and present obstacles of each approach toward corporate accountability, each also contains future possibilities that hold out some promise.

1. Antitrust Action

Past Record. The Sherman Antitrust Act of 1890 rode into existence on a surge of Populist sentiment in the country that marked the beginning of modern American attempts to regulate business in response to popular demand. The Sherman Act made illegal any contract, combination of businessmen, or conspiracy "in restraint of trade" and any attempt to monopolize interstate commerce. This legislation, still the cornerstone of government antitrust efforts, was a major breakthrough in civilizing business —or so we are to believe. In fact, the act, like most political acts, was much more a response to popular outcry than a substantive reform. One candid senator said at the time that the Sherman Act was simply the result of a political need "to get some bill headed: 'A Bill to Punish Trusts' with which to go to the country."[27]

Whatever potential the act did have for bringing business practices more in line with the public interest was erased by the lack of an adequate enforcement staff to make its provisions a reality. For years, the Justice Department's Antitrust Division staff consisted of five attorneys who were supposed to police the whole economy.[28] In addition, the Supreme Court cut down the act's potential by reading into it the "rule of reason." In the *Standard Oil* case, the Court said in effect that Congress did not really mean it when it said specifically that *"every"* contract, combination, or conspiracy in restraint of trade and *"every"* monopoly or attempt to monopolize was illegal. The Court said that Congress really meant to prohibit only those conspiracies that caused an "unreasonable" or "undue" restraint of trade. In his dissent, Justice Harlan said the Court had "deprived" the Sherman Act "of practical value" given what it was designed to do.[29] In fact, revealing the act's impotence, within a decade of its passage there occurred the greatest merger wave in American industrial history.

"Enforcement" of the Sherman Act has been at least as much of a charade as the initial passage of the act itself. There is, of course, much fanfare about the enforcement which does occur. Antitrust action against those devils—the ruthless, conniving, conspiring eastern captains of industry—became a national religion, and Teddy Roosevelt was its star evangelist, the Billy Graham of "trust-busting." When the Supreme Court upheld the breakup of the Northern Securities Company, the railroad holding company run by such giant bad guys as J. P. Morgan and E. H. Harriman, the first Roosevelt exclaimed that the Northern Securities prosecution showed "in signal fashion" that "the most powerful men in this country were held to accountability before the law." But in fact the great antitrust prosecution did not harm the economic interests of the Morgans and Harrimans, and the concentration of economic power in the hands of a few continued as always, as it has to this day. "The actual result of the antitrust laws," wrote the late Thurman Arnold, who later became a vigorous antitrust prosecutor in the New Deal days, "was to promote the growth of great industrial organizations by deflecting the attack on them into purely moral and ceremonial channels." Arnold saw Theodore Roosevelt as the man "with his big stick that never hit anybody."[30]

Like Roosevelt, Woodrow Wilson also had a popular program against the bad boys of big business, while at the same time relying on eastern businessmen as his most influential advisers and contacts with American society. The Progressive Movement was aimed at correcting some of the more obvious abuses of the system, not at general reform of the whole system; Progressives in power always thought "within a capitalist framework."[31] During the New Deal, antitrust prosecution under Assistant Attorney General Thurman Arnold was much more vigorous by comparison. Rather than conduct a moral crusade hunting for a few egregious offenders, Arnold kept the economic objective of the consumer interest in a revived economy uppermost in his enforcement efforts. But even Arnold undertook "no such general assault on bigness" as Wilson boasted of in his campaign

222 WITH JUSTICE FOR SOMEWITH JUSTICE FOR SOME

rhetoric.* Arnold's main concern, like that of the New Deal generally, was how to get the country back on its feet again economically, not how to make corporate power accountable to the public it serves.

Present Obstacles. The great obstacle to making corporate power accountable to elected political power is two-fold: the private political power corporations exercise behind the scenes, and the lack of public political power of a popular movement to demand such accountability. Present-day antitrust policies are evidence of both obstacles.

Because of the obvious imperatives of technological coordination in a national telephone system, American Telephone and Telegraph is a planned monopoly with its rates and profits regulated by government. But there are no such imperatives in the manufacturing of telephone equipment; there competition could exist, no doubt to the benefit of consumers. But it doesn't. AT&T buys its telephone equipment from its wholly owned subsidiary, Western Electric. This situation is a classic violation of antitrust laws, according to experienced antitrust attorneys. A study made by the Federal Communications Commission that regulates AT&T estimated that Western Electric could cut its prices on telephone equipment sold to AT&T by about 37 percent and still operate at a 6 percent profit. Such a reduction would, of course, also reduce the telephone rates we pay. That study was done in 1939. Ten years later one of the FCC investigators who had moved to the antitrust division of the Justice Department persuaded the department to sue AT&T asking that it be divested of its ownership of Western Electric.[32]

Little happened during the waning years of the Truman Administration, and it fell to the new Republican Attorney General, Herbert Brownell, to do something about the case. Brownell

---

* From 1890 to 1946, 198 defendants were sentenced to prison for violating antitrust laws. Seven of these were businessmen, and until the electrical company price-fixing cases in the early 1960s, no important business executives were imprisoned. Meanwhile, 108 labor union members have been sentenced to prison for violating the Sherman Act. What better proof of our dominating business culture?

asked AT&T's vice-president and general counsel, T. Brooke Price, to visit him at his vacation retreat at the Greenbriar Hotel in White Sulphur Springs, West Virginia; in the resulting discussion of the case, Brownell's main concern, according to Price's memo on the meeting, was that "A way ought to be found to get rid of the case . . . he thought we could readily find practices that we might agree to have enjoined with no real injury to our business."

There were a number of other such cozy meetings of the minds between government and business in the case. Brownell came to the Washington hotel room of AT&T officials to talk. His assistant, Edward Foote, had Price out to dinner in his Washington home during which he told Price he thought the government's case was weak and it would be "silly" to bring it to trial. Later, Foote met another AT&T official while on vacation in Boca Grande, Florida; the official flew there specifically to see Foote and iron out some of the details of the pending settlement of the case. The consent decree that resulted did not require AT&T to divest itself of Western Electric, which was the main idea of the suit in the first place. Several attorneys in the antitrust division objected to the consent decree; one, Victor Kramer, who had supervision over the case, refused to sign the decree, saying it was inconsistent with his oath of office to uphold the laws of the United States, in particular the law known as the Sherman Antitrust Act. Frederick Kappel, then head of Western Electric and later AT&T, suggested, according to Goulden's book on AT&T, that Western Electric officials "[u]se discretion . . . [d]on't brag about having won victory or getting everything we wanted. . . . Antitrust suit disposed of, but still have politicians, etc., to think of."

New York's crusty public-spirited Congressman Emanuel Celler had his antitrust subcommittee conduct an extensive study of the Justice Department's consent decree program, particularly the AT&T consent decree. After months of research and testimony, Celler's committee report sharply criticized Attorney General Brownell for having shown "partiality toward the defendants incompatible with the duties of his public office." It said that "giving his adversary 'a friendly tip'" which is how Price characterized his West Virginia tete-a-tete with the Attorney General was "hardly in keeping with the ethics of the legal profession" and with the lawyer's obligation to maintain our adversary system of justice.

The fact that it took an extensive congressional investigation with the power of subpoena to uncover this pattern of events is as important as the events themselves. Who knows how much more we could learn about the behind-the-scenes ways of corporate power and the illicit collusion between government and business which leads consumers to lose out? It would be nice, for example, if Congressman Celler could renew his investigation to interview the antitrust division personnel who anonymously tell of the repeated and frustrated attempts to re-open the AT&T Western Electric case during the Kennedy and Johnson Administrations of the 1960s. At least twice the Assistant Attorney General for antitrust approved staff recommendations to re-open the case, and twice the forwarded recommendation for legal action got lost in the higher circles of political decision-making.

There are other examples of political influence frustrating antitrust enforcement. In the Penn Central merger case of the late 1960s, the Antitrust Division vigorously opposed the merger in hearings before the Interstate Commerce Commission and the three-judge U.S. District Court. When it got to the Supreme Court, the Justice Department capitulated; Antitrust Division personnel understood that the sudden change of tune was the result of an earlier political understanding between Robert Kennedy and Stuart Saunders, then head of the Pennsylvania Railroad. And frustrated staff recommendations in 1964 to prosecute the National Farmer's Organization (NFO) over withholding livestock from the market, along with the division's complete capitulation in a 1967 suit that was begun against NFO on milk price-fixing, were commonly understood at the division to be the result of the case being too sensitive a "political football."[33]

The automobile industry, which is the American industry most dominated by giant corporations, is also the best example of frustrated antitrust enforcement. In 1961, a team of antitrust lawyers began a five-year study of General Motors. The resulting complaint alleged that of over one hundred mergers and acquisitions that built GM into the behemoth that it is today, more than forty of them were illegal restraints of trade under the antitrust laws. The draft complaint called for the breakup of the company by court order; it was leaked to the press in 1967, probably by a frustrated Justice Department lawyer. At the time, the 1968 elections, in which President Johnson was assumed to be running for re-election, were approaching. The *Wall Street Journal* cited the political risks LBJ would run of losing business support if he approved the suit. It quoted one antitrust lawyer's prediction that "the GM suit will be brought only if Johnson feels his closeness to business has become a political liability in an election year."[34] No suit was ever brought, disappearing behind executive secrecy somewhere between the Antitrust Division and the White House. No public explanation has ever been offered.

GM has had some minor antitrust suits brought against it over the last decade calling for divestiture of its locomotive, bulldozer, and bus manufacturing operations. They were all dropped or settled out of court without requiring divestiture.[35] In addition, in early 1968, a Los Angeles grand jury concluded an eighteen-month investigation with the recommendation that all the major car companies be criminally indicted for conspiring to restrain the development and marketing of antipollution devices, a conspiracy in the absence of which, the L.A. County Board of Supervisors suggested, air pollution due to cars in the Los Angeles area "would have ceased to be a problem in 1966."[36] The Justice Department rejected the grand jury's recommendation for criminal indictments; the grand jury almost brought them anyway, but was persuaded not to by the Antitrust Division lawyer who had worked with it. A year later, after the 1968 elections and just ten days before Johnson left office, the department brought a civil suit against the car companies instead. Over the protestations of twenty congressmen and the legal officers of half a dozen cities and states, the new Republican Administration settled the case out of court in September, 1969, with a consent decree in which the car companies, in effect, refused to admit they did anything wrong and then promised never to do it again. Finally, in December, 1970, Ralph Nader revealed that of eleven division attorneys who studied the GM monopoly problem between 1966 and 1970, *all eleven* urged some form of antimonopoly relief. The list includes Donald Turner, former head of the antitrust division, who, a month after he had left his official post and while a consultant to the agency, recommended that GM be split into three and Ford into two parts. No action has been taken on any of the recommendations.

Meanwhile, GM continues to control over half the car industry, Ford about another 30 percent of it,[37] and the antitrust laws remain unused as a tool to restructure the American economy and begin to make those who run it accountable to the public it serves. Galbraith echoed Thurman Arnold's charge of thirty years ago when he said in a 1967 congressional hearing that antitrust efforts to deal with the structure of the economy are a "charade" because they "legitimize the real exercise of market power on the part of the large firms by rather diligent harassment of those who have less of it."[38]

Harvard law professor Donald Turner, who ran the Antitrust Division under LBJ, has long advocated strengthening the antitrust laws to facilitate breaking up existing monopolies and oligopolies (which are near-monopolies, like the car companies). While still in office as Assistant Attorney General, Turner admitted at a congressional hearing, "I suppose it is highly likely that if I sent such a proposal forward to the Administration, it would not be rushed over to the (Capitol) Hill the following morning." At the hearing, run as a seminar discussion, Galbraith kept insisting that there was politically no chance the giants of industry would be broken up by antitrust enforcement. In a later speech, referring to the unrefuted Galbraith charge, Turner simply referred to the clear "inadequacy of antitrust in dealing with monopoly and oligopoly—whatever the reasons may be. . . ."[39] Senator Russell Long suggested a reason during the congressional panel discussion:

> . . . Something which is wrong continues to get worse and worse until the public becomes aware of it, and it continues

to get worse still until everybody becomes so outraged about
the matter that something has to happen and then Congress
has to pass a law. . . .

But as far as moving against one of these major companies goes, I agree that there is no prospect of it until the
public becomes upset, enraged and aroused about it—and
then you cannot justify voting any other way.[40]

Future Possibilities. Senator Long, who is the kingpin for the oil
industry's lobby in Congress, should know about the exercise of
corporate power. The senator also comes from a famous Louisiana political family with a definite populist flavor in its past.
Clearly, if antitrust is to be a meaningful approach to making
corporate power accountable, it will come only with a strong,
concerted populist-type push from the public.

While we're waiting for such a movement, or nurturing it,
there are things we can do. Even vigorously employed, antitrust
would be an imperfect tool for bringing about corporate accountability. It is aimed at business practices which restrain
trade, not business practices generally, such as deception, corruption, or dangerous products. Nor does antitrust deal directly
with questions of control of corporate decisions through directors, management, and the corporate structure generally. Though
antitrust enforcement could, after a mammoth legal battle, restructure the American economy, debate rages as to how much
bigness is necessary to maintain the present high level of consumer production and technological innovation in American
industry. But then, as discussed below, there is the value question of whether we desire or can afford to maintain that size
level. Antitrust cannot find ways for the American public to be
involved in such value decisions.

Still, if antitrust can't do everything, it can do a lot to help
bring corporate power under control. While we build a movement to prod the Justice Department's Antitrust Division by
petitioning Congressmen and through the work of public interest
advocacy groups in Washington—there are other points of pressure. Antitrust works on a strange theory of enforcement of public laws; it relies mostly on private parties to bring suits which

228 WITH JUSTICE FOR SOME

get treble damages under the antitrust laws as the main sanction to deter corporate offenders. This is largely due to the small staff of the Antitrust Division, which, even if its priorities were appropriate to the task, could not compel corporate accountability to the public. The lack of resources is due mainly to the determined hostility of New York Congressman John Rooney, chairman of the House Appropriations Subcommittee, in charge of the Antitrust Division budget.

Without private treble damage suits, the deterrent of the public law is piddling. Lee Loevinger, chief of the Antitrust Division during the 1961 electric company price-fixing cases, said that the $430 thousand in fines GE paid was for GE "no more severe than a $3 ticket for overtime parking for a man with a $15,000 income."[41] The maximum penalty for antitrust violations was raised from $5 thousand to $50 thousand in 1955; it will soon be raised to $500 thousand. Today, that is about .1 percent of the net income of any of the country's 500 largest corporations. Thus, how much will a corporate executive considering committing an antitrust violation that would increase his company's income by 2 percent (or $1 million) think about the deterrence of the law, with its $500 thousand fine? The conspiring companies did pay $500 million in private damage settlements. Half of that was written off through a special tax ruling in which the Internal Revenue Service determined that such payments, stemming from criminal conviction for antitrust violations, were a "necessary business expense." But even GE will think twice about shelling out $250 million, so there is still some deterrent left in private treble damage suits.

Private suits brought as class actions are particularly potent weapons, because covering a whole class of consumers, the damages sought are much greater. With the growth of consumer awareness, such suits are now expanding to include as plaintiffs not just the usual business competitors, suppliers, and purchasers who are injured by the conspiracy in restraint of trade, but also consumers, state and city governments, and other public agencies who have suffered. One example is the recent Pfizer drug price-fixing case settlement for $100 million, mentioned in Beverley Moore's chapter on public interest law firms. Another is the ruling by a U.S. District Judge in Los Angeles that claims against the car companies for their alleged anti-pollution device conspiracy could be made not just by those damaged through a "commercial relationship," as the companies urged in legal arguments, but also by local governments and the general public.[42] If such cases succeed, huge settlement payments and an effective deterrent would be generated not just by other aggrieved businessmen but by the public at large. That would certainly be a significant step toward public corporate accountability.

2. Federal Regulation

Federal "interference" or "regulation" or "underwriting" of business, depending upon your point of view, has gone far beyond the confines of antitrust into the miasma of legislation that established regulation over certain industry practices. In what is called the "fourth branch" of government, Washington has six major "independent regulatory agencies"—the Interstate Commerce Commission (ICC), the Federal Trade Commission (FTC), the Federal Communications Commission (FCC), the Federal Power Commission (FPC), the Civil Aeronautics Board (CAB), and the Securities Exchange Commission (SEC).

The degree to which they defend the public interest against corporate malevolence, and the extent to which they have been captured by those they supposedly regulate, is considered in necessary detail in Robert Fellmeth's chapter on *The Regulatory-Industrial Complex*. Through the mechanisms of job interchange, preferential access, control over appointments, and a general *simpatico* between regulator and regulated, industry has not been compelled to be any more responsive to the public interest than before the agencies were created. In fact, if anything, the situation has worsened, since the agencies often *protect* monopoly profits and corporate practices from public scrutiny. Fellmeth also suggests ways of improving federal regulation, which, if implemented, might make it a meaningful approach to corporate accountability.

The work of critics like Nader, Senator Nelson and Congressman Rosenthal, now ex-FTC Commissioner Philip Elman and

FCC Commissioner Nicholas Johnson also document the emergence of this updated power elite, until—as in the last sentence of Orwell's *Animal Farm*—you can look at the regulators and then at the regulated and not tell any difference between them.

3. *Shareholder Democracy*

"Shareholder democracy" is an attempt to achieve accountability, not through the outside force of government, but by action inside the corporate structure. It is an attempt to curb the extremely broad discretion and broad social decision-making power of corporate management, which is largely unrestrained by government regulations or economic conditions. With the large corporations, it is now corporate power that controls the market, not the reverse.

Past Record. The concept of "shareholder" or "corporate" democracy—namely, that shareholder votes control corporations just as citizen votes control governments—is coupled with the idea promoted by the New York Stock Exchange called "people's capitalism"—namely, that vast multitudes of Americans, not just the robber barons of old, own stock and participate in the network of corporate democracies. One corporate manager, Paul Gaddis, has described the shareholder as "the agent of legitimacy for management," and the larger the number of shareholders in the country, the stronger is "the anchor to legitimacy." Two pages later, he says that "the idea of shareholder control" is "probably always a delusion."[43]

So was "people's capitalism." It is true that stock ownership has greatly dispersed since the early days when one or two or a handful of businessmen owned large blocks of stock through which they controlled their corporations. There are now over thirty million Americans who own stock, over one-tenth of the population; but the vast majority of them own only a few shares or only a small part of any company. You may "own" a tiny bit of something, but it doesn't mean you "control" your "property" in any way—all it means is you get a check every quarter. One study done in 1953 found that 80 percent of all personally held stock was in the hands of 1.6 percent of the adult population.[44] The non-personally held stock is in the hands of investment institutions run by pension fund managers and others. They do not exactly represent "people's capitalism" either.

Nor does shareholder democracy exist. For one thing, all shareholders can really do is vote out one set of directors and vote in another—which they never do (except occasionally in large blocks of shares or in very small companies). The Board of Directors nominates its slate of new directors, and shareholders can only vote that slate up or down. Our "shareholder democracy" is very much like political elections in the Soviet Union: there are no opposition candidates. This state of affairs has been brought about by the diffusion of ownership of the large American corporations.* When companies used to be owned by a few people, it was different: they also controlled the companies. There was "shareholder democracy" then, but the shareholders were a few men with names like Gould and Rockefeller and Vanderbilt. With the diffusion of ownership to many people, as Berle and Means pointed out in their classic study in the thirties, there resulted a divorce of ownership from control, and it no longer meant anything in the classic capitalist sense to "own" a few shares of stock—you did not control anything through them.

A lot of people take—or used to take—the idea of shareholder democracy very seriously. One result was elaborate regulation by the SEC of shareholder voting by proxy, to try to give shareholders a fair chance to vote on company resolutions and directors. For example, management must file with the SEC its proxy statement, which it sends out every year to all shareholders, containing the resolutions to be voted on at the annual meeting. Most shareholders just send in their proxy, voting with manage-

---

* Thus, the twin ideals of "people's capitalism," proclaimed by the New York Stock Exchange, and "shareholder democracy," proclaimed by the SEC and the corporations are antithetical. The more diffusion of ownership (or "people's capitalism") you have, the less shareholder control, and vice versa.

ment and never make it to the annual meeting, which Galbraith calls perhaps "our most elaborate exercise in popular illusion."[45] * A shareholder can, with difficulty, get a proposal of his own put on the proxy statement for shareholder vote, but except for a handful of corporate democracy crusaders, almost no one bothers. As Bazelon points out, perhaps the perfect puncture of the corporate democracy myth is the fact that shareholder democracy "would hardly exist at all apart from the efforts of a handful of individuals." Then he cites figures: in 1956, out of two thousand proxy statements filed with the SEC, only 3 percent contained shareholder proposals (which was supposed to be a big reason for the SEC regulation). And of those 102 shareholder proposals, 78 were sponsored by the two Gilbert brothers and John Campbell Heinz, who are the major perennial meeting-going advocates of corporate democracy.[46] The fantasy of shareholder democracy is even more widely debunked and ridiculed than the myths of antitrust enforcement and government regulation by administrative agency.

Present Obstacles. The annual corporate meeting time, Spring, 1970, was the spring of popular discontent. The new left in several cities launched attacks on a number of the country's major corporations, including AT&T, GM, Gulf Oil, GE, Honeywell, Boeing, United Aircraft, and Commonwealth Edison of Chicago. The attack consisted of conducting muckraking research projects on corporations, demonstrating and getting into annual meetings to discuss corporate policies on issues like pollution, war products, and employment discrimination. AT&T demonstrators, three thousand strong, were driven back by mounted police in Cleveland; Honeywell demonstrators, fifteen hundred of them, were maced in Minneapolis; and United Aircraft demonstrators were arrested in Hartford. It is not clear just what specific changes in corporate policies the demonstrations

---

* Because of the danger of disruption, the GE chairman said at the 1970 meeting, as reported in the Chicago Tribune, that "management has taken the precaution of voting previously so that business will have been totally conducted."

caused, if any; but they did make a lot of corporate executives very nervous and much more attentive to defending their corporation's practices as they affect society. They never had to do that much before; in the past it was always just profits and losses at annual meetings.[47]

One of the spring offensives was particularly well-organized and methodical. There were no demonstrations at the GM annual meeting in Detroit; and the Campaign to Make GM Responsible worked entirely within the system—as we are forever told to do—to bring about change. It did not do any better than the demonstrators. Of course the four young lawyers who work for the Project on Corporate Responsibility, which ran Campaign GM and which controls 12 out of GM's 287 million shares, never expected to win. They hoped rather, as Ralph Nader said in announcing the Campaign, to "highlight the fiction of shareholder democracy." In 1971, a better organized Campaign GM—Round II—carried on that effort.

Campaign GM is a good example of the insurmountable obstacles to establishing shareholder democracy in our widely held major corporations today. The inflexible tenacity with which GM fought the campaign (based, to repeat, on 12 out of 287 million shares) is itself instructive. The first thing GM did was to present elaborate legal arguments to the SEC as to why none of the Campaign's proposed resolutions should even be *presented* for a vote at the annual meeting or in proxy material. The Campaign's three major resolutions were, first, to establish a special shareholder's committee chosen by management, the UAW union, and the Campaign, to do a year's study of GM's social impact and decision-making process; second, to expand the company's twenty-five–man board to include three new members representing the public interest; and third, to amend the corporate charter to include specific prohibition of any act detrimental to public health, safety, and welfare, or of any violation of federal and state law. The Campaign had six other resolutions calling for action by GM on auto safety, new car warranties, anti-pollution research, support for mass transit, plant safety, and more new car dealerships for blacks.

The SEC ruled against GM and ordered them to include the Campaign's first two resolutions in their proxy statement to all shareholders. But it still did not give them a chance to win a shareholder's vote. For one thing, GM could argue at length against the Campaign's proposals in the proxy statement, while the Campaign was limited to only one hundred words in their favor. And management can be pretty persuasive in telling you it knows best; in fact, GM has not lost a shareholder vote in a quarter century. Campaign GM sent out its own proxy statement with longer versions of its views to two thousand institutions which it *thought* owned GM stock. (Most GM shareholders are individuals with small holdings, 79 percent owning one hundred shares or less; institutions account for only 12 percent of the shareholders.) But there was no way the Campaign could reach all 1.3 million GM shareholders: first, it didn't have the list and couldn't get it from GM; second, it didn't have the money for such a mailing, and couldn't get that from GM either.[48]

But GM was not taking any chances. It included in its proxy statement mailing a special twenty-one–page pamphlet on "GM's Record of Progress," which cost $81 thousand in additional postage alone. Then GM printed full-page ads on its anti-pollution record in 148 newspapers around the country, which a leading national newspaper ad man says cost about $300 thousand. GM also went after votes as if it were a real political campaign with the outcome hanging in the balance. It told the treasurer at Syracuse University, which holds a few thousand shares, that it was going to contact all the university's trustees, according to the Campaign. It also lobbied vigorously with banks in New York and Philadelphia, one of which showed slight signs of wavering, but then saw the light. At the annual meeting in Detroit on May 22, Campaign GM got six million votes for its resolution, or 2½ percent of the total vote; management had 237 million votes on its side.[49]

The outcome really was never in doubt; the only interesting speculation was how much worry the Campaign would cause in Detroit. Meanwhile, the myth goes on. In introducing the special GM progress pamphlet, Chairman James Roche wrote to the 1.3 million shareholders, "If you have any questions, I hope you will write to me." He doesn't really hope that; anyway, he won't know if they do write, unless he sees the mountain of 1.3 million letters in the warehouse. The GM chairman also writes to any shareholder who sells his stock, asking him to reply by letter if the sale of the stock has been related to "any aspect of the corporation's policies or operations."[50] It would almost have to be so related. Does the chairman really want to hear from all the *former* shareholders as well? How would he really enjoy such a mail-in?

Future Possibilities. Even in the shareholder democracy approach to corporate accountability, there are significant possibilities for changing, or at least exposing, the system. The SEC's order of GM to include Campaign GM's resolutions in its proxy statement and the U.S. Court of Appeals for the District of Columbia's decision in the Dow Chemical case[51] suggest that the SEC's proxy rules may be of increasing value in promoting significant shareholder challenges, at least symbolic ones, to corporate power. We may never see such a challenge actually defeat management in a shareholder vote, but you don't necessarily have to win a vote to win a victory. Management can be embarrassed into action by unfavorable publicity, while still having all the votes it needs. That has happened with the Rochester companies of Xerox and Kodak, which have taken on substantial job training programs for minorities due to the public pressure—such as the pressure at Kodak's 1967 annual meeting, brought by FIGHT, the Rochester black activist group which Saul Alinsky helped organize. GM, while denying the need for reform, has also made some changes. At respectable distances between the active phases of Round I and Round II of Campaign GM, GM appointed a black director, a "public policy committee" to advise the company on public issues, and a vice-president to run a new department on environmental problems.

Exposure of how the system actually works is a prerequisite to building the political power to change it. Thus Nader suggests that projects such as Campaign GM and Alinsky's new "Proxies for People" movement "are never going to be successful in a 51 percent manner" and should not be judged that way. The value of Campaign GM is that it

> . . . forced a corporation such as General Motors to look out at its support structure—the banks, colleges and others who hold large blocks of its stock—for the first time. It required General Motors to surface and use its power.

Alinsky has a dream of one day filling Yankee Stadium with thousands of shareholders of a major corporation, having them thunderously vote "yes" on a proposal, only to have the chairman announce that management votes "no" with its 90 percent of the votes in proxy returns; the thousands in the stands therefore lose. "I'd just love to see that happen," says Alinsky; "I'd like to see him try to call 80,000 people out of order."[52] This tactic assumes the Alinskys and Naders can get a strong enough movement organized before the corporate managers catch on and make more moderate changes to head off such dramatic exposure. Reform is always a race between the exposers and the farsighted establishment. Nothing helps reform so much as a good, obvious shortsighted enemy for an organizing target.

Exposure is contagious too. While Campaign GM was finding out and educating people about how GM works, it also revealed how other institutions worked in conjunction with GM. Campaign GM was asking GM to exercise its public responsibilities, and it was also asking shareholders to exercise their responsibilities as owners. It turned out many did not want to, showing that even many shareholders did not like shareholder democracy. At Harvard University, a majority of students, faculty, and alumni favored Campaign GM's resolutions; but the Harvard administration voted for the GM management. Harvard's noted Nobel laureate Dr. George Wald had always objected to the radical student view that Harvard was "just another part of the power structure." When the GM-Harvard relationship emerged, he called it "a slap in the eye for all of us, . . . expos[ing] an entirely unrealized degree of complicity."[53]

There remains the question of whether shareholder democracy—or rather shareholder influence on corporate action—is a good thing even if feasible. Viewing shareholders as part of the general public, which is the real corporate constituency to which corporations must be made to answer—shareholder influence is a worthwhile approach. When viewed in the narrower sense— simply as an attempt to get shareholders to exert their powers of ownership over corporate management—the approach raises serious questions about its validity, or at least its priority compared to the major task of corporate accountability to the public. Abram Chayes points out that if corporate power, like other governing power, is to operate with the consent of the governed, the shareholder is really not the true class of the governed that we need be most concerned about. In fact in a sense he is *least* subject to corporate power, because all he has to do to escape it, *qua* shareholder, is sell his stock.[54] The shareholder as public citizen will remain just as subject to corporate pollution as the rest of us, but he is no longer part of the corporation's shareholder constituency. It is the corporation's constituency of the general public that cannot escape. What we need is not shareholder accountability, but public accountability. To the extent that the shareholder democracy approach confuses that distinction, it hides the real issue and is harmful. To the extent that it understands that distinction and comes out on the public side of it, it is helpful.

CONCLUSION

In his famous 1962 Yale Commencement speech, President Kennedy pleaded for a clearing away of the old ideological rifts and devil theory myths that have dominated economic thought in the past. He said that the key problems of the economy now were not social and political, but the technical and managerial. It was a stirring speech, eloquently delivered. But today, a decade later, the opposite is true. Though there are plenty of technical and managerial problems left to solve, the key problems of our economy now are social and political.

We know the American corporate structure is technically capable of producing an unparalleled glut of goods and services; it has done precisely that and has made us the richest country in human history. The critical examination of corporations and the search for corporate accountability go on not because of technical failing, but because of the social crisis—because we now face at once a productive economy and a sick society.

To meet this crisis, we have two tasks before us, both already begun but far from finished: the tasks of questioning values and organizing for power.

Questioning Values

An economy should be judged by what it adds to the wealth of a nation, and to the wealth of nations. Beyond that goal, judgment should measure its effect on men, on politics, and on culture of the society.

That is a good statement of the conventional view, made by Eugene Rostow in 1959.[55] Today, the signs all about us indicate that such a view is seriously in question, particularly among the younger generation. This developing "counter-culture," as Theodore Roszak calls it, agrees with R. H. Tawney, who wrote in 1920 that we must place economic activity in "its proper place as the servant, not the master, of society."[56] An economy can no longer be judged by its wealth, but must be measured by its effect on men, politics, and values. Such considerations are now primary, not secondary as Rostow suggests. There are areas of the country, and many in the world, where there is little wealth, and the economy and psychology of scarcity still operate. Some parts of the counter-culture feel passionate concern for such problems, but generally in America we have an economy not of scarcity but of abundance. Many raise questions about the unhealthy passivism that our emphasis on the consumption encourages and the undue sense of power and potency which comes from material acquisitiveness.[57]

But even assuming our American way of life is healthy for us as individuals, there is serious question whether we can afford to maintain it. Certainly if the present unequal distribution of it continues apace, the country is likely to be in shambles from internal strife. From a world view, the question is even more critical. The United States makes up 6 percent of the world's population, and every year it consumes about 60 percent of the world's consumable resources.[58] It is not possible—either ecologically or, as more of the world awakes to such facts, politically—for such a situation to continue indefinitely, or even for very long. But if the American economy is to continue expanding, as economists thinking only of economic facts say it must, then such an imbalance will have to continue, and even increase.

Finally, assuming our economy is good for man individually and politically, there is serious doubt about whether we can afford to maintain it ecologically. The summertime city suffocations from lingering pollution air pockets bring the imminence of the ecological crisis home as well as any alarming warnings from ecologists. But changes in the economy radical enough to save the ecology of the country will require much more than technical and managerial or even political measures. Behind the economist's worship of an expanding G.N.P., demand-creating advertising, and social status through material possession lie basic cultural Western beliefs of man's dominance over nature. Theologians have pointed to the command of Genesis for man to be "fruitful and multiply, and fill the earth and subdue it, and have dominion over the fish of the sea and over the birds of the air and over every living thing that moves upon the earth."[59]

But Christianity (as compared to Eastern religions' great respect for nature) is not the only Western belief at the root of the problem. There are many non-religious capitalists loose in the land, ravaging it like good Christians. Bethlehem Steel, through a subsidiary called Beth-Elkhorn, is strip-mining the Kentucky hills bare. Said one strip mining supporter, "I don't believe God would have put all this coal here if he hadn't intended for it to be taken out." Bethlehem has already mined millions of tons of coal, but their man in eastern Kentucky gave a straight capitalist reply to the suggestion of conservationists that the company should be satisfied; he told a reporter in amazement, "You can't just walk away from ten million tons of high-grade metallurgical coal." In announcing the company's strip mining plans, the Bethlehem man said, "If there's something wrong with my company, there's something wrong with the country."[60] It's not just the company or the country or Christianity or capitalism; it's the whole Western culture. When it comes to industrial irreverence for nature, Marxism is no better. The key problems of the economy, then, are neither technical and managerial nor political in the sense of the old ideological quarrels that President Kennedy wanted to cast aside; the key problem is broader still: it is cultural.

Thus, as often happens, the debate is on two levels, and those on the superficial level cannot understand why those on the deeper level are not satisfied. It is like the debate over Vietnam. President Nixon says he is taking the ground troops out, but his most searching critics want to know not just about ground troops, but also about general military and economic support for undemocratic countries around the world, about the dominance of military-industrial power at home, and about domestic priorities. So, too, when the corporations talk about anti-pollution devices and equal employment plans, that is fine as far as it goes. But on questions of whether such headlong consumption is psychologically healthy or politically wise or ecologically possible to continue—on such basic questions the corporations are resoundingly silent.

Organizing for Power

Beyond blind rejection, the corporations are silent on another matter too: restructuring the economy and society for public participation in running corporate America. The Harvard treasurer said that Campaign GM, mild as it was, represented the "entering wedge" to a complete change of American business. GM Chairman James Roche called it a way of challenging "the entire system of corporate management in the United States."[61] If so, the corporations have brought it on themselves by their unresponsiveness to suggestions for change and their silence in the face of the great issues facing our society and, in fact, our civilization. If they will not change, will not bend, will not even talk or listen, there is only one way to move them: organize the political power that forces change.

We have never really had the kind of sustained public consumer movement necessary to force a restructuring of the whole system. The Populist movement was too shallow: in the economic field, it chased a lot of foreign Eastern devils and thought it got them, but didn't. It won more respectability than accountability for big business. The Progressive movement was more thought out, but in practical politics it resulted only in correcting the worst abuses, while leaving the general system of unaccountable corporate power intact. The New Deal was broader; it went beyond chasing devils and the most blatant abuses, but its goal was economic recovery (along with what reform was necessary for recovery), not a restructuring that would provide public corporate accountability. The New Deal was also a reform from the top brain trust down, not from a popular consumer movement up. It never cared about forming such a movement, and never did form one.[62] FDR's political magic was enough to sustain it.

The kind of movement we need is not a new idea. The Progressive thinker Herbert Croly suggested it when he spoke of the need for the individuals who make up the public to join together in a counter-organization with enough strength to stand up to the other massive organizations that dominate modern life, those of government, business, and labor. Galbraith suggested it with his theory of countervailing power.[63]

Ideas of how to carry out a reconstruction of the system are not lacking, and more would be forthcoming if we had the kind of political movement necessary to enact them. Without such a movement, no idea is worth trying and all are just dreams. Our past attempts in providing some corporate accountability, abortive as they have been, contain basic concepts on which to build a program of reconstruction: the concepts that at some point, somewhere, a corporation can get too big, too powerful, and too monopolistic for the public good; that government, with enough public power behind it, can and should regulate business for the public good; and that shareholders, as part of the general public, might be able to influence corporate conduct, or at least expose its current undemocratic management.

At the first level of corporate accountability, that of shareholders, Georgetown law professor Donald Schwartz, who served as counsel to Campaign GM, has suggested a variety of ways shareholders could take advantage of improved proxy rules, develop corporate monitoring procedures, nominate directors, and elect directors as representatives of the public.[64] Campaign GM coordinator Philip Moore thinks about involving the public in corporate decision-making not just in the narrow ways that the consumer is the supposed "invisible hand" guiding corporate decisions, the labor union simply the occasional collective bargaining agent, and the shareholder the much revered and much ignored phantom "owner." Moore thinks about giving the public control, or at least very substantial influence, at every point where the corporation has contact with the public. The incisive English economist R. H. Tawney had very similar ideas when he wrote a half century ago that "proprietary rights" should be "maintained when they are accompanied by the performance of service and abolished when they are not," and that "producers" should "stand in a direct relation to the community for whom production is carried on, so that their responsibility to it may be obvious and unmistakable, not lost, as at present, through their immediate subordination to shareholders whose interest is not service but gain."[65]

That "direct relation" can take many forms. In some cases, it might be public ownership like the Tennessee Valley Authority, only with meaningful community participation or control as well. In some cases it might be nationalization, only again not in the sterile form done elsewhere where the managerial control of the technocrats has not lessened. And we should be open about what we are doing, as Galbraith has said: "The Democratic Party must henceforth use the word socialism. It describes what is needed. If there is assumed to be something illicit or indecent about public ownership, it won't be done well."[66] Increasingly, there is talk about experimenting with the "worker's control" model from Yugoslavia. Says the director of the Honeywell Project, "We want control of the corporate power to pass from the board to the employees and the representatives of the community."[67]

With the existence of such an efficient movement, even the problem of corporate social responsibility could resolve itself.

With corporations accountable to outside public forces concerned about the public good—concerned about, as Tawney says, service instead of gain—corporate executives can go on acting simply in their own interests, as the conservatives so desperately want them to do, only their own interests will be not to antagonize this constituency who demand more equitable corporate policies, with the sanction being loss of customers. At this point Friedman approaches Galbraith, for even the former has admitted that the corporation should engage in public service work and follow public-spirited policies *if* it is in their long run interest to do so. A militant constituency can make this so.

Perhaps it is all too good to be possible. But there have been mass popular movements in America in the past that have faced down corporate power, at least on some level. Those movements were far from complete successes, but surely we can learn from them and build on their legacy. Nor is the current racial and generational strife necessarily an unsurmountable obstacle. What this country needs is a genuine Populist, not the bogus, divisive shouters like Agnew and Wallace with their occasional Populist tinges.[68] Perhaps before long, the black movement will understand that the government as presently formed cannot do what must be done, and that business will not do it, and that those two facts are related: because business, the dominant culture caught in its own narrow ideological prison, will not, therefore government cannot. For as the socialist Michael Harrington writes, "to take office is not to take power, particularly in a capitalist society where so much power lies beyond the reach of the electorate."[69]

An American electorate that learns that lesson about the relative strength of corporate and electoral power will become very aroused. That is the lesson Ralph Nader's investigators, with their muckraking reports, aim to teach; it is the truth the radical black and white movements already understand, and the environmental one is moving toward; it is Justice Douglas's point when he says that the establishment today is our George III; it is the organizing point Saul Alinsky hopes to activate middle class whites around. There is a common ground that unites all these people and movements; maybe, with luck, we can find it.

The Regulatory-Industrial Complex

ROBERT C. FELLMETH*

What is essentially happening to America is the collusion of the two great forces in our society: government and industry. The removal of any mutual check results in a single, monolithic power bloc, behind which internal secrecy and vigorous public relations can cloak corruption and favoritism, incompetence and failure.

The original American idea was to create a government responsive to general public needs and to regulate economic forces where necessary in the public interest. American government chose minimal direct regulation, opting for the use of self-governing systems through laws changing financial or legal relationships between groups. Bureaucracy was minimal and the market system was used to allocate resources according to mechanisms automatically responsive to the public will. Reasonably simple laws and types of grievances, and a legal arena accessible to those victimized by the occasional swindler, sufficed.

But as industry grew in size and power and impact, important changes occurred. Many self-regulating systems began to break down. Railroads and oil companies, initially, then other industries, began to obtain and exercise monopoly power beyond the scope of any market check. These problems proliferated as gov-

---

* Robert Fellmeth graduated from Harvard Law School in 1970 and is working as an aide to Ralph Nader. He has co-authored two books on government agencies: *The Nader Report on the Federal Trade Commission,* and *The Interstate Commerce Omission,* and is currently working on a book on land management in California.

ernment-granted monopolies, from patent protection to utility monopoly, became increasingly prevalent. Corporations began to circumvent market checks en masse by organizing themselves into industry-wide trade associations. The associations fomented industry-wide collusion on higher prices and on limiting the characteristics of products for more sales. Illegal tie-ins, price discrimination, and other anti-competitive patterns became widespread.

Meanwhile, other processes, accelerated by increasing economic concentration, were creating more difficulties for the self-regulating systems. For example, the advance of science and technology meant a glut of new and untried drugs and food substances which could be marketed at great speed and at great profit without opportunity for consumer response to dangers or fraud. Communications advances have facilitated mass, immediate marketing of useless or dangerous goods and items. Those products which posed hidden, gradual, cumulative threats to health (e.g., from radiation, cancer related additives) were particularly free from market control. And more recently, the pollutive by-products of a growing industrial complex pose a danger as external costs are created, which the basic free enterprise system does not assess, and are borne by society.

In all of these areas, and in others, the public has cried out for action. Government responded by creating regulatory bodies with quasi-judicial, legislative, and executive powers to supervise areas of the economy where self-regulating systems had been undermined. Such a response, in lieu of re-arranging basic legal or financial relationships, was often unimaginative, but in some cases there was little apparent recourse. Legislation established the Interstate Commerce Commission, the Food and Drug Administration, the Federal Trade Commission, the Civil Aeronautics Board, the Atomic Energy Commission, the Securities and Exchange Commission, and many others on the federal and state levels.

An early reaction of the regulatory-industrial complex to itself is best illustrated in the advice given by the Attorney General of the United States in 1892, Richard Olney, to a railroad executive who suggested that the five-year-old Interstate Commerce Commission be abolished:

> The Commission, as its functions have now been limited by the courts, is, or can be made of great use to the railroads. It satisfies the popular clamor for a government supervision of railroads, at the same time that the supervision is almost entirely nominal. Further, the older such a commission gets to be, the more inclined it will be found to take the business and railroad view of things. It thus becomes a sort of barrier between the railroad corporations and the people and a sort of protection against hasty and crude legislation hostile to railroad interests. . . . The part of wisdom is not to destroy the Commission but to utilize it.[1]

In order to better "utilize" the ICC and other regulatory bodies, industry has increasingly organized politically. Massive trade associations have accordingly grown in power, and are now:

1. indirectly or directly financing the campaigns of elected public officials;
2. offering lucrative jobs to government officials and administrators;
3. arranging the appointment of industry officials or representatives to government posts;
4. encouraging government-industry "cooperation" through special "advisory committees" made up of industry officials to agencies;
5. supporting large and high-powered legal staffs to delay or circumvent enforcement of the law;
6. employing and contracting for services of academicians, consultants, and "think tanks" to "objectively" verify industry views;
7. financing a horde of professional lobbyists to plead, influence, wheel and deal, wine and dine agency officials, legislators, and their staffs. Many are hired from, and are old friends of, agencies and legislative committees; and

8. sponsoring the industry conference-and-convention-circuit which, by sheer volume of events, often hampers an agency's effective enforcement of the law, and enables personal contact outside Washington in intimate surroundings between industry and government officials, with the opportunity for the granting of small but very effective special favors.

The purpose of this raw "utilization" of government by industry was twofold. First, it was to prevent meaningful regulation where it impeded profits; second, it sought to obtain government protection from regulation by other units of government and from self-regulating systems which might still have some power. Hence, the ICC protects trucking companies from competition by generally prohibiting new competitors and allowing companies to collusively set rates free from market restraint. And supposed "regulation" of everything from drugs to auto warranty honesty makes private court action more difficult. The capture of these "regulators" is a *fait accompli* for many industries, enabling free exercise of abusive and dangerous monopoly power. Thus, the most vicious attacks on the Nader Reports, which advised the abolition of the FTC and the ICC, were not from the agencies but from the industries involved.

A more detailed description of the methods of institutional corruption and of the concealment of the end result is crucial to understanding the kind of restructuring increasingly compelled.

I. THE EMERGING REGULATORY-INDUSTRIAL COMPLEX: BUILDING THE LIAISON

The existence of permanent representatives of industry in Washington, a political advantage the general public does not possess, has helped cause the corporate acculturation of Washington agencies by the industries they supposedly regulate. Most important decisions are made in the middle levels of the bureaucracy; it is at this stage that policy is the most malleable, and it is at this stage that industry has both formal and informal input.

A. Informal Contact

Most agencies stay in constant informal contact with industry leaders and lobbyists. Thousands of letters of complaint from consumers alleging fraud or pollution lead agencies into secret conference with industry executives, who then help draft new rules which invariably meet only the agency's public relations needs. The consumer has the opportunity to propose amendments—but only at the public hearing stage, when policy is fairly hardened. Very few, if any, agencies contact consumers, small businessmen, or workers on any ad hoc basis when policy is in the formative stage.

An important part of informal influence is the entertaining of agency personnel by their regulated industries. File cards are kept by industry on most key officials, noting birthdays of sons and daughters, anniversaries, hobbies, favorite foods, and more. Consequently, officials are subject to a constant barrage of soft-sell gifts and favors. With most of these practices, it is not the monetary value that is designed or expected to influence the recipient; it is their cumulative impact—that people in a particular industry care about and like that official.

The extent of this process is documented in the Nader Reports from the summer of 1969. For example, the eleven Interstate Commerce commissioners have taken approximately 220 *trips* during the past 2½ years. One commissioner has publicly estimated that 25 percent of the expenses are borne by industry with the rest being borne by government. The chance to visit the home state at government expense because of industry invitation is an example of this process. The recent chairman of the ICC, for example, has visited West Virginia (her home state) some nineteen times in the past 2½ years, at government and industry expense, due mostly to industry "invitations." More recently, a high ICC official, Neil Garson, was obliged to resign after admitting that he had falsified some records, collecting government expense money and actually traveling at industry expense. Ironically, Mr. Garson was widely acknowledged as the most honest official in that agency.

B. Formal Advisory Groups

Industry contact directly or through the thousands of highly paid lobbyists is given formal status at the malleable stage of agency policy-making through a second aspect of the government —the "advisory committee." Most agencies have many such "committees," unknown to the public, which meet and express opinions about prospective decisions. The ICC, for example, has *seventeen* such bodies. Agencies rarely if ever include consumers or consumer representatives (e.g., from Consumer's Union), or small businessmen, workers, or academicians. They are universally dominated by large corporate and trade association officers.

The process has gone so far that it is used even where there is the likelihood of public attention. Thus, the president is brazen enough to reward his party's large contributors by appointing them to the National Industrial Pollution Control Council. Members include the directors and executive officers of: Union Carbide, Monsanto, American Cyanamid, Chemargro Corp., Procter and Gamble, Lever Brothers, American Can Co., and so on. The list reads like a Who's Who of America's major polluters. Those few who are allegedly into anti-pollution technology do not even purchase, in at least one case (Monsanto), their *own* pollution control equipment. The list does not include the major firms specializing and leading in pollution control technology and production. It does not include a single small businessman or consumer representative. It ends its membership with the presidents of the U.S. Chamber of Commerce, National Association of Manufacturers, and National Industrial Conference Board.

A usually mild Senator Metcalf was moved to remark:

It is now 6 years since the Department of Health, Education, and Welfare prodded by the House Natural Resources and Power Subcommittee, first attempted to inventory industrial waste discharges. That inventory was stopped, year after year, by a business advisory committee similar to the one which the President has now appointed. . . .

250 WITH JUSTICE FOR SOME

Let us tell it like it is: The purpose of industry advisory committees to Government is to enhance corporate image, to create an illusion of action and to impede Government officials who are attempting to enforce law and order and gather the data upon which enforcement is based.[2]

The formation of additional groups such as this one proceeds year after year. They now number in the hundreds. Most are not visible and few are publicly known. How many of us knew of the new pollution advisory group? And how much easier it was to quietly appoint to the General Advisory Committee of the Federal National Mortgage Association, eighteen officers or directors of banks, insurance companies, and other financial enterprises with mortgage business. If these agencies and groups seem remote to us, it is no accident, but their failures affect all of us, every day. They affect us when we're blatantly lied to by advertisers, when cancer-producing additives are knowingly allowed into our food products, when auto executives ignore warranties and charge fortunes for car repair parts, and when the most profitable (and least competitive) industry in America is the necessary-to-life drug and medical supply industry. In the numerous areas where laws already exist, these groups can blunt enforcement. Where laws do not exist, they can stop or neutralize legislation since most proposed legislation originates from within the regulating agencies.

C. Public Lobbying

Apart from these expenditures for trade association financing and for theoretically illegal campaign contributions to elected officials, the public is forced to pay for yet a third aspect of the liaison—its own persuasion through public lobbying. We are treated to astronaut Wally Schirra arguing at great expense over nationwide television and radio for "equitable regulation" for America's "great" railroads. These expenses are not clearly separated from the "increased costs" the railroads have claimed as the basis for some five general and massive rate increases in the past three years. Despite their monopoly power, a complete lack of regulatory review guarantees railroad success.

Tangential to this, of course, is industry public relations designed not to influence policy, but to persuade that problems do not exist or are being solved by voluntary action out of the goodness of the corporate heart. There are very few cases indeed where actual corporate expenditures toward minimizing the harm created by products or production ever approach even that part of the advertising budget devoted to the glorification of the little that is done. And even that is generally undertaken merely to prove that more cannot be done or that more is not necessary: witness current auto and oil industry public relations drivel.

D. Job Interchange

A fourth and critical aspect of the regulatory-industrial liaison is job interchange. Many agencies and departments are substantially comprised of former employees of the industry regulated, with close ties resulting. Conversely, attorneys view agency employment as little more than an opportunity to learn the trade for later industry practice. In fact, high officials who are often otherwise unqualified for executive positions with industry are admittedly offered such employment with industry while still in government. And indeed, over one-half of the former commissioners of the Federal Communications Commission who have left in recent years are now high executives in the communications industry. Over fifty Food and Drug Administration officials have left the agency for high posts in the food industry in recent years.

This process of the "deferred bribe" has become the normal and accepted way of maximizing the other mechanisms of influence. All but two of the commissioners leaving the Interstate Commerce Commission in the past decade (ten of twelve) have gone into the transportation industry directly, or have become "ICC Practitioners," lawyering for the industry. This job interchange process reinforces the informal influence effect in two ways: those who have served with agency or industry usually maintain close personal ties with old friends; and those still in the agency have their present views shaped by anticipated, future interests.

E. *Appointments and Hiring*

The fifth aspect is the appointment and hiring process. Any potential congressional action to control or break into the regulatory-industrial combination is negated by both pork-barreling and campaign contributions. Industry, through a variety of devices, invests millions into the campaigns of those key congressmen able to influence agency appropriations or appointments. The result, unsurprisingly, is the appointment of political and corporate hacks who are completely unqualified and can be easily overwhelmed by industry domination of technical information flow. Only four of the current eleven Interstate Commerce commissioners have had any experience with law, economics, antitrust, rate regulation, or transportation. Two of these four are from the regulated industry. All eleven had political "sponsors" and most have a long record of party work.

All of these processes cause a convergence of regulatory and corporate views. Lobbyists spend man-years convincing their agencies of the need for implementation of industry determined policy. The natural competition between specific firms is obviated by an increasingly concentrated oligopolistic structure of American industry and by the existence of hundreds of "trade associations," which lobby on behalf of firms, often on a collusive basis. Since these lobbying expenses are deductible, and since they are trivial compared to the millions of dollars at issue in governmental decision-making, industry spends lavishly in such efforts. Countervailing arguments from the diffuse public concerning indirect economic or environmental effects are lacking. The consumer is unorganized, unfinanced, and unrepresented. And agency personnel, even if they do not come from industry or expect to go to it, come to adopt the views which are daily put before them. The result is both a bias toward corporate rather than public interest policies—as a few thousand industrialists control our national politics and priorities.

II. SECRECY AND PUBLIC RELATIONS:
HIDING THE LIAISON

Early in the summer of 1968, a citizen researcher working for
Ralph Nader walked into the director of personnel's office at
the Federal Trade Commission (FTC) and asked for the agency's organizational chart. He was told that no such chart existed.
Later, when a chart called the "Budget Control Records" was
discovered, which contained the nonexistent information, the
director nevertheless refused to release or disclose it on the
grounds that the document was an "internal memoranda" and
hence exempt from disclosure under the Freedom of Information
Act. When asked for the legal basis for this extraordinary interpretation of the act, the citizen was told that names and positions were (of course) public information, but the *salaries* of the
employees, which were listed on the far right-hand column of
the records, were confidential. Puzzled that the amounts of public monies paid public employees could be regarded as privileged
information, the student nevertheless suggested that the salaries
be simply covered in the copying process or scissored off. His
request was denied by the director of personnel and subsequently
by the executive director of the agency.

Only by a direct appeal to the entire commission, with the implicit threat of adverse publicity and of a law suit under the Freedom of Information Act, were the records made available. Even
then, however, the FTC sought to charge a prohibitive price of
$.60 per page for duplication. Since the chart was in a thirty-page
report format, and since the student had eight reports going
back to 1959, the cost of a single copy of the 240 pages was
$144. Finally, the agency agreed to make an office copy of the
records available for his perusal. Ironically, this copy *contained
the salaries* of all the employees, the supposed basis for the
original denial of the records. Almost two months had elapsed
for the student's original request to see what is perhaps an
agency's most fundamental document.

As graduate students and young professionals in the Ralph
Nader summer study groups of 1968, and then later in 1969 and

1970, engaged in the investigation of the responsiveness and effectiveness of the Washington bureaucracy, they were totally unprepared for the receptions they received—denials of the most elementary pieces of information, constant lying about events and the existence of documents, harassment of those who were discovered talking with them out of their offices, surveillance of those they were "allowed" to see, and, always, enormous delays.

Preventing an "open" government, at least as far as relations with the general public are concerned, became an early necessity for industry corruptors. They succeeded beyond their wildest aims. They have created a government which, on its own, will suppress details of industry collusion in order to project its necessary "public interest" image. The actual atmosphere of the bureaucracy is shrouded in secrecy that is buttressed by an effective enforcement mechanism.

The notion of an "open American government" is a myth. Fear of public disclosure of everything from already public reports to the most basic and innocent personal opinions pervades the entire bureaucracy like a poisonous fog. The Freedom of Information Act has failed. The only groups with easy access to details of government operation, those accorded preferential access, are large corporations and their representatives.

A. *Upper Echelon Fear: The Image and the Reality*

At the outset of the student investigations, two fundamentally different categories of fear were encountered. There was the fear of appointed officials and upper staffs that the students would embarrass them by disclosing information they preferred to keep confidential. Secondly, there was the fear felt by lower to middle level staff, who were often eager to discuss the workings of their agencies but feared for their job security and long-term career possibilities.

The fear of upper staff was manifest when Paul Rand Dixon, then chairman of the Federal Trade Commission, physically forced investigator John Schulz out of his office when the latter asked about the basis for an information denial. Mr. Dixon then proceeded to call up his upper staff to instruct them that the

"FTC investigators" were to be locked out, that no one was to communicate with them. Perhaps one reason for the banishment was that they had already learned too much about the agency. Yet Chairman Dixon went beyond this approach—he institutionalized his lockout. One year later the investigators were told by Dr. George Dobbs of the agency that *all* personnel had been instructed not to speak with them without the written permission of the Commission. At the same time, trade association representatives, lobbyists, industrialists and their legal representatives came and went as they pleased.

Another example is provided by Richard McLaren, head of the Antitrust Division of the Department of Justice. Mr. Nader was refused access to information in his quest to understand why the Justice Department had "consented" to a settlement of an indictment against the Automobile Manufacturers Association of America for "product-fixing." The indictment charged that the automobile corporations, through their association, had conspired to delay or prevent the implementation of pollution control devices over a sixteen-year period. The Justice Department settled the matter, without sanction, in a way that hampered consumers and cities from using the voluminous grand jury records in later, treble-damage antitrust suits against the auto companies and their trade association. A former high level attorney in the Antitrust Division interpreted the situation: "Listen, McLaren was appointed because of Bar Association politics, not Republican politics. And he'd be unhappy if damaging information were revealed which could hurt *both* the legal fraternity and his present bosses."

Why do these officials fear exposure of their agency's activities? It is because image is the reality of Washington. Officials and upper staff will keep their jobs only so long as they can accommodate the vector theory of politics, responding to those forces which threaten them. This end can usually be accomplished through private accommodation; but if there is a major threat to the favorable image of the agency through the action of an individual, officials and upper staff realize that they might be compelled publicly to investigate an issue. Thus, while there are thousands of potential "scandals" in Washington every week—

from the outright influence-peddling of Speaker McCormack's office to the FDA malfeasance on cyclamates—only those events which are likely to be publicized with the proper tone of outrageous surprise will force the matter into the public eye and will compel Congress or other officials to take some kind of scapegoat, retributive, and self-purging action.

In order to understand fully the nature of this image threat to upper staff and appointed officials, it is necessary to consider two aspects of the source of their fear. First, the agencies project themselves as active, aggressive, independent, honest, effective, increasingly productive, and dedicated champions of the diffuse and general public interest. It is a view they seek to retain. Second, there is the fact that industry, the special interest "constituency" of the agency, does not present a threat to that image. They are not going to complain of agency inaction in the prosecution of corporation violations of law. They are not going to expose political maneuverings or ask embarrassing questions. As a result, there is no need to erect a barrier to information acquisition and personal relations by these groups. But the very activities by industry groups which do not themselves pose a threat to the agency's image itself, do pose a threat if exposed. The revelation of private dealings between industry and special interests to the detriment of the public would do great harm to the agency's image, its lifeblood. Since there has been no previous substantial threat of disclosure of these activities, there has been no deterrent to these practices. Agencies consider it necessary to maintain this low-visibility situation in order to protect this regulatory-industry collusion. This goal also requires the enforcement of secrecy down to the lower levels of bureaucracy.

B. Lower Echelon Fear: Weaving the Shroud

The fear at the lower to middle level is different than at the upper levels. It is not the fear of an embarrassing disclosure *per se*, but of retaliation from superiors for relating something which might conflict with the official agency version. This is the fear that enabled Chairman Dixon to enforce successfully his illegal edict. Very few employees of the Federal Trade Commission would in fact talk with the student investigators after the order. For example, a young attorney at the Federal Trade Commission who had spoken with a student in the hall of the FTC office building in Washington, D.C., was subsequently warned by his division chief to "be careful of his conduct" because the FTC was "back on its heels under criticism." Fearing unfavorable job recommendations from the agency upon departure, he canceled a prospective interview and would not talk with the investigators in public further—although he did so in private.

The fear at the lower level is also manifested in a myriad of subtle ways. It is an official who refuses to be interviewed alone, but insists on having another attorney or his superior present. It is requiring that a stenographer be present to record verbatim what is said, or writing copious "memos to the files" after an interview. It is lower and middle staff refusing to reveal even the most innocuous information, afraid to express even their most basic opinions about their responsibilities. It can be seen in sweaty palms and nervousness during an interview.

The institutionalization of this lower staff fear is accomplished through sophisticated enforcement mechanisms.

1. *The Agency Line.* Most agencies carefully construct an official or unofficial "agency line" concerning controversial issues. Rarely do these responses have any relation to reality, but they are repeated with such uniformity, within and by the agency, that mere repetition imbues them with a kind of sanctity. Thus, the Federal Trade Commission cannot investigate ghetto frauds because of the "interstate commerce clause of the Constitution." The Interstate Commerce Commission can do nothing about homemoving frauds because it lacks "jurisdiction." And the Food and Drug Administration cannot move "too fast" against the marketing of dangerous drugs. Of course, outside the agencies these answers are derided by those familiar with the law or issues involved. But they all have a kind of magic circularity which prevents inquiry from progressing further. The reality, however, differs from the asserted assumptions. The relevant statutory and constitutional clauses allegedly restraining the FTC and the ICC in the examples above have been liberally inter-

preted for the past decade, but the agencies themselves have yet to utilize them. And the FDA *can* move quickly against an unsafe drug as it did against the antibiotic combination Panalba— after years of inaction. Thus, most of these bureaucratic positions are self-fulfilling prophecies.

The agency line is generally expressed through form letters in response to complaints from consumers and through news releases and testimony to Congress. It is often codified, however, in the agency's annual report. The categories now and then change, but the tone and purpose of the annual report remain constant. It is designed to project an aura of careful progress toward the solution of current problems. They are difficult problems, yes, but the department has made great strides, as the increasing numbers of enforcement actions from year to year in all quantitative categories prove. And although the problem is not quite yet solved, solution is imminent. For instance, one can go back to the initial case before the Interstate Commerce Commission, the first large regulatory agency created back in 1887, and read about a group of small farmers complaining that the railroad refused to supply them with boxcars because they claimed a shortage. One can then follow this matter from annual report to annual report, through the 1920s and all the way to 1970. Each year one learns that the "boxcar shortage" problem, which once again forced many of America's small farmers to dump their harvest, will be solved in a very short time. There is never an indication that the ICC, in reality, has done virtually nothing in the area except protect big business, refusing to prosecute cases of massive violation of the law submitted by the agency's own special agents in the field. Thus, the only way to increase numbers year after year is to prosecute more trivial, less important violations, a mis-emphasis not reflected by annual report tables. Therefore, agency personnel in the field are directly told to meet a certain quota[3]—and told that it does not matter what kind of case it is, as long as they do *more* than was done last year. The agency line thus becomes not only the philosophy of the agency but its goal.

Consequently, the lower to middle level employee soon learns that it is hands off big business, hands off innovative prosecutions to counter innovative violations of law, and hands off offending those who might threaten political presure—i.e., major campaign contributors to key congressmen, industries dominated by former upper staff personnel or by the company the employee's superior just joined.

2. *Structure.* Although not set up for this express purpose, agencies are structurally arranged to aid in the enforcement of secrecy. First, most are highly compartmentalized. Departments are divided into bureaus, sections, offices, and desks. A veteran of twenty years or more in one office is likely to have no idea what is transpiring in the office down the hall. These natural lines of communication permit the isolation of a given report, meeting, or incident among a limited group. Those who would most likely reveal it are among the younger employees at the GS-9 to GS-12 levels, those who have less to lose by exposure of complicity with industry. But because of the compartmentalization, together with a policy of letting only a few of the younger staff participate in any one decision or matter, it is relatively easy for the entrenched upper staff to trace down leaks. For example, a report produced by the ICC's relatively small cost-finding section will not be widely known in detail outside that section. The officials ordering suppression of a given event or document (usually by discontinuing it just short of final publication) will usually consist of a small group of from one to five upper level officials.

3. *Surveillance.* Complementing agency structure is a pervasive fear and anticipation of surveillance, including electronic surveillance.* The student investigators were frequently told by employees at lunch or at their homes that they feared an electronic bug in their office. Most of them suspected other agencies

---

* Robert Kennedy, while Attorney General, was discussing a serious policy matter with one of his staff, when he commented that he wanted to convey the problem to FBI Director J. Edgar Hoover. His aide said, ominously, "He already knows by now," at which point Kennedy, understanding his meaning, began shouting, "Do you hear me, Edgar, do you hear me, Edgar?"

Also, Tom Wicker has recently reported that a major Democratic contender for the presidency would only be interviewed *outside* his normal office because he feared that his office was bugged.

or their superiors, and some pointed to the disturbingly lucrative business conducted by electronic device manufacturers with large industrial concerns. Many of these surveillance gadget companies have large and busy offices in Washington, and agency officials feel that any criticisms about policy expressed by them may be relayed to the industry's friends and to their contacts higher up in the agency. Since offensive surveillance development is advanced over antisurveillance detection and jamming, there is little these men can do to verify or alleviate their fears even if they have the resources to do so.

Non-electronic surveillance is just as prevalent and intimidating. A high official in the Nixon administration asked two departments the students were studying to submit detailed memos on their activities, including a list of all personnel interviewed. The ICC circulated a memorandum requesting staff to record how much time the students spent talking with them and to summarize the contents of the conversations.[4] Other agencies went even further. The Assistant Secretary of the Department of the Interior (DOI), Carl Klein, first agreed to cooperate with our study of the Federal Water Pollution Control Agency (FWPCA), which is within DOI's jurisdiction. Later, however, he refused to permit the students to interview any of the public employees in the agency or department. Mr. Klein persisted in his lockout, until rising pressures of adverse publicity compelled him to rescind his illegal bar.

Mr. Klein then attempted to regroup, however, requiring the students to schedule centrally all interviews and appointing two subordinates to "monitor" all interviews. Although the sixteen investigators working on this study, as well as the employees interviewed, were painfully aware of this policy, Mr. Klein was nevertheless brazen enough to deny it publicly to the *Washington Post*. He stated that "as far as I know" there are "no monitors." However, Mr. Klein's own staff assistant, Jeffrey Stern, and the FWPCA director of the Program Analysis, Richard Nalesnik, were specifically assigned to monitor our interviews. They openly acknowledged their role as such on several occasions. Further, they were told to report to Mr. Klein himself, and to his deputy, Robert L. McCormick, who also admitted the existence of the policy. Not only Mr. Klein's misuse of power in his "monitoring," but also his willingness to lie—no matter how obvious the lie might be to personnel within the agency—must impress agency employees who might be tempted to speak their minds. Of course, it must be understood that this kind of monitoring is rarely, if ever, required of the daily deluge of visitors from trade associations, corporations, and other special interest groups.

4. *Sanctions.* The critical element necessary to enforce secrecy and strict adherence to the agency line is the power of effective sanctions. The obvious sanctions are the denial of sought-after rewards, such as grade level advances. In addition, there are other sanctions, ranging from a sudden surge of undesirable assignments to the more extreme measure of dismissal. Even if matters do not progress to this point, their potential use is a sufficient deterrent to older, security-conscious bureaucrats.

5. *Natural Selection.* These sanctions of advancement denial, undesirable assignments, and dismissal are rendered most effective by a complementary system of natural selection. Agencies to some extent recruit and to a greater extent promote personnel who will be most affected by these sanctions. Those who question assumptions or who demonstrate aggressiveness or imagination are generally discouraged. The turnover rate at the lower professional levels (GS-9 to 12) of most agencies is staggering, partly because only those lacking in creativity and critical capacity are made welcome; the Peter Principle prevails. Many agencies rotate out, usually by the voluntary resignation of the discouraged or disgusted, one-third or more of the new recruits at these levels each year. Those that remain acquire an increasing interest in job security as they rise to more powerful positions. Their opportunity for new careers, especially without favorable job recommendations from the government, declines as the years pass. They become adjusted to passive acceptance of pre-set explanations. Eventual complicity with the interest group domination of agency officials provides yet greater incentive for obedience to the agency line. Often, the men most susceptible to

control move from complicity to a role of active suppression enforcement themselves.

The intensity of the process can be imputed from the longevity of those who have survived the selection process to reach positions of power at upper staff levels. At the ICC, for example, the average tenure in the agency of the present bureau directors is thirty-one years. And a tangential aspect to the lack of new blood infusion is the development of cronyism, illustrated by the FTC, where *every* attorney bureau director in 1968 came from a small Southern town, as did Chairman Dixon, who promoted them.

The interaction of some of these forces: structure, surveillance, sanctions, and natural selection, is illustrated in one particularly salient example: the case of ICC special agent Frank Lawrence. During the summer of 1969, the investigators had learned that there were numerous improprieties regarding the relationship between one specific freight forwarder, regulated by the ICC, and high ICC officials. The freight forwarder, U.S. Freight, is a large company which, together with two other firms, dominates the freight forwarding industry. It was learned that the ICC's managing director was especially intimate with the company. There was evidence that he attended the company's cocktail parties, that he called U.S. Freight executives to report on the activities of rival freight forwarders within the ICC, that he vacationed on the U.S. Freight Company yacht, and that he had been offered a lucrative job by the Freight Forwarders Institute (located at the same address as the Washington office of the U.S. Freight Company).

To this extent, his activities are not unlike the agency's relationship with industry generally. Then, in 1967, special agent Lawrence, attached to the ICC's Chicago office, submitted a "Compliance Survey" (a preliminary investigative report), which documented evidence of the systematic and massive bribing of traffic managers by U.S. Freight. Agent Lawrence received no reply and no further instructions from Washington, despite numerous inquiries. Finally, Washington instructed Lawrence not to file the usual follow-up investigative report, but instead to submit an informal memorandum to his superior. Although upset by this extraordinary request, given the substantial evidence he had compiled and the seriousness of the violation, he complied with the request. Nothing happened. Agent Lawrence inquired further and was explicitly told to drop the matter. During this time and to the present day, the Bureau of Enforcement, the agency's prosecutorial arm, had never even seen the report to evaluate it for the desirability of prosecution. The bribing did not cease.

Agent Lawrence's unwillingness to let the matter drop quietly was rewarded with a denial of his "within grade step increase" (normal pay raise based on years of service). He discovered that his submissions to Washington were returned to him with hypercritical comments. Much of the commentary was clearly absurd, such as "this is not a violation of the Interstate Commerce Act," when in fact identical cases abounded in agency records and with Court affirmation. Nearly every submission, although identical in nature and quality to his previous surveys and reports submitted during his nine years as an ICC investigator, was suddenly unsatisfactory. These tactics were designed to harass Mr. Lawrence into more obeisant acceptance of the Washington upper staff desire not to offend U.S. Freight. Other special agents were affected by what they knew was happening; most were afraid it could happen to them, and all of them got the message.

Since sanctions might not be enough to keep him in line, it was determined that more extreme measures would be taken to protect the natural selection processes from contamination by prosecution-minded investigators. Mr. Lawrence was told that he should resign. If he failed to resign, the year of bogus criticism would be used against him in a dismissal action. This "documentation," even though self-created, would require that he defend himself with a major effort and thousands of dollars—which he could not easily afford. Further, a successful dismissal would mean bad job recommendations; he would have to start all over again, although near forty.

In an unusual but happy turn of events, Mr. Lawrence refused to resign, choosing instead to contest the issue. At this point, his behavior deviates from the normal reaction of quietly resigning.

Attorneys researched the supposed evidence of his "incompetence" and documented in detail its falsity. They demanded a full hearing and requested as witnesses a substantial portion of the agency's upper staff. At first, the agency, contrary to elementary principles of due process, attempted to hold a "kangaroo" hearing. The same man bringing charges against agent Lawrence chose three ICC employees from whom Mr. Lawrence was to choose one as his hearing examiner. And this same official bringing the charges also partially controlled the promotion of the employees chosen as possible hearing examiners. Meanwhile, the ICC expressed its intention to hold a "closed door hearing." Mr. Lawrence's attorneys expressed the intention of obtaining a court order to compel an open hearing (a closed hearing can be waived by a defendant since *he* is the supposed benefactor of the privacy); when they requested an open hearing with press and public, and included as witnesses much of the agency's upper staff, the ICC suddenly backed down. In an unprecedented move, the letter of dismissal "was rescinded." Shortly thereafter the managing director resigned on four days' notice.

The student investigators were later told through sources in the General Counsel's office that the matter was dropped only after the commission was told that if Lawrence were to take the matter to court, he could compel the public release of his personal file, including the collection of bogus criticisms and returned, unacted upon, reports of genuine violations of the Interstate Commerce Act. The evidence could not be destroyed, since agent Lawrence had wisely Xeroxed everything he had sent or received. He could release it publicly in his defense. More recently, the agency has shifted to a tactic which would retain the prohibition on release, harassing Lawrence until he resigns on his own.

There are occasional cases making national news, such as efficiency expert Fitzgerald, fired for reporting inefficiency in the construction of the C-5A airplane. There are hundreds of less visible Frank Lawrences in our federal bureaucracy. There are thousands who are so emasculated or intimidated at an early stage, that they become willing accomplices; eventually, many become corrupt enforcers themselves.

C. *The Freedom "From" Information Act*

The Freedom of Information Act was generally regarded as the formal guarantee of the open and public system promised by every administration. The act *required* the disclosure of *all* information at reasonable fees to *anyone* who desired it *unless* the information fell within one of the nine carefully defined exemptions.[5] There was no notion of "standing" here, that legal artifact which prevents the enforcement of many personal and civil rights on procedural grounds. This was truly to be an act to enable the public to inquire into the nature of the government it was financing and authorizing. Further, the act placed the burden on the *government* to demonstrate that a document fell within the purview of one of its exemptions. The Attorney General of the United States reaffirmed this emphasis in his memorandum to all executive agencies, that ". . . there be a change in Government Policy and attitude . . . [now] all individuals have equal rights of access."[6] President Johnson praised the act with enthusiasm during his address upon signing it on July 4, 1966: "I have always believed that freedom of information is so vital that only the national security, not the desire of public officials and private citizens, should determine when it must be restricted."[7] Yet all these pious hopes were shattered when it came down to agency implementation.

The first ominous hint at how the act would be enforced came when numerous officials testified against the act before Congress. As soon as the act became law, however, a number of them then declared that the provisions had been in effect for years and that they anticipated no need to change agency information policy because of it.[8] These contradictory statements presaged the non-enforcement of the act. The following describes the experiences of the Nader students as case examples of what occurs when citizens, not corporations, try to breach the bureaucratic wall.

Although the 1969 Nader group had initiated three suits on specific denials of information requests, it was impossible to sue for every piece of information or document illegally withheld.

Hundreds of documents were denied over the course of the summer. Since the act lacked provisions for punishment, and hence lacked any deterrent effect, bureaucrats at the upper level were and are able to flout its terms with the most overweening arrogance. The devices employed by federal officials to avoid compliance with the act betray an ingenuity which could usefully be employed in the solution of problems under the agency's or department's jurisdiction.

1. *Denial that Information Exists.* Those students investigating the Interstate Commerce Commission during the summer of 1969 occasionally requested information they were holding in folders; they then heard agency officials tell them with straight faces that the documents requested were not kept or were "not in the form requested."

The investigation of the Civil Aeronautics Board (CAB) yielded declarations that the following information and statistics are not kept:

a. Speeches and personal appearances made by members of the CAB;
b. Records of the costs of investigations conducted by the CAB;
c. Enforcement actions by the CAB's Bureau of Enforcement against air carriers for violations of law;
d. Complaints charging racial discrimination by the airlines;
e. The number of initial decisions of CAB hearings examiners appealed to the Board in accordance with its regulations.

If all of this information is in fact not collected by the agency, that in itself would seem to indicate a low level of agency performance. Of course, most of it does exist, as was later discovered by continued pressure and staff leaks.

2. *Failure to Collect Information.* Many agencies and departments meet the problem of suppression at its source: they collect only the kind of information which can be used by special interests, not by consumers or those who might wish to judge agency performance. The ICC, for example, does not even bother to count or classify all of its thousands of letters of complaint from consumers. It keeps no data whatsoever on its most-used sanction, the "request for voluntary compliance."

The FTC was asked, in a series of questions concerning its

system for priority evaluations, if it records the size or sales volume of violators of deceptive practice statutes. The agency's response was: "Annual sales are not maintained as general information in deceptive practice matters. This is simply because sales volume is frequently one of the many considerations in assessing the impact of a particular practice." Of course, if no information is kept, sales would seem to be not "one of the many" factors, but no factor at all. Three other omissions illustrate this bureaucratic sloth: the FTC fails to keep track of expenditures allocated for prosecution of violators of their laws; it fails to monitor actively the advertisements it supposedly polices; and it fails to seek out fraud in the ghetto, where it is more pervasive—and most damaging.

In a more basic sense, the FTC, ICC, Federal Water Pollution Control Agency (FWPCA), Food and Drug Administration (FDA), and other agencies fail almost universally in formulating their own sources of information about the industries they regulate. Agencies and departments "trust" the corporations they are entrusted to regulate to provide nearly all of the information upon which the "regulation" rests. Thus, the ICC accepts without detailed verification railroad estimates of increased expenses justifying massive rail hikes. It relies substantially on the Association of American Railroads to supply information about car shortages.

3. *Minimal Disclosure and Distribution.* The Federal Trade Commission disclosed only in a formalistic sense assurances of voluntary compliance and compliance reports, documents which concern sanctionless requests by the FTC to businessmen to cease illegal activity. First, the only text of such reports which the commission permitted to be made public was extremely general and conclusory. A single copy of each was placed in ring binders in the docket room of the agency's central office building in Washington, D.C. No copies were made or distributed to anyone, and no news releases on them were issued. It is an exaggeration to say that these texts were made "public." Public assurances of voluntary compliance and compliance reports contain language such as "[X firm] has ceased to carry on its business in the manner disapproved of and will not do so again."

All detailed communications from challenged businessmen, the real substance of such cases, were held absolutely confidential. In other words, there is little likelihood that the public would ever learn of a businessman's transgressions. The handling of these records permitted the FTC to proclaim, when challenged, that such information is public, while effectively keeping it from the general public.

Other examples of partial secrecy at the FTC included the treatment of consent orders—which are settlements of alleged corporate violations—and of news releases. Proposed consent orders were made "public" without publicity. A single copy was placed at the central office, and it remained there for only thirty days. Even given these conditions, when Stanley Cohen of *Advertising Age* first requested access to several consent orders in the thirty-day open file, he was told by the staff that the information was confidential. Only an appeal to some sympathetic commissioners brought him the information which had officially been declared "public." News releases, even where they are issued about deceptive practice cases, are typically laced with such opaque legalisms that, even in the opinion of members of the trade press in Washington, it is difficult to extract any usable information from them.

There have been more direct tactics to limit physical access to supposedly "public" information. Two investigators discovered that some pamphlets they had been reading in a Department of Agriculture (Pesticides Regulation) library were removed overnight when officials learned of their interest in them. The students had previously been given permission to read the pamphlets by the librarian. Agency officials justified the removal with the comment that it was not "any of their business."

4. *Contamination*. Many agencies arrange their records in such a way that public information is inextricably intertwined or connected with allegedly confidential information. Separation is then ruled "impossible." The Department of Defense is a veteran deployer of this tactic. For example, it refused to reveal information on the quantity of oil being pumped from the bilges of naval ships. Its refusal was based on the grounds that this information, although not confidential in and of itself, was

going to be included in a report which *would* contain some operational data that *was* considered classified.

Likewise, the Department of Labor has claimed that it can release nothing from its files on the Walsh Healey Act since *part* of the file is considered confidential—even though the requested information is admittedly public and admittedly separable. This refusal is particularly irritating since it includes the withholding of information going back to 1936, when the act was first passed. Thus, there is no way to evaluate the administration of the law in its one-third of a century of existence.

5. *Delay*. If none of the first four tactics is available, an agency will use delay to wear down and discourage those seeking information. The first device which facilitates this process is the establishment of a multilayered appeal procedure. Most agencies require a denial (after a written request) by the managing director or general counsel (sometimes one, then the other), and finally a written request and a written denial by the chairman or appointed head of the agency or department. Delays of several weeks between each tier are common. Yet even more common are simple delays by individual officials in response to information requests. For example, Richard McLaren took three months to answer (and deny) the simple request by one student to interview four attorneys in his Antitrust Division.

6. *Misuse of Exemptions*. Probably the most direct and popular technique, when all of the above are inappropriate, is the broad interpretation of the exemptions of the Freedom of Information Act which specify allowable secrecy. The act states that, among others, "investigatory files," "inter-agency or intra-agency memoranda," "internal rule or procedure," and "information given in confidence" need not be divulged. Although each of these exemptions permitting limited secrecy was carefully framed and deliberated to prevent their misuse, the agencies have interpreted them so broadly that they completely swallow the act.

Anything from the field is part of an "investigatory file." Department of Labor records ten to fifteen years old on Walsh Healey Act violations are still "under investigation for prospective prosecution." And the Federal Trade Commission, immediately after the passage of the act, seemed to classify every noun in the language as "under investigation." Every company, every advertisement, *everything* was confidentially "under investigation." It was puzzling how few of these matters ever appeared on the agency's formal docket. Those that did appear, sometimes from continual requests for information, then remained there interminably.

The extensive delays occurring during "investigations" in numerous broad problem areas permit the open-ended use of the investigation exemption under the FOIA. Action rarely results even after investigations which last decades. FTC investigations into the food industry, odometers, petroleum, analgesics, soft wood lumber, lottery game gimmicks, and many others have taken from four to forty years.* Often, investigations end without result, then are reinitiated when pressure from consumers once again builds for action or disclosure.

In sum, a law which was to help guard the guards is being adroitly avoided; the obvious reason for the "massive resistance" is that those whom the law would regulate are also those who implement the law. It is analogous to the futile practice of filing complaints against the police with the police, but it is far more serious. Information, particularly timely information, is the sine qua non of a functioning democracy. When citizens lack access to information channels, while organized, special interests have easy access, a corporate oligarchy, not a representative democracy, results. The problem is further exacerbated in the domain of the Fourth Branch of Government. Here are men who wield large power but who are unaccountable to any electorate.

D. Preferential Treatment

The emergence of a two-pronged approach to information disclosure both exemplifies the problem of citizen access and the

---

* Of the 4.17 years it takes the FTC, on the average, to open an investigation and issue an order, over two years are spent on the "investigation." One case has been on the docket since 1947. Another case was in process for more than five years before the FTC learned that the defendant company had been dissolved, one year after the start of the investigation.

reason for agency secrecy. Corporations, lobbyists, and trade associations do not receive the kind of reception described by the anecdotes above. They are able to obtain desired documents and can substantially affect agency policy toward legislation, prosecution of cases, and information policy. In a culture where information is the currency of power, they are consistently able to get early or preferential access to documents, and then respond to an attentive agency audience.

In August, 1969, the existence of a Civil Aeronautics Board (CAB) report on the handling of various consumer complaints by the major airlines was discovered. The report revealed unprecedented consumer discontent with the air industry. This report was denied to the Nader group because it "mentions the names of airlines." Of course the information *was* released to some of the airlines and to their trade association. Thus, the supposed reason for the confidentiality, that someone might get an "undue competitive advantage," loses its credence, since the airlines had the opportunity to exchange among themselves the specific information involved.

The National Highway Safety Bureau pre-released to General Motors an Army medical team report on off-base accidents which showed high carbon monoxide levels in auto crash victims' blood. After its secret receipt of the report, the company recalled several million cars for a "carbon monoxide hazard." Under pressure, the National Highway Safety Bureau, months later, released the report publicly. The report clearly should have been released to General Motors, which has an interest in the safety of its product, but why not also to the public as well? They are driving the cars and *they* paid for the study. The fact that the agency feels it has something to hide was made apparent when the agency denied any knowledge of pre-release to General Motors.

Reports are frequently suppressed to protect favored corporate interests, such as the Bureau of Mines' Report on abandoned mine land collapse beneath housing developments, an ICC Report on competition in the truck industry and on diversification of the railroads, the report by the Task Force on Product Information outlining the government's testing results on a variety

of products, a report about the growing crisis in food adultera-
tion, another about the present water pollution problem, and
even several about the bureaucracy itself by the Civil Service
Commission. Yet whatever trouble we encountered relative to
industry access pales in comparison to a consumer writing a
letter from Oregon. Delay and polite evasions can easily wear
down even the most zealous long-distance and individual critics
of specific agencies and policies.

E. Conspiracy of Silence

At first thought, journalists would appear to be in a position to
learn of and to systematically expose these conditions. Journalists, however, do not generally watch an agency's operation day
to day. Their editors are not interested in in-depth studies or in
documented odysseys for the acquisition of a given piece of information. Further, journalists have deadlines to meet on their
specific assignments; they therefore cannot afford the time and
persistence required to obtain concealed information or penetrate
the fabricated reasons for its denial. And usually, because they
are not lawyers, they are subject to the usual legal esoteria most
agencies inflict when denying information. Because of its lack of
permanence, aggressiveness, thoroughness, and expertise, the
Washington Press Corps, with notable exceptions such as Jack
Anderson and Morton Mintz, will rarely find out about the
existence of the report, secret conference, or deal. And not content to rely upon its defensive approach *vis-à-vis* journalists, the
bureaucracy takes the offensive by offering numerous information, trivia, and stories. The more active the journalist with
regard to the agency, the more material he will be fed. There is
an attempt to get the journalist dependent upon the agency for
his information, and hence dependent upon conveying the
agency's story, however trivial that story is.

Academicians, a second potential research group, do not discover these conditions for several reasons. First, they are professionals in a system which discourages this kind of investigation.
They learn that there are proper questions to ask and proper
modes of inquiry. Their approach is to seek some extremely spe-

cialized point of law or political science or sociology, or formulate an a priori thesis and then defend it ad infinitum. This latter approach is by analogy similar to the phenomenon of the "territorial imperative" described by some biologists. Academicians are not only led toward prolonged excursions into irrelevance, but their so-called "rigor" seems to exclude detailed personal investigation. To issue a report which identifies names and deals in specifics is often considered, disdainfully, as "indulging in personalities." Empirical research is considered less intellectual and less important than the juggling and rejuggling of conceptual problems. Thus, academicians are not willing to take the initiative in such a way that would enable them to learn of the existence of suppressed information. Even if they were to establish its existence, they would not have the persistence to keep asking for it or to determine why they are denied it.

The third group capable of finding and publicizing the corruption, as well as correcting much of it, is the legislature. But much of the process of collusion has reached well into the legislative branch, as commentary above makes clear. Pressure from organized economic groups "back home" results in a pork-barreling environment of favor trading. Everyone supports the tax loophole, special privilege, or public works project of others so that those in his district will receive reciprocal votes of approval. This preoccupation dominates legislative activity.

Further, excessive campaign costs mean reliance on those able to contribute much. Although there is a federal corrupt practices act meant to remedy excessive influence from this source, contributions merely come from dummy committees to dummy committees, usually consisting of corporate officers or directors and trade association employees. Those legislators who are not substantially "bought" in this sense are often deep in debt. The advancement of liberal loans by banks to members of Congress (particularly those on the banking subcommittees) is an illustrative result of this process. Another is a sudden influx of legal business for a legislator's law firm.

Even assuming a will to challenge special interests, the tools do not exist for effective inquiry and oversight. The seniority-committee system stifles independent or wide ranging inquiry.

Staffs are pitifully small. Three, for example, work part time overseeing the regulation of America's surface transportation. And the turnover here is very high, with about one of the three leaving every year.

The cumulative result of this lack of scrutiny is that corporations have the first advantage of operating their realm with little visibility and no "personality." (Who can even name one member of U.S. Steel's Board of Directors?) And corporate secrecy is absolutely essential for the continued corruption of the political system. Ironically, as in other areas, industry is trying to project the opposite image. Campus newspapers are flooded with ads showing Motorola or Ford executives with sincerity implied from newly sideburned faces. Ads contain supposedly real "dialog" between serious campus types who want to know if "individuality" will be respected in the corporation, which seems "kind of like a machine." The personal corporate answers are soothing assurances, of course, with much self-congratulatory prose on how much a "dialog" is needed and how this company and president stand ready to let it all hang out. Corporate responsibility and accountability, however, as described in the previous chapter, is a sham.

This author, on behalf of the Harvard Law Civil Rights–Civil Liberties Research Committee, in 1969, individually invited the presidents of America's one hundred largest corporations to Harvard Law School for a symposium and dialog under any circumstances and at any time that suited their convenience. Those firms placing campus ads were included. *None* accepted, despite the cooperation of faculty and the dean of the Law School in the effort. Not one would come—any time.

Senator Metcalf ran into a similar problem several years earlier.

In 1964, Senator Lee Metcalf and Vic Reinemer, authors of "Overcharge," wrote to 103 private power companies in response to an advertisement which stated that these companies would "answer any question you may have quickly, without making a federal case of it." They asked the companies what attorneys and legal firms were retained by their respective companies in 1963, and what was the compensation for each. Of the 103 companies, only 20 responded accurately to the question, four of which retained no attorneys.[9]

III. TRYING TO CHANGE THE COMPLEX

The reinvigoration of this regulatory-industrial complex, not only in terms of solutions to substantive problems, but more importantly in terms of a defensible legal and governmental process, requires radical change. But there are certain interim reforms which could feasibly be attempted first. These should be attempted before the complete restructuring of the state is compelled.

1. The appointment process must be changed. Officials must be appointed on the basis of qualification. This seems to be a simple truism, but it will require public attention to appointments previously made before an audience of industry enthusiasts. Appointments must not be "cleared" with industry, as is presently the norm. Legislation should be passed prohibiting appointment of anyone with a substantial interest in the industry to be regulated.

2. Job interchange, at least the "deferred bribes" of upper level appointees, must be ended. This can be done by requiring, as a condition of appointment, that anyone taking a position may not accept employment for or compensation from an industry regulated by that government body for at least five years after leaving the government post.

3. There must be an adversary process in agency proceedings, with someone representing the counter-corporate side. There must be independent consumer counsel, with a full staff within each agency, as well as strong consumer representation on all formal advisory groups.

4. The Freedom of Information Act must be given some teeth. A summary judicial procedure must be established for easy and quick public appeal. Time limits should be set out to prevent agency refusals even to deny information (without which legal recourse is impossible). Exemptions should be statutorily

limited to make more difficult current abuse. A time limit should be placed on the applicability of many of the exemptions justifying suppression—particularly the investigatory file exemption. Disclosure requirements should be set out, with maximum reproduction charges set at no more than $.05 per sheet, plus minimal labor cost. Each agency should be required to collect specified minimal information about agency operations and required to make available to the public the document identification or labeling schemes of the department. Finally, the deliberate or repeated failure to disclose information which is clearly not within one of the exemptions should be grounds for contempt of court, with criminal sanctions applied.

5. The nation's regulatory agencies must be restructured for greater accountability and effectiveness. First, their adjudicatory functions should be separated from the prosecutorial, either along the lines of present agency jurisdiction or combined in one large Commerce Court. This will remove much present unfairness, particularly for the small businessman unable to play the very expensive agency-legal game. The judges will no longer be directing the prosecutors. Second, the agencies must confine themselves to policy-making, rule-making, and prosecutorial activity under the leadership of a single, visible, and accountable leader. The notion of "independence" fostered through "group decisions" and multilayered agency authority has simply not worked, as has been pointed out in the recent Ash report.

6. There must be tight policing of campaign contributions from industry, with prohibition and contribution disclosure requirements actively enforced. In addition, there should be a change in tax laws permitting deductions for contributions to candidates by private individuals, thus broadening the contributive base of officials. Further, free television time should be required and provided for candidates to minimize the importance and necessity of heavy financial aid for this purpose.

7. Tax law enforcement relating to lobbying must be changed. At present, corporations are in fact deducting their lobbying costs as business expenses. Individuals who are attempting to counter special interest bias, however, and who are not attempting to influence for economically selfish advantage are denied

the same privilege. In fact, organizations formed to represent a general interest threaten their entire tax-exempt status to the extent they try to influence electors and legislative acts. If possible, this should be reversed. Lawful attempts to influence election outcome and legislation should not result in exemption removal from "charitable" or "public interest" organizations. On the other hand, these activities, if connected directly or indirectly with enterprise based on economic gain, should *not* be deductible, no matter how cloaked.

8. Congressional oversight committees must be given adequate staff to scrutinize their respective agencies and departments. Staffs are presently so small that it would require a ten-fold increase to achieve the scrutiny necessary for even elementary congressional control of the bureaucracy.

9. The seniority system must be ended to give Congress the opportunity to select its own representatives to oversee America's economy and to lessen the effectiveness of perpetual corporate control of a few identifiable congressmen—whose power position, following a corporate-financed campaign, is presently assured.

10. There must be active trust-busting of corporations, trade associations, and unions. Most, if not all, of America's top 500 corporations should be split into more competitive entities. In few corporations of this size are there appreciable economies of scale. The largest, General Motors, could just as easily be Buick, Pontiac, Chevrolet, etc., with no loss in efficiency, but great benefit to the consumer and the public. Any industry-wide research or agreement necessary for the public interest should be accomplished by or through the government.

11. Corporations must be opened up for greater direct public scrutiny. The notion of "protecting" corporate violators of the law from public exposure (a privilege individuals are not allowed) must end. Hesitancy to statistically compare individually named corporations according to public issues—whether they be cleanliness or accuracy or safety—must be overcome. To facilitate this, a comprehensive corporate disclosure law should be passed requiring more detailed breakdowns of corporate expenditures and holdings. Government should compile and

publicize numbers of complaints received from consumers by type of complaint for individual firms, with number of sales or size of firm included so meaningful comparison is possible.

12. There should be legal redress under federal and state laws for parties as a class. This is the only way general public interests can be directly heard within our judicial system. The law should leniently define representation requirements and establish a clear cause of action on a class basis for consumer grievances.

Consumers of the World Unite

EDWARD BERLIN, ANTHONY Z. ROISMAN,
and GLADYS KESSLER*

The prior two chapters on aspects of corporate-consumer relations are both grim and instructive. If corporations will not heed
the public interest, and if they are not to be held accountable to
their own shareholder electorate or to federal regulation, then
one visible and viable alternative remains to compel fairness in
the corporate-consumer arena: consumers must organize to meet
power with power. As labor and welfare and black organizations
have shown—groups whose techniques can be of service to consumers—the name of the game in America is not justice but
power. And power does not mean a few spokesmen leading
around a disinterested flock of 200 million consumers—for without a strong grass roots movement, the leadership at the top will
be merely shouting, or whistling, in the dark.

The consumer movement today has reached a level of development where its direction and purpose are no longer clearly apparent. For example, the traditional consumer view that goods
should be sold at the lowest price is in conflict with the current
consumer interest in safer and probably more expensive products.
By the same token, the growing consumer interest in goods

---

* The three writers are Washington lawyers who comprise their own
"public interest law firm," handling major cases in the consumer and pollution areas and publishing articles dealing with these same issues. Edward
Berlin was Assistant General Counsel of the Federal Power Commission,
Anthony Roisman worked in the Justice Department, and Gladys Kessler
worked as a legislative assistant on Capitol Hill and as an attorney with
the National Labor Relations Board.

whose production or disposal does not create environmental problems cannot be wholly reconciled with the consumer's desire for cheap and convenient products.

The resolution of these problems cannot and should not be made by a handful of consumer spokesmen but must be made by masses of concerned consumers who, equipped with the facts, decide whether a clean and usable river is worth an increase in the cost of electricity, or limitations on the use of electricity by consumers and producers of consumer goods. It is our own view that the consumers' desire to have cheap and convenient products must eventually give way to the greater need to preserve our dwindling usable environment for future generations. If the choice is ours, the electric canopener will go before a single fish dies of thermal pollution from a nuclear power plant. But, of course, that is precisely our point—the choice should not be ours alone. Our vantage point, which is fairly typical of today's consumer spokesmen, is of a predominantly Eastern, white, middle class professional. It is hardly representative of the mainstream of the consumer movement.

A problem closely related to the need for greater consumer participation in the consumer movement is the question of which consumers most need to participate. It is generally assumed that the more educated consumer is less in need of government controls of consumer goods, and that this consumer, if fully aware of the relevant facts about products, will make the wisest purchase. It is therefore not surprising that the main thrust of the consumer movement, which is largely influenced by the more educated consumer, has been toward consumer education and full disclosure of facts to consumers. *Consumer Reports*, the most respected and practical consumer publication, is clearly geared to the sophisticated audience which can presumably use the wealth of product information which is provided.

The major legislative battles which consumers have fought nationally thus far have been for the most part battles for more information. The Truth-in-Lending Act, a law requiring full disclosure of interest charges in virtually all credit transactions, is considered by most observers to be the first great victory of the consumer movement—a victory which took eight years to achieve. The theory behind the law is that full and consistent disclosures of credit terms would permit consumers to shop for credit. That theory is of little use to the black or Puerto Rican or Mexican-American consumer in an urban or rural ghetto, who lacks the mobility of the middle-class consumer and for whom there are no real credit choices. He now knows, as he knew all along, that the sources of cheap credit are not in his neighborhood, that he cannot easily get to where they are, and if he did get to them they probably would not extend credit to him anyway.

Much the same situation exists with the other full disclosure legislation which has been enacted or proposed, such as Truth-in-Labeling, Truth-in-Packaging, unit-pricing, disclosure of shelf-life dates, etc. The middle-class, educated consumer can probably take full advantage of these disclosures. The low-income consumer, who is frequently the victim of an inadequate educational system, may find the full disclosure of unit prices and shelf-life dates merely one more group of confusing, irrelevant figures.

The middle- and upper-income consumer is in a financial position to make the choice between cheaper products which are harmful to the environment and more expensive environmentally desirable products. To the welfare mother there is no choice because the more expensive product is simply not a feasible alternative. It may be that in the long run the welfare mother and the middle-class mother will both equally benefit from the cleaner environment, but today the immediacy of maximizing the purchasing power of a grossly inadequate income makes the welfare mother firmly committed to the lowest priced product.

Despite these differences between the low-income consumer and other consumers, and despite efforts being made by leaders in consumerism to involve low-income consumers, there is virtually no participation by low-income consumers in the traditional consumer activities. One exception has been the development of cooperatives, buying clubs, and credit unions. But these activities, which have been generated almost exclusively on the local level, have not led to greater participation by low-income consumers in decision-making about consumer problems and in construction of possible solutions. This is a development which has occurred outside the consumer "movement." Another exception, which demonstrates the real potential for the consumer movement, is in the area of housing, where local tenant strikes have led to the development of a National Tenants Organization.

In general, however, the consumer "movement" is much less concerned with specific local problems. It has concentrated its efforts to solve consumer problems on obtaining state and national legislation and appearances before administrative agencies and less on direct action against individual suppliers or groups of suppliers. This emphasis by consumers is, in our view, an important development. A national consumer movement which lacks an extensive grass roots consumer organization is neither a truly effective national force nor, as we indicated earlier, is it a force which honestly represents all consumers. The lack of effectiveness is apparent in two ways.

First, the movement is unable to generate the financial resources to be an effective national force. On such key legislative matters as consumer class action legislation and the establishment of a consumer utility counsel, consumer advocates have been virtually overwhelmed by the forces of the opposition. The industry representatives from retail trade associations, utility trade associations, and similar industry lobbying groups made opposition to these legislative proposals a full-time job. These groups, with their vast manpower and financial resources, conducted extensive personal discussions with congressmen, senators, and their staffs; placed stories in the press highlighting the opposition arguments; barraged their membership through trade publications and, as a result, generated substantial mail in opposition to the legislation. Consumers, on the other hand, were forced to rely upon small printings of unprofessionally produced pamphlets. The manpower used to educate and persuade legislators who were generally ignorant about the bills, was supplied on an *ad hoc* basis by other pressure groups whose priorities lay elsewhere. No really sophisticated, effective mass mailings were ever generated to sway the "doubting Thomases." And the consumers were never successful in really dramatizing the need for this legislation. The gross inequity between these two forces is evident in the fact that the consumer utility counsel bill met an untimely death in committee, and class action legislation never reached the floor of either house during the 91st Congress.

Another classic example of this financial inequality is the story of the Truth-in-Lending Act legislation. This act, supported by one of the Senate's most respected members, Senator Paul Douglas, struggled for more than eight years before passage. Truth-in-Lending merely requires that all who extend credit advise their customer of the total cost of borrowing, expressed as a percentage of the total price. It would be natural to assume that there would be little opposition in Congress to legislation which helped consumers make intelligent choices about credit and did so in such a totally innocuous manner. But the under-manned, understaffed, consumer movement, even though aided by labor union lobbyists, did not win the battle for more than eight years.

This dollar gap cannot be closed unless individual consumers in great numbers are prepared to make small but regular contributions to support a national consumer effort. Common Cause is asking and getting $15 per member per year from hundreds of thousands of people; if consumers want a consumer movement with serious impact, they must similarly "sacrifice." Large donations from a few committed and wealthy organizations are hard to find and place dangerous reliance upon a few sources of funds. Foundation support and other tax deductible donations cannot be attracted for an active legislative program.

A second aspect of the ineffectiveness of a national consumer movement is the inability of the national consumer movement to use one of the consumer's best weapons, local action. This local action, consisting of law suits, boycotts, demonstrations, letter writing campaigns, and the like, helps to dramatize consumer needs and put teeth into the national movement's demand for action.

Closely related to this need for local organizations as a pre-requisite to obtaining legislative or administrative action is the need for local organizations to implement those victories obtained through legislative and administrative action. Legislation such as the Truth-in-Lending or the Interstate Land Sales Registration Act, which guarantees the prospective purchasers of vacation property that they will be told the truth about the property, cannot function properly unless local consumer organizations conduct education programs to alert consumers to these disclosures and their meaning. Also, under the Truth-in-Lending Act, when violations occur, consumers have the right to sue the violator and collect damages and attorney's fees. Local organizations can operate complaint centers which ensure the vindication of consumer rights through non-legal action and arrange for legal counsel where legal action is required. Because the statute provides for the right to attorney's fees, there is no need to rely upon free legal assistance. A referral list of lawyers sympathetic to consumers could be established which could not only supply consumers with lawyers but supply lawyers who understand and who are as sympathetic to consumers as they are to paying clients.

On September 23, 1969, the Agriculture Department, after substantial pressure from consumers, adopted a regulation limiting the fat content of hot dogs to 30 percent. For the first time consumers had some protection from the growing use of fat by hot dog manufacturers to reduce the cost and the nutritional value of this basic meat product. However, this regulation, if enforced by the Agriculture Department without scrutiny by consumers, is almost certain to be a hollow victory for many consumers. For instance, subsequent to its September 23 announcement, the department indicated that although the 30 percent fat limitation was to be made effective on October 23, 1970, certain manufacturers would be given an additional period of time to comply with the law. This retreat was sounded without even a notice in the Federal Register or a chance for consumer response.

Even after the law was made applicable to all manufacturers, there was no indication that the department intended to pursue a vigorous enforcement program. Consistent with what has become a way of life at the Agriculture Department and many enforcement agencies, violators, rather than being prosecuted for the violation, are warned to discontinue their illegal acts in the future. This program of leniency cannot and has not encouraged voluntary compliance with the law.

One way to deal with this problem is to sue the Agriculture Department to enforce the law. But this is a difficult legal argument, where the department can hide behind the doctrine of administrative agency discretion and the need to obtain compliance within a limited budget. Another, and more effective means to ensure enforcement is through local consumer organizations conducting frequent compliance checks and initiating boycotts against all manufacturers who are in violation of the law. This could be particularly effective because there are many manufacturers of hot dogs and other sausage products and thus consumers have an easy alternative. The high perishability of these products is also a factor which improves the impact of the boycott. By announcing their testing and boycott plans in advance consumers should be able to achieve a high degree of voluntary compliance, particularly after their first effective boycott.

Although we feel the need for local consumer organizations is necessary both to involve a broader consumer constituency in the deciding of consumer goals and to make national consumer activity more effective, it does not follow that organizing local consumer action is an easy task. It has been tried for years, but the grass roots consumer movement is still in its infancy. The major, missing element is the direct involvement of the consumer in action at the local level. Through this involvement the consumer not only develops a greater commitment to the movement, but also satisfies the basic urge to be an active participant in a matter of great concern. These elements are substantially magnified once the consumer has tasted the sweetness of a victory which has closed down a fraudulent merchant, significantly affected the vote of a key legislator, or forced a landlord to roll back a rent increase and improve the quality of maintenance at an apartment building. And, as in any movement with momentum, success begets success.

There are five basic weapons that the consumer has at his disposal. While some involve less consumer participation in the sense of physical involvement, they all represent action taken by or on behalf of consumers. Even where the action is taken on behalf of the consumer, if it is undertaken with direct contact between the organization and their agent, such as a lawyer or lobbyist, there is a substantial feeling and reality of participation by consumers.

1. The first consumer weapon is *self-help*. Whether we are talking about skyrocketing meat prices, inadequate janitorial apartment house services, or shoddy retailing practices—all are vulnerable to the techniques of direct action. For example, tenants deprived of their basic right to a habitable apartment have used rent strikes with great effectiveness. In Washington (D.C.), St. Louis, and Ann Arbor rent strikes have succeeded, when other tactics failed, in alleviating basic tenant grievances. In Washington, the rent strike device has been used by tenants on every economic level: those in public housing projects; those in privately owned low-income tenements; and even by those in middle-income housing where a rent strike, started over precipitous rent increases, soon grew to include a full complement of tenant grievances. Thus, while used most successfully by low-income tenants to date, rent strikes are equally adaptable to middle-class tenants who are facing intolerable and frequent rent increases with diminishing maintenance.

This theory of a consumer strike—where consumers withhold payments, retaining the goods and forcing the merchant to seek relief in the courts—can apply to many other consumer problems. Whenever credit is extended and the merchant collects on the obligation, the consumer strike can be used to fight such unscrupulous practices as credit charges in excess of those allowed by statute, poorly made merchandise, refusal to honor service warranties, or harassing and humiliating telephone calls as a collection technique. Debtors can go on a credit strike, and if there is doubt about their ultimate liability, a fund should be set up in a local credit union where payments are deposited until the dispute is resolved in the courts.

A variation on this device is to withhold only a portion of the alleged payment due or impose a financial cost on the merchant by some other means. For example, a telephone customer dissatisfied with a portion of his service could withhold a portion of the amount due on his bill; or electricity users who are victims of power failures or brown-outs could withhold payment until they receive a five-day notice, which is usually two or three months after the initial due date, thereby interfering with the cash flow of the utility. The possibilities are—fortunately—quite endless. The consumer strike should be utilized as if it were a chess game in which each move should demonstrate the consumers' power, but not "overkill" the opponent and trigger a complete cutoff of service or court suit for nonpayment—at least not until the consumers are prepared to fight on that level.

The refusal to make payment for services which are faulty, defective, or have been secured through fraud or deceptive practices—which is just another way of describing a credit strike—is most effective when one or all of the following are present: an easily identifiable, visible, and unsympathetic local opponent; a financial situation in which the withholding of payment is crucial to the continuance of day-to-day operations; and a situation in which the target of the strike has real control over the conditions which need remedying.

Closely related to the strike is the boycott. Here, the consumer flatly withholds his patronage from a given establishment —whether a bus company in protest of discriminatory policies, a food store for exorbitant prices, or a retail merchant for deceptive advertising. Boycotts also require a local, visible, basically unsympathetic target as well as alternative sources of goods or services. Well-organized housewives in Denver were able to put an abrupt halt to rising meat prices a few years ago by their concerted refusal to purchase meat. The key is staying power and a reasonable alternative for the consumer. A boycott of every food store in a city is obviously doomed to failure because the consumer will feel the pressure before the stores. But, the labor union technique of whipsawing, where one merchant is boycotted while others remain in business, is an effective and powerful technique which can preserve alternatives for consumers and exert maximum pressure on the merchant. Picketing and publicity are virtual necessities for any successful boycott, and, again, substantial organization and coordination of community efforts are vital ingredients.

Consumers choosing the techniques of strikes or boycotts need to be prepared, once their impact begins to hurt, for defending themselves in court. In the credit strike situation, the creditor may harass the consumer at his place of work and complain to his employer about nonpayment of debts, or he may go to court and seek to garnish a portion of his wages (garnishment is a device by which a creditor, after establishing in court that money is owed to him, can have first claim on a stated percentage of a man's wages before the employee even receives them). In the boycott situations, the opponent will in all likelihood seek an injunction against picketing on grounds that there is inter- ference with his legitimate business relations, or that it is in- herently violent and disruptive. Moreover, boycott leaders could be sued for damages for disruption and loss of business. In all these instances, competent counsel can, through the planning of strategy and on-the-scene advice, minimize the legal problems and present defenses which have proved successful in similar situ- ations. For example, when picketing is used, a lawyer can greatly reduce the possibilities of a court injunction by advising on the number, placement, and route of pickets, the content of signs, and conduct during any demonstration. Similarly, depending on the jurisdiction, the establishment of a carefully insulated deposit account with a high degree of consumer participation may protect and immunize all participants from garnishment during the pendency of long drawn-out negotiations and court action.

For the strike or the boycott to be meaningful, communica- tion channels will have to be opened, such as communications from defrauded consumers to other consumers, warning them of fraudulent practices, and to the guilty entrepreneur, with the object of correcting his activities. To facilitate these communi- cation objectives a Neighborhood Consumer Information Center has been established in the District of Columbia by Howard University law students. When complaints are received from consumers, an "undercover" agent is dispatched to the store complained of and if the offending practice is repeated, the store officials are thereafter confronted with a demand for remedial action. If corrective action is not taken, citizens in the community are advised, through regular leaflet distributions, to avoid patronizing that establishment. The publicity continues until the practice is abated.

On a lesser scale the Louisiana Consumers League moved recently to tumble the communications wall by installing a consumers' "hot line" in Baton Rouge to give Louisianians shopping tips, information on unfair practices, and assistance generally on consumer matters. The hot line is supported and staffed entirely by volunteers who do the taping, transcription, and follow-up work on requests left by callers. The Louisiana hot line is patterned after the Virginia Citizens Consumer Council, which is now well into its second year.

Where the activity complained of is sufficiently evil and well-entrenched, resort to demonstrations and civil disobedience may be appropriate. For instance, where bankers have continued to increase interest rates without a showing of any higher costs to justify the increase, and in total disregard of consumer needs, a strike or boycott will not help the consumer who cannot get credit at a price he can afford. But pickets at the bank, who urge depositors to use credit unions or other depositories which have more response to consumer needs, coupled with "deposit-ins" where consumers clog bank deposit lines to make $1 deposits, may help the banker realize that he must be more alert to consumer interests.

2. Another weapon available to the beleaguered consumer is recourse to the appropriate *local administrative agency*. With such retail consumer problems as a fraudulently induced contract or deceptive advertising, the injured party can often turn to the administrative process for vindication of his grievances. More and more local consumer protection agencies are being set up at the state and municipal level. While they vary a good deal in terms of jurisdiction, authority, commitment, manpower, and funds, they should never be ignored when seeking a remedy.

Most of these offices require the complainant to submit a signed, written complaint giving all the facts. Whatever the ultimate disposition of the complaint, its mere filing may be extremely useful: it alerts the administrative agency to future shady dealings or actual misconduct by this particular business; the incident may constitute one of many such complaints on which the agency later bases its decision to conduct a public investigation or to file a lawsuit; and even though the complaint may cover abuses not within the authority of the agency, a sufficient number of such occurrences may justify the ultimate broadening of the agency's jurisdiction in order to empower it to cope with such problems. The local consumer's organization could function effectively by soliciting consumers with similar complaints, sending them on to the consumer protection agency, thus demonstrating the breadth of the enforcement problem in order to encourage a prompt response.

This analysis applies to a consumer's specific complaint about a particular factual situation involving a known party. The situation is quite different when the consumer(s) seek(s) broad affirmative, discretionary action from an agency. For example, the local consumer protection agency may have broad, but undefined, rule-making authority. An individual whose goal is to persuade or compel that agency to issue a regulation requiring all food stores to use unit-pricing is faced with a far different problem. In that instance, confronted with an unresponsive, indifferent, hostile, or just plain overworked agency, the consumer will have the challenge of producing action. Again, the need for an organized campaign cannot be stressed too much. In addition to manpower and money, an organized group will command the respect and attention which it is very difficult for the individual consumer to receive.

First of all the organization must gather and present a very compelling factual case for the agency to consider; it must use the agency's internal procedures and rules to the best advantage and attempt to force a public hearing; it will have to meet with and influence the various individuals within the agency who will have any impact on the final outcome; and, of course, it will have to be prepared to do *sub rosa* battle with representatives of industry who will be better financed, possibly better informed, probably better connected politically, and with a great deal more to lose. The organization would most likely, in a rule-making proceeding, hire outside counsel. At the very least, it must be prepared to expend a great deal of its own time and energies and those of its members in lobbying for the proposed regulation or it will die a quiet death by indifference and apathy.

An important aspect of administrative action is the need to provide support to those administrative agencies which respond to consumer needs. When Bess Myerson Grant, the head of New York City's Consumer Affairs Department, required that all food stores disclose the price per pound or ounce on all packages (unit-pricing) to overcome the confusion created by a mixture of package sizes, she needed and should have received widespread support in the form of consumer action. Support for merchants which did not oppose the regulation would be one example.

3. A third weapon available to the consumer is *litigation in the courts.* Here, he must usually engage a lawyer to represent him, and many legal obstacles are placed in his way. Ralph Nader, in his keynote address at Consumer Assembly '70, said that the greatest need in the consumer movement today is "the need for skilled manpower and plenty of it." But not just any kind of manpower. "The name of the game is lawyers," he said. "Ten thousand lawyers in Washington, D.C., represent special interest groups; perhaps a half-dozen lawyers represent the public interest full time." And in a speech before the New York State Bar recently, Bess Myerson Grant called for an end to "legal tokenism," and asked for lawyers in large numbers to work for the public interest.

On the local level, there are not usually many, if any, ordinances or regulations which give an aggrieved consumer a direct right to go to court and affirmatively present his case. For instance, a householder who purchases, on time, a dishwasher which then proves defective within a few months after purchase has few legal alternatives. In the ordinary course of events, that consumer will not appear in court until he is forced, in a defensive posture, to answer for nonpayment of the debt. At that point the consumer can attempt to defend himself by citing the breakdown of the machine, the refusal to honor a warranty, and perhaps a nonexistent service contract. But given the cost of a lawyer, the chances are the consumer will pay rather than have his goods repossessed, a procedure which has been used in some states even without going to court.

But what of the consumer who is not content to be forced into a defensive posture and who, upon realizing that he has been bilked, wants to bring an affirmative suit for return of his payments and damages caused by the faulty operation of the product? If there is specific statutory authority for bringing suit against those who use deceptive or fraudulent sales practices, the consumer is in a good legal position. However, most of the so-called "little Federal Trade Commission Acts," which outlaw the traditional deceptive sales practices, allow only the designated administrative agency to prosecute and rarely allow defrauded individuals to proceed on their own. In that event, the consumer can bring a common-law suit for fraud or breach of warranty, although these are usually difficult to win because the consumer will be unable to expend the resources necessary to establish the factual basis for his right to relief.

The overriding problem which faces the individual consumer who wants to sue—and this is just as much of a middle-class as a low-income problem—is the disproportion between what his recovery can be, at best, and the cost of maintaining his suit. The unfortunate fact is that it rarely pays the individual consumer to bring an affirmative suit on his own behalf because the consumer's complaint almost always involves a relatively small sum ($100 to $500) which is insufficient to warrant payment of an attorney's fee.

A most important answer to this problem—and one of incalculable importance in the development of "consumer rights" —is the procedural device called the class action. By employing this method, one aggrieved consumer may, in one lawsuit, sue on behalf of all others similarly situated to recover damages, costs, and attorney's fees for all others of the victimized class. Thus, one individual who has taken out a consumer loan from a bank, on which an illegally high interest rate was charged because of the bank's method of computing such interest rate, may bring one lawsuit on behalf of himself and every other similarly aggrieved borrower. That very case is now pending in the District of Columbia. Whereas the actual overcharge for the one plaintiff may be $75 or $100 (clearly not enough to pay the fees for a major lawsuit), the overcharge for the entire class consisting of thousands of consumers clearly warrants a major suit on behalf of the consumers.

Another important aspect of the class action is that where one individual suit can be settled out of court by the offending party, without any formal resolution of the alleged violation, a class action may not be compromised in this manner. For example, one individual may sue a used car dealer because his contract contained blank spaces when he signed it, and this practice violates local law. The individual might be entitled to completely void the contract and to receive substantial civil penalties. However, when that car dealer realizes that he has a losing case, and may face much unfavorable publicity in the process of a trial, he will offer to settle out-of-court with the individual; and to avoid all the expenses of litigation, it might be tempting for the individual to accept a settlement offer which voids the contract and gives him one-half the civil penalties to which he is entitled. But this out-of-court settlement is of absolutely no legal use to the many hundreds of other used car purchasers who have been defrauded by this dealer. If a suit is brought on behalf of an entire aggrieved class of used car purchasers, it cannot be compromised without court approval and until all members of the class are included in the settlement; now the merchant will not be able to avoid substantial liability for his action by a cheap settlement.

Moreover, in a class action it is possible to obtain an injunction on behalf of all other members of the class against the practices complained of. For example, in a suit in Washington, D.C., a woman sued on behalf of herself, and all other poor consumers similarly victimized to prevent a collection agency from illegally and unconstitutionally harassing those who supposedly had unpaid debts. In this instance, the primary thrust of the suit was not just to get money damages but to *stop* a widespread and pernicious practice which had caused loss of employment, humiliation, and impairment of reputation to many people.

Class actions have been used with increasing success and popularity in the last few years as people have come to realize their practical and social utility. In addition to avoiding a multiplicity of suits and thus saving the court's time, the class action makes it worthwhile for private lawyers to sue for small recoveries-per-plaintiff which are sizable in the aggregate. Since the courts usually set the legal fees in relation to the size of recovery, private lawyers should have little hesitation about their ultimate remuneration in such suits where a legitimate complaint is involved.

Many states still do not allow class actions or view them very restrictively. However, the use of this device to vindicate consumer claims is achieving growing acceptance throughout the country. On the federal level, class action legislation is still pending in Congress, having failed to pass the 91st Congress. The legislation originally introduced by Senator Tydings (S. 3092) and Congressman Eckhardt (H.R. 14585) would permit consumers to bring class actions based on violations of state law in the federal courts. Passage of such legislation, penned *New Republic* writer David Sanford, would be "Giving the Consumer Class."

A local consumer organization could substantially assist the use of consumer class actions by receiving and investigating consumer complaints and, where an illegal practice by a merchant or group of merchants is found to be widespread, the organization could refer the case to an attorney who could file a class action on behalf of all the victims of the illegal practice. This effort by consumer organizations would be extremely important because lawyers, to whom such consumer complaints might normally be brought, are apparently prohibited from solicitation of other aggrieved consumers for the purpose of bringing a class action. It is an "ethical" restriction by the profession which Beverly Moore, in the following chapter, seeks to undo.

4. A fourth weapon available to the consumer is *legislative action*. Municipal, state, and federal legislators are increasingly anxious to be considered "consumer advocates" and, therefore, often have a welcome mat out for consumer groups. However,

effective lobbying which produces legislation and changes in legislative attitudes, as opposed to glad hands from legislators, requires a sustained, informed, and sophisticated effort.

Here again, it is absolutely essential for consumers to be organized. While individuals will be treated politely in most legislative anterooms, little or no attention will be paid to their views. The first question asked any lobbyist by a receptionist is, "Whom do you represent?" And the bigger the organization you represent, the more militant it is, the greater numbers you can produce on any given issue, the more weight your position will carry. For example, the Uniform Consumer Credit Code (a deceptively titled anti-consumer piece of complex credit legislation) was about to sail through a joint House-Senate study committee of the Arizona legislature in 1969. The local AFL-CIO decided to vigorously oppose the legislation. It presented carefully documented testimony against the bill highlighting its 39 percent interest rates. It issued publicity releases and got excellent coverage in the local press. It lobbied individual legislators. Once alerted to the intensity of consumer opposition, as well as being presented with a more balanced view of the legislation's pitfalls, the study committee decided not to issue a favorable report.

The first rule that every lobbyist must learn is to know his issue, including *all* the pros and cons, better than anyone else on any side. Next, he must understand the procedural framework governing the bills he is concerned about: what, if any, legislative committees will consider the bill; have hearings been held; will he be allowed to testify; what are all the rules governing the amendment process; and what are the procedural requirements and technicalities for final passage of the bill? He will need to understand all the politics of his legislation: who are his opponents and what is the nature of their opposition; who are the neutrals and uncommitted and what pressures can be exerted to win them over; with what other organizations or interest groups can he form alliances; how strong is his own side and which of his friends are really dependable when it comes down to a decision? More than anything else, legislative action requires hard and persistent work. People must be talked to at great length, they must be educated as to the issues, and they must be given short and cogent fact sheets which describe the lobbyist's position on the legislation.

The local consumer organization is not only essential as an organizer of these activities, but its membership, properly briefed, will be the lobbyists. A well-informed, astute, amateur lobbyist, speaking to his or her own legislator, may well be more effective than the professional lobbyist. Certainly such "amateurs" should accompany the professional to impress the legislator with the intense involvement of his own constituents.

5. The final consumer weapon is one that should be used regardless of the other four weapons that may be used, and it may be the most powerful one of all: *the press.* The influence and utility of publicity must not be ignored or underestimated. From the very inception of any consumer campaign, personal relationships should be established with the appropriate individual reporters, and intensive efforts should be made to fully inform members of the press of what the outstanding abuses are, who the offenders are, what action is contemplated, and what progress is being made, if any.

Press coverage can be used in more than just the obvious way of exposing the abuses of a slum landlord or a fly-by-night roofing company which fleeces homeowners and ends up with a mortgage on their home. Effective and hard-hitting newspaper stories can put backbone in a hesitant administrative agency to enable it to issue complaints and undertake investigations it would never have otherwise considered. Any doubt about the power of the press to right consumer wrongs is certainly dispelled by the recent efforts of one Washington, D.C., reporter. Through his persistent exposure of the frauds being perpetrated by a door-to-door company selling intercom systems to unwary homeowners, community action was aroused to the point where the company was put out of business and its officials prosecuted. But this example also underscores the need for a concerted local consumer effort using all the available weapons. By the time the criminal was caught it was too late to give any relief to his many victims. If the fraud had been discovered by a consumer organization at an early stage, a suit could have been filed to enjoin the further operation of the business and to collect damages for the already defrauded consumer.

Even the courts can, in certain subtle ways, be influenced by press coverage. For example, a suit which presents novel and innovative theories of law, which might tend to be dismissed out of hand by a conservative court, may acquire added respectability and urgency because of the facts highlighted in a series of press articles.

The use of the press (if indeed one can ever be said to "use" the press) is a delicate and difficult matter which must be handled with sensitivity, care, and absolute honesty. It often requires a great deal of patience as well as canny timing; it is worth every ounce of effort and every second of time.

Obviously there is a great deal more to the development of a grass roots consumer movement than we have been able to discuss here. Our purpose has been to emphasize the need for greater active participation by consumers at the local level. Our experience with and work for the consumer movement has demonstrated beyond any doubt that every day consumers are losing important battles because they lack the ability to apply manpower and resources, both locally and nationally, to these problems. With a potential constituency of 200 million consumers it is outrageous that the movement must rely upon a handful of consumer spokesmen and a few major national consumer organizations to carry the fight.

This year millions of American consumers will buy automobiles whose safety has been compromised by an industry which devotes more effort to style changes than to crash protection; millions more will fret and fume at the myriad of confusing and complex labels and packages in their local food stores, unable to determine what is the best buy; millions of apartment dwellers will suffer through cold and drafty winters, hot and humid summers, mounds of uncollected garbage, and ever-increasing housing costs; electric appliances will burn out and lights will dim from electric "brown outs," while electric utilities continue to feed millions of kilowatts of full power electricity to commercial users; doorbells will ring in millions of American homes and fast talking door-to-door salesmen will peddle $400 vacuum

cleaners and $1,200 intercom systems by the truckload to con-
sumers who can neither afford nor want the product; newspaper
ads will herald huge closeout sales, while earlybird customers
who respond to the "bait" will be "switched" to high-priced,
non-sale, non-advertised items; and on and on.

What is shocking is not that these and other injustices will be
perpetrated on consumers, but that the consumers, if they
united, could eliminate these abuses.

The Lawyer's Response:
The Public Interest Law Firm

BEVERLY C. MOORE, JR.*

I. A ROLE FOR THE LEGAL SYSTEM

On June 23, 1970, federal judge Inzer B. Wyatt approved a settlement in which major pharmaceutical companies agreed to pay $100 million to terminate a lawsuit charging them with illegally fixing the price of the drug Tetracycline since 1954. *West Virginia v. Charles R. Pfizer & Company*[1] was no ordinary antitrust case. Instead of the usual business competitors, the suing parties included virtually every state government, several major cities, numerous hospitals, and the class of all consumers who had purchased the drug during the price fix. Forty-two thousand individual consumers submitted claims in response to notices placed in newspapers throughout the nation. Since it was impossible to locate and reimburse all individual consumers, the court gave the remainder of the settlement fund to the state governments to be held in trust "for the benefit of consumers generally."

Pfizer is the first case in which consumers, as distinguished from competitors and distributors, have recovered for price fixing. The unfortunate fact is that "class actions"—where many sim-

---

* Beverly Moore is a lawyer in Washington, D.C., where he is working for a new public interest law firm, The Public Interest Research Group, and also collaborating on a study of antitrust enforcement. He was Comments Editor of the *Harvard Civil Rights—Civil Liberties Law Review* during 1969–70 and also worked in the campaign of the late Joseph Yablonski for the presidency of the United Mine Workers Union.

ilarly harmed people bring suit—are very rare. Most lawsuits involve injuries of a distinctly personal nature, such as individual wills, divorces, auto accidents, and bad debts. As the subject matter of these ordinary lawsuits indicates, the potential plaintiff is likely to have suffered a major personal or financial crisis before taking the drastic and expensive step of actual litigation. Cases like *Pfizer* involve a quite different type of legal injury, a mass produced "invisible tort." Thousands or even millions of similarly situated persons are damaged in a relatively minor way, yet precisely because the injury to each individual is so small, so remote in origin, and often wholly unnoticed, no single victim is likely to seek redress in the courts.

The average consumer falls prey almost daily to a long list of silent, unseen injuries. He is overcharged on most of his purchases by oligopolistic market structures which a vigorous antitrust policy should have eliminated long ago. Yet the consumer has probably never heard the word "oligopoly," nor does he understand the impact on the price he pays of such corporate schemes as resale price maintenance agreements, mergers, exclusive dealerships, or tying arrangements, all of which may be actionable offenses under present antitrust laws.

He would not realize generally that 1.6 percent of the American people own 32 percent of all privately owned wealth and 82.2 percent of all stocks, or that 11 percent of all spending units hold 60 percent of net private wealth while 45 percent have net assets (including homes and automobiles) of less than $5,000. Similarly, 500 industrial corporations control one-half of all sales and receive 70 percent of all profits from manufacturing and mining. Also, 2,632, or .2 percent of all active corporations, hold 65 percent of total corporate assets and receive 66 percent of total net corporate income. The 600 largest have average assets of $1 billion. Not one of the 200 largest concerns is controlled by a majority of its stockholders; 84.5 percent are management controlled and more than half of industrial markets are oligopolistic.

He is also unlikely to learn of the inflated freight rates that the Interstate Commerce Commission allows inefficient carriers to charge for many consumer goods in order to subsidize more powerful raw material shippers with below cost rates. Similar resource misallocating distortions in "regulated" airline, telephone, and power company rate structures will just as surely escape the victimized consumer's attention.

But if direct gouging should inconceivably miss its mark, the highly sophisticated deceptions of sellers will almost certainly ensnare Adam Smith's "rational economic man." Modern advertising has been quick to capitalize upon the increasing affluence of the consumer.

The function of advertising in capitalist theory is to perform an "informational" service that will facilitate rational consumer choice. In reality, much of the economy's $20 billion annual advertising budget is devoted to creating and manipulating consumer preferences. Unconsciously, the consumer may purchase *not* the advertised product, but the sexual allurement, social status, or carefree youthful setting in which it is advertised. Through constant identification of its wares with a brand name —e.g., "Bayer," not "aspirin"; "Clorox," not "bleach"—heavily advertising oligopolists are able to entrench their market power to the exclusion of virtually identical but less well-known brands. A Consumer's Union study demonstrates how products are also packaged in a manner calculated to dazzle and baffle. Five experienced, college educated housewives were dispatched to a large supermarket with a list of seventy items to be purchased according to the package offering the largest quantity at the lowest unit price. The results: thirty-two correct purchases, thirty-eight incorrect choices. The five-woman project staff labored for six hours with an electric calculating machine, analyzing 286 differently packaged offerings, to compute the right answers.[2]

More blatant practices range from outright fraud and defective products to the friendly encyclopedia salesman who offers a "free" set of books if the customer will subscribe to the company's "research service." There is also the home improvement company that first promises to pay the consumer large sums for referrals of additional customers, then sells the installment loan contract to a "holder in due course," and soon thereafter disappears. At a more subtle level, it is typical for oligopolists to compete in every area except price and quality—thus the prizes, giveaways, trading stamps (costing the consumer at least $800 million in 1964), and other gimmicks to divert the consumer's attention away from the product that he is buying.

Indeed, consumer deception is so widespread as to raise grave doubts about the legitimacy of the American economic system. In theory, the consumer is sovereign; economic resources are allocated in the most efficient manner according to the consumer's desires as expressed through his purchases in the market place. But under present conditions the premise of consumer sovereignty must give way to the reality of corporate manipulation of consumer preferences.

The real tragedy is that the consumer's present plight can still be remedied, or at least publicly exposed, by a vigorous and widespread program of "public" legal action, of which *Pfizer* is but a rare instance. Consumers have the same rights as businessmen to sue for treble damages under the antitrust statutes or to challenge transportation and utility rate schedules. There are many consumer protection statutes currently in force which deal with false advertising, lack of "truth-in-packaging," and of "truth-in-lending," and other deceptive practices. Ironically, such statutes are more often used as the basis for lawsuits by businessmen than by unorganized, unknowing, and relatively impecunious consumers.

In addition, there are numerous statutes entrusting consumer protection responsibilities to administrative agencies such as the Federal Trade Commission and the Food and Drug Administration. Yet, the absence of consumer pressures for administrative action has resulted in massive nonenforcement of the law by agency officials. Of course, existing consumer protection laws, even when enforced, are often inadequate and cannot or will not be sufficiently strengthened by judges or regulatory agencies. Again, however, consumers have not exercised their right to wage intensive legislative campaigns for new laws that would, for example, require sellers to disclose per unit prices and estimated useful lives of their products.

Consumers are by no means the only passive victims of invisible torts. The still uncalculated damages to property, health, and the general environment from all forms of pollution continue to mount. Though armed with numerous statutes, administrative agencies, common law nuisance doctrines, and a general public outcry, the apathetic victims of pollution have thus far refrained from a significant legal counterattack.

Thousands of local zoning ordinances and building codes restrict the access of the non-affluent to better schools, housing, sanitation, and social services. The mass media is largely concentrated in the hands of the three major television networks and the one-to-a-city daily newspapers; an intricate set of multiple- and cross-media ownership patterns link broadcast facilities, newspapers, publishing houses, cable television, and the emerging computer, satellite, microwave, and laser transmission technology, and vertical control ties in the talent agencies, syndicated columnists, wire services, copyrights, and other sources of program material. "Network television programming follows the classic pattern of oligopoly behavior—imitation, restricted choice, elaborate corporate strategies, and reliance on the 'tried and true.' "[3] As the institution with the single greatest impact upon American culture and values, television rarely displays the diversity of ideas necessary for informed social change. Finally, the "democratic" political system, throws the burden of voter registration to the individual citizen, leaves the financing of candidates to wealthy elites, and lets elections be determined by the power of incumbency (although 65 percent of the electorate are unable to name their congressmen). Voter turnout is outrageously low—45 percent in off-year congressional contests—and the composition of Congress reflects numerical majorities within geographical single-member districts, not the proportional strength of various political ideologies throughout the nation. Indeed, only a tiny fraction of the electorate even have logically structured political ideologies.[4]

The average American's perception of the "system" is more a reflection of ingrained mythology than of empirical reality. His nation may have cultivated God, Motherhood, and Apple Pie, but it is rare in history that a civilization with such an enormous potential for justice, progress, and material affluence has instead produced so much death, waste, and human misery.

Only some of the many invisible torts have been discussed.

The cost to each passive victim involves what welfare economists call an "external diseconomy," a cost of production borne not by the producer but imposed by him upon an unwilling and often unknowing public. Air and water pollution are frequent examples; so, too, in a general sense, are any devices, such as price fixing or oligopolistic market structures, by which producers are able to charge other than perfectly competitive prices for the goods they sell. Such external diseconomies are by no means a purely academic concern. Their total cost to society staggers the imagination, for we are talking about billions of dollars each year in misallocated resources and undeserved corporate profits. The damage from manipulation of consumer preferences alone must constitute a significant fraction of the gross national product.

The American economy is primarily a self-regulating mechanism. External diseconomies simply reflect the failure of the invisible hand of the market to function in a manner that is consistent with capitalist economic theory. But the concept of the external diseconomy has even wider applications. Racial discrimination and a general lack of basic political knowledge among voters are, respectively, social and political "diseconomies."

A lawsuit like *Pfizer* demonstrates how the legal system can redress the injuries brought about by external diseconomies, but the infrequent occurrence of such suits demonstrates how the legal system in fact reinforces those injuries.* As the present, but unutilized, availability of legal remedies for many of these invisible torts tends to suggest, the role of the legal system should be to force the "internalization" of all external diseconomies, to require each polluter to bear the cost of his own pollution, to prevent or to redress any non-optimal wealth distribution or resource allocation, to eliminate impediments to political equality. Consequently, when exploited consumers or pollution victims fail to or can't bring internalizing lawsuits like *Pfizer*, where the

---

* The approximately $30 million that individual consumers received of the $85 million settlement in *Pfizer* is far overshadowed by the $3 *billion* in treble damages that they might have recovered had the case been brought to trial. Despite the apparent enormity of the settlement amount, the price-fixing drug companies actually retained 95 percent of their illegal profits.

drug companies were compelled to pay for their over-pricing, there arise what might be labeled "external dislegalities."

In short, for self-regulating models to work justly, the legal system must maintain the structural and the informational preconditions. Right now, the models are a sham because the predicates are nonexistent. The problem is compounded by the inevitable tendency for uncontrolled economic power to lead to political power, which diminishes the chance of establishing in fact the assumptions of the models, such as competitive markets and an informed consumer.

II. THE LEGAL PROFESSION AT WORK

It is apparent that there exist many "paper rights" which are simply not being enforced by the classes of people who are their potential beneficiaries. When we ask why consumers have not done these things, we observe that the injury to an *individual* consumer from a price-fixed or deceptively advertised product is very small, perhaps $50, perhaps only a few cents. On the other hand, the aggregate injury to the *class* of all consumers who purchased the product may amount to millions of dollars. Because the injury is so minor, the consumer probably will not even perceive that it has occurred. It is an "invisible injury," or "invisible tort," as a consumer lawyer might refer to it, and modern technology has given rise to mass production of these invisible torts.

Suppose the alert consumer or pollution victim does propose to bring a lawsuit to recover his losses. He will find that legal expenses far outweigh his own potential recovery. Even though the antitrust statutes provide that the consumer-plaintiff may recover litigation costs from the losing defendant, who will finance the suit prior to its final outcome? Unlike corporations, labor unions, and other powerful interests, consumers and pollution victims are largely unorganized; they have no spokesman with the resources necessary to vindicate their legal rights. Why should one pollution victim pay dues to a conservation group when he knows that if the group can raise money from other sources and mount an effective legal campaign to stop pollution, he will have benefited at no cost to himself? Other groups, such as the poor, may be organized, but in their case organization does not generate funds.

This dilemma can be solved by two devices: the class action and the contingent lawyer's fee. The class action allows the individual victim to sue as a representative of all similarly situated persons and to recover in their behalf the aggregate damage to the entire class. He then distributes the proceeds to absent class members. Unlike the consumer, the pollution victim faces the difficult problem of apportioning his losses among many contributing polluters. Thus he will desire to sue the entire class of polluters—i.e., class plaintiffs v. class defendants. The contingent fee is an arrangement by which the lawyer for the class agrees to charge no hourly fee and, if need be, to advance expenses out of his own pocket, in return for being paid a fixed percentage— perhaps 25 percent—of the total damage recovery. The possibility of a multi-million dollar recovery will induce the lawyer to risk his own money (if he has any) on a class action, whereas he would have been forced to turn down an individual's lawsuit.

The class action is an absolutely essential weapon if public interest lawyers are to aid the drive for fundamental changes in American society. At present, however, while class actions can be brought in federal courts when a specific federal statute is involved (such as an antitrust law), the states have been more hostile.[5] New York's highest court recently refused to allow a class action in behalf of consumers who had signed standard form installment credit contracts that were identical in all material respects, including the illegal provisions and the damage to each member of the class.[6]

Consumer class action legislation now before Congress would confer broad jurisdiction upon federal courts to entertain certain types of consumer suits as class actions.[7] There appears to be substantial support for these bills—and substantial opposition from the Nixon administration and from business interests such as the United States Chamber of Commerce.[8] Chief Justice Warren Burger has stated publicly that class actions would overburden the crowded federal courts. He apparently believes that the class victims of "invisible torts" do not have the same constitutional right to utilize the federal courts as do individuals and corporations, or that federal judges lack the intellectual competence to deal with complex legal matters. In the fore-front of the opposition to federal consumer class action legislation has been the American Bar Association's Antitrust Section.[9] As the organized legal profession's spokesman on antitrust matters, this ABA group is dominated by lawyers who represent *defendants* in antitrust cases.* Richard McLaren, a former ABA Antitrust Section chairman who is now chief of the Justice Department's Antitrust Division, has been a major Nixon opponent of the class action bills.[10]

It is not that these lawyers are "evil" men, only that most of their professional careers have been devoted to defending the actions of organized and economically powerful interests. Their views of what the legal system is supposed to accomplish differ from public interest lawyers.' Unfortunately, this observation is not limited to antitrust law. Through superior ability to recognize its own need for legal advice and to pay handsomely for it, corporate power has virtually cornered the talents of the legal profession. The wealthier commercial interests are the primary clientele of the largest and most prestigious law firms. For example, a 1960 study of New York City lawyers found that for solo practitioners, 23 percent of clients had annual incomes above $20 thousand, while 47 percent fall below $10 thousand. For firms with more than fifteen lawyers, however, 80 percent of the clients had annual incomes exceeding $20 thousand and only 1 percent earned less than $10 thousand.[11]

In turn, the lawyers in the largest firms receive the highest compensation** and are by far the most competent in terms of

* If consumer class actions would further overcrowd court dockets, the solution is more courts. The ABA argues also that a large portion of the damage recovery may be siphoned off by attorney's fees and that most of the individual consumer victims, being unidentifiable, will not share in the remainder. But the federal law requires that attorneys' fees in class actions must be approved by the court. And it would be desirable to make the corporate law violator pay damages even if no individual victim can be identified, because of the deterrent impact.

** According to ABA statistics, of the approximately 325 thousand American lawyers in private practice (far more per capita than any other nation), educational qualifications. The New York survey revealed that only 47 percent of the solo practitioners had four-year undergraduate degrees and that only 19 percent had attended a full-time law school, compared with a 77 percent rating in both categories for members of firms with more than fifteen lawyers. That it is the corporate dollar, not the citizenry's need for legal services, that fuels the legal process and structures the profession is reflected in the business-oriented content of both law school curricula and bar examinations, which together prepare and screen a steady supply of business-oriented lawyers.

But since the wealthy few cannot consume the services of all lawyers, the bulk of the profession (the least competent) are reserved for the bulk of the citizens (the less affluent). This arrangement has the coincidental advantage of preserving the myth of equal justice for all citizens both among the public and within the profession. On the rare occasions when the typical middle-class citizen does seek legal advice, a lawyer is likely to be far less valuable to him than to his corporate exploiters. The "little" lawyers who represent average citizens do not bring consumer class actions, nor do they press their clients' interests before administrative agencies or legislative committees. Rather, most of their professional expertise is siphoned off into what is essentially legal featherbedding—uncontested divorces, simple wills, real estate title searches, and automobile accidents. Most of these services could be performed much more efficiently by non-legal personnel, no-fault insurance schemes, computer technology, and other devices.

The real problem is not that a lot of lawyers are spending a lot of time doing unproductive things. There does exist an increasing number of lawyers, like David I. Shapiro who devoted seven years to the *Pfizer* case, who would engage in public interest legal work if they had the right clients. Yet the average citizen, unlike the corporation, is unable to recognize his legal problems and

---

nearly half still practice alone. But their incomes are the lowest, averaging $7,870 in 1961; their numbers declining, and their work the most trivial and least rewarding. Lawyers who are partners in firms had average incomes of $18,200 in the same year.

therefore does not seek out public interest lawyers for advice. For example, a Missouri Bar Association study discovered that 36 percent of that state's residents had never used a lawyer and that 78 percent had done so only once in the past five years.[12] The following examples are from a survey in Cambridge, Massachusetts, with the percentages of persons interviewed who failed to perceive the situations as ones in which lawyers could be helpful: (1) a person's wife is suing for a divorce (44 percent); (2) a person is evicted from his home for no apparent reason (48 percent); (3) a finance company threatens to repossess a person's car (77 percent); and (4) a person's social security payments stop without explanation (84 percent). The Cambridge survey also found that the ability to recognize legal problems declines with income—again the poor are disproportionately victimized by unequal access to critical social processes.[13] If these statistics accurately reflect the average citizen's familiarity with the above "commonly recognized" legal situations, one can imagine how far from his mind is any thought of asking a lawyer to challenge any of the numerous "invisible" legal injuries that daily afflict him and millions of others. Another study found that only 3 percent of consumers even think of seeking advice from a lawyer after discovering that they have been defrauded.[14]

Corporate power is especially tempted to employ the skills of its lawyers where opposition from the victims of its invisible torts is unlikely. Consequently, corporate pressure is extremely influential at the administrative and legislative levels of the legal process, where it usually succeeds in preventing the enforcement of whatever laws that have been passed to curb its abuses. Lawyers for a corporation subject to regulation by an administrative agency quickly build up close working relationships and warm friendships with agency personnel. Primarily because the public, which would benefit from agency regulation, does not press for larger legislative appropriations, the agency must subsist on a starvation budget. When an agency does move against his client, however, the corporate lawyer is quick to negotiate a "consent settlement." The agency agrees not to prosecute and the corporation, while continuing to deny its guilt, merely promises not to violate the law in the future. Nearly all regulatory agencies have adopted this enforcement philosophy of "voluntary compliance," which of course eliminates any deterrent effect the law might have had upon other corporate violators.

The irony is that regulatory agencies like the Food and Drug Administration were first envisioned to fill the legal representation gap created by public indifference to invisible torts and the resulting external dislegalities. As it turns out, the administrative process, like the judicial process, is an adversary process. When one adversary (the class of invisible tort victims) is absent, the other (corporate power) will of course triumph by default. The law begins systematically to confer benefits, whether or not earned, upon the party present. An unequal distribution of the knowledge that legal advice is needed has perverted the American legal system so that it now acts as an invisible hand, not for redressing injustice, but for facilitating it.

The obvious solution to this legal problem recognition gap is for the public interest lawyer himself to tell the consumer or other potential client that his legal rights are being invaded. However, centuries old professional restrictions on commercial publicity, advertising, and the solicitation of legal business by lawyers pose a major roadblock to such an activist role for socially conscious attorneys. One of the lawyer's Canons of Ethics reads: "A lawyer who has given unsolicited advice to a layman that he should obtain counsel or take legal action shall not accept employment resulting from that advice . . ."[15] Lawyers who violate this rule may be and have been disbarred.*

One would think that a lawyer who stirs up a suit against, for example, an industrial air polluter should be commended, not condemned. One justification offered for these anomalous rules is that they are necessary to prevent "frivolous" suits. For exam-

---

* The Canon does permit the lawyer to advocate litigation, but it then prohibits him from representing in actual lawsuits those for whom his advocacy has been persuasive. Thus, there is hardly an incentive for the lawyer to conduct the empirical research and construct the legal arguments necessary even for mere advocacy. Similarly, the bar has long allowed lawyers to solicit the "non-fee generating" cases of indigents who are unable to pay legal fees. A contingent fee arrangement is not regarded as a non-fee generating case.

ple, disgruntled stockholders sometimes bring "strike suits" against allegedly incompetent or dishonest managements with the hope not of winning on the merits, but of forcing the corporation to enter into a compromise settlement by which it may avoid the heavy costs of protracted litigation. What is overlooked by the bar associations is that a lawsuit does not become frivolous by virtue of its having been solicited. And there are means of coping with the problem other than by preventing the lawyer from proposing a meritorious lawsuit to a potential client. "Strike settlements" should be unlikely in federal court class actions because the judge must approve any compromise agreement. Solicited plaintiffs could be required to post bonds to cover defendants' legal expenses in cases that were later ruled frivolous. In addition, lawyers who solicit frivolous cases could be held liable for the legal expenses of defendants.

The rules against advertising and soliciting are also considered necessary to prevent "overreaching"—the lawyer's taking undue advantage of his solicited client. The evil of "overreaching" is the injury to the solicited client who has been duped into paying fees to a lawyer who makes extravagant promises but knows that his client's lawsuit will never succeed. Here again the abuse is neither confined to lawyers who solicit nor a characteristic of all solicited cases. And there are alternative remedies. Among them would be to breathe new life into the tort of negligent representation by providing incentives for solicited clients to sue their negligent lawyers. Or lawyers could be required to supply solicited clients with a list of other attorneys specializing in similar cases. (Incidentally, the bar rules in many jurisdictions prohibit lawyers from holding themselves out as specialists in a particular area of law).

Another bar association argument for prohibiting advertising and soliciting by lawyers is simply that such activities tend toward "commercialization" which reflects adversely upon the "dignity" of the legal profession. But if stirring up lawsuits is good instead of bad, and if frivolous suits can be prevented by other means, it is difficult to perceive why soliciting legal business must be "undignified." Advertising, either by lawyers or by businessmen, can be deceptive or misleading. It may also be highly informational to the potential consumer of legal services who, even if he does recognize his need for a lawyer, will find little aid from the Yellow Pages in determining which one of many lawyers is best suited to handle his particular legal problem.

Certainly lawyer advertising should be regulated to insure substantially "informational" content. The present absolute ban on both advertising and soliciting, however, forecloses the possibility of rating systems by which clients might evaluate the relative competences of various attorneys. It eliminates competition between lawyers both for new clients and for each other's clients.

Who benefits? Certainly not the members of the public who are potential litigants. Aside from corporations protected by public ignorance, the large firm lawyers who already have a number of steady commercial clients stand to gain. Since these lawyers do not need to solicit new clients, the present arrangement reinforces their financial security and enhances their professional authority over clients who sometimes have little ability to look elsewhere. And since these more successful attorneys thrive upon a business clientele, they can easily solicit informally through the country club scene. One is not at all surprised to hear, therefore, that the large firm corporate-commercial lawyers and their medium-size firm counterparts from the South dominate the bar associations which enact the Canons of Ethics.* Like labor union members and business corporations, lawyers, doctors, and stockbrokers are not above dividing markets among themselves through the rules of their professional associations.

The advertising and soliciting rules will make the work of public interest lawyers very difficult. They may also be unconstitutional. In three cases, *NAACP* v. *Button* (1963),[17] *Brotherhood of Railroad Trainmen* v. *Virginia State Bar* (1963)[18] and *United Mine Workers* v. *Illinois Bar Association* (1967),[19] the Supreme Court has already moved much further in that direction than the American Bar Association was willing to admit in the revised *Code of Professional Responsibility*, which it adopted in late

---

* For example, a survey of American Bar Association membership among Detroit lawyers discovered that 78 percent of the lawyers in firms with more than ten members were also ABA members, while the same was true of only 29 percent of solo practitioners.[16]

1969. In *Button* the NAACP and its independent tax exempt affiliate, the NAACP Legal and Educational Defense Fund (LDF), invited the parents of black schoolchildren to meetings at which staff lawyers solicited them as plaintiffs in lawsuits to desegregate southern school systems. In *Brotherhood of Railway Trainmen* and *United Mine Workers*, labor unions referred all injured members with workmen's compensation claims to certain lawyers who had agreed to charge reduced contingent fees in one case or to salaried lawyers on the union payroll in the other. Through its "group legal service" program the Mine Workers' Union was able to reduce the legal expenses of injured workers from $500,000 to $12,400.[20]

Bar associations charged the lawyers with soliciting clients through lay intermediaries who acted as "runners" or conduits. In all three cases the Supreme Court held, in effect, that the questioned practices were protected by the First Amendment's guarantees of access to the courts and freedom of association. To no avail, the ABA, forty-four state bar associations, and the bars of four major cities petitioned the Court for a rehearing in *Brotherhood of Railway Trainmen*. The Supreme Court decisions establish the right of one layman to solicit another's participation in a lawsuit. The question that remains is whether the public interest lawyer himself may initiate the solicitation—or whether the average citizen can claim a First Amendment right to be aided in recognizing his legal problems by soliciting lawyers. Resolution of this issue is more properly the subject of a law review article.[21]

Even before *Button*, one federal court refused to consider charges against a lawyer who solicited stockholder suits against managements for violating Congressional statutes designed to regulate the securities transactions of corporate "insiders." The judge declared:

[T]he cry that the suit is being brought for the benefit of the attorney only is raised in the majority of these actions . . . yet I have had no case cited to me, nor have I found anywhere the Court took it upon itself to inquire into the circumstances surrounding the purchase of the stock or the arrangement between the stockholder and his attorney. That no court has done so appears consistent with the interpretation placed on the statute and the obvious purpose of Congress in enacting Sec. 16(b).[22]

The statute to which the judge referred forbids specified corporate officials and large stockholders from buying and selling their company's securities within a six-month period, the purpose being to prevent windfall gains to persons who might be in possession of "inside information" not yet generally available to the investing public. To enforce the provision, Congress not only provided that stockholders could recover these insider profits for the benefit of their corporations through private lawsuits, but it also declared that lawyers representing such stockholders could recover reasonable attorney's fees from the losing defendants. Since the average stockholder cannot be expected to understand the shenanigans of high finance, and since he is not personally entitled to the damage recovery, the Court reasoned, in effect, that Congress must have intended soliciting lawyers, acting as "private attorneys general," to be the primary enforcers of the statute. Here, institutionalized solicitation has transformed the legal process into an invisible hand to correct economic injustices. Similar benefits should be conferred upon persons other than upper middle class stockholders.

The objective of the soliciting public interest lawyer may be to get *his* cause, not the client's, into court. If so, there arises a direct conflict with the traditional conception of the lawyer's role as the servant rather than the master of his client's desires. The issue was recently dramatized by a group of law students who picketed the Washington offices of Lloyd N. Cutler, a Washington lawyer. Mr. Cutler had succeeded in negotiating a consent decree on behalf of his client, General Motors, who had been accused by the Justice Department of conspiring with Ford, Chrysler, and American Motors to delay the development and introduction of pollution control devices. The students, protesting the consent decree as a sellout, argued that Mr. Cutler should exert more pressure upon his client to act in the "public interest."

Mr. Cutler reported that neither the picketing students nor anyone else had an exclusive right to define the "public interest." He is right, provided there *are* lawyers to represent consumers, pollution victims, and all other interests. If all interests are not represented, then the picketing students would be justified in urging Mr. Cutler to "control" his powerful clients. But no lawyer need control his client when all people are clients and all clients are equal. The legal process should then function as a pluralistic marketplace of competing claims and ideas, with logic as the arbiter.

Lawyers may choose which clients they will represent. Lawyers may also terminate their services when their clients' objectives clash with their own values. To rebut the argument that public interest lawyers are a self-constituted elite,[23] a strong case can be made that the best legal advocates for changing the status quo are lawyers who believe in their clients' causes, not for their own sake, but because of a detached commitment to abstract principles that dictate the merits of those causes.

A public interest lawyer is often a lonely pioneer in a long neglected area of the law. If any previously unrepresented interests come forward to accept his services, the legal system is that much better off for the added diversity of input. A vital function of the public interest lawyer is to offer the legal forum and innovative legal theories that will enable new interests to coalesce. When the legal mavericks disappear, we should begin to worry that the dynamism of the legal system is coming to a halt. The dilemma posed by the public interest lawyer is not whether he will exercise elitist control over his clients; it is whether he will have the moral courage to search out his client's true desires and, if they conflict with his own, to tell his client to find another lawyer, even if it means passing up a tempting test case opportunity. The public interest lawyer himself is no hypothetical construct; he exists—in minuscule numbers. These public interest lawyers work primarily in three general areas: (1) civil rights, civil liberties, draft resistance, and the defense of "movement" radicals charged with criminal activities; (2) legal services for the poor; and (3) environmental pollution and (to a lesser extent) consumerism. Not all of these public interest lawyers are "independent professionals" who define "the public interest" for themselves and thus force the client to choose between that position and another lawyer. Particularly in the poverty law and radical "movement" fields, public interest lawyers are apt to adhere to a "client control" relationship not unlike that between Lloyd Cutler and General Motors. But how and by whom the public interest is defined is of less immediate concern than the development of institutional structures for the delivery of public interest legal services and the generation of a dependable financial base to support it.

III. FINANCIAL SUPPORT

Though armed with the class action and the right to solicit clients, the public interest lawyer will constantly be seeking additional financial support. The contingent fee would make this unnecessary if every injustice gave rise to a private right to sue for damages. Unfortunately, this just is not true. In addition to innumerable varieties of lawsuits seeking injunctive relief only, there are proceedings before administrative agencies and opportunities to lobby before legislative bodies. These two areas are of fundamental importance because actions here often determine whether courts will later be open to private class suits like *Pfizer*. And we have already seen that it is at these levels that corporate interests are least opposed and most successful.

To the cost of ordinary legal representation must be added the expense of maintaining an extensive investigative apparatus. Pollution and consumer exploitation are not easy to measure, but lawyers for the public will need documented evidence of the extent and impact of widespread low visibility legal injuries. The exact amount of damage must be calculated and apportioned, and more efficient methods developed for its distribution among millions and collection from thousands. The evidence, arguments, and demonstrated practicability of these "public" lawsuits must be so devastatingly irrefutable that even hostile judges cannot rule against them without publicly admitting that the "system" is unjust and unresponsive. Achieving such results will require no less than major scientific undertakings and a permanent system of surveillance over the activities of all levels of government, large corporations, and other centers of private power.

A surveillance apparatus will also be necessary to monitor compliance with legal victories. Successful test cases create only paper rights. It has been the experience of many lawyers that it is easier to persuade a court to issue an injunction than a contempt citation for violating it. Throughout the process of gaining new rights and securing their enforcement, public interest lawyers must constantly utilize the press to inform and to mobilize public opinion—to impress upon judges, administrators, and legislators the visibility of their pending decisions. This, too, will cost money.

Since resources will be limited, lawyers who work for a "public interest law firm" (PILF) will have to accept considerable financial sacrifices. On the other hand, PILF lawyers must be among the most competent and innovative in the entire profession, for they will be confronted with the most difficult of legal problems and opposed by the most talented attorneys that their wealthy adversaries can hire. It appears that there will be many volunteers. A rebellious minority of law students is already demanding changes in their business-oriented curricula in order to equip themselves for careers in public interest law. New courses in such areas as poverty law, consumer protection, and environmental conservation are springing up on many law school campuses.

A large and increasing proportion of these idealistic students are refusing to be channeled into the usual commercial law firms by their law school placement officers. But while they are finding that there are few public interest job opportunities available, even for lower pay, a threatened manpower drain has touched off a vigorous reaction by the largest and most prestigious firms. To lure students back into the fold these firms are offering attractively packaged "*pro bono*" programs. That is, the employment offer to each new associate contains a guarantee that without any reduction in salary he will be allowed to spend 10 to 15 percent of his "firm time" on non-fee generating "public service" cases, such as volunteer work for local legal aid offices or other poverty law projects.[24]

To what extent, then, is the need for a PILF diminished by

the *pro bono* activities of private firms? At the outset it must be recognized that the relatively small number of firms large and affluent enough to support *pro bono* programs cannot begin to satisfy the total unfilled need for legal services. In addition, the largest firms that are in the best financial position to offer such charity also have the most numerous paying clients, thus increasing the probability of a real or imagined conflict of interest between paying clients and *pro bono* clients. These conflicts are naturally resolved in favor of those who pay—*pro bono* clients quickly become second-class clients.

For example, when the Campbell Soup Company placed glass marbles in soup samples used for television commercials, to make it seem as if there were more vegetables in its product, the response of the Federal Trade Commission was a mere order that Campbell refrain from such conduct in the future. A group of George Washington law students were not satisfied with the "penalty." They wanted the FTC to order Campbell to go on television and tell the American people about their marbles, what a deterrent to deceptive advertising that would be. So they demanded the right to intervene in the case as representatives of all consumers and sought to retain an attorney from the prestigious Washington firm of Arnold & Porter. After an initially favorable response the students were told, on orders from a senior partner, that although there was no direct conflict of interest, Arnold & Porter could not represent them. The partner reasoned that it would not be in the interest of the firm's corporate clients generally for consumers to gain the right to intervene in FTC proceedings.

Nevertheless, in several major cities a growing number of young lawyers with available *pro bono* time are participating in the programs of outside civil rights and poverty law organizations. Such organizations operate as clearinghouses, matching needy clients with available *pro bono* lawyers from firms throughout an entire city. For example, the Ford Foundation financed Boston Urban Areas Project has successfully mobilized the *pro bono* resources of many Boston firms on a variety of legal fronts: aiding black unions, providing business law assistance to small ghetto enterprises, working to improve the administration of justice in lower criminal courts, bringing lawsuits to force local adoption of available federal food assistance programs for both adults and schoolchildren, and numerous other projects. The Boston project stands out among the many other projects sponsored in major cities by the conservative Lawyers Committee for Civil Rights Under Law. Elsewhere, the Chicago Council of Lawyers, the closest thing yet to an independent public interest bar association, monitors judicial appointments, serves as a focal point for *pro bono* contributions, and organizes task forces to handle specific projects. The New York Council of Law Associates is primarily a *pro bono* clearinghouse largely populated by younger members of the corporate firms and more closely connected with the established bar.

The large firms, however, have viewed such developments with jealous suspicion. These firms had established the *pro bono* programs primarily as a public relations device to attract graduating law students, but organizations like the Washington Lawyers Project seemed to be receiving all the credit. In part to recapture the limelight, several of the larger firms, including Washington's Arnold & Porter and Hogan & Hartson, have already set up their own "Public Service Departments." These are being managed by full-fledged partners and accorded equal status with the firms' regular commercial law departments. One task of the managing partner is to entice his younger associates to devote their *pro bono* time to "public service" clients represented by and identified with the particular firm. By depleting the manpower of the citywide clearinghouses and by further fragmenting the direction, coordination, and control of *pro bono* activities, the movement toward independent Public Service Departments within each of the larger firms can only exacerbate the lack of bold and systematic approach characteristic of too many citywide programs. Already, the Washington Lawyers Project—an important coordinating body—has died.

Even if private law firms were willing and able to supply the necessary resources, to entrust to their charity the responsibility for eliminating external dislegalities seems anomalous. The *pro bono* lawyer is commercial lawyer 85 to 90 percent of his time and a PILF lawyer for the remaining 10 to 15 percent. Consequently, it is difficult for him to perceive himself as working in a systematic and orderly fashion to eradicate widespread injustice. The primary motivation for his handling *pro bono* cases at all is to quell his moral unease (or guilt, perhaps). He is likely to accept almost any *pro bono* client who walks into his office as long as the case is "interesting" and "relevant" to current social problems. Aside from these broad criteria he sets few priorities. And, handling one isolated *pro bono* case at a time, he seldom builds an expertise in a single area of public interest law. Would General Motors entrust its fate to a part-time corporate lawyer?

In contrast, the PILF lawyer views his role through a vastly wider perspective. His primary concerns are not necessarily for clients who walk through his door, but often for those who must be solicited; not for particular individuals, but for large classes of invisible tort victims; not for the isolated lawsuit, but for a comprehensive series of related legal actions at all levels of government. Appreciating his limited resources, he develops an ideology, a set of priorities derived from legal cost-benefit analysis, and a systematic method for attacking carefully selected injustices.

IV. LESSONS FROM OTHER GROUPS

The impression gained from numerous personal interviews is that even those public interest lawyers who denounce "elitism" would welcome a systematic, principled, "affirmative action" legal program—albeit one developed and controlled by client classes. Who will supply millions of dollars annually to finance such efforts?

The federal government does finance an analogous operation— the Office of Economic Opportunity's Neighborhood Legal Services Program (NLSP), which is authorized to provide free legal services to indigents in all non-fee generating civil cases. In 1970, while the private bar grossed $4.5 billion, Congress appropriated only $60 million for the NLSP's 2,000 young and inexperienced lawyers to represent the 35 million people classified as poor. Even the ABA estimates that the NLSP budget is sufficient to cover only 25 percent of the legal needs of the poor.

The ABA has now decided to lobby for increased NLSP appropriations. There is little opposition within its own ranks; after all, more indigents bringing lawsuits means more legal business for private defense lawyers. On the other hand, the organized bar has been highly successful in preventing NLSP lawyers from handling any cases that might generate contingent fees for private lawyers. Thus, NLSP is foreclosed from involvement in a broad range of cases where damages or attorney's fees are recoverable. NLSP cannot bring purely injunctive class actions if the combined wealth of the non-indigent members of the class is sufficient to hire a private attorney.

Nevertheless, the efforts of several NLSP offices have measurably improved the condition of the poor. The paragon example is the California Rural Legal Assistance (CRLA) program, which in two lawsuits against state agencies saved California poor people $310 million. Especially in the area of welfare law, NLSP suits throughout the nation have forced government agencies to grant significant concessions to the poor. But the political reaction has been severe. Responding to the phenomenal success of CRLA, California Senator George Murphy introduced legislation that would give any governor an absolute veto over the NLSP in his state. His theory was that Governor Reagan could threaten to veto CRLA's appropriation unless it agreed not to bring suits against state agencies. The Murphy Amendment passed the Senate by a vote of 45 to 40, but failed in the House.

The Murphy Amendment stands as a constant reminder that the government will never finance a NLSP capable of bringing about significant social change. Even now a governor's veto of NLSP offices in his state can be overridden only by the National Director of OEO. But because of its own precarious political position, OEO is more likely to compromise, making concessions in exchange for the governor's withdrawal of his veto. Local bar associations, which have the right to "comment" upon NLSP operations in their respective areas, possess similar political leverage with OEO. The Baltimore Bar Association, for example, vetoed that city's NLSP program until it was guaranteed a majority of the seats on the local governing board and a veto over program expansion and test cases.

The same power is exercised by the United Fund or Community Chest, which supply the 10 percent local contribution required for federal funding. There have been instances of these monies being cut off because of NLSP suits against police departments or other sensitive local institutions. Debilitating political intimidation may be expected to increase as NLSP offices shift their emphases from attempting to serve every client with an individual problem—an impossible task with its present budget—to bringing politically controversial poverty law test cases. The recent decision of OEO to fund CRLA on a temporary basis rather than to overrule the Reagan veto, the plan to place regional political appointees in control of OEO lawyers, and the ouster of NLSP chief Terry Lenzner are examples of the political leverage that local officials are only beginning to exercise against a program that can embarrass them. The lesson: no PILF dependence upon government financing.

Would it be possible, then, for the PILF to raise sufficient funds from the private sector? There are, in fact, a sizable and growing number of nonprofit legal organizations operating as PILF's in specific areas of the law. None are financed by the government. The most well known is probably the American Civil Liberties Union (ACLU), which since 1920 has been in the forefront of legal battles to enforce the Bill of Rights. It is a nationwide organization with a permanent staff, more than 200 local chapters organized into statewide affiliates, and over 130 thousand "members" who provide about $3 million annually in mail-solicited contributions. Another well-known organization is the NAACP Legal and Educational Defense Fund (LDF), the self-styled "legal arm of the entire civil rights movement." Its resources in 1969 exceeded $3.1 million, also derived primarily from thousands of small, mail-solicited contributions. Active in thirty states, LDF maintains its own permanent legal staff, national headquarters, and several regional offices.

Both of these organizations utilize the test case method to achieve their objectives. The ACLU's primary resources are its cooperating attorneys. These are lawyers in private practice throughout the nation who spend their *pro bono* time on ACLU cases. Many are among the approximately three thousand members active at the local chapter level where policy is formulated through the selection and rejection of cases. The ACLU National Board takes positions on major policy issues, and a minuscule permanent staff continually litigates a number of important test cases. But the organization as a whole is highly decentralized.

LDF also has cooperating attorneys, 400 of them who in 1969 handled 600 separate lawsuits. But unlike the ACLU, the LDF national office has developed a centralized structure by which it has been able to set specific legal priorities and implement them systematically. First, the national office chooses the lawsuit it wishes to bring and maintains its own lay soliciting organization (plus continuous contact with the NAACP membership) to enlist the types of clients it needs. Second, LDF's permanent legal staff develops arguments and briefs in support of the positions it intends to litigate. Third, both the solicited client and the supporting materials are delivered to the attorneys in the field, significantly lightening their own burdens. And fourth, LDF pays these cooperating attorneys $60 per day plus expenses while engaged in litigation supplied or approved by the national office. Consequently, some LDF attorneys are able to devote up to 90 percent of their time to the organization's work.

Thus, there is a major difference between LDF and ACLU. The former sets specific goals and the entire organization works to achieve them. The latter merely announces general policies and provides little logistical support or compensation to induce cooperating attorneys to follow prescribed courses. In fact, the ACLU engages in relatively little active solicitation at the local level. Numerous potential clients with civil liberties problems seek out its well-known services, and choosing among the competing applicants is the gist of local ACLU priority setting. It may well be that this approach is best suited to the often localized setting of political oppression.

White racism is much more of a uniform, national problem, but it would be erroneous to imply that LDF is "undemocratic" or that it forces cooperating attorneys to litigate personally unappealing issues. The limited number of cases offered by the national office in a sense restrict the choice of its cooperating attorneys, but no more than the nonsoliciting private lawyer is restricted to clients who seek out his services. As long as a wide range of choices is kept open, the LDF (or PILF) attorney can reject a particular case and still expect to be offered a more interesting issue in the near future. The LDF cooperating attorney may, if he wishes, solicit his own clients, and the national office may still provide compensation. However, most LDF attorneys find it more convenient to rely upon the initiatives of the national office, which is often able to supply highly desirable types of clients whom attorneys in the field would be hard pressed to solicit on their own.

The LDF strategy is peculiarly appropriate for the innovative legal battles that must be waged in behalf of invisible tort victims. Unlike the decentralized ACLU approach geared toward guarding against deprivations of personal liberty, a multi-faceted PILF must protect people who do not even realize that they are being harmed. The primary defect of many of the smaller PILF's is that they scatter their meager resources among too many different objectives. The result is that no one problem area receives sufficiently thorough treatment to bring about fundamental change. Even where test cases have established significant precedents, resources are not available to implement these "paper" rights. Some of these smaller organizations might opt to be subsumed under the umbrella of a much larger, centralized PILF. The advantage of such an arrangement is that through pooling resources, more intensive efforts can be devoted to each concern. Furthermore, a large superstructure might provide the smaller units with a perspective that would encourage them to map out coordinated priorities. There is a real problem, however, in maintaining independent decision-making power for each member organization without sacrificing efficiency.

Another approach is for each of the smaller organizations to specialize. The calculated shift to a law reform emphasis has led to specialized NLSP organizations such as the Massachusetts Law Reform Institute and the Western Center on Law and Poverty. Another organization, the James Madison Constitutional Law Institute, feels that by concentrating its legal efforts in a particular area such as birth control, it can raise funds for an attack on abortion statutes from wealthy but conservative benefactors who would never contribute to a more general "civil rights movement." In the civil liberties field, organizations like the National Emergency Civil Liberties Committee, The National Lawyers Guild, and the Lawyers Committee for Constitutional Rights have concentrated upon the defense of radical political movements.

While existing organizations may become more effective by limiting the scope of their activities (and the size of their constituencies), a PILF must still devise new funding devices in order to attack the broader external dislegalities and to police compliance with legal victories. Following the examples of ACLU and LDF, several million dollars might be raised each year through mail solicited contributions. Additional funds could be raised through advertisements in newspapers, magazines, and perhaps television and radio, if financing were available for a sustained campaign. A fundamental conflict arises between centralized control over greater and more "efficiently" utilized financial resources, on the one hand, and the autonomous, small-group, anti-bureaucratic PILF structures that currently predominate, on the other. The LDF model partially overcomes the conflict between unified policy direction and individual lawyer initiative. Bureaucratizaton does take its toll on how well policies are carried out, and there is substantial evidence that small, unstructured groups are the best setting for innovative problem solving. The familiar problem is then to distribute the funds in a way that will maximize the legitimate decision-making autonomy of the recipient PILFs.

Each of the civil rights–civil liberties organizations possesses a tax exempt component which allows private donors to deduct their contributions for personal income tax purposes. Accompanying the tax exempt status, however, are strict requirements that no tax exempt funds be used for partisan political purposes or for "influencing legislation." The latter restriction means that a PILF cannot use tax exempt funds, including foundation grants, to engage in legislative lobbying, an integral part of the legal process, while another tax law allows its corporate adversaries to deduct expenses of lobbying for or against a bill directly affecting their business interests.

The tax exempt Washington Research Project serves as an example of how this dilemma may be avoided. A small, foundation-financed group of six experienced lawyers and five Vista attorneys, Project's litigation and administrative agency representation touches upon a variety of subjects most relevant to southern blacks: school desegregation (with LDF); racial discrimination by federal contractors, private employers, and labor unions; health care for average citizens; federal grants under the Elementary and Secondary School Act; and hunger cooperatives in Mississippi. But the Washington Research Project *Action Council*, on paper an entirely different legal entity, consists of Project personnel engaging in legislative lobbying with non-tax exempt funds. The legislative lobbying components of organizations like the Washington Research Project can usually be run on a financial shoestring because much of the empirical data and subject matter expertise necessary to prepare testimony may have already been generated through the litigation or "educational" activities of the tax exempt component.

Students can be important research and investigation resources for the PILF. The Law Students Civil Rights Research Committee, for example, maintains chapters at thirty-two law schools through which students conduct research aiding lawyers who are engaged in civil rights–consumer–poverty law litigation. Similar law student conservation groups are beginning to take root. Many law schools are moving in the direction of clinical legal education by setting up programs in which students participating in actual litigation receive course credit. It may also be possible to tap the budgets of undergraduate student governments for some public interest legal work. Ralph Nader associates have already organized OSPIRG (Oregon Students' Public Interest Research Group) and MPIRG (Minnesota), student-controlled PILFs to be financed by increases in university fees. (Those who disapprove are entitled to refunds.) The proposals are awaiting approval by the respective boards of higher education, and similar drives are well under way in Illinois and Ohio.

A new Washington-based, public interest firm, the Center for Law and Social Policy, has entered into an agreement with the Yale, Michigan, Pennsylvania, Stanford, and UCLA Law Schools for twenty to twenty-five law students to serve as center interns for six-month periods. Each student will receive an entire semester's credit for participating in the Center's seminars and litigation activities. In addition, the cooperating law schools will combine to provide and pay half the salary of two law professors who will each spend a year in residency at the Center. The Center plans to focus upon a wide array of consumer-conservation issues at the federal regulatory agency level: predatory credit practices of furniture and appliance stores, deceptive food labeling, unsafe toys and household products, and enforcement of minimum federal standards for hospitals participating in medicare and medicaid programs, FDA certification of drugs tested only in private laboratories, FHA barriers to construction of low-income housing, and FCC media licensing (with the RFK Memorial's Citizen's Communication Center).

Likewise, a handful of students from Clark College in Atlanta serve as interns at the Washington Research Project and receive course credit in connection with Project seminars. Ralph Nader's Center for the Study of Responsive Law has already demonstrated the student potential. The product of the first handful of "Nader's Raiders," who investigated the Federal Trade Commission in the summer of 1968, was an influential report which documented that agency's gross incompetence and often willful nonenforcement of the law. By the summer of 1970, there were 196 subsistence paid "raiders" investigating not only numerous federal agencies but state and local governments, corporations, and labor unions as well. The effort is still expanding, and it serves as the best existing prototype for a PILF investigative apparatus, generating massive empirical data for nationwide legal action, and doing so on a financial shoestring.

Thousands of students and hundreds of thousands of small contributions may ease the financial burden of the PILF. A few wealthy donors might be found to provide an endowment which produces a modest but steady annual income, an example being the James Madison Constitutional Law Institute. And there are rare examples of PILFs being financed entirely by a single philanthropist, such as Philip Stern in Washington, or by a single organization, such as the Chicago-based Businessmen for the Public Interest. Labor unions have apparently not been fully explored. The Center for the Study of Responsive Law receives royalties from sales of the various "Nader's Raiders" reports, as well as income from a charitable trust.

Foundations can be relied upon, if at all, only for closely monitored seed money and special projects. Once initial funding is provided, most foundations would expect the PILF to become self-sufficient in a relatively short time. Moreover, congressional reaction in the 1969 Tax Reform Act to the liberal activities of many foundation-financed operations has had a significant deterrent effect upon the larger foundations. Edgar Cahn has faced severe funding cuts for his Citizens Advocate Center, which monitors federal grant-making in poverty related areas. The Environmental Defense Fund (EDF), a scientist-lawyer group in the forefront of the legal battle against air pollution and pesticides, apparently saw the writing on the wall and has turned to the ACLU-LDF mail solicited contributions approach. The PILFs are beginning to compete among themselves for the limited grants available. It is rumored that the Ford Foundation changed its mind about funding a PILF proposal of conservationist Yale law students because of possible political repercussions. Reversing itself, Ford decided to go ahead with the grant after the students had altered their proposal to include a prestigious board of directors. But the Internal Revenue Service took the strange position that preserving the environment through litigation might not be a "charitable" activity for the purpose of obtaining a tax exempt status. IRS commissioner Randolph Thrower froze the pending exemption applications of the National Resources Defense Council and all other newly formed PILFs until a "study" could be undertaken. This action precipitated the first unified lobbying campaign of the Washington public interest bar, aided by a sympathetic press, expressions of concern from corporate firms with *pro bono* programs, and opposition from Nixon ecologist Russell Train. Thrower promptly reversed himself when congressional hearings were announced.

The lesson—and the parallel to the abortive Murphy Amendment—was clear. Even before the tax controversy arose, Ralph Nader was using funds raised from speeches, articles, private donations, and a $425,000 invasion-of-privacy damage settlement from General Motors to finance non-tax exempt PILFs free from the restrictions imposed by foundation grants. PIRG (Public Interest Research Group) is a 14-man subsistence-paid outfit which seeks to catalyze action on a wide variety of fronts. New groups to be organized, given seed money, and spun off as relatively autonomous non-tax exempt entities include a black law firm to police ghetto consumer frauds, a women's rights firm, and an antitrust-oriented CARG (Corporate Accountability Research Group). The black and women's firms are expected to be fee generating, thus partially solving the financing problem.

V. A PROPOSAL

Through all of these devices a PILF might raise several million dollars each year. More funds than these will be needed if the PILF is to justify its existence as an institution capable of efficiently concentrating enough resources upon eliminating specific external dislegalities to bring about lasting changes. *The only way by which the PILF can assure itself of such revenues is to earn them by the same means that private lawyers do.* In other words, unlike any of the organizations discussed, the PILF must solicit fee-generating cases like *Pfizer* and from them earn sufficient funds to defray the cost of its entire operation in excess of donations. In a sense, the PILF must make its own "monopoly profits."

Aside from consumer antitrust class actions, there are numerous other statutes under which multi-million dollar lawsuits might be brought in both state and federal courts. Some such as the federal Truth-in-Lending Act, explicitly provide for private lawsuits; others are silent. But some statutes and administrative regulations which do not explicitly allow private suits have been interpreted by the courts to provide a basis for private damage actions. The rationale for this judicial doctrine has been that persons whom the statute was designed to benefit might serve as private attorneys general to enforce it. Scores of unenforced statutes and regulations designed to protect the victims of invisible torts could become the subject of PILF test cases requesting the right to bring class actions. Large groups of persons might then bring suits under federal statutes regulating air and water pollution, or deceptive packaging and advertising. Since contingent fees may run as high as one-third of the damage recovery, the possibilities for a well-financed PILF are substantially enhanced if these multi-million dollar class actions can succeed. One drawback is that years pass and hundreds of thousands of dollars in expenses are incurred before damages are recovered in these protracted cases. Pointing to one of his law partners, David I. Shapiro said, "that man kept me alive for the last seven years" (while Shapiro worked on the *Pfizer* case).

There exist today private, nonsoliciting law firms substantially engaged in public interest law which manage to survive financially. In New York City, for example, several young lawyers styling themselves as a "law commune" earn moderate incomes while representing clients like the Black Panthers and handling scores of non-fee-generating matters. Much of their revenue is derived from Wall Street fees charged to publishers and booksellers fighting obscenity statutes, and wealthy parents whose children wish to avoid the draft. Another example is the conservation–consumer-oriented Washington firm of Berlin, Roisman, and Kessler, which managed to break even financially in its first year of operation. It hopes to capitalize eventually upon contingent fees from class actions, like one which it has already filed seeking $25 million in damages from all of the national banks in the District of Columbia for charging usurious interest rates.

Based upon the various PILF models that have been discussed, a nationwide organization can be envisioned. It is not suggested that there be a single, monolithic PILF; there should be several, each corresponding to a segment of the ideological spectrum. Nor is it contemplated that a small self-appointed group would determine the PILF's priorities and direct its policies. Although it would certainly have priorities, the primary function of the PILF would be to disperse financial resources, empirical data, and solicited clients to lawyers, including those employed by presently existing PILFs, who agreed with the national organization's policy priorities. The PILF's policy makers would be elected by and accountable to its lawyers and lay members. It is important to distinguish between the "national" PILF and the scores of autonomous local PILFs for which it will serve primarily as a clearinghouse for logistical support, information exchange, and strategy coordination. That national policy priorities must be imposed in order to distribute limited financial resources is simply unavoidable. But national PILF power over the pursestrings will at least provide otherwise nonexistent funds for non-fee-generating legal action in the environmental area, for example. The alternative is for the public interest antitrust bar and other fee-generating pursuits to retain all of the contingent fees that either efforts produce.

Basically, there would be three component parts—Central Coordination and Research, Litigation, and Lobbying—although the "legal" structure would be manipulated in order to retain tax exempt status for as much activity as possible. The first component, Central Coordination and Research (CCR), would function as the PILF's investigative apparatus as well as its primary policy-making, priority-setting, and strategy-planning actions. The investigation branch would be directed by a large staff of social scientists and other professionals scattered throughout the branch offices, employing thousands of student researchers at subsistence wages, many of them receiving academic credit for their work. While conducting intensive empirical research and monitoring the activities of government and the private power structure, the investigators would detect violations of law, oversee compliance with injunctions, organize victims of invisible torts into legal action groups, and solicit ideal clients for test cases and class actions.

With its broad overview of external dislegalities, CCR would be best suited to devise and implement basic policy decisions. To this end it would continuously mold the massive data from investigations into scholarly publications and sample legal briefs for lawsuits. To implement its priorities it would maintain a constant flow of necessary empirical data, legal briefs, solicited clients, and other logistics to salaried litigating lawyers who would constitute the litigating component.

At each PILF branch office these litigating lawyers would be associates of private "public interest" firms but all would be members of a national law firm subsuming the network of local firms. Whereas the private commercial law firms have their various corporate, tax, securities, and personal injury departments, these "public interest" firms would encourage specialization in consumer antitrust, deceptive trade practices, hazardous products, environmental pollution, administrative agency law, poverty law, civil rights–civil liberties, as well as a corporate and securities practice emphasizing the rights of invisible tort victims. To encourage development of expertise in these areas of public interest law, each litigating lawyer might be required to devote 75 percent of his time to cases solicited or approved by CCR. Such an arrangement would also enable the PILF to avoid compensating lawyers who would otherwise handle PILF cases without charge as a *pro bono* service.

Each PILF litigating lawyer would receive a fixed salary, varying in accordance with experience, ability, and time spent on PILF cases, regardless of the actual amount of fees he received from his clients. Any fees recovered in excess of his salary and expenses, including multi-million dollar class action contingent fees, would be forwarded by each lawyer to a central fund. The revenues of this fund would be used to pay the salaries of the remaining PILF lawyers and to make up the entire deficit of the CCR component through the "purchase" of the logistical support received.

Because of the PILF's limited resources, the salaries of these lawyers would not be as high as those earned by attorneys working for the large commercial firms. The socially sensitive lawyers who are willing to accept this sacrifice would, however, be able to devote up to 25 percent of their time to more remunerative non-public interest work. Moreover, the experience of LDF demonstrates that in an organization as large as the PILF the priorities set by CCR can be easily meshed with the personal preferences of the litigating lawyers for cases involving certain types of legal issues.

Since this financing scheme is dependent upon successful multi-million dollar class actions, it might be feared that commercial firms would quickly enter the public interest field to compete for the PILF's "monopoly profits." But such an intrusion should be welcomed as a means of freeing the PILF for concentration upon even more challenging external dislegalities. It must be assumed, however, that without investigative and logistical support comparable to that of the PILF, private firms will be no more active in the fee-generating invisible tort field than they are at present. Indeed, private tort firms might develop into a profitable market for the sale of "left-over" PILF investigative data. The possibility of a tort firm seeking venture capital from the public to sustain long-term suits may be farfetched now but possible in the future.

The third and final major component of the PILF would be a non-tax exempt legislative lobbying organization. It could draw upon sets of proposed statutes ranging from "model" to "utopian" compiled by the CCR component. Its most important function, however, would be to establish a political nexus between the PILF and the citizenry to make certain that the public is fully apprised of the successes *and* the failures of the legal battles being waged in its behalf, and particularly of the political figures to be held responsible. For while the PILF can be expected to fail in many of its efforts to change the system; its real value may be in exposing the precise nature of the basic injustices which presently permeate the society. Change will never come, "by any means necessary" or otherwise, until these basic injustices are protested in a manner which explains their specific consequences to the average American. Thus every lawsuit commenced by the PILF, win or lose, becomes a political act. After all, there are only two possible corrective mechanisms for social injustice. One is the reformist path of the law; the other is the risky business of violent revolution.

The Law School Response:
How to Sharpen Students' Minds
By Making Them Narrow

ERIC E. VAN LOON*

For some years now I have been concerned about the effect of our legal education on the idealism of our students. . . . They bring to this School a large measure of idealism. Do they leave with less? And if they do, is that something we can view with indifference? If they do, what is the cause? What do we do to them that makes them turn another way?[1]

—*Former Harvard Law School Dean Erwin Griswold*

When the 1969 academic year opened at Yale Law School, returning professors and students discovered a group of their fellows camped in the school's courtyard. The object of the several-weeks "Camp In," as one of the participants put it, was "to build trust in an atmosphere in which trust and easy-going smiles are alien." Lapel buttons read "Make Love, Not Law Journal." A few weeks later Yale Law experienced its first student strike in 145 years.

Earlier at Harvard Law School—a spawning ground for Wall

* Eric Van Loon is a 1971 graduate of Harvard Law School, where he was Editor-in-Chief of the *Civil Rights–Civil Liberties Law Review* and has been active in movements for educational reform. He holds an M.Sc. from the London School of Economics. His earlier article, "Who Are the Activists?" appeared in *American Education*.

Street lawyers—two hundred students staged an all-night "Study In" at the library to demonstrate dissatisfaction. At Georgetown Law, student discontentment forced the cancellation of classes and the administration invited Ralph Nader and Arthur Kinoy to suggest ways to rejuvenate the law school.

Legal education has not one problem, but many. Cast in a business mold, law schools face appeals for commitment to more public service. Increasingly bright and sensitive students resent the auditorium education and the endless dissection of appellate decisions. Professors who care deeply about teaching sense malaise, but seem prisoners of the system which created them. Anxious deans cast wary eyes on a notoriously low-budget enterprise. The outside bar, anxious about its reformation, protects commercial law by requiring it on bar entrance examinations.

What happens to the law schools will have widespread repercussions. The lawyer is still, as Justice Brennan recently remarked, "the indispensable middleman of our social progress."[2] If the law schools redefine their role, it is inevitable that the profession will also change.

I. THE TROUBLE WITH LAW SCHOOLS

Fundamental tensions exist between what law and legal education have been, and what a new generation of law student wants them to be. Rooted in obsolete pedagogy and new student values, the tremors embrace basic questions: Should the lawyer's chief function be defending clients or attacking inequities? Should schools teach normative or "hired gun" morality? Is their highest loyalty to students or to law firms? Should they maintain tradition, or try to reshape it?

One basic source of conflict is the law schools' responsibility for the role law currently plays in society. While De Tocqueville marveled at the lawyers' leadership in American life, many law students are challenging the myth of the lawyers' public spiritedness. For many, the legal profession has become the servant of the haves rather than the guardian of the have-nots. In the ghetto, the landlord evicts the tenant for nonpayment of rent, but the housing code goes unenforced. Buyers defaulting on exorbitant interest installments have their furniture repossessed, but purchasers of defective products are rarely reimbursed. Batteries of lawyers help General Motors negotiate deals, while tenant unions and neighborhood development corporations hunger for legal counsel. And on a recent issue before the FCC, 116 lawyers argued industry's case; consumers were represented by 4 ad hoc groups. More completely, 300,000 lawyers earn $6.4 billion annually for private services, while the 35 million poor are served by a thin OEO Legal Services budget of $56 million. Through 1964, less than ¼ of 1 percent of the money spent on legal services nationally was spent on legal aid.[3] As Mr. Justice Stone complained a third of a century ago,

> Steadily the best skill and capacity of the profession has been drawn into the exacting and highly specialized service of business and finance. . . . At its worst, it has made the learned profession of an earlier day the obsequious servant of business and tainted it with the morals and manners of the market place in its most anti-social manifestations.[4]

Remarkable as it may seem, the distended deployment of legal resources is seldom attacked by law schools: they have themselves fostered the imbalance. Curricular offerings illustrate the orientation. In the first year, criminal and personal injury law, affecting great numbers of citizens, receive less thorough treatment than contracts or commercial property transactions; the course on legal procedure draws chiefly on business examples. The second-year law student is advised he is not a real lawyer without the three business-oriented courses known popularly as Making Money, Counting Money, and Keeping It from the Government (Corporations, Accounting, and Taxation). While these three are nominally optional at Harvard, for example, 94 percent of the student body follows faculty urgings to elect them. Courses on estate planning abound, but few schools teach environmental planning; consumer law is only beginning to receive attention.

Curricular offerings also reflect the legal interests which attract the largest fees. Economic history chronicles how law builds institutions which advance the economic interests of particular groups. Traditionally, most of America's legal talent has been applied to the problems of the rich, breaking new ground in the law of tax, securities, and banking. The economic instruments of today's poor include credit unions and cooperative businesses and housing, but graduates of the finest law schools enter practice with barely an introduction to how their legal training might be used to attack the problems of the poor and the cities.

Law faculties also pride themselves on objective teaching of "how to think like a lawyer," imparting analytic skills and extolling rationality. Nonetheless, the courses impart an ethic biased toward business, for the business problems used to teach the lawyer's skills infiltrate the "value vacuum." Each day the student must play the role of corporate lawyer to be able to respond in class; he has no choice. The accompanying values transfer to him by osmosis. Reflecting on the heavily commercial tone and content of legal education, the dean of a major law school explained:

> Almost inevitably our students are led to feel that it is in [business and finance] that the great work of the lawyer is to be found. By methods of teaching, by subtle and often unconscious innuendo, we indicate to our students that their future success and happiness will be found in the traditional areas of the law. . . .[5]

The stress on purely logical reasoning also denigrates other values. Shortly before the end of his twenty-one-year deanship of Harvard Law School, Solicitor General Erwin Griswold admitted:

> Much of our current instruction encourages . . . a tendency to look inward at the consistency of the system rather than outward at the relation of the system to the real world, and its impact on people and events. . . . [There is] an exulta-

tion of rationality over other values which are of great
importance to our society.[6]

Law school teaching is also characterized by a conceptual framework that filters out everything but "legal" reasons. When a
recent Corporations class was asked to justify a company's giving
a pension to a retiring employee, students strained to find a
clever legal reason such that it could be deducted from profits
to decrease taxes. Half the period passed before someone thought
to answer that the employee deserved it, since he had no other
means of support. As this anecdote illustrates, the lawyer comes
to view his professional responsibility as analogous with his
client's interest. He justifies taking a client whose actions he
disapproves by rationalizing that the lawyer on the other side
will insure that justice is done. "Balancing the public interest" is
considered in many courses, but the purpose seems to be to give
the lawyer "policy arguments" to write into his brief only when
they support his client, or precedent is against him.

Two studies recently reported in the *Journal of Legal Education* confirm that law schools are far from value free. One, a
limited study at the University of Florida, showed a shift in student political outlooks. Entering law school, barely a quarter of
the class described their political views as "right of middle"; in
the third year, however, the figure had grown to 42 percent.
(Forty percent entered with a "left of middle" outlook, but this
was reduced to 24 percent in the third year.)[7] The second study,
by the National Opinion Research Center, covering 135 schools,
revealed that attendance at law school eroded commitment to
public service by converting students to private practice. Surprisingly, the "conversion rate" was highest (85 percent) at the
schools with the most diverse student bodies and broadest curricular offerings; at the state schools the number converted was
only 63 percent although the percentage uncommitted at entry
was the same at both kinds.[8] "It is not easy," as Ralph Nader has
lamented, "to take the very bright young minds of a nation, en-
velop them in conceptual cocoons and condition their expectations of practice to the demands of the corporate law firm,"[9] but

this is what the law schools acculturation process has done to all but a few resistant graduates.

The second wellspring of law student discontent is obsolete pedagogy. Chief among the indictments is that law school is boring. The same teaching medium is used in almost every course: students read appellate court decisions (cases) and assemble for classes with 75 to 150 others. Rather than lecture, the professor brings out key concepts by asking questions of random students (the Socratic method). Theoretically, every student answers vicariously, since he may be called on next, and everyone criticizes the answers in an orgy of analysis. But the weary repetition of dissecting businessmen's problems, three cases a class, thirteen classes a week, thirty weeks a year is an educational anachronism.

In 1870, the institution of the case method and its combination with Socratic dialog worked a revolution in legal education. In those days legal education was aimed at eighteen-year-olds who came to law school with no previous college education and often little training at all. A century later, admissions offices screen honors undergraduates who have completed independent study programs and research seminars. Many hold graduate degrees or have managed political campaigns. "To such students," says Yale Professor Robert Stevens, "the first year of law school, with its strange mix of intellectual rigor and the patronizing atmosphere of first grade, is no longer readily acceptable. Students who are turned off in their first year are unlikely to develop intellectual excitement in the second or third."[10]

Legal education also suffers from the narrowness of its approach. Only rarely are students given a problem and told to develop strategies for its solution. The case method's inquiry begins after the events have occurred, the trial is over, and the parties are appealing. Judge Jerome Frank's indictment from thirty years ago remains appropriate:

Students trained under the Langdell (case method) system are like future horticulturists confining their studies to cut flowers, like architects who study pictures of buildings and nothing else. They resemble prospective dog breeders who

never see anything but stuffed dogs. And it is beginning to
be suspected that there is some correlation between that
kind of stuffed dog study and the overproduction of stuffed
shirts in the legal profession.[11]

This cloistered atmosphere is less defensible because, while
legal training is more of a preparation for interaction in society's
institutions than many other academic endeavors, law school remains more campus-bound than many graduate departments.
Many students never visit a courtroom or a prison or speak with
anyone in legal difficulties. Instead, qualification is based on
completion of an academic exercise; and while academic excel-
lence is vital, a system which treats it as the only important
criterion is unbalanced. Although one can acquire skills important to a lawyer outside as well as inside the classroom, neither
the selection of professors nor student grading reflects this. Student honors are based almost exclusively on performance on
exams, as is the unique closed-circuit pattern of professorial recruitment. The typical faculty member earned outstanding marks
as a student, and edited the school's law review. After graduation he clerked for a judge and spent a couple of years in a law
firm; then he joined the faculty. His law school experience is the
most formative and most important element in his legal background. In professorial recruitment, admits one professor, "ed-
itorship of the law review at a leading school is worth more than
a partnership in a leading firm."[12]

The academic mold also imposes other costs. Outside the
classroom, almost all faculty attention to an individual student's
work takes the form of making fine grade point distinctions on
anonymous student examinations. When a student does work
with a professor on litigation, this is almost never entered on his
transcript. Clinical legal education receives the schools' blessing
—but rarely its credit. Most schools feel that internships in government agencies cannot become part of the law school curriculum because no teacher can grade it; certification for the profession
takes priority over student learning.

The nationwide prevalence of the Harvard mold is also astonishing. Fully one-quarter of the nation's law professors are Harvard graduates, with the result that law schools seldom have the luxury of competing models. Men with common training and careers tend to hold similar views, especially on educational matters; even minor innovations appear radical.

Underlying these troubles is the shared suspicion of students and professors that law schools are losing their traditional role. Just as the Oxford Classics degree is becoming obsolete as preparation for the modern world, the day of the gentleman's lawyerly "finishing" training is passing. The budding decision-maker of an earlier day could undergo a rigorous analytic honing at law school and emerge qualified to run a business, guide a government agency, or try a case, but today's corporate counselor must understand statistical decision theory and give tax advice for corporate planning. Government whiz kids must know systems analysis, cost-benefit analysis, and program planning and budgeting systems, for which general courses in contracts and commercial transactions do not prepare them. Increasingly, government and business schools are teaching the crucial skills, and law students are troubled that their schools seem oblivious to evolutions in related disciplines. "The traditional parameters of legal education," warns Charles Maechling, Jr., of the National Science Foundation, "threaten to leave law out of . . . research and planning on vital national problems."[13]

II. A NEW BREED OF STUDENT

Despite the problems, a new generation of students, approaching the profession with new principles, is growing up in the law schools. Yale Professor Charles Reich expressed their credo when he wrote: "The lawyer will no longer be serving merely as the spokesman for others . . . [but] must carry the responsibility of his specialized knowledge, and formulate ideas as well as advocate them."[14]

As a generation nursed on Kennedy eloquence, teethed on the trials of Mississippi summer, and educated in the years of Berkeley, Columbia, Chicago, and Vietnam, today's law student body has become more committed to political activism. More than 800 law students acted as New Mobe legal staff during the November, 1969, Mobilization March against the war, and a Harvard student, expecting ten or fifteen responses, got 125 volunteers to represent welfare recipients at hearings before the Massachusetts Welfare Board.

Part of the increased politicization is attributable to new elements in the student body. The number of black students, who were virtually nonexistent at "white" schools only four years ago, has skyrocketed since the formation in 1968 of the Council on Legal Education Opportunity and the Rockefeller Foundation-financed special summer study program. Similarly, the number of female law students has taken a quantum leap to where blacks and women constitute more than 20 percent of the student body at many schools. Many of them are political activists and, to an extent, their very presence serves to heighten sensitivity to groups which are discriminated against, but much of the activity is also attributable to the spirit of the time. "Today we have many students," reports Yale Associate Dean Henry Poor, "who wouldn't have been caught dead in a law school five years ago. They would have been in graduate school. But the immediacy of the urban crisis has made a dissertation seem ivy-towered."

One factor drawing new elements to law schools, is an emerging pantheon of legal heroes. Justice William O. Douglas has long kindled the hope that our legal system can evolve to be sensitive to the needs of all citizens. Now, however, he has been joined by a group of younger men who can inspire the idealistic college student. Harvard Law graduate Ralph Nader is, of course, a central figure with his uncompromising indictments of government, the legal profession, and the law schools. Elsewhere in the hierarchy, men such as William Kunstler from the Chicago Conspiracy trial, Panther lawyer Charles Garry, and Professor Arthur Kinoy embody the title "counsel to the movement." Richard Goodwin, Jeff Greenfield, and Adam Walinsky affirm that the legally trained can influence national policy as political aides. Jean and Edgar Cahn, who head the Urban Law Institute and the Citizen's Advocate Center, respectively, are models of the contribution that can be made via the private, public service law institute.

As the pantheon suggests, the new breed brings to law school new career aspirations. In 1958, the editors of the *Harvard Law Review*, then headed by Richard Goodwin, noted that "the opportunities offered by the large [private law firms in New York and Washington] seem more attractive than ever." A decade later, that attraction dims. None of the thirty-nine *Harvard Law Review* editors of 1970 plans to enter Wall Street practice at graduation, although starting salaries shot from $10 thousand to $15 thousand in a single year. Nor are their classmates enamored of the prospect: barely half of the class of 1969, reports the Harvard Placement Office, entered any sort of private practice at graduation. The year the salary increase took effect, the percentage of graduates entering private practice from Yale and Virginia Law Schools dropped from 41 percent to 31 percent and 63 percent to 54 percent respectively; at Michigan only twenty-six graduates went to Wall Street compared with a previous average of seventy-five.[15] Many were taking draft deferable jobs, and some will turn to private practice after military service or a judicial clerkship. Nonetheless, "the distribution of prestige among post–law-school jobs," reports Professor Frank Michelman, "has changed drastically in the last six to eight years. Today, landing a job with a big city firm is not status, not ego-satisfying. It's not chic, to say the least, to be out for money."

Students are also taking more active measures to reform the profession. Growing numbers of students spend their summers working for Ralph Nader investigating, among other things, large law firms. In the autumn of 1969, several student groups sent questionnaires to law firms requesting information on minority group hiring practices, the amount of law firm time granted to public service work, and firm standards concerning the ethics of their corporate representations. The purpose was to give students more information about the law firms they would be interviewing for possible jobs. Although the Harvard probe was signed by more than 300 students and endorsed by eleven student organizations, three-quarters of the firms refused to reply; the 110 answering firms generally sent polite evasions. A recruiting partner of the Covington & Burling firm in Washington called the questionnaire "a monstrosity"; others accused it of being "naive . . . prejudiced . . . prying"; a Pittsburgh firm canceled its interview appointments; and the organizers were threatened by some with retaliation when they seek admission to the bar.

The New York firm of Milbank, Tweed, Hadley and McCloy announced a policy of granting their lawyers 200 hours of "firm time" per year for *pro bono publico* work (for the public good). Students answered that this represented only forty minutes per ten-hour day, a scintilla of their resources, and issued a leaflet denouncing their clients' South African dealings. Representatives from the Cravath, Swaine & Moore firm discussed client South African investments until 1 A.M. with a roomful of critical students; their interviewers were picketed the following day. Ropes & Gray, a prestigious Boston firm, was picketed for its ties with the Eastern Associated Coal Company which opposes mine-safety and miner-health legislation. And Washington law students picketed the offices of the Wilmer, Cutler & Pickering firm for persuading the Justice Department to disregard a federal grand jury recommendation and, later, not to go to court against the major auto companies for an alleged conspiracy to suppress anti-pollution exhaust devices.

In the meantime, placement offices, long the bailiwick of the corporate firms, are being pushed—with some success—to make a greater effort to find jobs in the public sector. Between 1964 and 1967 the number of public defender offices in the United States nearly doubled (from 139 to 266), the number of civic legal aid offices grew by more than 130, and more than 1,000 new positions for attorneys were created.[16] Nonetheless, the student demand for jobs in the public sector exceeds the supply. One factor exacerbating the shortage is the Nixon Administration: many students who would otherwise look for federal positions choose not to join the Nixon-Mitchell-Kleindienst team. The Justice Department, Attorney General Mitchell confirmed recently, has been having recruitment problems, since many young lawyers disagree with administration policies.[17] "The whole system is breaking down," laments one. "There was an incentive for an immigrant's son like Felix Frankfurter when F.D.R. was President, but who wants to hobnob with Nixon?"

The economics of the new law, however, pose difficult problems. One reason why law schools teach commercial law and estate planning for the rich is that only they have been able to afford legal services. When a claim or tax return is small, $25-per-hour legal fees are not warranted. Many attempts to practice law for the poor without a government subsidy have become "poverty practices" for the practitioner as well as his clients. While new forms of class actions may make public service practice self-sustaining in the future, government funding must carry the burden for now. But reliance on the government brings dangers with it: the threat of a fund cut-off may deter the aggressive pursuit of rights, and government's apparent assumption of responsibility gives the bar greater leeway to rationalize noninvolvement. Where it has not been affirmatively obstructive, it has remained largely aloof from the new quest for justice. "As [private] lawyers become increasingly removed from the social and public problems and concerns that society deems most exigent and vital," warns Justice William Brennan, "they may become narrow in point of view, unduly circumscribed by the private and parochial interests of their clients, and lacking in perspective and breadth of vision."[18]

A few firms are getting the message. In October, 1969, Piper & Marbury, the largest Baltimore firm, opened a ghetto office to provide free legal services; the Boston firm of Foley, Hoag & Eliot has appointed a *pro bono* senior associate for two years to do welfare, civil rights, and consumer cases; and Hogan & Hartson, the third largest Washington firm, is establishing a Community Services Department, headed by a partner and staffed full time by two associates. Like other firms, Hogan & Hartson acknowledges that one motivation was to enhance recruitment.[19]

Gradually, the new breed is making its impact felt, demanding a new vitality from the schools and a new responsibility from the profession. Slowly both are reassessing their values and assumptions. But true reform remains distant.

III. REFORM AT THE FRINGE

Facing basic disenchantment, law schools have begun marginal reforms, adding new courses and offering new options, but the thrust of the mainstream is intact.

Catalogs display seminar smorgasbords of new relevance. Columbia teaches Law for the Poor in an Affluent Society; Chicago, the Urban Public School System. At the University of Southern California students read snippets of Sartre, Fromm, and C. Wright Mills, as well as Holmes and Frankfurter. "Concentrations" in Urban Law, International Law, and Law and Third World Modernization are also springing up. While some of these offerings reflect major faculty efforts to develop new and excellent subject matter, others are disappointments. Sometimes, the "new" offerings are little more than old courses with new titles, for thin law school budgets have not been stretched to provide real diversity. The number of courses is also misleading; though much is offered, little may be chosen, for the student is allowed only one seminar, though the catalog lists eight. At one school, courses on environmental and consumer protection, racism in law, and criminal procedure were all scheduled to overlap with one on constitutional litigation, so that choosing one entailed foregoing the others.

But the worst feature is that the offerings come too late. The Harvard student interested in Urban Legal Studies, for example, must endure required first-year courses and the second-year business trio before he reaches most courses for which he came to law school. Seminars are closed until his third year, when apathy has set in or his energies are concentrated on lining up a job. Nor do the tenets of legal education change; the focus on auditorium classes and appellate court decisions persists, while credit and grades remain tied to exams.

Interdisciplinary exposure is another mutation of the traditional curriculum, brought about by the addition of economists, psychiatrists, and urban planners to the faculty. Harvard's Dean Derek C. Bok admits, however, that the impact has been minimal. "In the past thirty years, there has been a flurry of adding specialists from other disciplines to law faculties, but this process has scarcely affected the heart of the curriculum where almost all students spend most of their time."[20] Occasional courses in other university departments and joint degrees with government and business schools are also becoming familiar features of the law school catalog, but many fear that these may postpone the fundamental changes needed in the law schools themselves.

At scattered schools, new centers for advanced study and empirical research are viewed as signs that law schools are recasting their molds. Columbia's Center for Civil Rights Research, Boston College's Consumer Law Institute, and the Harvard Center on Law and Education are examples. Unfortunately, for the average student, these centers remain peripheral to the curriculum except for a few imaginative courses and projects.

In the eyes of many, clinical legal education—work in community activities, neighborhood law offices, and consumer and poverty litigation—has become the saving grace of legal education. Praise for these efforts is high, but their role in the school's official certification for the bar remains small. Little of this outside work is awarded credit, and those clinical-related courses so honored are usually listed as experiments. Nor is the clinical director generally tenured, if he is a member of the faculty at all.

One departure that could introduce new vistas into legal education is the Intensive Semester concept pioneered at Yale and adopted in Stanford's Extern program. Under this arrangement, students receive regular law school credit for independent off-campus research or for internships lasting up to six months. Before and after "sabbaticals," students work with faculty members to enrich their experience. Daniel J. Freed, the professor responsible for developing Yale's program, explains that Yale is trying to identify institutions where social, legal, and educational problems are emerging in which student work can make a contribution. Generally, he says, the best learning experiences are ones which students put together themselves. The intensive semester enables them to get involved on a full-time basis in the kind of activities lawyers undertake outside law school, while allowing them to see why institutions fail, and giving them insight into strategies for social change. The intensive semester faces widespread resistance, however. Harvard and Chicago have turned down a proposal (accepted by five other law schools) that six students receive credit for a semester of work at the Center on Law and Social Policy in Washington, D.C., where they would work on litigation before federal regulatory agencies. One reason given for the rejection was that the project's being in Washington precluded professorial supervision. (Not even for the Harvard Law School would they move the federal government to Boston!)

Another innovation with much potential is the independent, student-initiated project. Students pick a problem, select a professor to advise them, and develop a work plan to execute it. The most elaborate such undertaking has been the Boston Urban Services Project involving eight Harvard students who developed a theoretical framework and a plan for decentralizing Boston city services. The "Boston Eight," as they were tagged, worked more than a year with the Office of Mayor Kevin White. Participant Steve Arons reflects: "Over three semesters and a summer the law school awarded credit for the equivalent of four regular courses. It was our most significant learning at law school." Very few such projects have been granted approval. The vague bias that time is better spent on regular courses in regular classes reviewing appellate decisions lingers on.

At Rutgers Law School, Professor Arthur Kinoy's clinic on Constitutional Litigation—combining active involvement with academic reflection—is probably the most significant innovation in legal education. Students in the seminar spend a semester working as junior partners (not research assistants) with lawyers actively trying cases. They share the lawyer's schedule, interviewing clients, mapping strategy, and examining points of law. Weekly, the seminar discusses one of the cases with the lawyers in charge and occasionally everyone drops everything to do emergency research for one of the cases. Kinoy's clinic is based on Jerome Frank's proposal that law schools include a law office where teachers combine teaching and practice while litigating constitutional questions. One feature that keeps motivation at a peak is emphasis on "people's law," a Justice Brandeis phrase meaning the development of theories and ideas to meet the needs of people battling on the frontiers of legal rights. Kinoy's students have labored to defend the Chicago Conspiracy defendants and the accused Panther 21 in New York, to put the Newark Police Department under receivership, and to forbid state agencies from keeping dossiers on political activists. The clinic is open to second- and third-year students regardless of their grades. "Just because a student did miserably in Corporations or Tax," argues Kinoy, "doesn't mean that he won't catch fire in work he finds more relevant." Supreme Court victories in the *Adam Clayton Powell* v. *John McCormack, Dombrowski* v. *Pfister,* and *Jones* v. *Mayer* cases (sometimes against large prestigious law firms) suggest that the quality of student work is high. The Kinoy clinic violates much that is sacred in legal education, however. The professor is an activist, as well as a scholar. Students receive extensive credit for assisting him, and others, outside the law school. No other school has yet followed suit.

A final significant development in legal education is the growing social impact of a number of law student organizations. At many schools, groups of students are banding together to research issues in poverty, welfare, and pollution law. The oldest and largest organization is the Law Students' Civil Rights Research Council with chapters at seventy-nine schools from Vanderbilt and Chicago to Boalt Hall at Berkeley. Others work with legislative programs for congressmen and state officials. New journals are also springing forth to carry the "New Law" beyond the campus. At Harvard, the *Civil Rights–Civil Liberties Law Review* has entered its sixth year with articles on air and water pollution, and the law students' challenge to law firms and bar associations. Columbia is publishing the *Journal on Law and Social Problems;* Yale, N.Y.U., and Michigan have begun similar publications in the last year. Established journals also reflect changes in tone and emphasis. The *California Law Review,* for example, published a review of Bob Dylan's "The Lonesome Death of Hattie Carroll" and Arlo Guthrie's "Alice's Restaurant," analyzing the picture they paint of the law and its impact on the New Youth Culture.

For the most part, however, the core curricular content re-

mains largely immune to the influence of the excitement surrounding it.

IV. POSSIBILITIES FOR REJUVENATION

For legal education to regain vitality, fundamental changes are
required. The most important is a reorientation to whom law
serves. Law schools must ask themselves how well they are providing society the social service it is their purpose to provide.
"Equal Justice Under Law," the inscription on the Supreme
Court Building in Washington, will continue to ring hollow for
California grape pickers, disadvantaged blacks, youths jailed for
possession of marihuana, court-martialed soldiers, and exploited
consumers, unless law schools alert their students to these needs
and train them to help. A basic reworking of the core curriculum would be an appropriate place to begin the rejuvenation.
Courses such as Property, Contracts, and the Rules of Procedure
should reflect their relevance to the least fortunate as well as the
financial oligarchy; the regular course on Corporations could include material on the application of traditional corporate techniques to the development of the ghetto.

To reduce the potential of internal law school strife, a second
basic reform should be the full inclusion of students in the decision-making process. In education, the young draw on the wisdom of the experienced to equip themselves for the tasks of their
own choosing. Decisions on curricular offerings, which reflect a
compromise between professorial expertise and student interest,
need to be executed jointly, for faculty decisions handed down to
student recipients who did not participate in their formulation
have been partly responsible for the present lag in preparing
students for new demands being made on the profession. Yale
Law's Fall 1969 student strike centered around student participation and complaints of unfair disciplinary action against four
blacks. Though the boycott lasted a day, its impact endures.
Elsewhere, faculty meetings and some administrative committees
are being opened to student membership, but a true educational
community will not be achieved until key committees such as
faculty appointments also include students.

Law schools must also move away from the certification syndrome, with its grade point emphasis, toward a goal of developing all students to their fullest. It is demeaning to both professors and students, as Justice Arthur Goldberg told the Harvard Law class of '71, to spend endless hours making fine but artificial distinctions. When the system's grade-certification orientation results in the exclusion of valuable learning experiences, the time for change is apparent. The standards of "how can we grade it?" and "how can a professor supervise that?" must be abandoned for a focus on whether something is an educational exercise that benefits students.

It is also time for law faculties to reexamine their assumption that the course is the basic learning unit and the classroom the most conducive learning environment. After a point, students learn more by grappling with problems than by attending class; after seventeen years in the classroom, that point of diminishing returns looms large. To revitalize legal education, litigation seminars, student-initiated projects, and semester internships must become a central part of every law school's program. Perhaps a clinical experience should be required as it is in medical school. Although growing numbers of educators are proposing that law school be reduced to two years (Stanford has recently offered an optional two-year degree), a better goal is to make law school three full years of excitement and challenge.

Another way to infuse new life is to get new people. Superior law grades are not the most important criterion for selecting faculty members; alternative paths of professorial recruitment must be opened. Outstanding practitioners from government or practice can impart as much to students as those whose chief accomplishment is legal editing. Hopefully, these new faces will infuse new materials and fresh approaches into legal education.

Finally, law schools have an obligation to reexamine the mixture of skills they hope to impart to their graduates. Interdisciplinary approaches and policy orientation must become a part of every lawyer's training for, as Professor David Cavers of the Executive Committee of the American Association of Law Schools has observed, "schools that produce many of our solo and small-firm practitioners, most of the counsel for our criminal defendants, and probably most of the lawyers who hold state and local legal offices (including judgeships), should recognize the opportunity that these facts afford. They can claim with little, if any, exaggeration that their graduates will have greater responsibility for the well-being of urban society than will the lawyers who represent great corporations or hold federal office."[21] Reflecting on the lawyer's role as intermediary and negotiator, another critic of legal education has suggested a mandatory course in interpersonal psychology or group dynamics. Decision theory and sociology are other important areas where the lawyer's awareness should be expanded.

The demands being made on legal education are great, but no greater than what the urban crisis is demanding of much of society, and of lawyers in particular. If the law schools do not respond, the bar may face eclipse as the "rightful leader in the preservation and development of American institutions." But if legal education in the 1970s can recapture the spirit of innovation that swept it exactly a century before, the bar in America can conform more closely to its philosophical tenets. As Professor Arthur Sutherland wrote in concluding his history of the Harvard Law School: "The familiar is not the necessary. What has been habitual in the law, and in education for it, may be deadening if it fails to accord with new demands of society. . . . The School must be ready to put away former things even when these in their own time have demonstrated great value. . . . Our universe is changing. We had better accept it changes and all."[22]

The 1970s: A Decade of Repression?

HARVEY A. SILVERGLATE*

The signs are strong that the stage is now being set for an up-
swell of political and intellectual repression in the 1970s. As
society accelerates its war against crime, drugs, freaks, civil disorder, and "dangerous" political doctrines and organizations, the
higher ranks of government join the lower echelons, such as the
police, to wage the battle. Thus, "law enforcement" tactics which
only recently were officially condemned and used only by undisciplined lower level law enforcement officers, are now being
given a veneer of respectability and even legality. What is perhaps more frightening is that the judiciary is being recruited in
this effort, affirming questionable practices in the name of necessity and law and order. Consequently, the forces of repression
in the 1970s may well be led not by local police, but by a
coalition headed by the President of the United States, the Attorney General, the Director of the Federal Bureau of Investigation, and the Chief Justice of the United States.

Historically, the American constitutional system, with its long
list of personal liberties preserved in writing and in court decisions for the benefit of the American people, has been the
chief protector of the right of citizens to say and do things which
others may dislike. Various public opinion polls and other studies

* Harvey Silverglate graduated from Harvard Law School in 1967, and
is now a partner in the Boston firm of Zalkind, Klubock & Silverglate, which
specializes in draft, drug, and civil liberties cases. He has written many articles in the civil liberties and criminal fields.

have consistently shown that large numbers of Americans—perhaps even a majority—do not approve of certain of the liberties embodied in the Bill of Rights, particularly as interpreted and broadened by the Supreme Court; yet the system has achieved sufficient durability and rigidity by virtue of its being based upon a written document, drawn up by the eminent "Founding Fathers," and interpreted by a Court composed of men with life tenure.

At crucial times in the history of the nation, however, we have seen that no amount of rigidity or historical respectability can withstand pressures of society's demand that individual liberties be curbed. At such times, any general agreement that the Bill of Rights should be kept intact has fallen apart at the seams, and our codified written system has been worse than ignored—it has been turned around and used as an instrument of repression against the free individual. It is this remarkable ability of the American constitutional system to act as both the rigid bulwark of our liberties and as the resourceful and diligent persecutor of our unpopular fellow citizens in time of national fear or stress that has led analysts to talk of citizens receiving "due process of law" during good times and of their being "due processed to death" in bad times. We have witnessed within the last few years events which indicate that the decade of the seventies may bear witness to more of the latter than the former. When a citizen is "due processed to death," he finds himself receiving all of the trappings of fair treatment and fair trial according to law; but he soon notices that the law has become sufficiently distorted that it cannot function as a wall between the dissenting individual and the demanding society.

The danger is not only that during the onset of legal repression many individuals will suffer; there is also the possibility that by embodying the concept of repression too deeply into the legal system and by making actual substantive and procedural changes in our laws, we may inflict irreparable injury upon the Bill of Rights, making it impossible for the nation to return to traditional libertarianism even after the current crisis of fear and disorder has passed.

LOWER LEVEL REPRESSION

Repression by police and lower court authorities is endemic in our society; yet, it must be distinguished from deliberate attempts by the policy-making organs of government to stifle dissent, which can be termed "legal repression." In the absence of higher level "legal repression," intimidation and abuse of authority by the lower officials is not condoned. To carry it out, members of the lower law enforcement echelons are forced to resort to secrecy, truth-stretching, outright lying, or even perjury. As a result of this type of harassment numerous victims have won jury verdicts under one or more of the federal Civil Rights Acts. For example, one such statute enables an aggrieved citizen to file suit against persons who acting "under color of law" deprive them of their civil rights.[1] Another statute provides for redress against those who conspire to violate a person's civil rights, including persons other than officers acting in the name of or "under color of" the law.[2] These are the statutes most commonly used in "police brutality" cases, where an officer of the law abuses his position and illegally acts as the tormenter of the citizen rather than as his protector. Such statutes are necessary to deter unlawful official conduct. It is not sufficient that an illegally arrested and unlawfully charged defendant merely obtain an acquittal of the criminal charges brought against him. The law gives aggrieved citizens access to the courts to punish officials who act illegally, which is important since public prosecutors may be slow to move against police and other officials who abuse citizens' rights.

Yet, it would take a flight of fancy to believe that the Civil Rights Acts or any other remedies available to a citizen, as well as the protections given a defendant at a criminal trial, are sufficient to protect the average citizen who incites the wrath of his would-be protectors. Most victims of repressive and discriminatory police and judicial behavior do not have the knowledge or resources to invoke the proper remedies and to lay the foundations at the early stages for such action. Furthermore, even the sophisticated victim must run the gauntlet of official prevarication in taking his case to the courts. Even if those obstacles are met and overcome, it is a general practice for municipalities to soften the blow against policemen who have civil rights suits brought against them or money judgments returned against them by providing the officers with legal counsel at no personal cost and by assuming the payment of any damages.

Some degree of disrespect for constitutional rights has long been evident in the police and lower court establishments. Defense attorneys handling routine, nonpolitical criminal cases have always known about these problems. For example, one trial court judge in Massachusetts was reported several years ago to have reminded a Boston criminal attorney arguing for the federal constitutional rights of his client that, "This is Massachusetts, and the federal constitution does not apply." Other municipal and police court judges as a matter of course penalize a defendant for choosing to exercise his Fifth Amendment privilege against self-incrimination. Lawyers and citizens alike, particularly black citizens, have long been aware of the propensity of some policemen to routinely engage in technically unlawful conduct in the area of "stop and frisk" and "search and seizure." Such illegal conduct is often encouraged by the inability of minority group citizens to protest effectively the invasion of their rights, and by the willingness of some lower court judges to look the other way in the face of often obvious police perjury on the witness stand. Thus, the judge or jury might believe the arresting officer as he testifies that when he approached, the defendant dropped a marihuana cigarette onto the sidewalk; therefore, the arrest of the defendant was lawful, since no search of the defendant's person preceded the circumstances which gave the officer probable cause to believe that the defendant was committing a felony. It often does the defendant little good to claim that he was stopped for no reason (other than the color of his skin or his style of dress) and subjected to an illegal search on the street. Many attorneys suffer a feeling of dismay and anger (not to mention embarrassment as the client wants to know "how can they get away with that?") as some lower court judges hear and believe, or profess to believe, the marihuana-cigarette-on-the-sidewalk story as it is repeated verbatim by police officers on the witness stand day after day.

Legal procedures make it difficult for a defendant to obtain justice on an appeal once the factual record is established in the trial court. The judge or jury in the trial court determines what transpired factually, and it is at that stage that the police version of events often becomes accepted. An appellate court, in reviewing the validity of a conviction by a lower court, is often bound by the lower court's determination of the facts and limits itself to reviewing the correctness of the legal principles applied to the facts found by the court or jury. By the time a case reaches the appellate court, what actually was a blatantly illegal street search of a long-haired "hippy-type" might be determined because of fact findings by a judge or jury, to be a perfectly legal search and arrest.

The legal system is further structured to make police perjury easy. Many crimes in the statute books make it unlawful to engage in conduct which does no injury to persons or property, but which goes contrary to prevailing standards of acceptable morality. Such crimes are often called "crimes without victims"—the kind of behavior termed by John Stuart Mill as "self-regarding conduct," indicating that such behavior affects and concerns only the individuals who voluntarily engage in it. Such "crimes" include, among others, obscenity, fornication, adultery, blasphemy, drug use, gambling, and public drunkenness. Since there are no victims of such crimes and no concrete evidence of their commission in most cases, courts are faced with a credibility contest between defendant and arresting officer.

Perjury is also encouraged by the vague wording of a great number of criminal laws, such as those against "disturbers of the peace," "loitering," and being "idle and disorderly." An arresting officer often can make a conviction stick if he can convince a court that what the defendant says was merely loud talking on a street corner was actually shouting, which disturbed the orderly passage of pedestrians and disturbed the surrounding area and people there. Usually the only victims of such "crimes" are the defendants persecuted for committing them.

Criminal laws against "self-regarding conduct," which is often engaged in by large numbers of people, combined with the vague language of many criminal laws, serve to allow police and prosecutors to engage in discriminatory, selective law enforcement. Thus, even if no police perjury is involved in a particular case, and the defendant committed some crime of a "moral" nature, the police often choose to arrest, and prosecutors often decide to charge such persons for reasons other than the "enormity" of their infractions. Persons who are unpopular or who harbor thoughts and philosophies at odds with those of local officials are most often the persons charged with such crimes. A tremendous amount of prosecutorial discretion is placed in the hands of law enforcement personnel very low on the echelon.

Society would doubtless benefit if the criminal law were reserved for those antisocial acts which do injury to persons and property. Even those policemen least concerned with the truthfulness of their testimony in court would hesitate to lie in a case involving a crime the commission and existence of which would have to be proven by evidence other than the officer's own testimony standing alone. Thus, a policeman could not easily charge a defendant with murder if no body were found; nor could he charge a man with armed robbery if the victim could not identify the "suspect" as the man who committed the crime. Persons are not so easily framed for the commission of crimes which do indeed have victims other than the sensibilities of a police officer or prosecutor.

It is because of these elements in our legal system that it has been possible for our courts to convict innocent citizens with all of the trappings of due process of law. The system has thus allowed its lower level members, including the police and the police courts and municipal courts, to punish unpopular citizens, while the upper echelons of the system in the executive, judicial, and legislative departments can earnestly believe, or at least lead others to believe, that the system affords liberty and justice for all.

Yet even under such circumstances, society as a whole seems to disapprove of illegal conduct aimed against any particular group of citizens. There is some comfort in the fact that violations of the citizen's liberties are officially condemned, and periodic efforts to correct blatant abuses often surface to public scrutiny. In the wake of a series of murders of white and black civil rights work-

ers in the South in the early sixties, when local and state prosecutors refused to bring charges against, or when juries refused to
convict, the alleged murderers, federal authorities brought prosecutions under the Civil Rights Acts. Juries still did not always
return a favorable verdict, but the point was made that higher
authorities disapproved of such conduct. An atmosphere was
maintained in which violators of individual liberties at least had
to act in secret.

The serious problem which America will be facing in the decade of the seventies is the transition from repression emanating
almost exclusively from lower echelon levels, officially condemned from above, to a more subtle, but probably more effective form of official, legal repression aimed against those engaged
in radical challenges to the system. At such times the upper
echelons set the tone and rallying cry and spearhead the drive by
using the courts against prominent radicals, while the reins on
the police are loosened to make lower level repression more
effective, less fraught with risks for the police, and more respectable. In such an atmosphere, the usual lower echelon repression
is not supplanted; it is supplemented and nourished.

OFFICIAL CRACKDOWNS: PAST AND PRESENT

Today is not, to be sure, the first time that the phenomenon of
official repression has appeared on the American scene. Indeed,
periods of repression alternating with periods of relative freedom
have been part of our national cycles since the Sedition Acts of
1798 were created to "protect" the infant republic. As has already
been pointed out, lower echelon repression, not officially recognized or sanctioned, has long been with us. But many times
before the current decade higher echelon levels within the administrative, executive, or legislative branches have added hys-
terical voices to the outcries for law and order.

During times of real or imagined "emergency" facing the nation, the courts have offered varying degrees of resistance to another branch of government which has overstepped its bounds.
During the Civil War, President Lincoln suspended the writ of
habeas corpus by executive order, thereby purporting to deprive

courts of their jurisdiction to review the legality of arrests, and the judiciary found itself hard pressed to make its weight felt. When, in 1861, a petition for *habeas corpus* was presented to Chief Justice Taney of the Supreme Court on behalf of one John Merryman,[3] who it was claimed was arrested at night and illegally confined at Fort McHenry near Baltimore, the Chief Justice issued the writ to be served upon Brevet Major General Cadwalader, who commanded Fort McHenry. The writ ordered Cadwalader to bring the prisoner before Taney the next day. However, when the United States marshal attempted to serve the writ, he was unable to get past the outer gate. Cadwalader claimed that he was duly authorized by the President to disregard the writ of *habeas corpus*. The Chief Justice, obviously a bit piqued, excused the marshal from making service because "The power refusing obedience was so notoriously superior to any the marshal could command." Taney then proceeded to commit his opinion to writing, ordered that the prisoner be turned over to the civil authorities and that his opinion should be filed and "laid down before the president, in order that he might perform his constitutional duty, to enforce the law, by securing obedience to the process of the United States." Shortly thereafter, Merryman was released from Fort McHenry, turned over to civilian custody, and indicted for treason.[4]

The Civil War period was notorious for such incursions of personal liberty and the refusal of the executive to be fully cooperative with the judiciary. Only after the conclusion of the war did the Supreme Court become bolder, striking out on behalf of the civil liberties of citizens. Justice Davis commented why in 1866: "Congress was obliged to enact severe laws to meet the crisis; and as our highest civil duty is to serve our country when in danger, the late war has proved that rigorous laws, when necessary, will be cheerfully obeyed by a patriotic people, struggling to preserve the rich blessings of a free government."[5]

During the First World War, First Amendment rights fell under heavy attack. There was great difficulty in knowing what speech was protected and what was not. In one case decided March 3, 1919,[6] Justice Holmes wrote a majority opinion upholding a conviction under the Espionage Act[7] based upon circulation of an antidraft pamphlet urging citizens to oppose military conscription. Mr. Justice Holmes here formulated his classic analysis:

> The most stringent protection of free speech would not protect a man in falsely shouting fire in a theatre and causing a panic. It does not even protect a man from an injunction against uttering words that may have all the effect of force. The question in every case is whether the words used are used in such circumstances and are of such a nature as to create a clear and present danger that they will bring about the substantive evils that Congress has a right to prevent.

Using this new "clear and present danger test," the Court and Holmes found that the defendant fell within its ambit.

A couple of months later in another Espionage Act case,[8] the majority again upheld the conviction of a defendant who had circulated printed pamphlets designed "to excite, at the supreme crisis of the war, disaffection, sedition, riots, and, as they hoped, revolution in this country for the purpose of embarrassing and if possible defeating the military plans of the government in Europe." This time Justice Holmes dissented, blasting the majority with the admonition that "We should be eternally vigilant against attempts to check the expression of opinions that we loathe. . . ." His own First Amendment loophole of "clear and present danger" had been used against him, now being enlarged to suppress nondangerous speech. The best minds on the highest bench of the land were thus wrangling over so basic an issue as the First Amendment. One had Justice Holmes' own waivering and his frank statement that "The character of every act depends upon the circumstances in which it is done" and that "when a nation is at war many things that might be said in time of peace are such a hindrance to its effort that their utterance will not be endured so long as men fight and that no Court could regard them as protected by any constitutional right."[9] How, then, was the average citizen to feel secure in deciding what he might, or might not lawfully do?

It was around this period, just after the First World War, that American concern for internal subversion reached the point of frenzy. Under the leadership of A. Mitchell Palmer, the then Attorney General of the United States, radical organizations were subjected to a series of blitzkrieg-like raids. Alien radicals were ordered deported from the country. The President, Woodrow Wilson, was gravely ill during these episodes, and he was in no condition to exercise the restraint over his Attorney General which one might have expected from this source of moral rectitude. This was not to be the last time in American history that a "law and order" Attorney General was to acquire substantial sway over official treatment of civil liberties without a salutary restraining hand reaching out from the White House. A similar problem was to spring up in the 1970s, only this time presidential restraint was to be absent not because of incapacitation or illness of the President, but because the rooting out of dissidents and extremists was to become an official national policy.

The Second World War had its own brand of court-sanctioned incursions against the civil liberties of citizens. Perhaps most notorious was the relocation and segregation of citizens of Japanese descent who lived on the West Coast.

In 1943, when the war was at its height, Chief Justice Stone, in an opinion for the Court,[10] upheld the conviction of a Japanese-American for violating an act of Congress and an accompanying order making it a misdemeanor knowingly to disregard restrictions placed upon all persons of Japanese ancestry residing in areas of the West Coast. The restrictions consisted of a curfew placed upon Japanese-Americans by the military commander. Chief Justice Stone pointed out that the Constitution "does not demand the impossible or the impractical," and, while claiming the Court would not review in detail the factual basis of the government's finding that these citizens posed a danger, he went on to note that there were facts and circumstances "which support the judgment of the war-waging branches of the Government that some restrictive measure was urgent." Even Justice Douglas professed not to have as much knowledge of the facts of the situation as was in the possession of the military authorities. "The point is that we cannot sit in judgment on the military requirements of that hour."[11]

It was not until nearer the end of the war, after the tide had turned in favor of the Allies, that Mitsuye Endo,[12] another American of Japanese ancestry, received a ruling from the Supreme Court declaring that the government had no right to detain her in a relocation camp under the auspices of the War Relocation Authority. True, Justice Douglas, in the opinion for the Court, managed to distinguish the Hirabayashi situation from the Endo situation by resorting to interpretation of the Executive Order involved; but one might make an educated guess as to what the outcome of that case might have been had it reached the Supreme Court when the national emergency was at its height.

Thus, during times of national emergency or danger the executive and legislative branches have assumed extraordinary powers to curtail liberties which at other times were relatively freely accorded to individuals. These incursions came from the very top echelons of government, and they were often validated by the highest Court in the land, which sometimes did and sometimes did not admit in all frankness that it was only because of the presence of an emergency that the incursions were being upheld. Justice Holmes is to be congratulated for his frankness in making it clear that the dangers of the times affect the breadth of individual liberty, but it also must be admitted that it is precisely that doctrine which opens up a Pandora's box, particularly when less Olympian judges than Holmes sit on the bench. It is quite simple to detect when a crowded movie theatre is or is not burning, and when a false alarm would or would not cause a riot. But simplicity ends there. We pay a heavy price for resorting to the "balancing process" whereby the state's interests are purportedly weighed against the individual's.

Perhaps the most memorable example of official repression that comes to the contemporary mind is the McCarthy era in the early 1950s. Individual citizens found themselves helpless and stifled in the face of often wild accusations of Communist or left-wing taint made by the senator from Wisconsin. Even the United States Government was hard put to fend off the charge that 215 Communists inhabited the ranks of the State Department. It is well to remember that the Communist witch hunts of the fifties were not technically illegal. They resulted from a mass hysteria, promoted by a powerful senator, and nurtured by official silence. President Eisenhower did not enter the battle against McCarthy until the senator attacked his army.

The McCarthy era was not an aberration, or if it was, then we have seen other such aberrations appearing periodically. Just a few years after the demise of Joe McCarthy, the United States Supreme Court[13] upheld the validity of the McCarran and Smith Acts,[14] which require that the American Communist Party register as a foreign agent, and which also provide penalties for belonging to an organization knowing that the organization advocates the violent overthrow of the government. A member of the four-man minority dissent, Justice Hugo L. Black, declared that the majority was condoning governmental action which banned "an association because it advocates hated ideas." Joe McCarthy might have been dead, but his immortal soul was still lingering.

Indeed, Justice Black correctly understood what the majority of the Court was allowing the government to do. The majority condoned such practices at the highest levels of government. Repression had taken a legal form, and the law not only failed to protect dissidents, but it was also turned directly into an instrument to control the growth of dissent. America began to get a taste of why it was worse to have repression by bad laws rather than repression despite good laws.

Good laws might be ignored at the lower echelons; but bad laws handed down from the highest levels are even more dangerous. When a repressive law is passed and then enforced under Supreme Court imprimatur, only a fool could mistake the message that all stops have been pulled out in the battle against liberty in its own name.

The Supreme Court is thrown into a position of extreme pressure and tension during periods of governmental and popular outrage over "crime in the streets" or "subversion and anarchy." The Supreme Court has often stood up to such pressures, at least for a time. In a 1967 opinion,[15] for example, the same Supreme Court which upheld the Smith and McCarran Acts struck down the Subversive Activities Control Act of 1950,[16] which forbade Communists from working in defense plants. Perhaps the Court felt that the witchhunts had gone far enough. Then–Chief Justice Earl Warren observed in the Court's opinion that in the course of promoting and protecting the national defense we must take care in maintaining and defending "those liberties . . . which make the defense of the nation worthwhile."

THE CURRENT CRISIS

The current problem—call it "emergency" if you will—facing the American Republic seems for the first time to involve less of a threat of attack from without than it does revolution from within. Of course, most of this nation's prior bouts with legal repression have revolved around the friends or supposed friends of the nation's enemies. Japanese-Americans on the West Coast were suspected of being at least emotionally sympathetic to the enemy Japanese Empire. And the victims of the McCarthy era were thought to be the internal allies of Soviet Russia, a fifth column.[17]

But the current threat is apparently seen by the government as involving something more sinister—an internal threat not tied to any particular foreign power, but tied rather to an indigenous revolutionary doctrine, promulgated by militant blacks and by white radicals. Historians and political analysts up until quite recently felt that development of a revolutionary movement in America was impossible in view of the "consensus" whereby nobody really wanted to destroy the pie-making apparatus, but rather everyone wanted a larger slice of it. In the demonology of no less an "authority" than J. Edgar Hoover, the Black Panthers have replaced the Communist Party as the most serious threat to the internal security of the United States. And the FBI Director, in making this analysis, added that "despite its record of hate, violence, and subversion, the Black Panther Party continues to receive substantial monetary contributions from prominent donors."[18] And the enemy will be thwarted, not merely by the classic devices used for years by police against "undesirables." Law and order will be protected by resort to respectable and lawful legislation—respectable because it is created by Congress in the name of preserving law and order, and lawful because much of it will probably survive Supreme Court scrutiny, if indeed the High

Court chooses to scrutinize much of this legislation. The Court might instead refuse to exercise discretionary Supreme Court review, and thus allow the lower courts to be "hatchet men." Thus, not only can the Party be destroyed, but its respectable donors and supporters can be frightened away.

"Only emergency can justify repression," said Justice Brandeis during the First World War. The emergencies in our nation's past have almost always been war emergencies, or threats from without supported by collaborators from within. Yet the non-war, internally generated revolution of today, and the reaction that has begun to set in, encompass the creation of a substantial body of statutes and law enforcement practices which may be with us far longer than the "Red raids" of Attorney General Palmer, or the ravings, rantings, and witch hunts of the McCarthy era. Repression of Communists in the State Department or at defense plants was a mere game compared to the repression of elements of contemporary society whose revolutionary doctrines are rubbed into the public consciousness daily by means of mass demonstrations, inflammatory rhetoric, threats of violence, and periodic violence.

To combat this threat, Congress endeavors to punish more than revolutionary action. It threatens to punish revolutionary thought, and it threatens to discover the presence of such revolutionary thought in an individual's head by eavesdropping as those thoughts pour out of his mouth in private conversation. A celebrated example of the government's preference to punish "thoughtcrime" rather than substantive criminal acts is the draft conspiracy trial of baby doctor Benjamin Spock, the Reverend William Sloane Coffin, Jr., and three other draft and Vietnam War opponents in a showcase trial held in Boston in 1968. The defendants were accused of conspiring to interfere with the operation of the Selective Service System by organizing public rallies, writing and circulating dissident manifestoes, encouraging draft-age young men to resist the draft, and similar actions.

Four of the "Boston Five" were convicted; but, largely because the government chose to prosecute under the conspiracy theory, the convictions were reversed on appeal.[19] Most legal scholars seemed to believe that the government could have more easily obtained convictions and had them upheld if it prosecuted each defendant for a substantive crime. It is likely that the government chose the conspiracy route because to have done otherwise would have allowed a reviewing court to rule on the legality or illegality of many specific acts of dissent against the war and the draft. Such an appellate opinion could have read like a manual and guide to lawful, protected dissent. But conspiracy law is sufficiently broad and vague so that a conviction for conspiracy would have the effect of threatening any citizen who at any time expressed his views on the war or the draft to other persons, or who participated in any group or mass action program to protest the war. Even a Supreme Court decision would probably not be decisive enough to dissipate the vague, general fears that such an indictment might be expected to generate among many ordinary citizens.[20]

Similarly, the government invoked an even more vague, more ominous statute in prosecuting the "Chicago Eight" for conspiring to cross state lines with the intent of inciting riot, and in also accusing each defendant of crossing state lines with intent to commit some illegal act. The government tried to make out a case of a substantive violation against each defendant, presumably as a backstop to the general conspiracy charge against all of them, just in case the conspiracy statute did not hold up under constitutional scrutiny by a reviewing court. The jury acquitted all of the defendants on the conspiracy charge, and convicted five of them for crossing state lines with intent to incite riot. The specific acts committed by each defendant might in and of themselves have been lawful and protected by the First Amendment, but taken together along with the act of crossing a state line, the acts were enough to warrant jury conviction. Never before in our jurisprudence has a state of mind been such a crucial element in a criminal statute.

The extreme dangers of statutes passed as part of a program of legal repression are exemplified by the rare view of the jury decision-making process given to us when one of the "Chicago Seven" jurors wrote a series of newspaper articles on the jury's deliberations. The articles pointed out that while some jurors raised the question of the constitutionality of such a statute, they decided that it would be best to leave that question to the judges.[21] Apparently the jurors were not made aware of the high odds against any appellant convincing four justices of the Supreme Court to vote to review a case. Besides, the interviews with the jurors made it painfully clear that while they did not convict on the conspiracy charge, they did not do so partly because they compromised and convicted on the substantive charges. Thus, the presence of the broad conspiracy charge, despite the verdict of not guilty, had its effect on the jury's decision.

Juries, even though they are composed of ordinary members of the community who are assumed to possess all of the prejudices of "average" Americans or members of the "silent majority," often do return verdicts of not guilty in cases where evidence is exaggerated, fabricated, or where an earnest defendant, long hair and all, has convinced them of his credibility. This is possible even in the face of grossly unfair methods of jury selection, which virtually preclude certain elements of the population from obtaining juries composed of their peers. In Massachusetts, for example, persons under 25 years of age have long been exempted and for practical purposes excluded from jury duty.[22] A major complaint by observers of the Spock conspiracy trial in Boston was that the jury that tried the famed baby doctor had a conspicuous lack of women, and of course, mothers. Few blacks serve, and many of the best educated members of the community evade jury duty.

The composition of the jury is of crucial importance in the modern day conspiracy and political trials, since the government in such cases often charges, in broad, catchall, vague indictments, acts the commission of which are hardly in dispute. All that is in dispute is the conclusion that the conduct charged is either illegal or unwarranted. This is one of the hallmarks of the "political trials" which are becoming familiar spectacles. Thus, when the prosecutor of Alameda County, California, charged that the "Oakland Seven," who organized the militant "Stop the Draft Week" demonstration at the Oakland Armed Forces Induction Center in 1967, were guilty of conspiracy to commit the misdemeanors of trespass and resisting arrest, the jury was presented with unrebuttable evidence as to the actions of the defendants.

The defense did not try to deny the role of the defendants in the antiwar movement; rather, it tried to justify this role to the jury. The jury was allowed by the judge to take into consideration, in trying to determine whether or not the defendants had criminal intent, the defendant's belief as to the illegality of the Vietnam War and the defendants' right to resist unlawful, excessive police violence. An acquittal resulted.

Thus, the trial of a "political" case is not altogether hopeless. The Spock case was won on appeal. The "Oakland Seven" case was won at the trial level. But the government is not interested only, or perhaps even primarily, in winning cases and in putting dissidents behind bars. In fact, the appellate court in *Spock* would have allowed the government to re-try two of the defendants, but the government turned down the invitation and the indictments were dismissed. The point had been made—the government would follow, investigate, film, photograph, and prosecute selected enemies of the Republic who would serve as warnings and examples to others.

Furthermore, the government has weapons other than political trials, perhaps more potent weapons. The government can take steps to encourage lower echelon "law enforcement" officials and to signal an end to high level condemnation of uncivilized police tactics. The lower echelons are quick to take up the lead in restricting the exercise of civil liberties.

A recent example of the officially sanctioned encroachments on our liberties has been the growth of wiretapping. In 1967, the very same year the Supreme Court was appearing at its libertarian best, President Johnson took cognizance of a growing national uneasiness over the issue of privacy, electronic surveillance, and wiretapping, telling the nation:

> We should protect what Justice Brandeis called "the right most valued by civilized men"—the right to privacy. We should outlaw all wiretapping, public and private, wherever and whenever it occurs, except when the security of the nation itself is at stake—and only then with the strictest safeguards. We should exercise the full reach of our constitutional powers to outlaw electronic "bugging" and "snooping."[23]

The careful observer would have noted that the President's proclamation was not as sweepingly libertarian as it might have seemed at first glance. The ominous phrase "except when the security of the nation itself is at stake" springs out at the reader. Such language supplies the government and courts with the same opportunity to justify invasions of privacy as Chief Justice Holmes' famous dictum about not being allowed to yell "Fire!" in a crowded movie theatre has given the opponents of free speech to make serious incursions into the First Amendment. It is similar to the vague and broad "disturbing the peace" statutes which say very little as to the kind of conduct proscribed or the types of dangers to be guarded against.

Few men doubt the good faith of Justice Holmes when he sought to protect theatregoers, and perhaps it is too early in the historical record to judge the good faith of Lyndon Johnson in the privacy area. The fact is, however, that shortly after the 1967 State of the Union address, the Congress passed the most sweeping invasion-of-privacy legislation ever to be placed on the books. While prior law tended to circumscribe to a large extent the right of governmental agents or private citizens to utilize wiretapping devices, including both federal[24] and state[25] enactments, and while the courts seemed to be becoming ever more solicitous of the rights of the citizen,[26] in 1968 the whole privacy framework was dramatically torn asunder by the Omnibus Crime Control Act.[27] Wiretapping and eavesdropping by state, federal, and local law enforcement officers and agents were suddenly not only no longer forbidden, but these practices were actively encouraged under a procedure which offers little protection to the individual. Eavesdropping is permitted in cases involving the national security, but the Congress interpreted the area of national security so broadly that the act allows eavesdropping for such "national security" crimes as robbery, marihuana and narcotics traffic, and other assorted offenses posing a threat to "life, limb, and property." It would appear, then, that almost any crime will justify official snooping.

One can only guess how long it will take the "new" Supreme Court to come around to upholding the position of the President, Attorney General, and the Congress in this and other areas. The Omnibus Crime Control Act was apparently a success-ful attempt to short-circuit federal case law in the privacy area, law which had likened unauthorized invasions of privacy to war-rantless searches and seizures which violate the Fourth Amend-ment. Federal court case decisions[28] had predicated the right to privacy on the Constitution, but the Congress nevertheless vir-tually repealed that case law by passing a statute. One must assume that the Congress knows that no statute can supersede the Constitution, but until the Supreme Court would act, the statute was to provide a facade of legitimacy to governmental wiretapping. Of course, there was always the chance that the Court might abdicate its prior position and join the other high echelons of government aboard the repression bandwagon, thereby fully legitimating the statute in the process.

Under the Omnibus Crime Control Act, broad as it is, court orders are required for eavesdropping. However, in security cases eavesdropping can begin in advance of an order. Out of this narrowly carved exception, the Attorney General of the United States, John Mitchell, created a huge, yawning canyon in which no law or constitution was seen as a hindrance to governmental snooping. In 1969, Mitchell stated that the Federal Bureau of Investigation had eavesdropped into the affairs and lives of the "Chicago Eight" who were indicted for, among other things, conspiring to cross state lines with the intent to promote riot at the 1968 Democratic National Convention. Said the chief law enforcement official of the nation:

> While it may be appropriate for Congress to establish rules limiting the investigative techniques which the Executive may employ in enforcing the laws that Congress has en-acted, a serious question exists as to the power to restrict the President's power to gather information which he deems necessary to the proper exercise of powers which the Consti-tution confers on him alone. . . .

> The President . . . has the constitutional power to au-thorize electronic surveillance to gather intelligence informa-

tion concerning domestic organizations which seek to attack and subvert the Government by unlawful means.[29]

After all of the years of wiretapping and electronic surveillance by the FBI done in violation of state and federal statutes and court decisions, now at least the problem is out in the open. But faced with Attorney General Mitchell's bold admission of the practice, and his defense of its probity and legality, civil libertarians are hard pressed to devise an appropriate response. The government cannot now be embarrassed on account of its position and its actions, because the government has turned the sinner into a saint, the sin into a virtue. The government has legitimated its own activities by exercising its legislative prerogative.

As has already been pointed out, this legislation is as much symbolic as it is real. Thus, the inclusion in a recent Washington, D.C., crime control bill of the "no-knock" search rule does not really change the police practice very much. Attorneys and others involved in criminal cases report generally that police rarely knock on the door prior to entry onto a premises which is the subject of a search warrant. The no-knock law merely legitimizes a long-standing lower echelon law enforcement tactic. Similarly, few people are naive enough to believe that wiretapping begins with the Omnibus Crime Control Act. All that the act does is allow the fruits of this kind of surveillance to be used as evidence: it thus legitimates the prior practice. As criminal law expert Professor Yale Kamisar points out, this kind of legislation is a warning that the era of the Warren Supreme Court is over. "It's very symbolic," he states. "The political movement is now in favor of the no-nonsense, get-tough boys."[30]

These highly symbolic higher echelon steps have not been lost on the law enforcement officials below. At the current time all of the forces of legal repression, and illegal repression, are being turned against the Black Panther Party and its members. The Party's top leadership, including Eldridge Cleaver, Huey Newton, and Bobby Seale, are either fugitives from justice or are under indictment or sentence. But on a lower level, Panther leaders and members have been harassed and arrested under vague and

broad statutes while they have been passing out political literature. They have been attacked while gathered in the privacy of
their homes and headquarters. They have been shot by policemen
who have later charged that the Panthers opened fire on a small
army of policemen who came with peaceful, lawful intentions.
Panthers on the streets are subjected to continual illegal stops,
frisks, and searches. Many have been indicted and tried on seem-
ingly nonpolitical charges such as robbery and even murder, but
great doubts and questions have overhung the propriety of some
of the evidence in these cases. The Panthers apparently pose too
big a threat at times to give the state the luxury of "due processing them to death." Some Panthers have suffered more summary
dispositions at the hands of police.

If and when the Panther "threats" subsides, it is quite probable that the official wrath will focus even more intently upon
white radicals and students, whose revolutionary chants pose a
more generalized challenge and promise more thoroughgoing and
radical change to America than do the Panthers. The current
practice of beating student demonstrators into bloody submission
will probably give way to more permanent forms of punishment,
including long prison sentences meted out by the upper echelons
of the law enforcement establishment, and perhaps summary
executions performed by the lower echelons without substantial
interference from their superiors. Grave dangers face America,
and one fears that the current collision course may already have
too much momentum to be stopped. The lines are being drawn
ever more clearly, and many fair-minded citizens who abhor violence and persecution may be forced to choose sides in a battle
that they wish was not theirs.

If a man has broken a criminal law, that is one thing. If a dissident is charged with breaking a criminal law on the basis of
fabricated evidence, that is bad. But when that same dissident is
convicted because he has in fact broken a law which is so broad
as to encompass a whole range of activity—in which the right to
engage had, until then, been thought to belong to every American citizen—then legal repression has set in. Thus, the "Oakland
Seven" jury had to be reminded by the judge that much of the
evidence presented by the prosecution consisted of acts, such as

making public antiwar speeches, which are protected by the
First Amendment. The Spock jury was not so clearly informed,
which perhaps helped account for the verdict of guilty in that
case. The powers-that-be on the highest levels of the administrative and legislative branches have stepped into the act of repressing
the unpopular, the dissident, the nonconformists, the trou-
blemakers. They leave in their wake a record, a history, and a
plethora of legislation which it will be difficult to repeal even
after the passage of the nadir of the Dark Ages of the seventies.

But the forces of repression have gone well beyond mere indictments and legislation. Perhaps recognizing that zealous and
talented civil liberties and radical lawyers have managed to win
significant jury verdicts and overturn repressive legislation in the
appellate courts, these forces have begun an attack upon members of the bar who are "too zealous" in the defense of their
unpopular clients. The judge in the Spock trial treated defense
lawyers with a disdain which was not lost on the jury. Judge
Julius Hoffman in the trial of the "Chicago Seven" conspiracy
case treated defendants' attorneys without respect, refused to
allow the defense attorneys to speak uninterrupted, and then
sentenced them to jail terms of up to four years and thirteen
days. Perhaps the most outrageous and frightening recent case
was the decision by the Grievance Committee of the United
States District Court in Washington, D.C., finding Attorney
Philip J. Hirschkop guilty of professional misconduct and recommending that he be suspended or disbarred.

The Hirschkop case had a large segment of the liberal and
radical legal profession up in arms. In the first place, while the
behavior of the judge in the Spock trial did not go beyond un-
pleasantness for the attorneys personally, and while some feel
that the behavior of the attorneys in the "Chicago Seven" case,
while provoked by the judge, was nevertheless not justified, there
is little or no support among reasonable men for the action of
the Grievance Committee judges. Even the Ethics Committee
of the District of Columbia Bar Association voted 21–3 that
Hirschkop's court conduct in defense of the "D.C.9" did not
violate the canons of legal ethics. Hirschkop, one of the eminent
civil liberties attorneys in the country, a member of the National

Board of the American Civil Liberties Union, took on the defense in February, 1970, of a group of antiwar protestors. In the course of the trial, Hirschkop asked Judge John H. Pratt to disqualify himself from trying the case. "I will be brief, Judge," he said, out of the hearing of the jury, "because I firmly believe that I am just wasting my time. I think you have made up your mind before you have heard anything this morning. I am very discouraged about the proceedings this morning." The attorney protested that the judge was not allowing him sufficient latitude to defend his clients. "I am afraid of making this system rotten by not being able to do my job. . . ." He protested the judge's assumption, an assumption held by many judges and even attorneys, that an attorney should not put up a fight which makes life unpleasant in the courtroom. "I am not here to expedite [the case]. I will do it with all the dignity of a lawyer, and all the sanctions of a bar in mind, but I will not take part in greasing the wheels, not of justice, but of expeditiously packing these nine people off to jail as quickly as we can."

The American Civil Liberties Union termed the actions of the Grievance Committee "outrageous." "By recommending disbarment, the Grievance Committee is, in effect, serving notice on all attorneys who handle the defense of political dissidents—in the best spirit of the Bill of Rights—that their effectiveness in behalf of their clients is enough to bring them under attack," stated the ACLU. The *Washington Post* editorialized that "it is essential to the fair administration of justice that impecunious and unpopular defendants have able representation when they come to trial. The effect of the suspension or disbarment of Mr. Hirschkop would be to discourage such representation."[31] In addition to filing the complaint against Hirschkop, Judge Pratt sentenced him to thirty days in jail for contempt. And the Grievance Committee agreed with the trial judge that the attorney's statements were "prejudicial to the administration of justice." One wonders what kind of justice cannot bear an attorney attempting to dislodge a rigid judicial mind or expressing dismay at his failure to obtain a fair trial for his unpopular clients.

The campaign against attorneys who are either too successful or too vigorous has spread quickly and widely. Thus, even a non-political attorney such as famed criminal trial counsel F. Lee Bailey was censured by a Justice of the Massachusetts Supreme Judicial Court for using the news media to "generate a climate of opinion among the public" which would be "favorable to his clients and hostile to the prosecution."[32] And perhaps not so coincidentally the American Bar Association Special Committee on Evaluation of Disciplinary Enforcement chose this period of time to issue a new report entitled "Problems and Recommendations in Disciplinary Enforcement,"[33] which concentrates on creating more efficient machinery for processing complaints of misconduct lodged against attorneys.

This trend became crystal clear in the recent testimony of Nixon-appointed director of Selective Service, Curtis Tarr, at the hearings on the military draft held by the Special Subcommittee on the Draft of the House Armed Services Committee, which hearings were held in late summer and fall of 1970. "The spread of draft counseling is certainly one of the most alarming changes in America as it relates to the draft right now," reported Director Tarr to the Subcommittee. He attacked attorneys and draft counselors for aiding draft-age men "to avoid a legal obligation." "I am alarmed," said Tarr, "that in a nation like ours there is such a blatant open attempt to make it difficult for us to carry out the law." Tarr thus bands attorneys and draft counselors with a tinge of disloyalty, perhaps even a tinge of antidraft conspiracy, despite the testimony of a Justice Department official at those same hearings, who reported that the "procedural errors committed by local [draft] boards in classifying registrants are the greatest factor contributing to the high incidence of our prosecutive problems." Tarr thus castigated attorneys for trying to have the law enforced, rather than castigating draft boards for frequent and blatant violation of the rights of draft registrants. One wonders if the government will ever launch an attack on tax lawyers for helping their clients "avoid" taxes.

The prospects for an effective repression are enhanced, of course, by the contribution to efficiency that the computer has been making. With the FBI checking up on such activities of activists as their banking practices,[34] their reading habits,[35] their police and court records, and other personal details, and feeding such information into central data banks, one cannot hope for much longer to find or preserve privacy because of the proverbial inefficiency of governmental bureaucracy.[36] Technology will be no small aid to the repression of the 1970s.

As reported by Ben A. Franklin in the *New York Times* of December 27, 1970, the Justice Department's "civil disturbance group" has since its organization in 1969 collected 13,200 names in its computerized records of persons connected with riots or reported to have urged violence. The national computer file in the Transportation Department contains for police or governmental use the names and offense records of 2.6 million people who have had a driver's license suspended or revoked. The Civil Service Commission has more than 15 million names and index files and personnel dossiers, 10.2 million of them in a "security file" designed to provide "lead information relating to possible question of suitability involving loyalty and subversive activity." The hearings before Senator Sam J. Ervin Jr.'s Subcommittee on Constitutional Rights in the winter of 1971 revealed a shocking buildup of a domestic surveillance program of the Army. Thousands of citizens have been investigated, including leading political figures. As former military intelligence Captain Christopher H. Pyle testified at the Ervin hearings, "The United States today possesses the intelligence buildup of a police state." It turns out that the Army was able to beef up its spying system on the strength of evidence such as its February 1969 directive which warned of a "true insurgency, should external subversive forces develop successful control" of the racial and antiwar dissidents. As Tom Wicker noted in a March 2, 1971, column in the *New York Times,* "Now available are some almost unbelievable documents couched in Pentagon jargon, which show the kind of thinking that went into the surveillance program—if thinking is the word." Wicker goes on to point out that although government officials at first expressed a lack of knowledge about the whole area, "it is clear that Senator Ervin ought really to be looking into the highest levels of the Johnson Administration; for it was there that the Army got what authority

378   WITH JUSTICE FOR SOME

it had, and there that the Army's blundering, blunderbuss plans
got their approval." And now federal money is financing a
merger of all state and federally gathered information into a
single central data bank. It appears quite likely that within a
couple of years the government will have secret files and computerized memory banks on perhaps 30 or 40 million citizens.
One doubts that even then the government will possess sufficient
integrity and introspective powers to ask itself why it has to
doubt the loyalty of such a large number of its citizens. If government surveillance activities at least led to the asking of this
crucial question, then one would not be entirely dismayed at the
situation. But the king is going among his subjects incognito not
to gather their true opinions as to how the defects of the government might be remedied, but rather to learn whom to watch
and perhaps punish.

Many think that all of these problems will subside if and
when the war in Vietnam ends. This, however, appears unlikely,
since the American radical movement seems to have gone well
beyond the single issue of the war. Fundamental changes in
American society are being called for in perhaps the first indigenous American revolutionary movement since 1776. Our
society and governmental institutions appear to be reacting by
hardening their stance. Suddenly even small reforms aimed at
refining the American political and judicial systems and bringing
them closer to the democratic ideal, the classic "New Deal" and
"liberal" programs, are running into heated opposition. The Vice
President of the United States, Spiro T. Agnew, has coined the
phrase, "RadicLibs" for what he considers those "Radical Liberals" in and out of Congress and the Senate. The end of the war
might quiet the liberals, but it is not essentially at the liberals
that the machinery of legal repression is aimed.

Furthermore, if America's withdrawal from the Vietnam War
comes on terms seen as dishonorable, that very withdrawal may
provoke a reaction of its own, just as our less-than-victory conclusion of the Korean conflict immediately preceded the Mc-
Carthy era. When the richest and most powerful nation in the
world cannot subdue a relatively primitive country, the search
for a scapegoat might be expected to commence.

The longer our tensions last, the firmer will the machinery of legal repression become entrenched. The personnel of the Supreme Court may change entirely, and numerous oppressive statutes may fill the lawbooks. Analogies to the past, when liberty has emerged at least somewhat vigorous after periods of repression, may become inapposite, for we may soon experience a repression different not in degree but rather in kind. As Supreme Court Justice William O. Douglas has written, "A black silence of fear possesses the nation and is causing us to jettison some of our libertarian traditions."[37] Once jettisoned, some of them may never return. We may be in the process of creating new traditions.

Notes

Mark J. Green, *The Law of the Young*   Page 1

1. *In re* Gault, 387 U.S. 1 (1967).
2. M. Twain, *Dictionary of Humorous Quotations,* 203 (1949).
3. E. Waugh, *Decline and Fall* (1929).
4. *High School Student Unrest,* U.S.A. Special Report, published by National School Public Relations Association, Washington, D.C.
5. Divoky, *Revolt in the High Schools: The Way It's Going to Be,* SATURDAY REVIEW, Feb. 15, 1969, at 83.
6. 393 U.S. 503 (1969).
7. 286 F. Supp. 988 (N.D. Ill. 1968), *aff'd* 2–1, Kiley, J. dissenting, 415 F. 2d 860 (7th Cir. 1969).
8. 38 U.S.L.W. 2542 (Apr. 10, 1970).
9. Vought v. Van Buren Public Schools, 38 U.S.L.W. 2034 (E.D. Mich. June, 1969).
10. Zucker v. Poritz, 299 F. Supp. 102 (S.D.N.Y. 1969).
11. Eisner v. Stamford, 39 U.S.L.W. 2536 (July 2, 1970).
12. *See* 83 HARV. L. REV. 159 (1969).
13. Jones v. Day, 127 Miss. 136, 89 So. 906 (1921).
14. 158 Ark. 247, 250 S.W. 538 (1923).
15. Los Angeles Times, May 13, 1966, part 2, at 2, col. 7.
16. 269 F. Supp. 524, 528 (1967).
17. 261 F. Supp. 545 (N.D. Texas 1968).
18. Brownlee v. Bradley City Board, 38 U.S.L.W. 2568 (Apr. 10, 1970).
19. NEWSWEEK, Sept. 29, 1969, at 77.
20. Boston Globe, Sept. 21, 1969, at 6, col. 1.
21. CIVIL LIBERTIES, Feb. 1970, at 1.
22. New York Times, June 2, 1970, at 29, col. 2.
23. 381 U.S. 479 (1965).
24. People v. Overton, 20 N.Y. 2d 360, 229 N.E. 596 (1967).
25. 47–Kans.–, 456 P. 2d 1 (1969).
26. New York Times, Mar. 16, 1970, at 16, col. 1.
27. Buckley, NATIONAL REVIEW, July 10, 1969, at 33.

28. Ginsberg v. United States, 390 U.S. 629, 654 (1967) (Douglas, J. dissenting).

29. Pilpel, *Sex vs. the Law*, HARPER'S, Jan., 1965, at 35.

30. 394 U.S. 557 (1969).

31. TIME, Aug. 8, 1969, at 87.

32. New York Times, Aug. 30, 1970, Section IV, at 8, col. 2.

33. *Supra* note 31.

34. New York Times, Aug. 12, 1970, at 28, col. 4.

35. Yolles, "Pot Is Painted Too Black," Washington Post, Sept. 21, 1969, at 64, col. 5.

36. *Supra* note 32.

37. ATLANTIC, Oct., 1968, at 55.

38. NEWSWEEK, Sept. 7, 1970, at 22.

39. 390 U.S. 629 (1968).

40. 352 U.S. 380 (1957), *reviving* the *Hicklin* test of 1868, which measured a work's obscenity by the possible effect of isolated passages on those particularly susceptible.

41. 354 U.S. 476 (1957).

42. New York Times, Nov. 2, 1969, Sect. D, at 27, col. 5.

43. E. Glueck, S. Glueck, *Delinquents in the Making* (1952).

44. US NEWS AND WORLD REPORT, Mar. 11, 1968, at 11.

45. New York Times, Sept. 24, 1961, at 57, col. 3.

46. NATION, Jan. 30, 1924, at 106.

47. Hildebrand, *Why Runaways Leave Home*, 54 J. CRIM. L. 211, P.S. 216 (1963).

48. Bernstein, "D.C. Becoming Haven for Teenage Runaways," Washington Post, Jan. 25, 1969, at A16, col. 5.

49. Whitbread, *Runaways: the tragic story of why 500,000 kids leave home every year*, LOOK, July 25, 1967.

50. L. Beggs, *Huckleberry's for Runaways*, 37 (1969).

51. *Supra* note 48.

52. 378 U.S. 500 (1964).

53. *Quoted in*, Note, *The Tennessee Impact of the Gault Decision*, 35 TENN. L. REV. 632 (1968).

54. Forer, *Rights of Children: The Legal Vacuum*, 55 A.B.A. J. 1151 (1969).

55. Mack, *The Juvenile Court*, 23 HARV. L. REV. 104, 120 (1909).

56. Douglas, *Juvenile Courts and Due Process of Law*, 19 JUV. CT. JUDGES J. 1, 9 (1968).

57. Washington Post, Dec. 29, 1966.

58. *Quoted in* Dorsen and Rezneck, *In Re Gault and the Future of Juvenile Law*, 1 FAM. L.Q. 1, 4 (1967).

59. *In re Gault*, 387 U.S. 1, 28 (1967).

60. *Supra* note 58.

61. Kent v. United States, 383 U.S. 541 (1966).

62. *Supra* note 59.

382

382 WITH JUSTICE FOR SOME

63. *Quoted in* Bazelon, *Racism, Classism and the Juvenile Process,* 53 JUDICATURE 373 (1970).

64. New York Times, Nov. 2, 1969, Sect. VI, at 38.

65. New York Times, July 7, 1968, at 6.

Bruce Wasserstein, *The Courts and the Campus*   Page 38

1. Anthony v. Syracuse Univ., 224 App. Div. 487, 231 N.Y.S. 435, at 437 (1928).

2. Seavey, *Dismissal of Students: "Due Process,"* 70 HARV. L. REV. 1406, at 1407 (1957).

3. Dixon v. Alabama State Bd. of Educ., 294 F. 2d 150 (5th Cir. 1961).

4. *See Developments in the Law—Academic Freedom,* 81 HARV. L. REV. 1045 at 1056–1064 (1968).

5. Note, *Private Government on the Campus—Judicial Review of University Expulsions,* 72 YALE L.J. 1362 at 1409–1410 (1963).

6. Grossner v. Columbia Univ., 287 F. Supp. 535 at 546 (S.D.N.Y. 1968).

7. Green v. Howard Univ., 271 F. Supp. 609 at 612 (D.C. Cir. 1967).

8. Brown University, *Notes on College Charters* (1910).

9. *See generally Campus Confrontation: Resolution by Legislation,* 6 COLUM. J. L. & SOC. PROB. 30 (1970).

10. New York Times, Dec. 30, 1969, at 1.

11. Powe v. Milles, 407 F. 2d 73 (2d Cir. 1968).

12. Guillory v. Tulane Univ., 203 F. Supp. 855 at 858–859 (E.D. La. 1962).

13. Green v. Howard Univ., 271 F. Supp. 609 at 615 (D.C. Cir. 1967).

14. Carr v. St. John's Univ. 17 App. Div. 2d 632, 231 N.Y.S. 2d 410 at 414 (1962).

15. Sturm v. Boston Univ., 89433 Eq. Suffolk Sup. Ct. (Mass. 1969).

16. Coleman v. Wagner College No. 34869 (2d Cir. June 22, 1970).

17. Dixon v. Alabama State Bd. of Educ., 294 F. 2d 150 at 159 (5th Cir. 1961).

18. *In re* Gault, 387 U.S. 1 (1967).

19. 45 F.R.D. 133 at 138, 142 (W.D. Mo. 1968).

20. Esteban v. Central Mo. State College, 290 F. Supp. 622 at 630 (W.D. Mo. 1968).

21. Buttny v. Smiley, 281 F. Supp. 280 (D. Colo. 1968).

22. 1969 Cal. Sess. Laws, ch. 1427 Section 5 *adding* Sections 31291–31294 to CAL. EDUC. CODE (West Cal. Leg. Ser. at 2783, 1969).

23. Study by Urban Research Corporation of Chicago, *reported in* New York Times, Jan. 14, 1970, at 13, *advertised* at 51.

24. Goldberg v. Regents of Univ. of Cal., 248 Cal. App. 2d 867, 57 Cal. Rptr. 463 at 466 n. 4 (1967).

25. Dickey v. Alabama State Bd. of Educ., 273 F. Supp. 613 (M.D. Ala. 1967).

26. *Developments supra* note 4, at 1130.

27. Norton v. Discipline Comm. of East Tenn. St. Univ., 419 F. 2d 195 at 198 (6th Cir. 1969).

28. Siegel v. Regents of Univ. of Cal., 308 F. Supp. 832 at 834 (N.D. Cal. 1970).

29. Adderley v. Florida, 385 U.S. 39 (1966).

30. O'Leary v. Commonwealth, 441 S.W. 2d 150 at 157 (1969).

31. Esteban v. Central Mo. State College, 290 F. Supp. 622 at 626 n. 4 (W.D. Mo. 1968).

32. New York Times, Feb. 1, 1970.

33. Herman, *Injunctive Control of Disruptive Student Demonstrations,* 56 Va. L. Rev. 215, at 227 (1970).

34. Walker v. Birmingham, 388 U.S. 307 (1967); Shuttlesworth v. Birmingham, 22 L. Ed. 162 at 171 (1969).

35. F. Frankfurter & N. Greene, *The Labor Injunction,* 132–133 (1930).

36. Barker v. Hardway, 89 S. Ct. 1009, at 1009 (1969).

37. Tinker v. Des Moines Independent Community School Dist., 393 U.S. 503 (1969).

38. Grossner v. Columbia Univ., 287 F. Supp. 535 at 539 (S.D.N.Y. 1968).

39. Schwartz, *Comment,* 45 Denver L.J. 525, at 532 (1968).

40. New York Times, Sept. 20, 1970, Sec. 1 at 8.

41. New York Times, June 18, 1970, at 38.

42. *California: The Besieged,* Time, June 22, 1970, at 16.

43. *New York: Tommy the Traveler,* Time, June 22, 1970, at 16.

44. New York Times, Sept. 27, 1970, at 66.

Edward F. Sherman, *The Civilianization of Military Law*   Page 65

1. Dept. of Army, Office of the Adjutant General, AGAM-P (M) (May 27, 1969) DSCPER-SARD, Subject: Guidance on Dissent. *See also* DOD Directive No. 1325.6, Sept. 12, 1969.

2. Howe v. Clifford, No. 622–68 (D.D.C. 1968); Levy v. Parker, (D.M. Pa. 1969), *pet. for release on bail granted,* 90 S. Ct. 1 (1969); Daniels v. Laird, et al., Civil No. HC 140–70 (D.D.C. 1970); Stolte & Amick v. Laird, Civil Action No. 22,224 (D.D.C. 1970).

3. *Report of the Special Civilian Committee for the Study of the United States Army Confinement System,* Department of the Army (1970).

4. Message of the Commandant of the Marine Corps, New York Times, Sept. 4, 1969, at 1, c. 4.

5. S. 3117, 91st Cong., 1st Sess. (1969); S. 4168–78, 91st Cong., 2d Sess. (1970); S. 4191, 91st Cong., 2d Sess. (1970).

384 WITH JUSTICE FOR SOME

6. 1 *Journals of the Continental Congress* 1774–1789, at 90 (Lib. of Cong. ed. 1904–1937).

7. 346 U.S. 137, 139–140 (1953).

8. Quoted in *Hearings on H.R. 2498 Before a Spec. Subcomm. of the House Comm. on Armed Services*, 81st Cong., 1st Sess. 780 (1949).

9. Ansell, *Military Justice*, 5 Cornell L.Q. 1 (1919).

10. S. 64, 66th Cong., 1st Sess. (1919).

11. 24 *Md. State Bar Ass'n Transactions* 183, 188 (1919).

12. R. Everett, *Military Justice in the Armed Forces of the United States* 9 (1956).

13. Farmer & Wels, *Command Control—or Military Justice?*, 24 N.Y.U. L.Q. 263, 265 (1949) (citing the War Dep't Advisory Bd. on Clemency Report [1946]).

14. White, *The Background and the Problem*, 35 St. John's L. Rev. 197, 201 (1961).

15. S. DOC. NO. 196, 79th Cong., 2d Sess. 18 (1946).

16. *Report of War Dep't Advisory Comm. on Military Justice to the Secretary of War* 3 (1946).

17. Act of June 24, 1948, tit. II, 62 Stat. 604.

18. Letter from James E. Folsom to Edmund M. Morgan, Nov. 5, 1948, VI Morgan Papers (Harvard Law School Library).

19. Letter from Ernest W. Gibson to Edmund M. Morgan, Nov. 18, 1948, VI Morgan Papers.

20. Quoted in Statement of John Kenney, Under Secretary of the Navy, *Hearings on H.R. 2498 Before Subcomm. No. 1 of the House Comm. on Armed Services*, 81st Cong., 1st Sess. 780 (1949) in VI Morgan Papers.

21. Farmer & Wels, *supra* note 13, at 273.

22. Act of May 5, 1950, ch. 169, 64 Stat. 107, 10 U.S.C. §§ 801 et seq. (Supp. IV, 1968).

23. 1 U.S.C.M.A. 74, 1 C.M.R. 74 (1951).

24. 346 U.S. 137 (1953).

25. 11 U.S.C.M.A. 428, 430–31, 29 C.M.R. 244, 246–47 (1960).

26. H.R. 3455, 86th Cong., 1st Sess. (1959).

27. Mott, *An Appraisal of Proposed Changes in the Uniform Code of Military Justice*, 35 St. John's L. Rev. 300, 302 (1961).

28. *Comm. on the UCMJ, Good Order and Discipline in the Army* (1960) (Report to W. M. Brucker, Secretary of the Army).

29. Report of the Special Committee on Military Justice of the Assoc. of the Bar of the City of New York, Mar. 1, 1961.

30. Pub. L. No. 90-632 (Oct. 24, 1968).

31. 10 U.S.C. § 827 (c) (Supp. IV, 1968) (art. 27 [c] of the UCMJ).

32. New York Times, Oct. 25, 1968, at 4, col. 1; 115 CONG. REC. 12, 630 (daily ed. Oct. 15, 1968).

33. Weiner, *Are the General Military Articles Unconstitutionally Vague?*, 54 A.B.A.J. 357, 363 (1968).

34. United States v. Howe, 17 U.S.C.M.A. 165, 37 C.M.R. 429 (1967).

35. Priest v. Koch, 19 U.S.C.M.A. 293, 41 C.M.R. 293 (1970); Lowe v. Laird, *et al.*, 18 U.S.C.M.A. 131, 39 C.M.R. 131 (1969).

36. United States v. DuBay, 17 U.S.C.M.A. 147, 149, 37 C.M.R. 411, 413 (1967).

37. *See* F. Gardner, *The Unlawful Concert: An Account of the Presidio Mutiny Case* 143 (1970).

38. L. West, "The Command Domination of the Military Judicial Process," Aug. 10, 1969 (unpublished thesis in George Washington University Law School, Washington, D.C.), published in part as West, *A History of Command Influence on the Military Judicial System*, 18 U.C.L.A.L. Rev. 1 (1970).

39. United States v. Kinder, ACM 7321, 14 C.M.R. 742, 776 (1953) (quoting from the "Einsatzgruppen Case").

40. 395 U.S. 258 (1969).

Jean Murphy and Susan Deller Ross, *Liberating Women—Legally Speaking*
Page 104

1. B. Friedan, *The Feminine Mystique* (1963).

2. Women's Bureau, U.S. Department of Labor, Bull. No. 294, *Handbook on Women Workers*, Table 42, at 97 (1969).

3. *Id.* 133–134.

4. *Id.* Table 61, at 137.

5. *Id.* Chart S, at 180.

6. Blackstone, *Commentaries* 433.

7. Kanowitz, *Women and the Law: The Unfinished Revolution* (1969), gives a comprehensive summary of sexual distinctions in the law.

8. Lockner v. New York, 198 U.S. 45 (1905).

9. Cromer, "Sex Discrimination in Private Employment: The Conflict Between the Civil Rights Act of 1964 and State Labor Laws for Women," unpublished Master's Essay, University of Pennsylvania, 1967, at 13.

10. 110 Cong. Rec. 2580 (1964).

11. Men are given chairs in one of these states. U.S. Department of Labor, Women's Bureau, *Summary of State Labor Laws for Women* (1969), at 18. All the statistics used in this section, giving the number of states which have each type of law, are taken from this pamphlet. It gives information about all state labor laws applying to women and lists the specific states which have enacted each law.

12. Of the ten states which have minimum wage rates for women only, three have no rates in effect. Both men and women receive a day of rest in twenty-seven states, while in another thirteen states only women are covered.

13. Lunch breaks are required in twenty-three states of which three also cover men. Rest periods are given to women only in twelve states; no state gives men rest periods.

14. Richards v. Griffith Rubber Mills, 300 F. Supp. 338 (D. Ore. 1969).

386 WITH JUSTICE FOR SOME

15. *Summary of State Labor Laws for Women, supra* note 11, at 18: cross-ing watchman, section hand, express driver, metal molder, bellhop, gas or electric meter reader; in shoeshining parlors, bowling alleys as pinsetters, poolrooms; in delivery service on motor-propelled vehicles of over one-ton capacity; in operating freight or baggage elevators if the doors are not auto-matically or semiautomatically controlled; in baggage and freight handling; trucking and handling by means of handtrucks, heavy materials of any kind; in blast furnaces and smelters.

16. Remarks of Congresswoman Green, *quoted in* Phillips v. Martin-Marietta Corp., 416 F. 2d 1257 (5th Cir. 1969), at 13.

17. Quoted in C. Bird, *Born Female: The High Cost of Keeping Women Down* (1969), at 6–7.

18. 29 U.S.C. 206 (d) (1963).

19. Vladeck, *The Equal Pay Act of 1963*, 18 N.Y.U. Lab. Conf. 381, (1965) contains a summary of federal and state equal pay action prior to the 1963 act.

20. Moran, *Reducing Discrimination: Role of the Equal Pay Act*, Monthly Labor Review, June, 1970.

21. 284 F. Supp. 23 (D.N.J. 1968); 421 F. 2d 259 (3rd Cir. 1970); *cert. denied.*

22. Schultz v. First Victoria National Bank, 58 LC 32,074 (D.C. Tex. 1968), 420 F. 2d 648 (5th Cir. 1969); Wirtz v. Citizens' National Bank 58 LC 32,050 (D.C. Tex. 1968); Schultz v. First National Bank in Orange, 61 LC 32,269 (E.D. Tex. 1969).

23. Wirtz v. Oregon State Motor Assn., 57 LC 32,010 (D. Ore. 1968).

24. Goldberg, *Are Women Prejudiced Against Women*, Transaction, Vol. 5, April, 1968, at 28–30; Bem and Bem, *Training the Woman to Know Her Place: Power of a Non-Conscious Ideology*, Women: A Journal of Liberation, Vol. 1, Fall, 1969, at 9.

25. Langer, Working for the Telephone Company, The New York Review of Books, Vol. XIV, No. 6, March 19, 1970.

26. 42 U.S.C. § 2000e *et seq.* (1964).

27. 110 Cong. Rec. 2577 (1964).

28. C. Bird, *supra* note 17, at 12–14 documents the joke approach at length.

29. *De-Sexing the Job Market*, New York Times, Aug. 21, 1965.

30. The New Republic, Sept. 4, 1965, at 10.

31. 29 C.F.R. § 1604.1 (1965). New policies were announced in press re-leases of August 19, 1966, and February 24, 1968. Finally, 29 C.F.R. S1604.1 (a) (3), (b) and (c) were revoked on August 19, 1969, and a new subsection (b) promulgated in its place.

32. 29 C.F.R. § 1604.1 (b) (2) (1969).

33. Mengelkoch v. Industrial Welfare Comm'n., 284 F. Supp. 950, 956 (C.D. Cal. 1968), *appeal dismissed* 393 U.S. 83; Ward v. Lutrell, 292 F. Supp. 162, 165 (E.D. La. 1968); Coon v. Tingle, 277 F. Supp. 304 (N.D. Ga. 1967).

34. Rosenfeld v. Southern Pacific Co., 293 F. Supp. 1219 (C.D. Cal. 1968), *appeals pending* Nos. 23,983 and 23,984 (9th Cir.); Weeks v. Southern Bell Telephone Co., 408 F. 2d 228 (5th Cir. 1969); Bowe v. Colgate-Palmolive Co., 416 F. 2d 711 (7th Cir. 1969).

35. *See* Richards v. Griffith Rubber Mills, *supra* note 14 (voiding Oregon weight law under Title VII); Longacre v. Wyoming, 448 P. 2d 832 (1968) (voiding state law prohibiting the employment of female bartenders under a state fair employment practices act); McCrimmon v. Daley, 61 CCH Lab. Cas. 9352 (7th Cir. 1969) (reversing dismissal of challenge to Chicago bar maid statute), 2 FEP Cases 971 (N.D. Ill. 1970) (on remand, voiding same statute under both Title VII and the Fourteenth Amendment); Cheatwood v. South Central Telephone, 303 F. Supp. 754 (M.D. Ala. 1969) (invalidating company weight policy under Title VII). Caterpillar Tractor Co. v. Grabiec, 2 FEP Cases 945 (S.D. Ohio 1970) (voiding Illinois hours law under Title VII).

36. Cooper v. Delta Airlines, 274 F. Supp. 781 (E.D. La. 1967).

37. Diaz v. Pan American World Airways, 2 FEP Cases 525 (S.D. Fla. 1970).

38. Phillips v. Martin-Marietta Corp., 411 F. 2d 1 (5th Cir. 1969), *rehearing denied*, 416 F. 2d 1257, *rev'd* 3 FEP cases 40 (Jan. 25, 1971).

39. 416 F. 2d 1257.

40. The Court has never ruled that sex is an invalid basis for classification under the Fourteenth Amendment, no matter how gross the discrimination involved. *See*, e.g., Hoyt v. Florida, 368 U.S. 57 (1961); Muller v. Oregon, 208 U.S. 412 (1908); Bradwell v. State, 16 Wall. 130 (1872) (under the privileges and immunities clause). The quotes are from the oral argument at 50–51 available in the Supreme Court Library.

41. 347 U.S. 483 (1954).

42. Allred v. Heaton, 336 S.W. 2d 251 (Tex. 1960), *appeal dismissed*, 364 U.S. 517 (1960); Heaton v. Bristol, 317 S.W. 2d 86 (Tex. 1958), *appeal dismissed*, 359 U.S. 230 (1959).

43. de Rivera v. Fliedner, Civil No. 00938-69 (N.Y. Sup. Ct. 1969).

44. Seidenberg, *The Submissive Majority: Modern Trends in the Law Concerning Women's Rights*, 55 CORNELL L. REV. 262, 270 (1970), discusses, but does not cite, one such case, dismissed on technical grounds.

45. Kirstein v. Rector and Visitors of Univ. of Virginia, Civil No. 220-69R (E.D. Va., Sept. 8, 1969).

46. Mollere v. Southeastern Louisiana College, 304 F. Supp. 826 (E.D. La. 1969).

47. U.S. Dep't of Health, Education and Welfare, Children's Bureau, *Child Care Arrangements for the Nation's Working Mothers* 1 (1969).

48. F. Ruderman, *Child Care and the Working Mother* 10 (1968).

49. U.S. Dep't of Health, Education and Welfare, Children's Bureau, *What Is Good Day Care?* (1965).

50. Mead, *Some Theoretical Considerations on the Problem of Mother-Child Separation*, AMER. J. ORTHOPSYCHIATRY, Vol. 24, 477 (1954).

51. New York City Health Code, § 47.07 (1959).

52. 26 U.S.C. § 214 (b) (1964).

53. Leavy & Kummer, *Criminal Abortion: A Failure of Law*, 50 A.B.A.J. 52 (1964).

54. Members of a class on Women and the Law at New York University Law School interviewed various members of the legal profession in September, 1969, about prostitution and whether men were, or should be, prosecuted equally. One judge made the quoted remark in response to the questioning.

55. Robinson v. York, 281 F. Supp. 8 (D. Conn. 1968); Commonwealth v. Daniel, 430 Pa. 642, 243 A. 2d 400 (1968).

56. Maine Statutes 34, Sec. 854 (1969); N.Y. Corrections Law, Sec. 3-a and b; N.Y. Penal Law, Sec. 240.35.

57. New York State Family Act, § 712 (b) (1962).

58. L. Kanowitz, *supra* note 7, at 28–31.

59. Hoyt v. Florida, 368 U.S. 57 (1961). *See* Strauder v. West Virginia, 100 U.S. 303 (1880), reversing a black man's conviction for murder by an all-white jury.

Ronald Brown, *White Debt and Black Control: of Missionaries and Panthers*
Page 133

1. J. H. Franklin, *From Slavery to Freedom* 291 (1952).

2. T. B. Wilson, *The Black Codes of the South* 38 (1965).

3. A. Meir and E. Rudwick, *From Plantation to Ghetto* 54 (1968).

4. *See* Franklin, *supra* note 1, at 218.

5. *See* Wilson, *supra* note 2, at 38.

6. *Id.*

7. FREEDOMWAYS 12 (Spring, 1961).

8. 19 How. 393 (1857).

9. *See* Wilson, *supra* note 2, at 64.

10. *Id.*, at 58.

11. 167 U.S. 537 (1896).

12. 347 U.S. 483 (1954).

13. COMMONWEAL, June 13, 1969, at 360.

14. THE BUSINESS LAWYER, Sept. 1969, at 101.

15. LABOR LAW JOURNAL 372, June, 1969.

16. *See* J. Griffin, *Black Like Me* (1960), and G. Halsell, *Soul Sister* (1969).

17. 395 F. 2d 290 (1968).

18. CIV. RIGHTS DIG., Summer, 1969, at 30.

19. New York Times, Oct. 29, 1969, at 27, cols. 1–3.

20. New York Times, Sept. 23, 1969, at 56, col. 3.

21. *Id.*

22. *Id.*

23. EBONY, Dec. 1969, at 33.

24. *Id.*

25. New York Times Magazine, Sept. 14, 1969, at 130.

26. *Id.*

27. EBONY, Oct. 1969, at 176.

28. H. Cruse, *The Crisis of the Negro Intellectual* 93 (1967).

29. *Id.*, at 564.

30. CURRENT, Sept. 1969, at 51.

31. K. Clark, *Dark Ghetto* 11 (1965).

32. T. L. Cross, *Black Capitalism: Strategy for Business in the Ghetto* 203 (1968).

33. *Id.*, at 100.

34. *Id.*, at 17.

35. *Id.*, at 100.

36. *Id.*, at 32.

37. *Id.*, at 109.

38. *See* Cruse, *supra* note 28, at 93.

39. *Id.*

40. New York Times, Oct. 22, 1969, at 20, cols. 2–4.

41. 379 U.S. 184 (1964).

42. 366 F. 2d 1 (1906).

43. 6 How. L.J. 30 (1960), at 30 and 54.

44. CIV. RIGHTS DIG., Summer, 1969, at 32.

45. Note, *Equal Protection*, 82 HARV. L. REV. 1106 (1968).

46. Hughes, *Reparations for Blacks?*, 43 N.Y.U.L. REV. 1063, 1071–1072 (1968).

47. *Id.*

48. Act of Aug. 13, 1946, Chpt. 959 G 1, 60 Stat. 1049.

49. *See* Hughes, *supra* note 46, at 1063.

50. *Id.*, at 1072.

51. *Id.*

Fred J. Hiestand, *The Politics of Poverty Law*   Page 160

1. The client is real, one of many represented in the class action of Larez v. Oberti Olive Co., Cal. Superior Ct., Madera County, No. 16637 (1969), described more fully at *infra* 9–11. Alviso is a pseudonym.

2. Mills, "The Big City: Private Troubles and Public Issues," in *Power, Politics and People* 396 (Horowitz paperback ed. 1963).

3. Cal. Assembly Comm. on Agriculture, *The California Farm Labor Force: A Profile* 22 (1969).

4. Rep. of Cal. Leg. Analyst, *Budget Analysis for the State of California* 1970–71, A-35 (1970).

5. Cal. State Senate Fact Finding Comm. on Labor and Welfare, *California Farm Labor Problems* pt. I at 57 (1961).

6. Rivera v. Division of Industrial Welfare, 265 Cal. App. 2d 576, 71 Cal. Rptr. 739 (1968).

7. *But see* Romero v. Wirtz, CCH Pov. L. Rptr. 9133, a pending three judge federal district court suit filed by CRLA in 1968 challenging on constitutional grounds the exclusion of farmworkers from unemployment insurance coverage.

8. *The California Farm Labor Force: A Profile, supra,* at 99.

9. McWilliams, *California: The Great Exception* 157 (1949).

10. Alaniz v. Wirtz, CCH Pov. L. Rptr. 300.15; No. 47807 (N.D. Cal. filed Sept. 8, 1967).

11. 433 F. 2d 74 (9th Cir. 1970).

12. Bustos v. Mitchell, Civ. No. 3386-69 (D.D.C. 1970).

13. The statistical information cited herein about *alambristas* is taken from Diaz v. Kay Dix Ranch, 9 C.A. 3d 588 (1970).

14. *Diaz, supra* at 599.

15. *Quoted in* Baran, *The Political Economy of Growth* 249 (1957).

16. Gnaizda & Yeamans, "Is It 'More Blessed to Give than to Receive'?," a study of federally subsidized grower attitudes toward federal assistance to the poor, California Rural Legal Assistance, Inc., 1968.

17. Rodriguez v. Madera Unified School District, Cal. Superior Ct., Madera County, No. 15641 (1967). Judgment for defendants. No appeal taken.

18. Vega v. Madera County Welfare Dept., Cal. Superior Ct., Madera County, No. 15641 (1967). Judgment for defendants. Appeal pending, 5 Civ. 1144 (5th Dist. Cal. Ct. of Appeals).

19. This decision was ultimately affirmed in another case with a somewhat different emphasis by the United States Supreme Court, Wheeler v. Montgomery, 90 S. Ct. 1026 (1970).

20. Fuentes v. Mabey, No. F. 342 Civ. (E.D. Cal., filed Aug. 29, 1969).

21. CONG. REC., S. 12564 (Oct. 14, 1969).

22. 67 Cal. 2d 733, 63 Cal. Rptr. 689, 433 P. 2d 697 (1967).

23. CONG. REC., S. 12564 (Oct. 14, 1969), debate over S.B. 3016.

24. *See,* e.g., The Washington Post, Sept. 29, 1970, pat. H4.

25. Holmes, "The Poverty Lawyers' Work Is So Good It Has to Be Stopped," WASHINGTON MONTHLY (June, 1970).

26. J. Skelley Wright of the D.C. Circuit Court capsulized well the responsibility of the judiciary in Hobson v. Hansen, 369 F. Supp. 401, 508 (D.D.C. 1967) in stating that when a "politically voiceless and invisible minority" is involved in litigation, "these considerations impel a closer judicial surveillance and review of administrative judgments adversely affecting racial minorities and the poor, than would otherwise be necessary."

27. Silver, "The Imminent Failure of Legal Services for the Poor: Why and How to Limit Caseload," 46 J. OF URBAN LAW 217 (1968).

28. Carlin & Howard, "Legal Representation and Class Justice," 12 U.C.L.A.L. REV. 381 (1965).

29. For an early and perceptive treatment of how to balance community desires with the most effective legal service program see Lorenz, "The Application of Cost-Utility Analysis to the Practice of Law: A Special Case Study of the California Farmworkers," 15 KAN. L. REV. 409 (1967).

30. Most legal service programs are subject to funding control by local community action agencies because their clients fall within limited geographic communities that have OEO funded local Community Action Programs. CRLA, however, was established to represent the rural poor throughout the entire state of California, including many areas without community action agencies. CRLA's clientele, of course, needs a statewide firm, as many clients are migrant farmworkers who follow the crops up and down the state. Therefore, CRLA was not subjected to funding control by a community action agency as none exists to serve the community of California.

31. San Jose Mercury (San Jose, California), July 28, 1969.

32. Hernandez v. Hardin, No. 50333 (N.D. Cal. 1968). A dismissal without prejudice was entered on September 2, 1969 after the defendants entered into a stipulation to institute food programs in sixteen California counties.

33. Larez v. Shannon, 2 Cal. 3d 813, 87 Cal. Rptr. 871, 471 P. 2d 515 (1970).

34. Damico v. California, No. 46538 (N.D. Cal. 1969). The *Damico* opinion declined to decide whether the "divorce or deprivation" law conflicted with the equal protection of the laws, preferring to find it in violation of the Social Security Act.

35. Minsky, "Adequate Aggregate Demand and the Commitment to End Poverty," in *Rural Poverty in the United States* 579 (1968).

John Cratsley, *The Crime of the Courts*   Page 190

1. *See* President's Commission on Law Enforcement and the Administration of Justice, *Task Force Report: The Courts* (1967); *Report of the National Advisory Commission on Civil Disorders*, Chapter 13 (1968).

2. Leonard Downie, "Crime in the Courts: Assembly Line Justice," THE WASHINGTON MONTHLY, May, 1970, pp. 26–39.

Craig Karpel, "Defending the Poor: Lawyer as Hangman," The Village Voice, June 12, 1969, pp. 28–32, 51.

Jeremy Main, "Only Radical Reform Can Save the Courts," FORTUNE, Aug., 1970, pp. 110–114, 152–154.

3. Stephen R. Bing and S. Stephen Rosenfeld, *The Quality of Justice in the Lower Criminal Courts of Metropolitan Boston*, A Report by the Lawyers' Committee for Civil Rights Under Law to the Governor's Committee on Law Enforcement and the Administration of Justice, Boston (1970).

4. *Ibid.*, at pages 126–127.

5. The Boston Globe, Nov. 11, 1969.

6. *See* Rule 3:17 of the Supreme Judicial Court of Massachusetts es-

tablishing a Committee on Complaints, "including those concerning the conduct of any judge. . . ."
  7. The Boston Globe, Feb. 22, 1970.

David P. Riley, *Taming GM . . . and Ford, Union Carbide, U.S. Steel, Dow Chemical . . .* Page 207

  1. *See* the Council on Economic Priorities, *In-Depth Study, The Manufacture of Anti-Personnel Weapons* (1970), 2, 7, and section on the Honeywell Corporation.
  2. Washington Post, Apr. 11, 1970.
  3. New York Times, Apr. 29, 1970, at 61, col. 4.
  4. The figure on the number of corporations comes from "Congressional Consumer Investigations: What Do They Tell Us?" Remarks of Senator Philip A. Hart (D-Mich.) to New York Consumer Assembly, Mar. 7, 1970, 5. For figures on economic concentration, *see Hearings on Role of Giant Corporations Before the Subcommittee on Monopoly of the Senate Select Committee on Small Business,* 91st Congress, 1st Sess. 2 (1969).
  5. Berle, "Economic Power and The Free Society," in Hacker, ed., *The Corporation Take-Over* 98 (1965).
  6. *Hearings on Role of Giant Corporations,* 534. This was the subject of a classic debate between Adolph Berle and the late Prof. E. Merrick Dodd in the 1930s; see Berle, *The 20th Century Capitalist Revolution* (1954).
  7. For Bazelon quote, *see* Bazelon, *The Paper Economy* 10 (1963); *see also* Chayes, "The Modern Corporation and the Rule of Law," in Mason, ed., *The Corporation in Modern Society* 27 (1966). For GM comparison with foreign governments, *see* Nader, Statement announcing the Campaign to Make General Motors Responsible, Feb. 7, 1970, 4. For GM, Standard Oil, and Ford figures, *see* Galbraith, *The New Industrial State* 87 (1967).
  8. Bazelon, 195.
  9. Unless otherwise indicated in footnotes, these examples are from a list presented by Ralph Nader in *Hearings on S.860 and S.2045 Before the Subcommittee on Executive Reorganization of the Senate Committee on Government Operations,* 91st Cong., 1st Sess. 366–378 (1969). Information on the leaky pipeline explosion was supplemented by author's interview with Nader in January, 1970.
  10. *Hearings on Competitive Problems in the Drug Industry Before the Subcomm. on Monopoly of the Senate Select Comm. on Small Business,* 91st Cong., 1st Sess. Pt. 12, 5057 (1969).
  11. *See* Washington Post, Mar. 24, 1970, at A1, col. 1; and Apr. 8, 1970. Lawyers working with Nader at the Public Interest Research Group in Washington have brought a suit concerning the sufficiency of the warning.
  12. *See* Hart, Remarks, 3.
  13. The National Commission on Product Safety, *Final Report,* 2 (1970).
  14. *See generally,* Hart, Remarks.

15. This information comes from two sources: Phillips, *The Lockheed Scandal*, THE NEW REPUBLIC, Aug. 1, 1970, 19; and Sherrill, *The Convenience of Being Lockheed*, SCANLON'S MONTHLY, Aug., 1970, 40. For a defense of Lockheed, *see Target: Lockheed*, BARRON'S NATIONAL BUSINESS AND FINANCIAL WEEKLY, Aug. 17, 1970, 1.

16. *See* quotation from Proxmire Committee Report in Barnet, *The Economy of Death* 119 (1969).

17. Galbraith, *The New Industrial State*, 400; *see also* Nossiter, "Arms Firms See Postwar Spurt," Washington Post, Dec. 8, 1968, at A18, col. 1.

18. The quotation on the impairment of contracts clause is from Home Building & Loan Association v. Blaisdell, 290 U.S. 390 (1934), a Supreme Court decision discussed in Miller, *The Supreme Court and American Capitalism* 36 (1968). The Dickinson quotation is cited in Hofstadter, *The American Political Tradition and the Men Who Made It* 13 (1948).

19. For discussion of the trend of decisions and the exceptions to it, *see generally* Miller, *The Supreme Court and American Capitalism* (1948).

20. Miller, "Private Governments and the Constitution," in Hacker, ed., *The Corporation Take-Over* 138 (1964). For similar views *see* Arnold, *The Folklore of Capitalism* 191, 215 (1937); Brewster, "The Corporation and Economic Federalism," and Chayes in Mason, 25, 72; Berle, "The Developing Law of Corporate Concentration," 19 U. CHI. L. REV. 639 (1952). In one noteworthy case, a corporation was subject to constitutional due process when the Supreme Court prohibited it from infringing on the civil liberties of citizens in a company town. Marsh v. Alabama, 326 U.S. 501 (1946).

21. Bazelon, 183–4. In addition to labor organizing, Bazelon cites the example of the car dealers who, unsatisfied with GM's "private judiciary" set up to handle their complaints, lobbied the Automobile Franchise Dealers Act of 1956 through Congress; Bazelon, 81. Nader mentions the lack of free speech of professional employees in corporations in "The Profits in Pollution," *The Progressive*, Apr. 1970, 19, 21.

22. For discussion of tort doctrines, *see* Miller, *The Supreme Court and American Capitalism*, 26. For discussion of the problems with proxy fights and shareholder suits, *see* Rostow, "To Whom and for What Ends Is Corporate Management Responsible?" in Mason, 46–49; Bazelon, 189; Berle "Economic Power and the Free Society," in Hacker, 92; and the discussion below of Campaign GM.

23. Quoted in Gaddis, *Corporate Accountability, For What and To Whom Must the Manager Answer?* 47 (1964).

24. Bazelon quote at 183; *see also* Chayes in Mason, 31. The conscience-consensus view is presented in Berle, *The 20th Century Capitalist Revolution*; discussed by Brewster in Mason, 73; and criticized by Bazelon, 224–225.

25. Kahn, "We Look Forward to Seeing You Next Year," *The New Yorker*, June 20, 1970, 51.

26. Chayes in Mason, 37.

27. Hofstadter, *The Age of Reform, From Bryan to F.D.R.* 244 (1955) hereinafter referred to as Hofstadter; *see also* Arnold, 210.

28. Hofstadter, 247, 314.

29. Hofstadter, 251. Antitrust reformers generally agreed with Justice Harlan's view. *Ibid.* Miller says the decision rendered the Sherman Act "at best a sheathed sword," in Miller, *The Supreme Court and American Capitalism,* 64.

30. The Roosevelt quote on the Northern Securities case is in Hofstadter, 238; Arnold's quotes are in Arnold, 212, 217.

31. Hofstadter, 240, 305. *See generally,* Kolko, *The Triumph of Conservatism* (1963).

32. The sources for this discussion are: Goulden and Singer, "Dial-A-Bomb: AT&T and the ABM," *Ramparts Magazine,* Nov., 1969, 30; and *Hearings on the Consent Decree Program of the Department of Justice Before the Antitrust Subcomm. of the House Comm. on the Judiciary,* 86th Cong., 1st Sess. Pt. II, Vol. III (1958), and the *Subcommittee Report* of Jan. 30, 1959; and Goulden, *Monopoly* (1968).

33. Interviews with former antitrust division personnel, 1970.

34. Wall Street Journal, Oct. 31, 1967; reprinted in *Hearings on Planning, Regulation, and Competition: Automobile Industry—1968, Before the Subcomm. of the Senate Select Comm. on Small Business,* 90th Cong., 2nd Sess., 36, 39.

35. New York Times, Nov. 1, 1967; reprinted in *Hearings on Automobile Industry,* 41.

36. Text of Board of Supervisors' resolution reprinted in Nader, *Unsafe at Any Speed* 262, 264 (1965). For discussion of the Justice Department suit that followed, *see* Riley, "The Challenge of the New Lawyers: Public Interest and Private Clients," 38 G. W. LAW REVIEW 547, 561–564 (1970).

37. Economics professor Mark Schupack points out about the highly concentrated automobile industry: ". . . four firms make all of the domestic production. Consistently less than 10 percent of the sales in this country are of foreign automobiles. G.M., Ford, and Chrysler are among the five largest firms in the country. The three firms controlled $25 billion in assets at the end of 1967. No other industry has such vast resources concentrated in so few hands." Statement printed in *Hearings on Automobile Industry,* 920.

38. Galbraith, Statement in *Hearing on Planning, Regulation, and Competition Before Subcomms. of Senate Select Comm. on Small Business,* 90th Cong., 1st Sess., 4, 7 (1967).

39. The first Turner quotation is from the *Hearing* cited in note 38, at 28; the second quotation is from "Address to the New York City Bar Association," Nov. 14, 1968, reprinted in *Hearings on Automobile Industry,* 928.

40. *Hearing* cited in note 38, at 38.

41. Quoted in Welsh and Horowitz, "Clark Clifford, Attorney at War," *Ramparts Magazine,* Aug. 24, 1968, 46.

42. New York Times, Sept. 9, 1970, at 1, col. 3.

43. Gaddis, 61, 63.

44. Reagan, "What 17 Million Shareholders Share," N.Y. Times Magazine article (Feb. 23, 1964), reprinted in Trebing, ed., *The Corporation in the American Economy* 102 (1970).

45. Galbraith, *The New Industrial State*, 95.

46. Bazelon, 191.

47. For summary of spring campaigns on corporations, *see* Maeroff, "Stinging the Corporations," *The Nation*, June 22, 1970, 753; on their effect, *see* Schwartz, "Corporate Responsibility in the Age of Aquarius," Address Before the Committee on Federal Regulation of Securities, Section of Corporation, Banking and Business Law, American Bar Association, Aug. 11, 1970, 18.

48. Campaign GM described in more detail in Riley, "Can Lib-Rad Slingshots Dent the GM Giant?" The Village Voice, May 14, 1970, at 27. Campaign GM did attempt to get the list of GM shareholders through the SEC procedures, but got bogged down in the legal work required. The Campaign expects to get the list for its 1971 effort—at a cost of several thousand dollars.

49. Reported in Kahn, "We Look Forward to Seeing You Next Year," *The New Yorker*, June 20, 1970, 51.

50. *See*, L. L. L. Golden, "Public Relations—Full Disclosure," SATURDAY REVIEW, Oct. 12, 1963; reprinted in *Hearings on Automobile Industry*, 391.

51. In Medical Committee for Human Rights v. SEC, decided July 8, 1970, by the U.S. Court of Appeals for the District of Columbia Circuit, the Court found that it had jurisdiction to review the SEC's approval of Dow Chemical's refusal to include in its proxy statement the Medical Committee's resolution against making napalm. In remanding the matter for further SEC proceedings, the Court emphasized that the SEC's proxy rules were designed to, and should, encourage, not discourage, the inclusion of shareholder proposals in management proxy statements.

52. The Nader and Alinsky quotes are from Maeroff, "Stinging the Corporations," *The Nation*, June 22, 1970, 753.

53. Washington Post, May 24, 1970.

54. Chayes, 40.

55. Rostow, *Planning for Freedom: The Public Law of American Capitalism*, 3 (1959).

56. Tawney, *The Acquisitive Society* 183 (1920); on the counter-culture, see Roszak, *The Making of a Counter-Culture, Reflections on the Technocratic Society and Its Youthful Opposition* (1969).

57. Fromm, *The Revolution of Hope, Toward a Humanized Technology* 40 (1968). *See also*, Fromm, *The Sane Society* (1955); Fromm, *Man for Himself, An Inquiry into the Psychology of Ethics* (1947); Watts, *Nature, Man and Woman* (1958); and May, *Love and Will* (1969). The passivism and undue sense of power are not, as they may seem, contradictory, because

the sense of power comes from outer material things, leaving and encouraging inner passivism.

58. Barnet, *The Economy of Death* 46 (1969).

59. *See* report on theological conference, Fiske, "Christianity Linked to Pollution," New York Times, May 1, 1970; also, McCarthy, "The Lack of Reverence for Nature," Washington Post, Feb. 18, 1970.

60. Trillin, "U.S. Journal: Kentucky, The Logical Thing, Costwise," *The New Yorker*, Dec. 27, 1969, 33, 35, 36. On Marxism's irreverence for nature, *see* Roszak, 100.

61. The Harvard treasurer quote is in the Washington Post, May 6, 1970; the Roche quote is in his introductory note to GM shareholders in the special "GM's Record of Progress" pamphlet sent to all shareholders, Spring, 1970.

62. *See* Schlesinger, *The Coming of the New Deal* (1959).

63. For discussion of Croly's ideas, see Hofstadter, 246–247; Galbraith, *American Capitalism, the Concept of Countervailing Power* (1952).

64. Schwartz speech, 15–18.

65. Tawney, 180. *See also*, Taylor, "Crisis in the Modern Economy—Is the Corporation Above the Law?" *Harvard Business Review*, March, 1965; reprinted in *Hearings on Automobile Industry*, 400, 411: "When society has defined the duties of corporations to itself as securely as it has defined their duties to their shareholders, the public character of the corporation will have been acknowledged in the law."

66. Galbraith, "Who Needs the Democrats?" *Harper's Magazine*, July, 1970, 43, 60. But public ownership by itself—without changes in society's values and specific, powerful representation of the public interest in running public corporations—is not worth much. Barnet, 148–149; *see* discussion of public ownership in other countries in Harrington, "Whatever Happened to Socialism?" *Harper's Magazine*, Feb. 1970, 99. Marcus Raskin has suggested that the presidents of NBC, CBS, and ABC should be popularly elected. Seminar at Institute for Policy Studies, 1969; *see* Raskin, "The Dream Colony," in Stavins, ed., *Television Today: The End of Communication and The Death of Community* 5, 27 (1969).

67. Maeroff, 754. Massachusetts and other states authorize employee-elected positions on corporate boards. Germany has also experimented with employee and public representation. Chayes, 41; and Vagts, *Reforming the Modern Corporation: Perspectives from the German*, 80 HARVARD L. REV. 23 (1966), cited in Schwartz, 14. There is of course a big difference between representation and control.

68. Hints of the possibility of such a genuine populist movement can be found in the political base of such men as Senator Harold Hughes of Iowa, District Attorney Jim Garrison in New Orleans, Henry Howell in Virginia, and the call of Oklahoma Senator Fred Harris for a "common-sense populist coalition." New York Times, Dec. 31, 1969.

69. Harrington, 102.

Robert C. Fellmeth, *The Regulatory-Industrial Complex*   Page 244

1. R. Fellmeth, *The Interstate Commerce Omission*, XV (1970).
2. Cong. Rec., Apr. 16, 1970, at S. 5887-9.
3. *See*, for example, instructions from Washington to ICC special agents to this effect, reproduced in Chapter XII of *Surface Transportation, The Public Interest and the ICC*, by R. Fellmeth, issued on March 12, 1970.
4. *Id*.
5. U.S.C. § 522 (Supp. II, 1967). For discussion of no standing aspect, *see* Davis, "The Information Act: A Preliminary Analysis," 34 U. Chi. L. Rev. 761 (1967).
6. Attorney General Ramsey Clark, U.S. Dept. of Justice, Attorney General's Memorandum on the Public Information Section of the Administrative Procedure Act (June, 1967).
7. Statement by President Lyndon Johnson upon signing of Pub. L. No. 89-487, July 4, 1966.
8. Davis, *supra* note 5, at 763.
9. *Supra* note 2.

Beverly C. Moore, *The Lawyer's Response: The Public Interest Law Firm*
Page 299

1. United States v. Pfizer & Co., 281 F. Supp. 837 (S.D.N.Y. 1968).
2. *What's Happened to Truth in Packaging?* 34 Consumer Rep., Jan., 1968, at 41.
3. N. Johnson, *How to Talk Back to Your Television Set* 18 (1970).
4. *See*, e.g., A. Campbell, *et al.*, *The American Voter* (1960).
5. There have been notable exceptions. E.g., Holstein v. Montgomery Ward, No. 68 CH 275 (Ill. Cir. Ct. 1968), allowing a class action in behalf of "charg-all" customers who were automatically billed for certain creditor insurance premiums unless the company received affirmative notice to the contrary; Daar v. Yellow Cab Co., 63 Cal. Rptr. 724, 433 P. 2d 732 (1967), allowing a class action in behalf of overcharged taxi passengers.
6. Hall v. Coburn Corp., 160 N.Y.L.J., Aug. 8, 1968, at 2, col. 3, *aff'd*, 31 App. Div. 2d 892, 298 N.Y.S. 2d (1969), *aff'd*, No. 16 (N.Y. Ct. App. May 13, 1970).
7. H.R. 14585, 91st Cong., 1st Sess. (1969); S. 1980, 91st Cong., 1st Sess. (1969). These bills, sponsored primarily by Senator Joseph D. Tydings (D-Md.) and Representative Robert C. Eckhardt (D-Tex.) are generally referred to as the Class Action Jurisdiction Act.
8. "We must strongly reject any proposal authorizing consumer class actions." *Hearings on Class Action and Other Consumer Protection Procedures Before the Subcomm. on Commerce and Finance of the House Comm. on Interstate and Foreign Commerce*, 91st Cong. 2d Sess. 418–19

(1970) (Testimony of Charles S. Mack, Comm. Executive, Consumer Issues Comm., U.S. Chamber of Commerce).

9. *Id.* at 353–54.

10. *Id.* at 200–27.

11. Carlin & Howard, *Legal Representation and Class Justice*, 12 U.C.L.A. L. REV. 381, 384 (1965).

12. Standing Comm. of the California State Bar on Group Services, *Report on Group Legal Services*, 39 Cal. St. Bar J. 639, 652 (1964).

13. R. Rockwell, A STUDY OF LAW AND THE POOR IN CAMBRIDGE, MASSACHUSETTS 37, 41 (1968).

14. D. Caplovitz, THE POOR PAY MORE 175 (1963).

15. American Bar Association, Code of Professional Responsibility, DR 2-103(A) (1969).

16. Ladinsky, The Social Profile of a Metropolitan Bar, 43 Mich. St. Bar J. 76, 84 (1964).

17. 371 U.S. 415 (1963).

18. 377 U.S. 1 (1964).

19. 389 U.S. 217 (1967).

20. Record at 61. *See* New York Times, Feb. 11, 1967, at 29, col. 1.

21. Comment, *Controlling Lawyers Through Bar Associations and Courts*, 5 HARV. CIV. RIGHTS–CIV. LIB. L. REV. 301, 348–78 (1970).

22. Magida v. Continental Can Co., 176 F. Supp. 781, 783 (S.D.N.Y.) *aff'd*, 231 F. 2d 843 (2d Cir.), *cert. denied*, 351 U.S. 972 (1956).

23. *See generally* Note, *The New Public Interest Lawyers*, 79 YALE L.J. 1069 (1970).

24. *See* Note, *Structuring the Public Service Efforts of Private Law Firms*, 84 HARV. L. REV. 410 (1970).

Eric E. Van Loon, *The Law School Response:*
How to Make Students Sharp by Making Them Narrow   Page 334

1. Griswold, "Intellect and Spirit," in *The Path of the Law from 1967*, at 150 (A. Sutherland ed. 1968).

2. Brennan, "The Responsibilities of the Legal Profession," in *The Path of the Law from 1967*, at 89 (A. Sutherland ed. 1968).

3. Bellow, "The Extension of Legal Services to the Poor: New Approaches to the Bar's Responsibility," in *The Path of the Law from 1967*, at 116 (A. Sutherland ed. 1968).

4. Stone, *The Public Influence of the Bar*, 48 HARV. L. REV. 1, 7 (1934).

5. Griswold, *supra* note 1, at 149 and 151.

6. *Id.*, at 151.

7. Little, *Pawns and Processes: A Quantitative Study of Unknowns in Legal Education*, 21 J. LEGAL ED. 145, 149 (1968).

8. Zelan, *Occupational Recruitment and Socialization in Law School*, 21 J. LEGAL ED. 182, 186 (1968).

9. Nader, *Law Schools and Law Firms*, NEW REPUBLIC, Oct. 22, 1969, at 20.

10. Stevens, *Aging Mistress: The Law School in America*, CHANGE, Jan.–Feb. 1970, at 32.

11. Frank, *Why Not a Clinical Lawyer School?*, 81 U. PA. L. REV. 907 (1933).

12. Stevens, *supra* note 10, at 36.

13. Maechling, *Legal Research and the Problems of Society*, 21 J. LEGAL ED. 88 (1969).

14. Quoted in Nader, *supra* note 9, at 23.

15. Young, *Old Law Firms Take New Tack*, NATIONAL OBSERVER, Nov., 1969, at 10.

16. Bellow, *supra* note 3, at 115.

17. Interview with Joseph Califano, former Special Assistant to the President, by Mark Green, in Washington, D.C., Jan. 5, 1970.

18. Brennan, *supra* note 2, at 91 and 95.

19. Berman & Cahn, *Bargaining For Justice: The Law Student Challenge to Law Firms*, 5 HARV. CIV. RIGHTS–CIV. LIB. L. REV. 25 (1970).

20. Bok, *A Different Way of Looking at the World*, 20 HARV. L. S. BULLETIN 3 (Mar.–Apr., 1969).

21. Cavers, "*Legal Education in Forward-Looking Perspective*," in *Law in a Changing America* 150 (G. Hazard ed. 1968).

22. A. Sutherland, *The Law at Harvard* 369 (1967).

Harvey A. Silverglate, *The 1970s: A Decade of Repression*   Page 353

1. Civil Rights Act, 26 U.S.C. § 1983.

2. Civil Rights Act, 26 U.S.C. § 1985.

3. Ex parte Merryman, 17 Fed. Cas. 144, No. 9, 487 (C.C.D. Md. 1861).

4. Details of the case are set forth and discussed in Randall, *Constitutional Problems under Lincoln*, 162 (rev. ed. 1951).

5. Ex parte Milligan, 4 Wall 2, 18 L. Ed. 281 (1866).

6. Schenck v. United States, 249 U.S. 47 (1919).

7. Espionage Act of June 15, 1917, Comp. St. 1918, § 10212c, Title 1, Sec. 3.

8. Abrams v. United States, 250 U.S. 616 (1919).

9. Schenck v. United States, 249 U.S. at 52.

10. Hirabayashi v. United States, 320 U.S. 81 (1943).

11. *Id.*, at 26.

12. Ex parte Endo, 323 U.S. 283 (1944).

13. Communist Party of the United States v. Subversive Activities Control Board, 367 U.S. 1 (1961); Scales v. United States, 367 U.S. 203 (1961).

14. Internal Security Act of 1950, 64 Stat. 987, 50 U.S.C. 781 et seq.

Title I of the Act is the Subversive Activities Control Act. The Smith Act is found at 18 U.S.C. § 2385.

15. United States v. Robel, 389 U.S. 258, 88 S. Ct. 419 (1967).

16. 64 Stat. 992, section 5(a)(1)(D), 50 U.S.C. § 784(a)(1)(D).

17. See E. Goldman, Rendezvous With Destiny (1952).

18. New York Times, July 14, 1970, page 21.

19. See United States v. Spock, 416 F. 2d (1969). The Court of Appeals for the First Circuit indicated that two defendant-appellants, namely Coffin and Mitchell Goodman, could be re-tried for conspiracy, but the government chose not to re-try them. Hence the indictments were dismissed.

20. The views of the author regarding the Spock case are set forth in more detail in a book review appearing in the Book Section of the Boston Sunday Herald-Traveler, Oct. 19, 1969, at 1.

21. The series of articles by the juror, Kay S. Richards, appeared in several major newspapers. E.g., the Boston Sunday Globe, Feb. 22, 1970, at 28.

22. General Laws of Massachusetts, Chapter 234, Section 1.

23. State of the Union Address, 1967.

24. Communications Act of 1934, 48 Stat. 1064, 47 U.S.C. § 151, particularly 47 U.S.C. § 605.

25. General Laws of Massachusetts, Chapter 272, Sections 99–101; Commonwealth v. Spindel, 351 Mass. 673 (1968).

26. See, e.g., Berger v. New York, 388 U.S. 41 (1967); Katz v. United States, 389 U.S. 347 (1967).

27. Pub. L. 90–351, 18 U.S.C. § 251 et seq.

28. Refer to footnote 26.

29. Quoted in Mayer, On Liberty: Man v. the State, 112–113 (1969). See also The New York Times, June 14, 1969, at 1, col. 5, reporting on a brief filed in the United States District Court for the Northern District of Illinois by United States Attorney Foran in the case of United States v. Rubin, one of the "Chicago Eight" conspiracy cases.

30. New York Times, July 26, 1970, p. 7.

31. American Civil Liberties Union, "Civil Liberties," No. 271 (Sept., 1970), p. 8, discusses the case.

32. The Boston Globe, September 17, 1970, p. 7.

33. American Bar Association, Problems and Recommendations in Disciplinary Enforcement (Preliminary Draft, Jan. 15, 1970).

34. "F.B.I. Accused of Checking War Foes' Bank Files," New York Times, July 7, 1970, p. 5.

35. "Whaddya Read?," New York Post, July 11, 1970, p. 24.

36. Tom Wicker, "A Right Not to Be Data-Banked?," New York Times, July 7, 1970, editorial page.

37. W. O. Douglas, Points of Rebellion, at p. 6 (1970).

Mark J. Green, former editor of the *Harvard Civil Rights–Civil Liberties Law Review*, is an attorney now working for Ralph Nader in Washington, D.C.; and Bruce Wasserstein is a recent graduate of Harvard Law School, where he was managing editor of the same review.